Thomas Aquinas and Teilhard de Chardin

Thomas Aquinas and Teilhard de Chardin

Christian Humanism in an Age of Unbelief

DONALD J. GOERGEN, OP

PICKWICK *Publications* · Eugene, Oregon

THOMAS AQUINAS AND TEILHARD DE CHARDIN
Christian Humanism in an Age of Unbelief

Pickwick Publications
An Imprint of Wipf and Stock Publishers
199 W. 8th Ave., Suite 3
Eugene, OR 97401

www.wipfandstock.com

PAPERBACK ISBN: 978-1-6667-3849-0
HARDCOVER ISBN: 978-1-6667-9926-2
EBOOK ISBN: 978-1-6667-9927-9

Cataloguing-in-Publication data:

Names: Goergen, Donald [author]

Title: Thomas Aquinas and Teilhard de Chardin : Christian humanism in an age of unbelief / Donald J. Goergen O.P.

Description: Eugene, OR: Pickwick Publications, 2022 | Includes bibliographical references and index.

Identifiers: ISBN 978-1-6667-3849-0 (paperback) | ISBN 978-1-6667-9926-2 (hardcover) | ISBN 978-1-6667-9927-9 (ebook)

Subjects: LCSH: Thomas, Aquinas, Saint, 1225?–1274 | Teilhard de Chardin, Pierre | Creation | Christianity—Philosophy | Theological anthropology | Cosmology | Jesus Christ—Person and offices

Classification: BD418.3 G64 2022 (print) | BD418.3 (ebook)

10/19/22

Dedicated
to those
whose vocation in life
is that of bridgebuilding.
In gratitude for love and friendship.

And he said to them, "Therefore every scribe who has been trained for the kingdom of heaven is like the master of a household who brings out of his treasure what is new and what is old."

—MATTHEW 13:52

Contents

Acknowledgments

It takes more than one person to write a book. There are many for whom I am grateful. Vivian Boland, OP, Ann Garrido, and Michael Demkovich read portions of the manuscript and gave me feedback. Stan Drongowski, OP, Samuel Hakeem, OP, and Ann Willets, OP, have been a source of constant support. I would be negligent not to mention my two wonderful sisters in that same regard, Janet Haack and Judy Wittkop. Amy Mudd and Rose Holt were also encouraging. Scott Steinkerchner, OP, was of great help in assisting me with proper formatting, footnoting, and many other details. I also thank my editor at Wipf & Stock, Robin Parry, as well as Wipf & Stock for their openness to publishing the book. There are the many students whom I have taught in the past fifty years, but I especially think of several classes for whom I was privileged to teach seminars on St. Thomas at the Aquinas Institute of Theology in St. Louis, Missouri. A hermitage with the Sisters of Charity in Nazareth, Kentucky; the Sacred Heart Jesuit Retreat Center in Sedalia, Colorado; and the St. Catharine Motherhouse of the Dominican Sisters of Peace in Kentucky provided stimulating settings for some of the writing. I also wish to thank my Dominican brothers in the Province of St. Albert the Great and at the St. Pius V Priory in Chicago. As I complete my work on the manuscript, the war in Ukraine continues, and I would like to acknowledge the heroic example of President Volodymyr Zelenskyy.

List of Abbreviations

WORKS BY THOMAS AQUINAS

SCG — *Summa contra Gentiles* [On the Truth of the Catholic Faith]. 5 vols. Translated by Pegis, Anderson, Bourke, and O'Neil. New York: Doubleday, 1955–1957.

ST — *Summa Theologica*. 3 vols. Translated by the Fathers of the English Dominican Province. New York: Benziger Brothers, 1947–1948.

WORKS BY PIERRE TEILHARD DE CHARDIN

AE — *Activation of Energy*. Translated by René Hague. London: William Collins Sons, 1970.

AP — *The Appearance of Man*. Translated by J. M. Cohen. New York: Harper & Row, 1965.

CE — *Christianity and Evolution*. Translated by René Hague. New York: Harcourt Brace Jovanovich, 1971.

DM — *The Divine Milieu*. Translated by Bernard Wall. New York: Harper & Row, 1960. This is the translation from which I take quotations. There is a later translation by Siôn Cowell.

FM — *The Future of Man*. Translated by Norman Denny. New York: Harper & Row, 1964.

HE — *Human Energy*. Translated by J. M. Cohen. New York: Harcourt Brace Jovanovich, 1969.

HM	*The Heart of Matter*. Translated by René Hague. New York: Harcourt Brace Jovanovich, 1978.
HP	*The Human Phenomenon*. Translated by Sarah Appleton-Weber. Portland, OR: Sussex Academic Press, 2003. This is the translation from which I take quotations. There was an earlier translation by Bernard Wall.
HU	*Hymn of the Universe*. Translated by Simon Bartholomew. New York: Harper & Row, 1965.
MM	*The Making of a Mind, Letters from a Soldier Priest, 1914–1919*. Translated by René Hague. New York: Harper & Row, 1965.
MPN	*Man's Place in Nature*. Translated by René Hague. New York: Harper & Row,1966.
SC	*Science and Christ*. Translated by René Hague. New York: Harper & Row, 1968.
TF	*Toward the Future*. Translated by René Hague. New York: Harcourt Brace Jovanovich, 1975.
VP	*The Vision of the Past*. Translated by J. M. Cohen. New York: Harper & Row, 1966.
WW	*Writings in Time of War*. Translated by René Hague. New York: Harper & Row, 1968.

Prologue

The world is shrouded in mystery. Yet the modern sciences have sought to penetrate that mystery. Is it just a question of time before our sense of mystery is eclipsed? Evolution has become a fact of life, even if there remain many missing pieces. Both time and space have taken on new, almost unbelievable, dimensions. Does this new awareness expand or diminish the role of religion? What is the future of religion in an increasingly secularized world? The Christian traditions, and all faith traditions, find themselves in a world where belief in a reality that transcends the world can no longer be taken for granted.

Our world has also become increasingly polarized. Politics, right versus left, economics, the gap between rich and poor, multiculturalism with its insights and pitfalls, gender consciousness: all seem to portray a world falling apart. "When things fall apart," what can we count on to hold them together?[1] As much as dialogue gets emphasized, the ability to learn from one another seems on the decline. The space between us and them, between me and you, widens. We huddle within our own comfortable enclaves, get news from those who think like us, and more easily categorize or demonize than attempt to understand and respect.

This is not only true in the world, but also in the churches. Battles rage. Tradition versus modernity. It is not desirable, of course, that we all think alike. Neither is it desirable that our brothers and sisters become enemies to be demolished at all costs. Have we lost a sense of a common human identity, of a common destiny, of the common good? What it means to be human is a question revisited these days in both religious

1. "Things fall apart; the center cannot hold." Yeats, "The Second Coming," in *Selected Poetry*, 99.

and non-religious settings. And the religions need to look at the blind spots in their own histories that have contributed to the rise of unbelief and the malaise within which we find ourselves, humanity searching for meaning outside the perennial wisdom traditions.

Into this arena, considering both the devastations and the progress of the last 150 years, where do we find the seeds for building a common future? In the past? In utopian dreams? In "advanced" civilizations? At the margins? All have something to offer. I take inspiration from the Gospel according to St. Matthew. "Therefore every scribe who has been trained for the kingdom of heaven is like the master of a household who brings out of his treasure what is new and what is old" (Matt 13:52). Neither tradition alone, nor the modern alone, suffices for the future. True, there has been a knowledge explosion, and in an evolving world an evolution of consciousness, but there is also the perennial sacred wisdom of our ancestors. They knew in ways we do not know, and we know much that they did not. It is only by plumbing the depths of the traditional wisdom traditions, with the knowledge and questions of our own times, that we can move more securely into the future. It is not only tradition or progress, but tradition as a story of progress. We stand on others' shoulders. We move forward with an awareness of where we have come from and an eye on where we are going.

Into this conflict-ridden arena, I have chosen to harvest the wisdom of two thinkers unsurpassed in their fields, to glean what may be helpful in our construction of a Christian humanism for our own times: Thomas Aquinas and Pierre Teilhard de Chardin. From the vantage point of the Catholic faith, and in the Christian world beyond that, as well as the wider history of rational wisdom, the depth of Thomas's insights and his contributions to the history of thought remain unsurpassed. This is not to say there are none his equal. Yet his synthesis remains a starting point for us today, not a closed book. He himself admits to changing his opinions on varied questions during his life. Were he alive today, he would continue to change his mind as he takes into consideration life's current questions and the expansion of scientific learning. Aquinas's thought is a trustworthy and stable foundation on which to build.

Teilhard de Chardin comes from a different period of history. He is not a thirteenth century philosophical theologian but a twentieth century priest-scientist. His scientific work, by its very nature, has had to give way to continued advances in paleoanthropology. But the insights with which modern science, particularly the reality of an evolving universe, challenged him, has led to a synthesis of faith with science and of an integration of traditional Christian thought with new frontiers. In this, the direction that he has set also remains unsurpassed. As a Catholic priest and professional scientist, he has demonstrated the compatibility of the two. Modernity and tradition need not be opposing forces even if they are mutually challenging. What do these two seemingly different thinkers have to offer us if we bring them into conversation with each other?

The two are not as different as one may think, even though many who have written of them place them in opposition to each other, as if one must choose between them. Both have taught us, however, to think more in terms of both/and rather than either/or. It is with that frame of mind that we should consider them. Both were open to new insights as well as grounded in a tradition which they would help to develop. Thomas took the risk of incorporating the natural philosophy and metaphysics of Aristotle into his understanding of God and creation at a time when teaching or studying Aristotle was considered a risk. Thomas went into the storeroom and took out something as old as Augustine and as new to his world as Aristotle, and the world is better for it. Teilhard likewise took a risk by integrating the facts of evolutionary biology into a mystical theology focused on a God of evolution. He too risked censure, given that the Church had not yet accepted evolution as compatible with the Christian faith. He too went into the storeroom and the world is better for it.

Thomas Aquinas and Pierre Teilhard de Chardin seem like such a contrast. One was a philosophical theologian, the other a natural scientist. One a representative of the medieval world; the other of the modern. One a Dominican; the other a Jesuit. They have, in fact, more in common than what first might meet the eye. Each had a tremendous appreciation for the material world: Teilhard's "cosmic sense," and Aquinas's theology of creation. Each had a feel for what ancient theology labeled "theandric," seeing the divine present in the human world: Teilhard's "divinization," and Aquinas's concept of a deifying grace. Each had a healthy appreciation of creation's anthropocentricity: Teilhard's emphasis on the human phenomenon, and Aquinas's appreciation of the spiritual nature of the human soul imprinted with the *imago Dei*. Each was christocentric, for it was in Christ that God, the human, and the material world come together. Both were bold and lived dangerously from an intellectual point of view. Each ran the risk of condemnation: Teilhard for his openness to evolutionary theory in the aftermath of Charles Darwin, and Aquinas for his openness to Aristotle at a time when Aristotle was not yet sanctioned by the Church.

Each did his work in an intellectually exciting time. Each also had a synthetic mind, which is perhaps what most brings them together and makes each a wise guide in his own right. Each had a deep conviction about the truth of the Catholic faith; yet each was committed to not letting that faith close off avenues of research in the pursuit of truth.

Beyond that, however, there are other similarities, ways in which they complement each other. Thomas's mature *Summa Theologiae* is structured into three parts. It is all about God, but God in relationship to creation, in relationship to the human creature's journey to God, and that journey illuminated by the life, death and resurrection of Christ. One *Summa*, three parts. Teilhard's evolution-inspired vision also sees God as an omnipresent reality manifest first in the cosmos itself, then in the human phenomenon, and lastly through Christ. Or to use his more distinctive words. creation unfolds from cosmogenesis, to and through anthropogenesis, to and through christogenesis, back to God himself who will be all in all (1 Cor 15:27–28). We have much to learn from each of them, as well as from many others than they, not by too quickly setting up opposition but rather by seeing wherein their convictions converge. I thus bring into juxtaposition two visionaries to see what they have to offer a renewed Christian humanism in an age of unbelief.

Even before becoming a Dominican, even before thinking that someday I would be Dominican, the thought of Thomas Aquinas constituted the core of an undergraduate major in philosophy at Loras College, Dubuque, Iowa. It was also during those undergraduate years that I first heard the name of Teilhard de Chardin, while studying French during the *cours d'été* at Laval University in Québec City, following my sophomore year. In one of the classes that summer of 1963 the name of Teilhard was mentioned. I had never heard of him but was not to be outdone by others in the class. I rushed out and purchased his works available at the time, to my knowledge only available in French. *Le phénomène humain* had come out in English but I did not know it yet, not until I returned to classes in the Fall. It was not until the following summer, however, that I began to read him. The summer of 1964 was bleak. I grew up on a farm. We rented. A tornado did significant damage to many of the buildings in late Spring. My mother was in the hospital. My grandmother was just home from the hospital and could not be left alone. I stayed with her in town while dad would go out to the farm to rebuild. She did not require great care but could not be without someone present. Within the course of a couple days, I was able to read the entire *Phenomenon of Man*. During that summer, the vision of hope outlined by Father Teilhard captured my heart, head, and imagination. His hopeful vision has never left me.

It was at Loras College that I was given what has remained a good description for me of the prophetic work of Father Teilhard. A philosophy professor, Dr. Moran, someone not inclined toward the thought of Teilhard, in a student-faculty disputation, described an experience he had as a young boy. He had been to a circus where he had seen a clown standing on his head juggling. He was fascinated by it. Only later did he realize that he had seen better clowns, better jugglers, and better acrobatic performances, but he had never seen one do all three. It has been Teilhard's synthetic mind that has made his contribution enduring. There have been more noted scientists, more scholarly theologians, and more profound mystics, but there have been few who have been able to do all three with such integration.

My deep appreciation for Aquinas did not come until later, although my undergraduate philosophical education had been Thomistic. Later, in 1969, having sat in on a series of lectures in Berkeley by Étienne Gilson, then having spent the summer of 1972 with Father James Weisheipl, OP, in Toronto, and teaching on a faculty with Fathers Benedict Ashley, OP, and Thomas O'Meara, OP, Aquinas could not be dismissed. It was, however, only when I began to teach the *Summa* myself that I "saw" something of what Thomas saw, as earlier I had "seen" something of what Teilhard had seen. The students to whom I taught the *Summa*, and from whom I learned much, came alive with an appreciation for his genius and synthetic mind. My seminars with students on Aquinas were some of the most stimulating times I had as a teacher. Although I could feel Father Weisheipl's deep love and understanding for Aquinas, it is in teaching that one gets taught, in teaching that one learns, as one is questioned. These two visionaries, Thomas and Teilhard, complement each other. One without the other would have left me incomplete. I now see the method and thought of Thomas Aquinas as the foundation on which to build, a holy teaching receptive to the challenges and wisdom that come from a modern mystic such as Teilhard de Chardin, with the hope that what is handed on to a future generation of theologians and evangelists will be an even more secured understanding of the faith for our age of unbelief.

In the first eight chapters that follow, in what constitutes part one, I approach Aquinas and Teilhard in parallel fashion, so that we can see how each sees creation, the human person, Jesus Christ, and God. One can see what similarities and what contrasts there may be. In the second part, I bring these two thinkers, along with others, into a reflection on the need for a renewed humanism if belief, and Christian faith, are to contribute to the challenges of our secular age.

With Thomas Aquinas, in explicating his thought, I will focus primarily but not exclusively on his *Summa Theologiae*,[2] since there will be more than enough just in the *Summa* for the space that I can allow. I will thus place references to the *Summa* within the text itself. With Teilhard de Chardin, however, I will need to refer to a wide variety of his essays and will thus place references to those in footnotes. In both cases there is no question of being able to go as deeply into a particular topic as one might wish. To cover the thought of each of them in relatively short chapters requires making choices about what to emphasize and which insights to develop in more detail. In each case, however, one will get a good sense or overview of their thought. Both were creative and bold thinkers even though situated in different times and places. Both responded to the needs or signs of their times. English translations of each, given the times in which they were translated, were not aware of the importance of inclusive language. I have chosen, however, to leave translations as they are, rather than attempting new translations, yet being sensitive to the impact of language where I can.

2. For those unfamiliar with Thomas's *Summa Theologiae*, it is divided into three parts and the second part is subdivided into two further parts. In references to the *Summa*, these are indicated by I, I-II, II-II, and III. Each part is further divided into what medievals called questions, or *quaestiones*, which were more like topics. These are referenced as *q*. 20 or *q*. 52, the subdivisions in each part of the *Summa*. A question is further subdivided into articles, usually phrased as questions, and these are indicated by *a*. 1 or *a*. 6. Thus, a reference such as *ST*, I-II, q. 69, a. 3 can be found in the first part of the second part of the *Summa*, question 69, article 3, which happens to be on the beatitudes, and whether they are suitably enumerated. Sometimes there may be a further reference within an article to the body of the article (*corpus*); or to a response to one of the objections, *ad* 2; or to a major statement from the Scriptures or one of the Fathers that precedes Thomas's own opinion, stated as "on the contrary" or *sed contra*.

Thomas Aquinas

Theologian, Scholar, Friar Preacher (1224/5–1274)

1216	Foundation of the Order of Preachers
August 6, 1221	Death of St. Dominic
1224/1225	Thomas's birth at Roccasecca (vicinity of Naples)
ca. 1230–1239	An oblate at the Benedictine Abbey of Monte Cassino
1239–1244	Student in Naples
1243/1244	Albert the Great arrives in Paris
April 1244	Thomas takes the Dominican habit
1244/1245	Forced detention of Thomas at Roccasecca by his family
1245	Thomas returns to the Dominicans
1245–1248	Student in Paris with Albert the Great
1248–1252	Student and assistant to Albert in Cologne
1252–1256	Teaching in Paris as bachelor of the Sentences, Composes the *Scriptum super libros Sententiarum*
1256	Thomas's inaugural lecture as a Master of Theology
1256–1259	Regent-master in Paris as Magister in Sacra Pagina
1259–1261	Thomas returns to Italy, probably to Naples
1261–1265	Conventual Lector in Orvieto; Completion of *Summa contra Gentiles*; *Super Job*; *Catena aurea* (Matthew); Corpus Christi Liturgy

1265–1268	Regent Master at Rome: *Prima Pars*; *Catena aurea* (Mark, Luke, John)
1268–1272	Second Paris Regency: *Secunda Pars*; *In Matthaeum*; *In Joannem*
December 10, 1270	Bishop Tempier's condemnation of Averroistic Aristotelianism
1272–1273	Regent Master in Naples: *Tertia Pars*
March 7, 1274	Thomas Aquinas dies at Fossanova, south of Rome
March 7, 1277	Condemnation by Stephen Tempier of 219 propositions
July 18, 1323	Canonization of Aquinas by Pope John XXII

Pierre Teilhard de Chardin

Scientist, Priest, Mystic (1881–1955)

May 1, 1881	Born at Sarcenat in the Auvergne in central France
March 20, 1899	Entered Jesuit novitiate at Aix-en-Provence
March 25, 1901	Took first vows in the Jesuit Province of Lyons
1901–1905	Student of philosophy on the island of Jersey (England)
September 1905	Assigned to teach physics and chemistry in Cairo
1908–1912	Four years of theology at Ore Place, Hastings, South England
August 24, 1911	Ordained to the priesthood
1912–1914	Studied paleontology at the Museum of Natural History, Paris
December 1914	Called into the French army and attached to the medical corps
January 22, 1915	Served in the front lines as stretcher-bearer during World War I
May 26, 1918	Made solemn vows
March 10, 1919	Demobilized
July 5, 1921	Handed in doctoral thesis on mammals of the Lower Eocene Period
1920–1923	Taught geology and paleontology at the *Institut Catholique* in Paris

1923–1924	First period in China, in Tientsin: Discovery of traces of Paleolithic Man
1924–1926	Interlude in Paris: the license to teach at the *Institut Catholique* revoked
1926–1927	Second period in Tientsin, China
March 1927	Finished *The Divine Milieu* (revised in 1932)
1927–1928	Another interlude in France
1929–1938	Back in China, first in Tientsin, then in Peking as of 1932, Discovery of *Sinanthropus*/Peking Man at Chou-Kou-Tien
1938–1939	In France and America
1939–1946	Second period in Peking, the time of the Second World War
1938–1940	*The Human Phenomenon*, substantially written while in Peking
August 6, 1944	Permission to publish *The Human Phenomenon* refused
1946–1951	In Paris: Autobiographical essay, "The Heart of Matter" (written 1950)
1951–1955	In America, with visits to South Africa
March 1955	"*Le Christique*" ("The Christic"), his last great essay, completed
April 10, 1955	Dies on Easter Sunday in New York City

Part One

Thomas and Teilhard

Two Visionaries

1

Thomas d'Aquino and Pierre Teilhard de Chardin

WE BEGIN OUR EXPLORATION with a brief exposition of the lives of these two visionaries.

THOMAS AQUINAS: THEOLOGIAN, SCHOLAR, FRIAR PREACHER (1224/5–1274)

Thomas Aquinas, or Tommaso d'Aquino, was born in 1224 or 1225, at the family castle at Roccasecca, in the county of Aquino, almost halfway between Rome and Naples, in the Kingdom of Sicily, one of the nine children of Landolfo and Theodora, the youngest of the four boys.[1] As the youngest son, in accord with what seems to have been a common practice, he was offered as an oblate to the Benedictine Abbey of Monte Cassino at the age of five or six, accompanied by his nurse or governess, where he became familiar with Benedictine life and received his earliest education.[2] His

1. The most authoritative biographies of Thomas Aquinas in English are Torrell, *Saint Thomas Aquinas*, and Weisheipl, *Friar Thomas d'Aquino*. A brief but authoritative introduction to the life of Thomas is found in Tugwell, *Albert and Thomas*, 201–66. A more recent biography emphasizing Thomas's context is Prudlo, *Environmental Portrait*.

2. An oblate, or *oblatus*, was a child given by one's parents to a monastery for education and possibly a future with that religious community. When he came of mature

aristocratic parents most probably had high expectations for him, possibly even as a future abbot. At the age of fourteen or fifteen, however, he left the monastery for studies in Naples where he would have studied the liberal arts and philosophy. These were turbulent times as there was tension between the popes and the emperor, Frederick II, who had established in 1224 a *studium generale* or university in Naples to train his own men for service within his kingdom. One had to steer a delicate balance between one's loyalty to the pope and to that of the emperor. Within Thomas's family, loyalties to one or the other could shift. At this time at the *studium* in Naples the study of Aristotle was flourishing, although at the University of Paris the study of Aristotle was technically forbidden.

It was during his years of study in Naples (1239–1244) that Thomas made the acquaintance of the Dominicans.[3] Around April of 1244 he chose to receive their habit, much to the displeasure of his family and particularly his mother, whose plans for Thomas were not that he be a mendicant. Thomas had received the habit, however, and remained steadfast in his commitment. So did his mother remain steadfast in her opposition. Thomas was being sent by the Order of Preachers from Naples to Paris, in the company of the Master of the Order, for further study, but his mother had arranged to have him taken captive north of Rome and returned to Roccasecca. He was detained for a little more than a year with attempts to dissuade him from his intent. Unable to so persuade him, his family allowed him to return to the Dominicans in Naples who sent him north once again and eventually, again in the company of the Master of the Order, to Paris, the intellectual center of Europe at the time, where he resided in the Convent of Saint-Jacques. It would not be mere hagiography to say that in these early years Thomas had already given witness to a strong devotional life as well as to a life of study. He was almost twenty when he had been detained by his parents in Roccasecca. His early years also formed in Thomas's mind the clear distinction between the temporal power of an emperor and the spiritual power of the church, for the context of his early life would have forced him to ponder the relationship seriously. Later in life he refused the possibility of being the archbishop of Naples or being made a cardinal. As Denys Turner well points out, an essential context for understanding Thomas is his Dominican life.[4]

---

age, the oblate was free to take vows or leave the monastery. The child was a gift to the monastery while at the same time a recipient of a monastic education.

3. For a life of St. Dominic, see Goergen, *St. Dominic*.

4. Turner, *Portrait*, 8–6.

Thus, most probably by Fall of 1245, Thomas was a student in Paris, although it is not clear in what his studies consisted. It may not have been theology but rather the completion of studies he had begun in Naples in which case he would have been associated with the faculty of arts. Perhaps he completed his studies of philosophy and began the curriculum in theology. At this time in Paris Thomas became acquainted with Albert[5] whom he later served as a secretary. Albert must have been impressed with Thomas because Thomas accompanied Albert to Cologne in 1248 after three years in Paris. He would have completed his theological studies in Cologne. At their General Chapter in 1248 the Dominicans had decided to establish a *studium generale* in Cologne where there had been a priory founded in 1221/1222 by Henry, a close friend of Jordan of Saxony, who had succeeded Dominic as Master of the Order. Albert was asked to help establish the new studium. He and Thomas would have arrived in Cologne by the Feast of the Assumption on which day, as Torrell points out,[6] was the laying of the first stone for the magnificent Cologne cathedral.

During his four years in Cologne (1248–1252), between ages twenty-three and twenty-seven, Thomas would have been a student of Albert's as well as having continued as his assistant. It was probably during these years that he was ordained to the priesthood. As Albert's assistant, he would have begun to do some teaching, which would have been commenting on the Scriptures. Thomas's primary professional activity during most of his life was that of a professor of Bible. One began by lecturing on the Scriptures, what was known as "cursory" lectures given by a bachelor[7] on the literal sense of the text. Thomas's commentary on the book of Isaiah comes from this Cologne period, as may be true of Jeremiah and Lamentations as well. Some of his commentary on Isaiah, or "lecture notes," have come down to us in Thomas's own almost illegible handwriting. Some of the side annotations on the book of Isaiah reflect Thomas's own spirituality as a Friar Preacher. After having completed his studies in Cologne, and already having begun lecturing on the Scriptures, Thomas was recommended by Albert to go back to the University of Paris to take up more formally a teaching career, although Thomas was quite young

5. Tugwell, *Albert and Thomas*, 3–129; Weisheipl, "Life and Works," 13–51.

6. Torrell, *Saint Thomas Aquinas*, 1:25.

7. A young man began his teaching career as a "bachelor," or teaching assistant, under a Master. As a Master, he was able to teach in his own right and have bachelors under his guidance for whom he was responsible. In Cologne, under Albert's tutelage, Thomas would have been a *baccalarius biblicus*.

at the time, only twenty-seven, when ordinarily one did not begin such before the age of twenty-nine. This gives witness to Thomas's abilities and the respect that Albert had for him as his student and teaching assistant.

As of September 1252, Thomas was back in Paris, for a second time, the intellectual center of Europe, but this time as a teacher rather than as a student. This four-year period would be a productive one in Thomas's life. His responsibility this time was that of teaching or commenting on the *Sentences* of Peter Lombard, the standard text of the time after that of the Scriptures.[8] He would be a bachelor of the Sentences (*baccalarius Sententiarum*) under the guidance of Master Elias Brunet de Bergerac, a Dominican from the Province of Provence, and eventually becoming a Master himself. During these years the teaching of Aristotle was legitimized only in the arts faculty at the University of Paris. Tensions between the arts faculty and the theology faculty flared up as they had before, as well as that between the secular faculty and the mendicants. These were intellectually stimulating but also troubled times at the university. Respecting Thomas's earliest commentaries on several books of the Bible which he had done in Cologne, his *Scriptum super libros Sententiarum* was his first truly significant original work, commenting on all four books of the *Sentences*, in which he held some opinions about which he later changed his mind. Other smaller works also come from this same Parisian period, e.g., *On Being and Essence* (*De ente et essentia*), which works already show Aquinas's familiarity with the thought of Avicenna[9] and Averroes,[10] Arab and Muslim commentators on the works of Aristotle.

8. In the thirteenth century the *Sentences* of Peter Lombard became the standard and obligatory text and perdured as such for three centuries. An excellent introduction to the intellectual and scholastic context within which Aquinas taught is that by Pieper, *Scholasticism*. On Lombard, see 94–99. For the intellectual ancestors and university context of Thomas's teaching, see Prudlo, *Environmental Portrait*, 97–101, on Lombard.

9. Avicenna (*ibn-Sina*) was born ca. 980 in Persia, present-day Uzbekistan, and died in 1037, age 56–57, in Persia, present-day Iran, during the Islamic Golden Age. He was a physician and philosopher and Islamic scholar, a child prodigy who had memorized the Koran by the age of ten, about whom it was said that he had read the *Metaphysics* of Aristotle forty times. Most of his works were written in Arabic but came to be translated in the thirteenth century. His was the leading school of Islamic philosophy in the twelfth century.

10. Averroes (*ibn-Rushd*) was born in 1126 in Cordoba, died in 1198 in Morocco, age 71–72, during the Islamic Golden Age, who emphasized the reconciliation of reason and faith and of Aristotelianism with Islam. He was a Muslim polymath and master of Aristotelian philosophy, wrote commentaries on Plato and Aristotle in their

Having commented on the *Sentences* as a bachelor, Thomas was set to become a Master or *magister*, a teacher in his own right, for which he had to prepare an inaugural lecture, for which he chose a text from Psalm 103.[11] The process for the inaugural lecture was established by university statutes. Thomas then became a Regent-master (*magister regens* or reigning master) in Paris as *Magister in Sacra Pagina*, a Master of the Sacred Page, or one authorized to comment on the Scriptures on his own authority and not as someone's assistant. It is unclear on which texts of Scripture Thomas commented during this period but that the authority to comment on the Bible was now a prerogative of his is clear. The Scriptures would remain the primary basis for his teaching for the rest of his life. According to university statutes, the three functions of a Master were: *legere, disputare, praedicare*, that is, to "read" or comment on the Scriptures verse by verse; to "dispute" or conduct disputations on doubtful questions, another avenue for teaching; and to preach, a significant responsibility on its own. Although Thomas would have preached more frequently, we have at least twenty of his university sermons. He would have preached at the university several times a year.[12] In addition, not from this period, there were later sermons on the Ten Commandments, the Creed, the Our Father, and the Hail Mary, all variously dated.

A Master had to hold disputations regularly. There were both private disputations conducted within one's own school, which for Thomas would have been the Convent of St. Jacques, and public disputations, such as those held twice a year during Advent and Lent. Thomas's disputed questions *De veritate* come from this first period of his regency in Paris and extend over that three-year period. He had been a bachelor commenting on the *Sentences* from 1252–1256. He continued in Paris as a Master from 1256–1259. His unfinished commentary on Boethius's *De Trinitate* also stems from this period, for which we have a copy in Thomas's own handwriting, and on which work Thomas is the only thirteenth century author to have commented. The primary responsibility as *magister*, however, remained one who could comment and teach authoritatively

Arabic translations, defended Aristotelian philosophy against al-Ghazali, believed the universe was created by God in contrast to Avicenna, who held to its eternity.

11. "*Rigans montes de superioribus suis de fructu operum tuorum satiabitur terra*" (From your heights you water the mountains, the earth is filled with the fruits of your works); Ps 103:13 in the Vulgate edition; Ps 104 in contemporary translations.

12. Pertinent to Thomas's preaching and academic sermons, see Aquinas, *Academic Sermons*.

the Bible. Teaching at the university during this first period for Thomas as a Regent-master, however, was not simply an academic affair; it was also a turbulent time. We are not able here to recount the history of the virulent conflict between the secular masters at the university and the new mendicant orders but Thomas's first polemical defense of the mendicants, *Contra impugnantes Dei cultum et religionem* comes from his first year as a *magister.*[13]

In 1259 Thomas departs from Paris to spend a couple years back in Naples, then four in Orvieto, and three more in Rome, before returning to Paris again in 1268. His stay in Naples is not attested by any documents but seems to be the most reasonable conclusion as to where he would have gone once leaving Paris. Having begun the *Summa contra Gentiles* before leaving Paris, he would have completed its four books by 1265 at the latest. We have a good portion of this work, described by Torrell as Thomas's second great work,[14] in his own handwriting. It would have been his first work of synthesis, a presentation of the Catholic faith for non-believers. In a way unusually self-revelatory for Aquinas,[15] he introduces this *Summa* with these words:

> In the name of Divine Mercy, I have the confidence to embark upon the work of a wise man, even though this may surpass my powers, and I have set myself the task of making known, as far as my limited powers will allow, the truth that the Catholic faith professes, and of setting aside the errors that are opposed to it. (*SCG*, Book I, chapter 2)

The first three books of this *Summa* present truths accessible to reason whereas the last book comprises truths known only through revelation. Thomas acknowledges here both his confidence in reason in the search for truth as well as its limits.

13. In English translation often called "An Apology for the Religious Orders," a treatise against the opponents of religious and mendicant life. Later works defending mendicant religious life include *De perfectione spiritualis vitae* and *Contra doctrinam retrahentium a religione.*

14. Torrell, *Saint Thomas Aquinas*, 1:332, also 101–16.

15. We gain more insight into Thomas's character from anecdotal stories that have a credible history, such as the time at which Thomas and some students were returning to Paris from Saint-Denis and a student exclaimed, "Look, Master, what a fine city Paris is! Wouldn't you like to be lord of it?" And Thomas replied, "I would rather have the homilies of Chrysostom on the Gospel of Saint Matthew." See Weisheipl, *Friar Thomas d'Aquino*, 121.

In September of 1261 Thomas was appointed lector for the Dominican priory in Orvieto. The role of lector involved giving the lectures in a local priory to those who had not been sent away to a larger *studium* of the Order, whether that be a general studium or a provincial one, which meant therefore most friars. Thomas would, among other lectures, have commented on books from the Bible and his highly praised commentary or lectures on the book of Job is attributed to his time in Orvieto. His commentary on Pseudo-Dionysius's *On Divine Names* may have also come from this period in Orvieto, or perhaps later during his years in Rome, reflecting the influence of Neoplatonism on Thomas's thinking. In addition to completing the *Summa contra Gentiles*, Thomas was also invited by Pope Urban IV to do the Office for the Feast of Corpus Christi, which in 1264 Pope Urban had instituted as a feast for the universal church. The Office gives witness to Thomas not only as a Scripture scholar and systematizer but also as a poet, as does the *Adoro Te* which would have been composed later.[16] The Office contains the renowned *Pange lingua* text. Orvieto became a significant city after the election of Pope Urban IV in 1261 as it then became the site where the Roman curia and pope met and resided when away from the inconveniences of Rome. Another work that Thomas undertook at the request of Pope Urban was the *Catena aurea*, a compilation of patristic texts explicating the texts of the four Gospels.

After four years in Orvieto, Thomas was sent to Rome, to Santa Sabina, the headquarters for the Order of Preachers, to establish a *studium* there for the Roman province. It was in Rome that he began the composition of his most mature work, his *Summa Theologiae*, and completed its first part or *Prima Pars*. Thomas also continued work on the *Catena aurea*. He had completed the work on Matthew in Orvieto but the work on the other evangelists remained. He also began the *Compendium theologiae*, never to be finished, at the request of his fellow Dominican brother, friend, and secretary, Reginald of Piperno.[17] Thomas was incredibly prolific and we are not able to take note of all his writings here, which

16. After considerable scholarly discussion, today the *Adoro te* is considered an authentic work of Thomas. Murray, *Aquinas at Prayer*, 239–55; Torrell, *Saint Thomas Aquinas*, 1:132–35.

17. Reginald (1230–290) was Thomas's *socius continuus*, or ongoing companion, assistant, and secretary, from 1259 on. He was not Thomas's only secretary but his only continuous or permanent one. Weisheipl writes: "Reginald was to spend the greater part of his life in the service of Thomas, going wherever he did, taking dictation, transcribing, serving Mass, hearing confession, and assisting in every way" (*Friar Thomas d'Aquino*, 145).

comprise theological syntheses, disputed questions, biblical commentaries, commentaries on works of Aristotle as well as other commentaries such as on Boethius, more polemical writings, as well as requests for expert opinions, along with liturgical texts and sermons.[18] He sometimes dictated to as many as four secretaries at a time.[19] After his experiment with the studium in Rome, Thomas was sent to Paris in 1268 as a Master for a second time.

Although personal details with respect to Thomas's life are few, the context and circumstances in which he lived can be well documented. As for reasons why the Order may have asked Thomas to return to Paris, various biographers list: (1) the renewed attack against the mendicant religious orders; (2) growing opposition in the theology faculty to Aristotle; and (3) the Averroist crisis. It is very possible that all of these were at play, as well as others. Thomas was in the midst of several critical battles. During this time, with respect to the first of these reasons mentioned above, Thomas wrote two more defenses of the mendicant orders.[20] With respect to the second, Thomas had to steer a middle course between those who were opposed to Aristotle and those who adopted Aristotle uncritically. One such question pertained to whether the world is eternal, a position held by Aristotle. Such seemed contrary to faith and the doctrine of creation. Thomas maintained in *De aeternitate mundi* (On the eternity of the world) that philosophically one could not disprove by reason the thesis that the world was/is eternal (supportive of the Aristotelian position) but that nevertheless, theologically, as faith teaches us, the world had a beginning. In either case the world could or would be dependent on God for its being.

Some of Thomas's opinions manifested differences between the Franciscans and Dominicans, the two mendicant orders, who were united when it came to a defense of mendicant life. One question about which there was such a difference was that of the unicity of the soul or substantial form in human beings. Although one speaks of a vegetative soul or life principle among non-sentient organisms, and a sentient soul

18. For a catalogue of Thomas's works, see Torrell, *Saint Thomas Aquinas*, 1:330–61; Weisheipl, *Friar Thomas d'Aquino*, 355–405.

19. For further discussion of Thomas and his secretaries, see Torrell, *Saint Thomas Aquinas*, 1:239–46.

20. *De perfectione spiritualis vitae* (On the perfection of the spiritual life) and *Contra doctrinam retrahentium a religione* (Against the teaching that deters one from joining religious life).

or life principle in the animal world, and a rational soul or substantial form among human beings, the question was whether there was one substantial form in a human person or three. Thomas maintained the oneness of a person's soul that performed all its functions in contrast to his opponents who held to a plurality of forms. Both disputes, on the eternity of the world and the unicity of the substantial form in human beings, reflect a tension between a more traditional Augustinianism and an emerging Aristotelianism. Although Thomas was more Aristotelian in the dispute about the unicity of the soul, he was also adamant in his opposition to what seemed to have been Averroes's interpretation of Aristotle which held to their being only one soul for *all* human beings, in which each person participated, which opinion Thomas refuted in his *De unitate intellectus contra averroistas* (On the unity of the intellect against the Averroists). The finer points of these disputes are not important for us here except that they indicate Thomas's engagement with the intellectual and hotly disputed questions of his day.

In addition to his teaching amid the controversies in which he was involved, Thomas's writings during this second period as Regent–master in Paris were extensive. His commentaries on the Gospels of Matthew and John stem from this period and perhaps portions of commentaries on the letters of St. Paul. Precise dating for many of Thomas's writings is difficult to determine. There were also further disputed questions. As significant as Thomas's commentaries on the Bible are, his commentaries on the writings of Aristotle, such as those on his *Physics*, *Metaphysics*, and the *Nicomachean Ethics*, are of great importance as well. As important as any work from this second Parisian period as Regent–master would have been, his continued work on his magisterial *Summa* stands out. The *Prima Pars* having been composed in Rome, he now continued with the two parts of the *Secunda Pars* and would have begun the first questions of the *Tertia Pars* which he continued later in Naples. These years in Paris (1268–1272) were as productive, if not more so, than any in Thomas's life. After four years there, and his second term as Regent–master completed, he departed from the Priory of Saint-Jacques in Paris and returned to his native land and the Priory of San Domenico in Naples. He may have realized that he would never return to Paris again where he had invested so much of his life's energies. He would not have known that only two years more remained for him.

In the Spring of 1272, Thomas took leave of Paris. His Roman province asked him to establish a *studium generale* in Naples. He was now forty-seven or forty-eight years old. He lectured again on letters of St. Paul as well as on the Psalms, the latter remaining unfinished. And there remained the completion of the *Tertia Pars* of his *Summa* to which he devoted further attention, but it too remained unfinished. His health had begun to decline. During his life, he would have walked on foot from Naples to Paris, to Cologne, back to Paris, then to Rome and back to Paris, and then again to Naples, although some portions of these trips may have been by sea. He was known to have been a joyful friar, humble, deeply contemplative, with a capacity for friendship, which topic was central to his theology of charity. There are testimonies to mystical experiences, such as at prayer in Naples when Christ was reported to have asked him: "You have written well of me, Thomas, what would you ask of me?" and his reply was, "*Non nisi te, Domine*" (Nothing but you, O Lord). He was devoted to the Eucharist as well as to the crucifix.

The graces in Thomas's life were not conflict free. As we have seen, particularly in Paris, he was at the center of ongoing and resurfacing tensions, disputes, and attacks, as well as challenges elsewhere. In 1270, while he was still in Paris, there had been the condemnation of thirteen Averroist theses by Stephen Tempier, the bishop of Paris, that put Aristotelianism under suspicion in the continued conflict between Augustinian conservatives and radical Aristotelians or Averroists, between whom Thomas had always tried to steer a middle course. The condemnation did not calm the waters but did leave Thomas's own writings open to scrutiny. After Thomas's death, however, on March 7, 1277, Stephen Tempier judged 219 propositions to be suspect, some of which were opinions of Aquinas even if he had not been himself a target of the bishop's action nor mentioned by name. Nevertheless, he became the object of continued critique, first by the Dominican archbishop of Canterbury, Robert Kilwardby, and then by the Franciscan, John Pecham, who succeeded Kilwardby as archbishop, who both considered some of Thomas's views heretical. Albert the Great himself, still alive when Thomas died, came to Thomas's defense as did others. The controversy surrounding Thomas continued from varied quarters, but he was defended by his Dominican Order and in 1323, forty-nine years after his death, he was canonized as a saint by Pope John XXII at Avignon, France.[21]

We need to return to the circumstances of Thomas's death. In late 1273, on the feast of Saint Nicholas, December 6, while celebrating Mass,

21. On the condemnations and controversies surrounding them, see Weispheipl, *Friar Thomas d'Aquino*, 331–50, and Torrell, *Saint Thomas Aquinas*, 1:296–316.

Thomas had an experience after which he never taught or wrote again, leaving his *Summa* unfinished at the treatise on Penance. His classic response to Brother Reginald's inquiry pertinent to Thomas's no longer writing was "Reginald, I cannot, because all that I have written seems like straw to me."[22] When pressed further, he added "compared with what I have seen and what has been revealed to me"[23] James Weisheipl sees the experience and events that followed as a result not only of a deep spiritual experience but also of a breakdown due to exhaustion from overwork that had been his self-imposed burden for a long time.[24] In late January or early February, 1274, he along with his *socius* Reginald were on foot to the Second Council of Lyons, the fourteenth ecumenical council, which was to be a council to work out a mutual understanding with the Greek East. On the way, he seems to have hit his head against a fallen tree. He became increasingly ill. Later, after having resumed the journey, Thomas, further weakened, asked to be taken to the Cistercian abbey at Fossanova where, after a week or two, he died on March 7, 1274. His condition had weakened ever since the earlier experience in December of 1273 when he discontinued writing although he would have had to be in fairly full health for him to have undertaken the journey to Lyons. He died the death of a saint, a scholar, and a servant of the Lord at the age of forty-nine. His remains, years later, in 1369, on January 28, were restored to the Dominicans and transferred to the Dominican priory in Toulouse. During the French Revolution the remains were transferred to the Basilica of St. Sernin in Toulouse and in 1974 to the Church of the Jacobins in Toulouse where they are venerated today.

PIERRE TEILHARD DE CHARDIN: SCIENTIST, PRIEST, MYSTIC (1881–1955)

Marie-Joseph-Pierre Teilhard de Chardin was a Jesuit priest and scientist. He was born in the Auvergne region of central France, not far from Clermont-Ferrand, on May 1, 1881, the fourth of eleven children, about seven months before the birth of Angelo Roncalli, the later Pope John

22. Weishiepl, *Friar Thomas d'Aquino*, 321–22; Torrell, *Saint Thomas Aquinas*, 1:289.

23. Torrell, *Saint Thomas Aquinas*, 1:289; and Tugwell, *Albert and Thomas*, 266.

24. Weisheipl, *Friar Thomas d'Aquino*, 320–23.

XXIII, whose Vatican Council Teilhard did not live to see.[25] His mother passed on to him her devotion to the Sacred Heart of Jesus as well as to his Blessed Mother to whom he later made a personal consecration. At an early age he was already enamored with the realities of the material world. He wrote later of a painful experience he had at the age of seven when he discovered that iron could rust and what seemed imperishable was corruptible. What seemed so solid was less so than it first appeared. Already a geological sensitivity, a sense of the earth, was making its appearance. At age eleven he was sent to a Jesuit boarding school where he made his first communion, Ascension Thursday, 1892. At the age of seventeen, on March 20, 1899, he became a Jesuit novice at the novitiate in Aix-en-Provence. Auguste Valensin, a novitiate classmate, and Pierre Charles became from that time on lifelong friends and confidants.[26] He made his first vows on March 25, 1901.

In 1901 the French government passed anticlerical laws restricting religious orders.[27] The following year Jesuit education was transferred to the island of Jersey, belonging to England, where Teilhard spent his next three years completing the juniorate, studying philosophy, and giving expression to his cosmic sense by exploring the island, during which years he excelled in the study of Latin and Greek and even composed verses in them. During this same time his oldest brother, Albéric, died (1902); a younger sister, Marguerite-Marie, acquired a lifelong illness; his older sister, Françoise, joined the Little Sisters of the Poor and became a missionary to China (1903); and his youngest sister, Louise, died of meningitis at the age of thirteen (1904). In 1905 Teilhard himself was sent to Cairo to teach physics and chemistry in the Jesuit high school there for

25. A biography of Teilhard that is both very reliable and very readable is Ursula King, *Spirit of Fire*. Considered definitive at the time is the earlier one by Cuénot, *Teilhard de Chardin*.

26. Auguste Valensin (1879–1953) entered the Jesuit novitiate in 1899. He and Teilhard shared formation together in the novitiate, then in Jersey and Hastings. Valensin became a professor of philosophy and was a disciple of Maurice Blondel. He and Teilhard shared an active and intimate correspondence: *Lettres intimes à Auguste Valensin*. Pierre Charles (1883–1954), a Belgian Jesuit, also entered the novitiate in 1899, but in Belgium. His theological studies were in Hastings, which he would have shared with Teilhard. He became a professor of dogmatic theology at Louvain in Belgium. One of his works, *Prayer of All Things*, manifests a kindred spirit with that of Teilhard. Charles, Valensin, and Teilhard remained friends throughout their lives.

27. Dansette, *Religious History*, II:185–323.

the next three years.[28] As in Jersey, Egypt also offered opportunities for geological exploration helping both to satisfy and stimulate his love of nature. It also allowed him to become acquainted with Islamic culture. After these three years of his Jesuit regency, Teilhard returned to England in 1908 to study theology for four years at Ore Place, Hastings.[29] In 1911, his sister Françoise died of smallpox in Shanghai, at the age of 32. Several months later Teilhard was ordained to the priesthood, August 24, 1911.

During his theological studies Teilhard was allowed to pursue his geological and paleontological interests through varied excursions in the area. During this time, he met and came to know Joseph Maréchal, SJ, who taught biology, experimental psychology, and mysticism at Leuven/ Louvain. He read and was influenced by Henri Bergson's *Creative Evolution* which was published in 1907. He was beginning to form his own appreciation of the relationship between matter and spirit. He met Charles Dawson which led to his later entanglement with the Piltdown fraud. It was during these years that Charles Dawson had supposedly discovered fragments of human cranial bones at Piltdown in Sussex, England, that would contribute to our understanding of human origins but which were later discovered, in 1953, by Kenneth Oakley to be a hoax perpetrated by Dawson, with whom Teilhard himself had worked on several occasions.[30] At the close of his theological studies in 1912 Teilhard was sent to Paris[31] for advanced studies in geology and paleontology at the Institut Catholique, the Collège de France, and the Museum of Natural History where he met Marcellin Boule,[32] a specialist on Neanderthal man and renowned professor of paleontology, which then became Teilhard's lifelong

28. See Teilhard, *Letters from Egypt*.

29. See Teilhard, *Letters from Hastings*.

30. Stephen Jay Gould (1941–2002), Harvard evolutionary biologist, in a critical conjecture (see *Hen's Teeth*, 201–50), suggested that Teilhard was complicit in the fraud, a hypothesis that could not be sustained. Much has been written on the fraud and who perpetrated it. See Walsh, *Unravelling Piltdown*. Also see King, *Teilhard and the Unity of Knowledge*, and his foreword to *Divine Milieu*, x, n6.

31. See Teilhard, *Letters from Paris*.

32. Marcellin Boule (1861–1942), also from the Auvergne region of France, was a French geologist, paleontologist, and professor at the Museum of Natural History in Paris from 1902–1936. He was known for his extensive research on Neanderthal man. Boule accepted Teilhard as a student of his for whom he became a mentor and whom he came to respect highly for his gifts. They became lifelong friends as well as colleagues although at times having different views on things. Teilhard blessed Boule's second marriage.

interest. As the previous years had been, these were also richly rewarding years for Teilhard. He also met Abbé Henri Breuil,[33] a prehistorian, and traveled with him to Spain to explore prehistoric caves.

Teilhard had just returned to England to begin his Jesuit tertianship when war broke out. He was declared fit for service, and in December of 1914 entered the First World War as a stretcher-bearer and was sent to the front lines. As is to be expected, his years in the war, and in the front lines, were formative years for him. He described it to his cousin who had also become a close friend, Marguerite Teillard-Chambon,[34] as "a baptism into reality."[35] We learn much from Teilhard's correspondence, earlier in his letters from Egypt, later from Hastings, at times to friends, but particularly during these years in his correspondence with Marguerite, a close confidante whom he trusted with his ideas as well as struggles, published in the collection *The Making of a Mind*. He was appreciated and recognized for bravery for his chaplain-like ministry and presence to soldiers in settings of great danger. Teilhard's first essays also come from this period. It was at this time that he wrote essays such as "Cosmic Life" (1916), "The Mystical Milieu" (1917), "The Soul of the World" (1918), "The Eternal Feminine" (1918), "The Priest" (1918), and others. During war, what has been described as a crucible for him, his ideas on God and the world became a more solidified vision. He would emerge from the war even more both priest and scientist. His "cosmic sense" had become melded with a "human sense" as well as a "christic sense." It was also during the years of war, May 26, 1918, that he professed his solemn vows. It was also in 1918 that he first met Léontine Zanta with whom he developed a personal friendship and became a correspondent.[36]

33. Henri Breuil (1877–1961) was a professor of prehistory at the Collège de France in Paris as well as at the Sorbonne, a Catholic priest noted for his study of cave art. He visited the Peking Man excavations at Chou-Kou-Tien, China, in 1931. He collaborated with Marcellin Boule and became a lifelong colleague and friend of Teilhard.

34. Marguerite Teillard-Chambon (1880–959), known as Claude Aragonnès, an author in her own right whose writings included a biography of Abraham Lincoln, was Teilhard's cousin, close friend, confidant, and correspondent. He entrusted many of his thoughts and early essays to her during the time of WWI. She introduced Teilhard to Léontine Zanta, who also became his lifelong friend. See n36 below. His wartime letters to her can be found in Teilhard, *Making of a Mind*.

35. *Making of a Mind*, 26.

36. Léontine Zanta (1872–1942), the first French woman to receive a doctorate in philosophy, a committed Catholic, was influenced by Henri Bergson under whom she had also studied. She played a significant role in the emergence of French feminism. Marguerite Teillard-Chambon had been a student of hers and introduced Teilhard

Following upon his demobilization in March of 1919, Teilhard returned to scientific studies in geology and paleontology, studying especially with Marcellin Boule at the Museum of Natural History. He later received his doctorate, with distinction, in 1922, with a thesis on mammals of the Lower Eocene Period in France. By 1920 he was teaching geology at the Institut Catholique in Paris. He became a lifelong friend of Édouard Le Roy,[37] professor of the philosophy of science and successor to Henri Bergson at the Collège de France, as well as of Maurice Blondel.[38] He saw his life as now devoted to research.

In 1922 Teilhard received an invitation to join a funded expedition exploring the Yellow River region in central China. He would be located at a Jesuit house in Tientsin, a port city not far from Peking.[39] This was the beginning of what would become something of a second home as he would eventually spend many more years in China. A four-month expedition in 1923 brought him to Mongolia and the Ordos Desert, their destination. So profitable was it that he and Father Licent, his Jesuit confrère in China, undertook a second expedition the following year. Just as the war had plunged Teilhard into the depths of reality, so this period in China expanded his horizons and enriched his life's experience. Whether in Cairo, Hastings, Paris, or during war, Teilhard was always open to what the experience had to teach him. It was from this first of his times in China that we receive Teilhard's "Mass on the World," signed Ordos, Easter, 1923.[40] His appreciation of the "cosmicity" of Christ was beginning to take full form. He also had to struggle, as a scientist committed

to her in 1918, after which they remained friends and correspondents. See Teilhard, *Letters to Léontine Zanta.*

37. Édouard Le Roy (1870–954) was a noteworthy French philosopher, mathematician, and disciple of Henri Bergson, whom he succeeded at the Collège de France and the Académie Française. A committed Catholic, he was accused of modernism and several of his writings were placed on the Index. He and Teilhard mutually influenced each other, became lifelong friends, and were correspondents.

38. Maurice Blondel (1861–1949) was a French philosopher who was best known for his philosophy of action and on the relationship between philosophical reasoning and Christian faith. He had an influence on the later movement known as *ressourcement.* Blondel, along with Henri Bergson and Édouard Le Roy, was one who had influence on the thought of Teilhard and with whom Teilhard became acquainted with the help of Valensin, who was a student of Blondel's. See Teilhard and Blondel, *Correspondence.*

39. See Teilhard, *Letters from a Traveller*, 65–194.

40. Teilhard, "The Mass on the World" (1923), *HM*, 119–34. Also see Thomas King, *Teilhard's Mass.*

to evolutionary theory, with the traditional exposition of the Church's teaching on original sin. Following the strenuous and successful expeditions, Teilhard returned to Paris in October 1924.

At a colleague's request, Teilhard had previously drafted some preliminary and tentative thoughts in a paper, "Note on Some Possible Historical Representations of Original Sin" (1922).[41] These reflections, having reached his Jesuit superiors in Lyons and Rome as well as the Holy Office, led his superiors to have him leave Paris and the Institut Catholique. It was the beginning of a lifelong struggle to bring his thoughts about Christianity and evolution to publication. He was to limit himself to publishing only purely scientific work. By June 1926 he had returned to Tientsin, this time under a cloud of suspicion. His friendship with George Barbour,[42] a Scottish geologist teaching in Peking, whom he had met earlier, continued to solidify. *The Divine Milieu*, a spiritual treatise and his first fundamental work, dates from this 1926–1927 period. He had completed it by early 1927. While having received the approval of his Jesuit superiors, it was not allowed publication by Roman authorities. From October 1927, through November 1928, he had another interlude back in France before returning once again to China for the third time, this time for about ten years.

Teilhard would be in China from March 1929 through 1938 and then again from 1939–1946. Except for brief periods back in Paris and in America, he would be primarily located out of Peking for the next sixteen years, which would produce significant scientific work as well as further explorations of his re-visioning Christianity in relationship to an evolving universe, further writings which were also not published in his lifetime. This time included his involvement as geologist in the excavations at Chou-Kou-Tien (known today as Zhoukoudian) southwest of Peking (known today as Beijing). Early in the 1920s, at the site, two teeth

41. *CE*, 45–55. We will be discussing Teilhard's approach to the doctrine of original sin in chapter 7.

42. George Brown Barbour (1890–977), of Scottish descent, was a world-renowned geologist. He and his American wife spent eleven years in China from 1920–932 where he met Teilhard and where they were involved in geological expeditions together, among which were the excavations at Chou-Kou-Tien. Later the Barbours settled in Cincinnati, Ohio, where he taught geology. The relationship between the two men continued and Barbour was one of Teilhard's companions who knew him well, both as a scientist and as a spiritual man. Barbour was a very religiously sensitive Presbyterian. He once referred to Teilhard as "our dear saint." One of Barbour's sons, Ian (1923–2013), became well known for his own work in science and religion.

had been found, which led Davidson Black, a Canadian, in 1927, to pursue excavations there to which specimens he gave the name *Sinanthropus pekinensis* or Peking man (later known as *Homo erectus pekinensis*).[43] In December of 1929 a Chinese scientist, Pei Wen-Chung (Pei Wenzhong) discovered a complete skullcap. Teilhard was given the task of determining the age of the geological formations in which the skull had been found, an important responsibility as Peking man may have been the earliest version of *Homo sapiens.* At the time, the discovery was a paleontological breakthrough in the study of human origins.

Almost fifty years old now, Teilhard was invited to be the official geologist on another expedition across Central Asia funded by the French Citroen car company—the *Croisière Jaune* or Yellow Expedition. Prior to this he had spent several months in Paris at the close of 1930, made his first visit to the United States in early 1931, where he lectured and visited New York, Chicago, and San Francisco. Teilhard joined the Yellow Expedition on May 8, 1931, which comprised over forty participants, mainly French, also Chinese, Teilhard being the only Catholic, through some almost inaccessible parts of China, lasting nine months. On New Year's Day, 1932, he celebrated Mass and all his companions were present. Following the Yellow Expedition, Peking rather than Tientsin became his Chinese home. During the time he had been on the expedition, his father had died on February 11, 1932, which he learned upon his return. His mother died four years later, February 7, 1936. On neither occasion was he able to be there. Following the expedition Teilhard wrote another essay, "The Road of the West: To a New Mysticism" (1932),[44] in which he viewed at the time the intellectual and mystical directions

43. Peking man, by which name he is most known, but scientifically now named *Homo erectus pekinensis*, or the upright man from Peking, was first known as *Sinanthropus pekinensis.* It comprises a variety of fossil specimens dating from roughly 600,000 years ago, discovered during excavations at Zhoukoudian (Chou-Kou-Tien) near Beijing (Peking). Most of the early studies of these fossils were supervised by Davidson Black until his death in 1934 when Teilhard took over, and later Franz Weidenreich, although Teilhard had been involved as far back as 1929 when he had returned to China after a brief period in which he had been allowed to be back in France. "*Homo*" is a genus of which there are several species, e.g., *Homo neanderthalensis, Homo erectus, Homo sapiens,* and others. Each has played a role in the attempt to trace the path to modern man. The consensus today is that humans first evolved in East Africa and traveled from there, as was the case with *Homo erectus.* A delightful account is Aczel, *Jesuit and Skull.*

44. *TF*, 40–59.

taken by the West as superior to those of the Eastern religions.[45] In his lifetime, apart from his purely scientific treatises, Teilhard wrote close to two hundred essays which were published posthumously. During this first Peking period (1932–1938) he stayed in contact with the excavations at Chou-Kou-Tien even as the Japanese began their invasion of China, joined Helmut de Terra in an expedition into India in 1935, made two trips to the United States (1933, 1937) as well as maintaining contacts in France, in addition to the continued field work in mainland China itself. At the end of this first Peking stretch he went to Japan (September 1938), the United States (October 1938), France (November 1938–June 1939) and the United States again (July and August 1939), at a time when war was again looming on the horizon in Europe, arriving back in China in late August of 1939. He had again visited New York, Chicago, and San Francisco where he had many contacts. During the months in Paris, early in 1939, he met Jeanne Mortier, who volunteered to become a secretary for him and later became an executor for his writings.[46]

Teilhard made many friends in his life: with philosophers like Maurice Blondel,[47] Édouard Le Roy,[48] Auguste Valensin;[49] with colleagues like George Barbour,[50] Davidson Black,[51] Helmut de Terra,[52] and Pierre Leroy, SJ;[53] with women who played a significant role in his

45. The most thorough treatment of Teilhard's approach to Eastern religions is Ursula King, *Eastern Religions*.

46. Jeanne-Marie Mortier (1892–1982) collected and conserved Teilhard's writings from the time of their meeting in 1939 until his death, became one of his correspondents, arranged for the publication of his writings after he died, and is significantly responsible for their accessibility today. She also arranged for the publication of the *Teilhard de Chardin Album* along with Marie-Louise Aboux, a photo album with commentary published both in French and in English in 1966.

47. See n38 above.

48. See n37 above.

49. See n26 above.

50. See n42 above.

51. A Canadian paleoanthropologist, friend, and collaborator with whom Teilhard had worked at Chou-Kou-Tien. He was credited with naming *Sinanthropus pekinensis*.

52. See n57 below.

53. Pierre Leroy, SJ (1900–1992) first met Teilhard in Paris in 1928 while preparing to go to China to work with Emile Licent, SJ, in Tientsin, and later succeeded Licent as director of the museum with which Teilhard himself had been attached on his first trips to China. They became close friends, the closest of confidantes. Separated after the war, they continued correspondence. Later Teilhard lived in New York and Leroy was for a year and a half at the University of Chicago. Leroy had earlier studied under Lucien Cuénot. See Leroy, *Letters from My Friend*.

life, like his cousin Marguerite,[54] Léontine Zanta,[55] Ida Treat,[56] Rhoda de Terra,[57] and Lucile Swan.[58]

During his second stretch in Peking (1939–1946), the years of the Second World War, Teilhard was much more confined. He worked diligently on *Le Phénomène Humain* which he considered to be his major *oeuvre* and had completed the manuscript by June of 1940, the same month in which the French surrendered to the German invasion. It was difficult during the war to get the manuscript to Rome for approval, which he did by April of 1944. Permission for publishing was denied although he had presented it as a scientific treatise. The refusal deeply disappointed him. Teilhard's cosmic sense included the human phenomenon and the birth of reflective consciousness as pivotal. Although his research remained scientific, his writings continued to be increasingly spiritual. Twenty-two essays date from August 1939 through February 1946. At the end of the war Teilhard was permitted to return to Paris. He set sail from Shanghai on March 27, 1946, and on May 3 was back in Paris, where he spent the next five years.

Back in France he was able to connect with the mid-twentieth century intellectual currents. He was involved in discussions with many, among them Emmanuel Mounier, a personalist philosopher; Gabriel Marcel, a Catholic existentialist; Paul Rivet, founder of the new Musée de

54. See n34 above.

55. See n36 above.

56. Ida Treat (1889–1978), an atheist and Marxist, was a professor and journalist based in Paris in the 1920s and 1930s, where she received a doctorate in letters and later a second doctorate in paleontology. Teilhard supervised her research at the Museum of Natural History, and they became friends and correspondents. See Teilhard, *Letters to Two Friends.*

57. Rhoda de Terra, the wife of Helmut de Terra (1900–1981), an accomplished geologist, became Teilhard's self-appointed secretary and a lifelong friend and correspondent. They had first met in the mid 1930s during one of the expeditions led by her husband in Kashmir and India. Teilhard and Helmut de Terra were close colleagues and close friends with whom he stayed when visiting America. It was in her apartment that Teilhard died on Easter Sunday in 1955. See Teilhard, *Letters to Two Friends*, 121–218, and de Terra, *Memories.*

58. Lucile Swan (1890–965), a sculptress and painter, was born in Sioux City, Iowa, studied at the Art Institute in Chicago, moved to Peking in 1929 (and remained there until 1941 when the United States entered the war against Japan who had been at war with China), worked on reconstructing the skull of Peking Man, and sculpted a well-known bust of Teilhard with whom she had fallen in love, whom he had met in Peking in 1929 (Teilhard and Swan, *Letters*).

l'Homme; Nicholas Berdyaev, a Russian religious philosopher; Vladimir Lossky, an Orthodox theologian; Dominique Dubarle, OP, a philosopher; and Bruno de Solages, rector of the Institut Catholique in Toulouse. In 1946 he had met Julian Huxley for the first time and a close relationship developed. With these there was always friendliness, not always agreement, as reflected in some of the discussions with Marcel. He was able to reconnect with his Jesuit friend and colleague Henri de Lubac.[59] In 1947 he was made an officer of the Légion d'Honneur and honored thus:

> He [Teilhard] may be properly ranked today, in the field of paleontology and geology, as one of the glories of French science, the international prestige of which he has done so much, through his personal relations with scientists of other lands, to develop and maintain.[60]

In 1948 he was nominated for a prestigious position in prehistory at the Collège de France for which permission to accept was refused. He corresponded with many, unbelievers as well, such as Lucien Cuénot,[61] a renowned biologist and father of Claude Cuénot, the early biographer of Teilhard. During the years in France, he returned to visit his native Auvergne and returned in 1948 once again to the United States where he was able to resume his relationship with George Gaylord Simpson whom he had met on earlier visits to the States. He worked to revise *Le Phénomène Humain* which he acknowledged was a tedious task for him and for which permission to publish was still denied. On the more gratifying side, his contribution to science was being recognized. In 1950 he was

59. Henri de Lubac, SJ (1896–1991), a French Jesuit priest, one of the most significant theologians of the twentieth century, a prolific author, taught theology at the Institut Catholique in Lyons, founded the *Sources Chrétiennes* series, contributed to the *nouvelle théologie* movement, was silenced in the 1950s but invited by Pope John XXIII and Pope Paul VI to contribute to the deliberations of the Second Vatican Council, and was made a Cardinal by Pope John Paul II. He was a friend, a knowledgeable and supportive expositor of Teilhard's thought without being his disciple, having published four books on Teilhard (in 1962, 1966, 1968, 1977), as well as many articles and introductions to some of Teilhard's own writings. He first met Teilhard in 1922 and they became correspondents from 1930 until 1949. See de Lubac, *Religion of Teilhard.*

60. Cuénot, *Teilhard de Chardin*, 247.

61. Lucien Cuénot (1866–1951) was a French biologist whose recognized work was in genetics. Teilhard held him in high esteem and cites him several times, e.g., in *HP*, 86, where he presents Cuénot's diagram of the tree of life. Pierre Leroy, SJ, had been a student of Cuénot's before having been sent to China. Claude Cuénot (1911–1992) who authored the distinctive biography of Teilhard, was one of his children. Claude became a correspondent with Teilhard as well.

made a member of the Académie des Sciences of the Institut de France. Later in 1950 he pondered the possibility of a visit to South Africa where interesting discoveries of Australopithecines were being made.

After a visit to South Africa, Teilhard spent his remaining years in the United States. He had made five visits to the United States (1931, 1933, 1937, 1939, 1948) before 1950 when he settled there more permanently. His life had not been easy, deaths in the family, deprived during much of his life of what Paris had to offer, writings under a cloud, growing heart disease, later struggles with some depression. On one occasion he was reported by Père Bergouioux to have said, "Pray for me that I may not die embittered,"[62] and on a different occasion, "It is absolutely necessary to keep smiling. The essential, and doubtless most fruitful, gesture is to smile, with something of love in the smile."[63] Prior to his departure from France, he had worked on a significant autobiographical essay, "The Heart of Matter" (1950). In 1951, now seventy years old, he was able to visit South Africa, the home of many remains from the early history of *Homo sapiens* and his hominoid cousins, the Australopithecines. From South Africa he sailed to America and lived with the Jesuits at St. Ignatius, 980 Park Avenue, New York City, for the next four years except for one further visit to South Africa in 1953 sponsored by the Wenner Gren Foundation in New York. Permission was given for a return visit to Paris in 1954. He was never confined in his interests or contacts, visiting in 1952 Albuquerque, Los Angeles, Berkeley, Glacier National Park, and Bar Harbor, Maine. In the months following his second return from South Africa Teilhard learned of the death of two of his novitiate classmates and close friends, Auguste Valensin and Pierre Charles, as well as that Piltdown man had been a hoax. His last major work, a testament to his Christian faith, and a summary of his vision of God working through Christ from within an evolutionary view of the world was "Le Christique," dated March 1955.[64]

On Easter Sunday, April 10, 1955, after celebrating his own Mass as well as attending Mass at St. Patrick's Cathedral, he died of a heart attack while visiting Rhoda de Terra. The funeral was the following Tuesday at his Jesuit residence on Park Avenue. A faithful son of St. Ignatius, he was

62. Frédéric-Marie Bergounioux, OFM (1900–1983) was a professor of geology at the Institut Catholique in Toulouse. See Bergounioux *L'âme sacerdotale*, 11; English translation in Almagno, *The Cord*, 173.

63. Cuénot, *Teilhard de Chardin*, 246.

64. *HM*, 80–102.

buried in the Jesuit cemetery at the Jesuit novitiate at St. Andrews on the Hudson, sixty miles north of New York City.[65] Later that same year Jeanne Mortier saw to the publication of Teilhard's *Le Phénomène Humain*, an English translation of which appeared in 1959 as *The Phenomenon of Man* and newly translated in 1999 as *The Human Phenomenon*. In 1962, seven years after Teilhard's death, the Holy Office issued a warning, not a condemnation, a *monitum*, pertinent to ambiguities and possible errors in some of Teilhard's writings. Three days before Teilhard's death, on Holy Thursday, Teilhard left in his journal a reference within which he saw his vision of Christ in relationship to the cosmos as an articulation of the vision of Saint Paul in 1 Corinthians, chapter 15, verses 26 to 28.[66]

Now that we have looked rather quickly at the lives of these two thinkers, let us think along with them about the cosmos, humanity, Christ, and God.

65. Near Hyde Park, NY, north of Poughkeepsie, since 1970 the home and property of the Culinary Institute of America.

66. See the testimony, dated April 7, 1955, that Teilhard left three days before his death. *FM*, 309. Also, Cuénot, *Teilhard de Chardin*, 387.

2

Thomas Aquinas's Theology of Creation

THE FIRST PART, OR the *prima pars*, of Aquinas's magisterial *Summa* begins with God, noting the reasonableness of belief in God's existence; discussing our use of language with respect to God, what can or cannot properly be said when speaking about God; and then moving from the nature of God and his omnipresence in the world to the Christian understanding of God as triune. He then moves to a discussion of creation. For Aquinas, God creates, and it is the Triune God who creates (*ST*, I, q. 45, a. 6). God is *both* Trinity *and* Creator. God is both three persons and yet one God, or perhaps better said, the one God subsists in three *hypostases*. For now, it may be good to leave the word *hypostasis* in Greek and save until later what Aquinas and the tradition before him understood "person" to mean.[1] What is important at this moment is to realize that Aquinas considers God as having revealed himself to be *both* Father, Son, and Spirit, *and* Creator. The fact that our world is created is for Aquinas a theological statement, a matter of belief (*ST*, I, q. 46, aa. 1–2). Our universe is not only a cosmos; it is also a creation. To Aquinas's theology of God, we will return later.[2] Our topic in this chapter is God's creation.

From the start, one must not only get God right, but one must get creation right. It is the first thing to be considered apart from God himself, even though it is not apart from God, but neither is it a part of God.

1. I discuss this in chapter 6 on Thomas's Christology.

2. I discuss some aspects of his theology of God in chapter 8.

God's creation, God's universe, is expansive. Not only is there a plethora of creatures, an unimaginable diversity of them, but pivotal to creation, at its apex so to speak, at its most amazing, is the human creature with all his or her complexity as a creature, who can think or reason—no small feat indeed—a rational animal with equal weight being placed on both words. As a creature, Aquinas considers the human being as a part of creation, a part of the natural world. He thus considers the human person within his theology of creation in the first part of the *Summa*. But the human person is also a spiritual creature and as such *capax Dei*,[3] open to the divine, open to that which lies beyond human nature as such. This world of grace and the virtuous life which it undergirds, at the heart of Aquinas's anthropology, is the subject of the second part of his *Summa*. For there is more to be said about the human creature than her creatureliness alone.

Within this human world there is one human being who theologically requires further attention beyond what is said of the rest of us, namely Jesus Christ and the story of his conception, birth, life, death, and resurrection. This Word Incarnate is the subject of the third part of the *Summa* which brings us back again to the God with whom Thomas began. We end where we begin, as T. S. Eliot pointed out in a different context,[4] for all comes from God and returns to God, the Neoplatonic theme of *exitus* and *reditus*.[5] God is the Alpha and the Omega according to the book of Revelation (1:8). We will return to God, as well as to his Only Begotten Son, but for now, what does Aquinas say of creation?

Our universe, the one in which we live, expanding as it is, with its billions of galaxies, unfathomable to the human mind, is created, that is, it comes to be out of nothing, *ex nihilo*, produced by God alone. In other words, for Aquinas if there is no God, there is nothing at all. Since the universe is created by an infinite intelligence, it is also intelligible, knowable, structured by a Mind and knowable by minds. It is also good, as the book of Genesis says. Mirroring its Creator, the universe is good, and like its Creator, creative, that is participating in the creative activity

3. See St. Augustine, *Trinity*, 378–79 (*De Trinitate*, XIV, 3.11).

4. "We shall not cease from exploration / And the end of all our exploring / Will be to arrive where we started / And know the place for the first time." Eliot, "Four Quartets," in *Complete Poems*, 145.

5. M. D. Chenu, OP, saw this theme as undergirding the basic structure of the *Summa*. See Chenu, *Toward Understanding*, 297–318. Also see Torrell, *Saint Thomas Aquinas*, 1:150–53.

of God.[6] Beyond the universe's creatureliness, and its intelligibility, and its goodness, it is manifestly diverse. The distinctions that exist among all the things that God has created is one of the first emphases in Aquinas's theology of creation. There is a sense of plenitude about it, a richness, a variety. There is no one creature exactly like another, even among the angels, especially among the angels. Aquinas's creation not only comprises material beings but spiritual beings as well. The plenitude of the universe requires it. As much as Aquinas appreciates matter and its goodness, the universe is not confined by being a world of matter alone. There is no scientific basis for materialism if by the latter we mean only matter, only the visible, only the empirically verifiable. There is more to the universe than what meets the eye, or a microscope or telescope, or is mathematically measurable.

There is also in God's creation the by-product of evil. God is not the cause of moral evil but evil exists in our world. The mystery of evil is one of the greatest conundrums for the human mind.

Besides the distinction between corporeal and spiritual creatures, there are distinctions or diversity in each realm, among the spiritual creatures or angels, among the completely corporeal creatures (that range from the elements of the periodic table to cucumbers and leeks, to tulips and orchids, to rabbits and zebras, to the chimpanzee and the australopithecines). And there is that distinct creation that is a composite creature, both corporeal and spiritual, the rational animal that we mentioned above, within which species there is also great diversity as well as remarkable individuality. According to Aquinas, each human person is a composite of a body and a soul, the latter being its life-giving principle as well as a source of individuality.[7] As a spiritual being, endowed with both intellect and will, or freedom and the capacity to think, the human person is also a moral agent, but that pertains more to the *secunda pars* of the *Summa*. Aquinas's complete anthropology is found in both the first part and in the second part of the *Summa*. That is a topic for a separate chapter. For now, let us examine each of the above statements in greater

6. Creation or the universe is not creative in the same way as the Creator is, who creates *ex nihilo*, but is creative in an analogous way, helping to bring forth that which was not there before, as a teacher does in bringing about learning in one whom he or she instructs, see *ST*, I, q. 117, a. 1. Aquinas makes it clear that only God creates in the strict sense of what creating means, see *ST*, I, q. 45, a. 1, *ad* 1; a. 5.

7. For a discussion of questions pertaining to the human soul in the thought of Aquinas, see Stump, *Aquinas*, 191–216.

detail to appreciate more fully what Aquinas can teach us about the universe in which we find ourselves.

The universe is created. It isn't that the universe just is! Only God just is. God *is* Isness, Being Itself. There is no distinction in God between *what* God is and *that* God is (*ST*, I, q. 3, a. 4). God always was, is, and will be. Eternity is one of the attributes of God, or one might say synonymous with God (*ST*, I, q. 10, aa. 2–3). What is eternal *is* God. Creatures are distinguished by the fact that they could not be. Only God cannot not be. Creatures are finite and contingent. They receive being from elsewhere. It is not of their essence to be. They are caused with that kind of causality called creation. God is not caused; God is the Uncaused Cause; God is the First Cause, the Cause of all causes and of all that is (*ST*, I, q. 2, a. 3; q. 3, a. 5). Creatures get their being from God. It is not their own, but on loan so to speak (*ST*, I, q. 104, a. 1). Creatures exist because they participate in Being. They aren't being itself. Participation is a significant theme in the thought of Aquinas.

> Just as that which has fire, but is not itself fire, is on fire by participation; so that which has existence but is not existence, is a being by participation. (*ST*, I, q. 3, a. 4, *corpus*)

> God is essential being; other things are beings by participation. (*ST*, I, q. 4, a. 3, *ad* 3)

> Therefore all beings apart from God are not their own being but are beings by participation. Therefore, it must be that all things which are diversified by the diverse participation of being, so as to be more or less perfect, are caused by one First Being, who possesses being most perfectly. (*ST*, I, q. 44, a. 1, *corpus*)

"Being" is an analogous term in Aquinas; it is to be understood in various even if related ways. We *are* but not in the same way that God *is*. Nor is it a question of degree. The kind of "Being" that God is (*esse*) is not the same kind of "being" that we have. Ours is participated being. We are creatures. This "procession" of creatures from God as the First Cause of all creatures is discussed by Aquinas in questions 44 to 46 in the first part of the *Summa*. God is not only the one by whom all come to be but is also their destiny, not only their first efficient cause but also their ultimate final cause (*ST*, I, q. 44, a. 4).[8] The mode of the coming to be of all that is

8. In the philosophy of Aquinas, grounded particularly in that of Aristotle, there are primarily four causes: efficient, final, material, formal. There is also exemplar causality and the principle of privation. There will also be in Aquinas references to First

not God is called "creating" because it presupposes nothing other than God himself; in other words, that which comes to be, comes to be *ex nihilo*, from nothing (*ST*, I, q. 45, a. 1),[9] only as a work of God who is its efficient and its final cause. Only God can create in the sense that Aquinas is using the word here, namely the production of being "from nothing" (*ST*, I, q. 45, a. 5). All that is not God is a creature, dependent on God for its "being" or existence. Creation is not a kind of change from something to something else, but rather denotes dependency on God.[10] Creatures are God-dependent. Aquinas also uses the word emanation (*emanatio*) in his theology of creation (*ST*, I, q. 45), creation being a particular kind or mode of emanation, of the way in which one thing comes forth from another. God is not in any sense a material cause of creation; creation is rather God's production of beings by the universal cause or the Cause of all causes.

There are degrees of participation in being on the part of finite beings. There is more being in a living creature than in a non-living one. A cactus has more being than a stone does; it participates to a greater degree in Being Itself. An eagle has more being than does an oak tree; it participates to an even greater degree. It is not only alive but sentient; it can move in a way a tree cannot. Socrates participated to an even greater degree in being than did fish in the Aegean Sea. He could think. So there are degrees of being but only one Being who is Being Itself. The stone is

Cause and secondary causes, and a principal cause and instrumental causes. Material and formal causes are known as intrinsic causes, intrinsic to finite corporeal beings. A material cause is that out of which something is made (its matter, even if that is just pure potentiality). A formal cause is that which makes something to be what it is, its form, that which answers the question, "What is it?" Efficient and final causes are not intrinsic to the creature. Final cause is that for the sake of which something is made or done, the purpose or goal. Efficient cause is that which "produces" it or brings it about, the agent of change, that which acts. It is what people in a scientific age ordinarily think of when they think of a cause. For an exploration of Aquinas's thought on causality in relationship to modern science's understanding of causality, see Dodds, *Divine Action*, esp. 46–53, 94–104. The approach of modern science is to reduce a more robust (and Aristotelian) approach to causality to efficient causality alone. See Feser, *Aristotle's Revenge*.

9. On *ex nihilo*, Denys Turner writes: "The preposition *ex* in *ex nihilo* does not govern the description of some state of affairs out of which whatever there is has been created. Rather it is the negativity of the *nihilo* that governs the *ex* here, in the creation of whatever there is, there is no out of it at all, no initial conditions, no primal soup, not even the 'formless deep' of the Book of Genesis, and for certain no 'random fluctuations in a vacuum'" ("Why Is There Anything?," in *God, Mystery, and Mystification*, 140).

10. *SCG*, Book II, ch. 18, #2.

closer to non-being than it is to Being Itself. Spiritual creatures (human beings and angelic beings) are as close to Being as creatures get. All creatures participate to varied degrees in being, but God does not participate, God *is* Being, in whose Being all finite creatures participate. "To create" means to give or share being with that which has none—thus to allow something new to exist. God is the Source of all being. God alone creates. The universe and all that is in it are created.

That which is created is intelligible. In contrast to many modern philosophers, Aquinas affirms that things in our world are knowable in themselves—*because they are created.*[11] They are mind related. All things exist first in the mind of God. Once they come to exist outside of God, created by God, they remain mind related. They remain correlated to the mind of God. They thus have an intelligibility about them for God is supremely intelligible, even if to finite minds incomprehensible. Created things are therefore also knowable to the human mind—even if not with the same degree of clarity as they have in the mind of God. To be a creature means to be intelligible, able to be comprehended, comprehensible. Aquinas's epistemology is realist and stands in contrast to modern philosophical idealists for whom all that we can know are our own ideas or the contents of our own minds. We can't get outside ourselves to know the real world as it actually is. Our human minds impose themselves on the world and we never know things in themselves. But, for Aquinas if things are created, they have an intelligibility. We can know them. We can know that something is true.

God is Truth Itself, but truth also resides in creatures as well, who participate not only in Being but also in Truth. Aquinas discusses how we know, the process whereby reality, real things in the world, creatures, impress themselves upon our human intellectual powers. The extramental world (a dog) impresses itself on our senses through a process of sensation, which sense data or images or percepts are the objects that our intellects actively convert into knowable objects to which our minds are receptive. Aha, it's a dog! The formation of what we perceive (in the real world) through a process of conceptualization (the percept becoming a concept) gives us understanding. We now know what something is and what it really is. Books of course have been written on this theory of knowing and it is not our purpose here to go into the details but only to emphasize that what is created is created as knowable. Aquinas accepts

11. Josef Pieper makes this connection between "being created" and "being knowable" in "Negative Element."

the definition of truth as *adaequatio rei et intellectus*, or the conformity of the mind to the thing itself, to that which is real (*ST*, I, q. 16, a. 1).

Aquinas discusses truth in many places[12] as well as in question sixteen of the *prima pars*. Knowledge is a way in which a thing known is in the knower (*ST*, I, q. 16, a. 1), not as it exists of course in the extra-mental world but with its own kind of existence in one's mind, as a de-materialized intelligible image or likeness. Truth resides both in the intellect and in things themselves as they are related to the intellect, as they are structured as knowable. For Aquinas, everything that is, is knowable, because there is a correlation between being and truth, or being and intelligibility. They are as it were convertible (*ST*, I, q. 16, a. 3). To be is to be knowable. Truth is considered a transcendental, something that transcends the categories in terms of which we ordinarily understand things.[13] God is Being Itself. God is Truth Itself (*ST*, I, q. 16, a. 5). We are. We thus participate in the Truth that God is. A creature is what it is because it first existed in the mind of God and now, as a creature, exists outside that mind but still conformed to what it was in God's mind, and is thus mind-related and intelligible. So, in one sense, there is only One Truth: in another, many truths (*ST*, I, q. 16, a. 6). One Creator, many creatures.

That which is created is also good. In question five of the *prima pars*, Aquinas indicates that goodness, like truth, is also a transcendental, in other words convertible or identical with being, distinct but not distinct in God, only distinguished by our human minds (*ST*, I, q. 5, a. 1). We distinguish Truth and Goodness, but in themselves they are not distinct. Truth is being insofar as it is related to the mind; the good is being insofar as being is *desirable*. We are good, creatures are good, because everything created participates not only in being but in goodness as well. Aquinas, following Boethius, states that all things are good by participation, except of course for God who is Goodness itself (*ST*, I, q. 6, a. 3, *sed contra*). To be good belongs preeminently to God (*ST*, I, q. 6, a. 1). God *is* Goodness, just as God *is* Truth. In one sense, one could say, properly speaking, that goodness belongs to God alone. But given Aquinas's emphasis on his

12. E.g., in the *SCG*, Book I, 60–62, and in *De Veritate*, q. 1. On the structure of the disputed questions *De Veritate*, see Torrell, *Saint Thomas Aquinas*, 1:59–69.

13. The transcendentals—unity, truth, goodness—cannot be subsumed within the Aristotelian "categories" of substance and the nine accidents, but rather are coterminus with being itself and transcend the categories. Everything that *is*, is one, true, and good, since "to be" is itself to be knowable and desirable. This is the philosophy of the transcendentals.

doctrine of participation, creatures are good also through participation in the goodness that God is. He writes:

> Everything is therefore called good from the divine goodness, as from the first exemplary effective and final principle of all goodness. Nevertheless, everything is called good by reason of the similitude of the divine goodness belonging to it, which is formally its own goodness, whereby it is denominated good. And so, of all things there is one goodness, and yet many goodnesses (*ST*, I, q. 6, a. 4, *corpus*).

It is a remarkable and enlightened statement. God alone is essentially good (*ST*, I, q. 6, a. 3), but that goodness is shared. We participate or share in it. We creatures are thus truly good as well, with a participated goodness. We are not just called good due to our participation in goodness; due to our participation in goodness we *are* good, ontologically speaking (not morally speaking). Thus, in one sense there is only one Goodness but in another there are many goodnesses.

This emphasis in Aquinas is one that he wishes to make as part of his desire to put distance between the truth of the Catholic faith and the teaching of the Manicheans that the material world is inherently evil. Thomas's own religious order, that of the Dominicans, in their founding moments, came to be as preachers refuting the errors of the Albigensians or Cathars, twelfth and thirteenth century Manicheans. It has often been stressed that Aquinas himself was so open to the philosophy of Aristotle because it would be a better tool for refuting the Manichees.[14] This anti-Manichean theme permeates much of Aquinas's theology for Manicheism presented a very different theology of creation, namely that it was created by an evil god. For Aquinas there is one God, one Goodness, yet many goodnesses, many creatures, who are formally good, good in themselves. The goodness of the created order is one of the major emphases in Aquinas's theology of creation. "Every being as such is good" (*ST*, I, q. 5, a. 3).

This leads to Aquinas's understanding of evil, which for him does exist, but no being *as such* can be spoken of as evil *in itself*, "but only so far as it lacks being" (*ST*, I, q. 5, a. 3, *ad* 2), the doctrine of evil as *privatio boni* to which we will come shortly (*ST*, I, qq. 48–49). Not only is goodness

14. There is a humorous anecdote recorded by G. K. Chesterton about an invitation to Thomas to dine at a banquet sponsored by King Louis IX during which Thomas, while daydreaming, blurted out, "And *that* will settle the Manichees!" suggesting his coming to the awareness that Aristotle would be more effective in helping to refute the Manichean heresy than Platonism would be (*Saint Thomas Aquinas*, 97–120).

in God identical with being itself; not only is the nature of goodness to be desirable and thus God is the most desirable reality there is; not only do we participate in goodness and there are thus many goodnesses; but goodness is by nature self-diffusive. *Bonum est diffusivum sui* (*ST*, I, q. 5, a. 4, *ad* 2; III, q. 1, a. 1). Goodness tends to communicate itself, particularly as a final cause, that is by drawing things to itself, as that which is desired (*ST*, I, q. 5, a. 4). For Aquinas the intellect is oriented toward the knowable, toward truth; the will, however, is drawn toward the desirable, toward goodness. Both Truth and Goodness, both intellect and will, are major players in Aquinas's thought. The more being something has the more desirable it is. As there is a hierarchy or degrees of participation in being, so likewise in goodness. The more being a reality has, the more like God it is. But there are traces of God in every creature for God is omnipresent in his creatures.

God is present in all that God creates. All of creation manifests the grandeur of God, according to the psalmist (Psalms 8, 19) as well as Gerard Manley Hopkins (1884–1889): "The world is charged with the grandeur of God. It will flame out, like shining from shook foil; It gathers to a greatness, like the ooze of oil . . ."[15] Aquinas would easily affirm the same sentiment based on his theology of creation. God is present in all things. In question 8 of the *prima pars*, he writes:

> God is in all things; not, indeed, as part of their essence, nor as an accident; but as an agent is present to that upon which it works. For an agent must be joined to that wherein it acts immediately and touch it by its power . . . Now since God is very being by his own essence, created being must be his proper effect; as to ignite is the proper effect of fire. Now God causes this effect in things not only when they first begin to be, but as long as they are preserved in being . . . Therefore, as long as a thing has being, God must be present to it, according to its mode of being. But being is innermost in each thing and most fundamentally inherent in all things . . . Hence it must be that God is in all things and innermostly. (*ST*, I, q. 8, a. 1, *corpus*)

So beings are not only good because they participate in the supreme goodness that God is, and not only intelligible because they participate in the truth that God is, but beings exist because they participate in being which most properly belongs to God who is Being Itself. Therefore, God is present to all things.

15. From "God's Grandeur," 66.

Nothing would *be* if God were not present to it as the source and cause of its being. God is ubiquitous, omnipresent, and immanent (*ST*, I, q. 8, a. 2), and in all things in a threefold way according to Aquinas (*ST*, I, q. 8, a. 3), what is sometimes referred to as the presence of immensity.[16] God is in all things by his essence, presence, and power: (1) God is in things after the manner of an efficient cause and thus in all created things for which he is the cause of their very being. God is not present to them as part of *their* essence but due to *his* essence (*ST*, I, q. 8, a. 3, *ad* 1). Arguing against Avicenna (*ST*, I, q. 45, a. 5), who maintained that not all things were created immediately by God, Aquinas argues that all beings are created by God for their very being is given by God, and thus God is present to all creatures by his essence which is Being Itself. (2) Arguing against Averroes, who maintained that not all things fall within the providence of God, such as inferior bodies, Aquinas argued that God is present in all things as a real presence to them (*ST*, I, q. 8, a. 3; q. 22, a. 2). As a thing known is in the one who knows, and a thing desired in the one desiring, so all things are present to God and in God as he is present to them and in them. (3) Arguing against the Manicheans to whom he refers, who maintained that spiritual and incorporeal things were subject to divine power, but corporeal things were subject to a contrary principle, Aquinas maintained that God is in all things by his power (*ST*, I, q. 8, a. 3). This threefold way of speaking is not so important as much as Aquinas's continued emphasis on God's real presence in and to all things. It is even more true to say that all things are in God who is also in all things (*ST*, I, q. 8, a. 3, *ad* 3).

In his response to the fourth objection in article three of question 8, Aquinas notes that there are three primary degrees of God's presence in things (or four):

1. God is present in *all* things and to all things by the presence of immensity, or as the cause of their being, and as governed by God's providence and power.

2. A. God is present to the rational creature in a special way in that the rational creature is a spiritual creature with intellect and will and created in the image and likeness of God (*ST*, I, q. 93). This

16. Teilhard will speak of this same presence of immensity. See "Cosmic Life" (1916), *WW*, 48: "God . . . is the Center who spreads through all things; his immensity is produced by an extreme of concentration." To be developed further in the next chapter.

simply manifests another degree of the presence of immensity, for God is more present to the rational creature than to other living beings, and more present in living than in non-living beings. The non-living, the living, the sentient, the rational, the incorporeal or purely spiritual: all denote degrees of the presence of being.[17]

2. B. There is another kind of presence, not just one of degree: "grace constitutes a special mode of God's existence in things (*ST*, I, q. 8, a. 3, *ad* 4). Grace is a unique mode of God's presence in human creatures which we consider in a later chapter.
3. "There is, however, another special mode of God's existence" in the human being, namely the hypostatic union, God's presence in Christ and in the humanity of Christ, whereby the human nature of Christ is united to the Person of the Word (*ST*, I, q. 8, a. 3, *ad* 4).

We may note in a previously quoted text that Aquinas had said: "Now God causes this effect in things not only when they first begin to be, but as long as they are preserved in being" (*ST*, I, q. 8, a. 1). God is causally present to creatures as their Creator, but that presence does not cease when the creative act, so to speak, is completed and something has come to be. Aquinas would distinguish the creative act itself, which is production of being *ex nihilo*, as distinct from God's continuing presence to things as he preserves them in being, which presence Thomas refers to as God's governance of the universe (*ST*, I, q. 103). At no point could a creature continue to be if God withdrew his presence from them (*ST*, I, q. 104, a. 1). This preservation is sometimes spoken of as conservation, God's continuing presence to creatures. In its own way it is a continuation of creation as God continues to preserve what he has brought forth. Aquinas's theology of God and of creation is permeated with the notion of presence and participation, each of which is understood in diverse ways or to different degrees.

God's creation is diverse. Central to Aquinas's treatment of creation, or of the universe, is his awareness of its immense diversity. He would not have been as aware, as later Charles Darwin was, of the multiplicity of species on planet earth but he would have seen that multiplicity as congruent with his theology. For Aquinas, it is fitting that there be

17. Ordinarily when Thomas speaks about substances, he speaks about them as incorporeal or corporeal. He does, however, also use the word "spiritual" when discussing angels. E.g., *ST* I, q. 50, a. 2. He also in *ST* II-II, q. 28, speaks about spiritual joy. Ordinarily, however, he refers to angels as incorporeal and immaterial.

a plenitude or richness to creation as it manifests the grandeur of God. In question forty-seven of the *prima pars* Aquinas talks about this distinction that exists within creation. This multiplicity comes from God himself for the very perfection of the universe consists in this diversity and is intended by God.

> Hence, we must say that the distinction and multitude of things come from the intention of the first agent, who is God. For he brought things into being in order that his goodness might be communicated to creatures and be represented by them; and because his goodness could not be adequately represented by one creature alone, he produced many and diverse creatures, that what was wanting to one in the representation of the divine goodness might be supplied by another. For goodness, which in God is simple and uniform, in creatures is manifold and divided; and hence the whole universe together participates the divine goodness more perfectly and represents it better than any single creature whatever. (*ST*, I, q. 47, a. 1, *corpus*)

God wills diversity. As in the book of Genesis, God sees that it is good (Gen 1:4, 10, 12, 18, 21, 25, 31). Even though the tulip is my favorite flower, the universe would lack a plenitude if there were no other flowers on the earth. Even though I have had a fondness for rabbits since my childhood, the universe would be lacking something if there were no trout, no parrots, no wild geese, no tigers. As we now know, the diversity within creation can stagger the mind. And we do not know all the species that may still be discovered or all those that have disappeared. There is much about penguins that one never knew, the varied species of them, the number of them that are becoming extinct, whether they reside only in cold water and the southern hemisphere, until explorations and discoveries were made. Aquinas would take pleasure in the awareness of the diversity within God's creation, see it as good, and be open to more diversity than that of which he himself may have been aware.

This sense of plenitude requires therefore some inequality, some distinctions, within creation. "For the universe would not be perfect if only one grade of goodness were found in things" (*ST*, I, q. 47, a. 2). Plants are more perfected, have more being, participate in more goodness, than do minerals, and animals do more than plants, and the human being more than other animals. This inequality is not something to be disparaged but rather appreciated. A stone as stone or a plant as plant lacks nothing of its own created fullness. This does not manifest any lack of appreciation for those creatures that may manifest God less fully. It is in the totality that the plenitude resides. As the wisdom of God is the cause of the diversity in the first place, so it is God's wisdom that is the cause of this differentiation or hierarchy or inequality within creation (*ST*, I, q. 47, a. 2). Without it we would have only flatness,[18] not true differentiation at all. Could this call for diversity suggest that there could be more than one world (*ST*, I, q. 47, a. 3)? Why not many? As contemporary as this question is,[19] it was also a question for Aquinas for whom in the end there is only one, although that oneness might encompass more than we ordinarily think. Even if there is a multiverse, or parallel universes, or a multitude of universes, as there is a multitude of galaxies, from God's perspective there is only one, since they would all be God's creation. Nothing rules out more diversity than we may currently know.

Aquinas's sense of diversity, however, extends beyond what we might ordinarily think when we think of the diversity of creatures. His understanding of the plenitude of creation requires that "the perfection of the universe requires the existence of an incorporeal creature" (*ST*, I, q. 50, a. 1). Although he may have considered the existence of angels something to be accepted as revealed, his theology of creation also suggests that the universe would be deficient without them. Considering the diversity of creatures, why would there not be spiritual beings as well as material beings, even though we cannot adequately picture them as they are lacking in any material base for our being able to imagine what they are like. But they fit a universe as diverse as ours is.

God created incorporeal beings as well as corporeal ones. God so loves diversity that among his diverse creatures are those who are not composites of matter and form. Aquinas frequently had recourse to Aristotle's hylomorphic doctrine, namely that substances, or "things that are," that exist in our world with some ability to stand on their own (like a tree, a kitten, Martin Luther King Jr.), are composed of two principles, "matter" or that out of which something is made and "form" or that which makes something to be what it is, gives it its quiddity or "whatness" or nature. Angels are finite but are pure form; they are composites of "essence" and "existence." Thus, they too could not be, even though they are not

18. Ken Wilber introduced this word to describe a universe without any hierarchy to it. See *Sex, Ecology, Spirituality*, 422–30. Although I do not agree with everything Wilber says, the book contains a wealth of wisdom and insight. Likewise, see his *Marriage*, 10, 56–57, 85, 135, for references to "flatland" and a critique of modernity.

19. See O'Meara, *Vast Universe*.

composites of matter and form. They are created and sustained in their existence by God, but they lack any material aspect. They are what they are, and each angel is what it is.

Aquinas gives quite a thorough treatment to angels, a good deal of emphasis to them. The major treatise on angels comprises questions 50 to 64 of the *prima pars*, but he also discusses them further in questions 106 to 14, where he discusses the ordering or hierarchy of angelic beings, how they communicate, their mission, how they guard us, and those that are bad, the demons. All in all, he thus devotes twenty-four questions comprising 118 articles on this topic. They are an important component of the created world even if beyond our perception. His treatment also helps us to appreciate that we are *not* angels, or simply angels with bodies, to which modern Cartesians open the door, but that we ourselves are animals[20] grounded in the physical world. Aquinas's treatment of angels is worth studying since it gives us insight into the nature of the created world, its diversity, its plenitude, its beauty, its connectedness to God—even if one might wonder how we can know so much about what is not visible to us, a challenge to a more empirically oriented world. Yet Aquinas himself was an empiricist in an Aristotelian sense. He maintained that knowledge begins with the senses and with the sensible world, but one can go from the physical world to the metaphysical, from the visible (the telescopically or microscopically as well) to the invisible. Modern empirical science studies the empirical world with its natural sciences but those sciences cannot prove that the totality of finite being is limited to what is sensible. For Aquinas the sensible world is a door to the suprasensible, which is the object today of other sciences.[21]

Aquinas discusses the multitude of angelic beings (*ST*, I, q. 50, a. 3), their incorporeality (*ST*, I, q. 50, a. 5), what it means for an angel to be somewhere (*ST*, I, qq. 52–53), what and how they know (*ST*, I, qq. 54–58), how the will differs from the intellect even among angelic beings (*ST*, I, q. 59), and given angelic wills, the nature of angelic love (*ST*, I, q. 60). Angels did not exist from all eternity (*ST*, I, q. 61, a. 2), nor were they necessarily created before corporeal creatures.

20. On our "human" animality see Turner, *Portrait*, 47–69; as well as Chik, "Thomistic Animalism," 645–76, and Vogler, "Intellectual Animal," 645–76.

21. E.g., see Tart, *End of Materialism*; Sheldrake, *Sense of Being Stared At*; among many others.

> For the angels are part of the universe: they do not constitute a universe of themselves; but both they and corporeal natures unite in constituting one universe. This stands in evidence from the relationship of creature to creature, because the mutual relationship of creatures makes up the good of the universe. But no part is perfect if separate from the whole. Consequently, it is improbable that God . . . should have created the angelic creature before other creatures. (*ST*, I, q. 61, a. 3, *corpus*)

Notice the probable character of Aquinas's opinion, as he is always careful about the degree of certainty one may have, always aware that there are other plausible opinions on the same subject; and note his holistic sense in affirming that it is the totality of the universe and not just a part of it that manifests its perfection. No part is complete apart from the other parts, apart from the whole. The incorporeal and the corporeal go together. He continues with how grace operates in an angel and whether they can sin and what the implications of the latter might be (*ST*, I, qq. 62–64). Over all one can see that Aquinas gives spiritual substances extensive treatment, one might even think overly extensive, except that in the medieval world an openness to belief in angels was strong and the theological tradition about them rich. Interest in them has rebounded in our own times. Aquinas's treatment of creation then moves from the incorporeal to the corporeal.

God created corporeal beings as well as incorporeal ones. In questions 65 to 74 of the *prima pars* Aquinas's emphasis moves to those creatures that are completely corporeal in contrast to the incorporeal ones that he had just considered. At the conclusion of this section of his treatment of creation he will consider the composite being that is both spiritual and corporeal, the human being. He begins his discussion of the creation of corporeal beings by assuring us that they too were created by God (*ST*, I, q. 65, a. 1) and proceed from God's goodness (*ST*, I, q. 65, a. 2). Although this has been emphasized before, he reinforces an anti-Manichean theology: "Certain heretics maintain that visible things are not created by the good God, but by an evil principle," but there must be "one principle of being from which all things in whatever way existing have their being, whether they are invisible and spiritual, or visible and corporeal" (*ST*, I, q. 65, a. 1). Everything was "brought into being for the reason that it was good for it to be" (*ST*, I, q. 65, a. 2), as Scripture attests in the first chapter of the book of Genesis.

Aquinas then considers in questions 67 to 74 the order of creation in seven days as it is biblically presented in the Genesis account. How literal is Aquinas's understanding of this order? For him, Scripture will always be the most authoritative voice. After Scripture there will be the patristic authorities supreme among whom will be Saint Augustine. Even in Scripture, however, there is room for metaphor and figurative speech (*ST*, I, q. 1, a. 9) as well as diverse senses in Scripture (*ST*, I, q. 1, a. 10). So, reliance on the authority of Scripture does not necessarily mean always understanding it in what today we would consider a literal interpretation.[22] Thus Aquinas takes up the question of whether the so-called seven days are really only one day, an opinion held by Augustine who maintained that "all the days that are called seven are one day represented in a sevenfold aspect" (*ST*, I, q. 74, a. 2). The seven days do not teach how things were produced temporally.

Aquinas respects Augustine's opinion, while at the same time remaining impartial and open to a temporal development in the production of corporeal creatures, as the account in Genesis suggests (plants, fish, birds, land animals, cattle, beasts of the earth). Aquinas sees the work of the first three days as making basic distinctions within creation and the work of the next three days as works that adorn that creation. Both Augustine and Aquinas respect diverse opinions when it comes to the "work" of creation. Neither takes the account in Genesis completely literally. The testimony of Scripture is to be respected but already early among the Fathers varied interpretations of the Genesis account arose. What does the word "day" mean? What is it trying to say? The highly symbolic and poetic text does not attempt to describe factually how the production of corporeal creatures came to be but that they were all created by God. It is also God who creates time itself, which came into being with creation (*ST*, I, q. 46, a. 3; q. 66, a. 4, *ad* 4, 5).

With corporeal creatures we now have those who are composed of both matter and form. In addition to their first efficient cause, namely God who brings them into being, and their ultimate final cause, once again God, although each creature may have more proximate final causes, all bodily creatures are also composed of two intrinsic principles, matter and form. This means that they are also capable of decomposition; they

22. Thomas's preference was for a literal interpretation, as that was understood in his day, as a reference to the text itself, in contrast to all the spiritual senses or allegorical interpretations whose value he also recognized, but as supplementary to the basic or literal meaning of the text. *ST*, I, q. 1, a. 10.

are subject to decay or the ravages of time. Some creatures are living and have a soul, a vegetative soul, which makes them both to be what they are and gives them life. Others have a sentient soul, also the principle of life as well as that which makes them to be this rather than that. These are the distinctions we find within creation. No creature is without form. Angels are pure form. Corporeal creatures comprise both matter and form. In living creatures this form is also known as a soul, a life principle. There are gradations in creation and among corporeal creatures as well. And there is one corporeal creature who is distinct because its soul is not mortal but immortal, and this is the human person.

And God created a human being, a rational animal, a corporeal and spiritual composite. Of the 119 questions in the first part of the *Summa*, almost a fourth of them are devoted to a discussion of human nature and the species we call *Homo sapiens* (*ST*, I, qq. 75–102). The supernatural life and destiny of human beings is reserved for the *secunda pars* of the *Summa*. In this anthropological section of the *prima pars* Aquinas discusses, often in great detail, the nature of the human soul; its intellectual and appetitive powers, the latter including free will, the former having both an active and a receptive dimension, as well as the operations of these two powers of the soul; the operations of the soul when separated from the body as well as when in union with the body, and when in union with the body the relationship between intellectual knowledge and sense knowledge; as well as the "coming to be" of the human person as an embodied soul or ensouled body and our first existence in a paradisal state.

All this lies within Aquinas's discussion of creation. One might ask why he does not treat of these matters in the second part of the *Summa* which is completely concerned with human and moral life. Why does he treat of the human being here? The answer is that he sees the human creature first as a part of creation, as part of the natural world. Those questions which go beyond human nature as such are the subject of the second part of the *Summa*. His treatment here indicates that he sees humanity not as apart from nature, apart from the universe, but as a part of the universe.[23] We are in the universe of corporeal beings even though we transcend them due to the immaterial nature of the human soul. The human for Aquinas is not something to be placed over against the natural

23. Alfred North Whitehead wrote: "It is a false dichotomy to think of Nature *and* Man. Mankind is that factor *in* Nature which exhibits in its most intense form the plasticity of nature" (*Adventures*, 85, emphasis in text). An excellent portrayal of the difficulty that comes from the separation of humankind from the natural world and a critique thereof is Tarnas, *Cosmos and Psyche*, esp. 1–70.

world as will happen come modern philosophy where the relationship between the thinking monad and the world out there become dichotomous in a post-Cartesian world view, where body and soul become separate substances.[24] In Aquinas's post-Platonic and pre-Cartesian hylomorphic understanding, the human being is a psychosomatic unity, a manifestation or creation of an intense union between the corporeal and spiritual, in which one finds two principles but not two antagonistic ones. The human being is a spiritual being but an embodied one. Man and woman take their place first in nature itself, in the universe, of which they are not only a part but the pinnacle of what one finds in the corporeal world.

In contrast to other medieval thinkers, Aquinas fought hard for the unity of the human person. She does not have a vegetative soul, a sentient soul, and a rational soul but only one soul which performs all these operations.[25] Aquinas also makes a distinction between *ratio* (reason) and *intellectus* (intellect, understanding, intuitive awareness). While not being distinct powers of the soul, they are nevertheless distinguishable in the way the power operates, the former being discursive, a specifically human way of knowing, for angels do not know discursively nor do the species in the animal world; while the latter, *intellectus*, has an immediacy to it, an intuitive quality, and is sometimes spoken of as a higher part of the mind (*ST*, I, q. 79, aa. 8–9). We have already referred to the fact that Aquinas is a realist when it comes to human knowledge. We can know the extra-mental world and we know it through a process involving sensation, sense data, sensory images or likenesses or phantasms, as well as a process of abstracting or producing through the active work of the mind intelligible species or forms which the mind receives and understands, but it is the world outside us which is understood and not simply the contents of our minds. Nor do our minds so impose its *a priori* workings in such a way that we cannot know things in themselves. Knowledge begins not with the mind but with the senses. Yet the human soul is a spiritual reality, capable of being sustained apart from the body, although then not a complete substance, since its nature is to be united to its body. The soul for Aquinas is created by God but not without its body (*ST*, I, q. 90,

24. Among the critiques of Descartes's dualism is that of Smith, "Replacing Descartes," 143–204.

25. This was one of the great controversies with which Thomas was engaged, that of the unicity or plurality of forms in the human being. E.g., see Weisheipl, *Friar Thomas d'Aquino*, 76, 288–90, 337–40. Torrell also discusses this controversy, *Saint Thomas Aquinas*, 1:187–90, 300.

a. 4). The body-soul unity is created as one reality and simultaneously, not one before the other. The body too is created even as it comes to be from the "slime of the earth" (*ST*, I, q. 91, a. 1; Gen 2:7)[26] but the human being emerges as a body-soul unity and as embodying the image of God.

The human being is created in the image of God. The theology of the *imago Dei* has a long history and goes back to the book of Genesis itself (1:26–27), receives strong emphasis in the Orthodox traditions, in the theology of St. Augustine, and in the doctrine of deification.[27] Aquinas takes this topic up in question ninety-three of the *prima pars.* His appreciation of God's creative activity reaches its summit in the creation of the human being as a being like unto God. This is central to Aquinas's theology of creation and pertains to the human person in her natural state. Even with sin, therefore, this image is not lost. It is constitutive of who we are. Aquinas affirms that we are in some respect like to God but not a perfect likeness (*ST*, I, q. 93, a. 1). This likeness of course does not imply that we are equal to God. "Therefore, there is in man a likeness to God; not, indeed, a perfect likeness, but imperfect. And Scripture implies the same when it says that man was made *to* God's likeness; for the preposition *to* signifies a certain approach, as of something at a distance" (*ST*, I, q. 93, a. 1).[28] Of course it is only Jesus Christ, the Only Begotten Son, who is a perfect Image (*ST*, I, q. 35, a. 2; Col 1:15). Nevertheless, this likeness unto God manifests the dignity of the human person within all of creation.

What are we to say then of God's presence in all things about which we spoke above? Does all of creation itself not manifest the glory of God? Just as there are distinctions within creation, so likewise here, not to the diminishment of God's omnipresence but to recognize the uniqueness of humanity within that creation. Just as life builds on that which is prior to it in creation and sentient life builds upon vegetative life, so rational or intellectual creatures build upon what was there in the universe. "But

26. Within the thought of Aquinas, on the relationship between primary and secondary causality and its relationship to evolution, see Dodds, *Divine Action*, 199–204.

27. The theme of deification will come up again when we consider Aquinas's theology of grace in chapter 4. With respect to the Orthodox traditions, see Christensen and Wittung, *Partakers*, esp. 95–159; Lossky, *In the Image*, esp. 97–110; and Papanikolaou and Demacopoulos, *Orthodox Readings*. For deification in the thought of St. Augustine, see Meconi, *One Christ*. Also, Meconi and Olson, *Called*. For deification in the thought of Aquinas, see Spezzano, *Glory*; and Williams, *Ground of Union*.

28. The NRSV translation of Genesis 1:26a is: "Let us make humankind in our image, according to our likeness." The Latin Vulgate translation has: "faciamus hominem ad imaginem et similitudinem nostrum."

some things are like to God first and most commonly because they exist; secondly, because they live; and thirdly because they know and understand" (*ST*, I, q. 93, a. 2). Aquinas does not hold that *all* creatures are made to God's *image* (*ST*, I, q. 93, a. 2) but he does see *traces* of God in all things (*ST*, I, q. 93, a. 6). "While in all creatures there is some kind of likeness to God, in the rational creature alone we find a likeness of *image* . . . whereas in other creatures we find a likeness by way a *trace*" (*ST*, I, q. 93, a. 6).[29] The likeness to God that justifies use of the word "image" is humanity's intellectual nature; the mind with its intellect and will constitute humanity's *imago* (*ST*, I, q. 93, a. 6). The human person's natural capacity for knowing and loving God; as well as a person's actually and habitually, even if imperfectly, knowing and loving God through the action of grace; as well as knowing and loving God perfectly as is true of the saints in heaven, all pertain to humanity's ability to be like unto God (*ST*, I, q. 93, a. 4). Although Aquinas carries with him the common medieval understanding of woman as not equal to man in all ways, nevertheless, since "image" refers principally to humanity's intellectual nature which "is found both in man and in woman" (*ST*, I, q. 93, a. 4, *ad* 1), no distinction is to be made between man and woman as regards their bearing God's image. Saint Augustine had said the same.[30]

Theological reflection, going back as far as Saint Irenaeus in the second century, made a distinction between image and likeness,[31] as does Aquinas (*ST*, I, q. 93, a. 9). Likeness can be considered in two ways, as something more general than image, having a wider usage, or it can be considered more narrowly, as a perfecting of the image. We are created as images but challenged to be more and more like unto God. Aquinas comes back to the preposition "*to*," namely that we are never perfect images although in this life we continue to perfect that image through a life of virtue. "But man is said to be both *image* by reason of the likeness; and *to the image* by reason of imperfect likeness" (*ST*, I, q. 93, a. 1, *ad* 2). Humanity's uniqueness consists in being able to be more like God than any other corporeal creature.

Although creation is good, evil does exist. Last, but certainly not of less importance, is the question of the reality of evil in our world. Aquinas

29. The emphasis is in the English translation of the text.

30. Augustine, *Trinity*, 329 (XII, 3, 12).

31. See Lawson, *Saint Irenaeus*, 8–9, 13–14, 154–61, 199–221; Quasten, *Patrology*, 1:311.

devotes two questions in the *prima pars* to this topic (48–49).[32] He is not concerned here, within his theology of creation, about moral evil, or sin as such; that is a major topic within the *secunda pars*. Here Aquinas is concerned about death, disease, decay in the world of life, vegetative and sentient life, as well as within nature in general. Today we are very aware of the ravages that nature reeks upon itself.[33] A tornado or hurricane can destroy property, trees, and human lives. Apple trees or tomato plants can be infected by parasites. A hawk looms down and kills a scurrying rabbit. A lion does not lie down with a lamb. Apart from the ways in which the human species may ravage the planet,[34] life on earth itself struggles to survive. There is pain in the animal world. There is the food chain. Species are not necessarily kind to each other. What do we make of these "natural evils"?

Aquinas again avoids any touch of Manicheism (*ST*, I, q. 49, a. 3). God is the first cause of all things. Is God thus the cause of evil (*ST*, I, q. 49, a. 2)? Evil is the absence of a good that is due to something (*ST*, I, q. 48, a. 1). The fact that an orange cannot see is not an evil; it is in the nature of the thing not to be able to do so. An evil is the absence of what rightly ought to be there. If a dog is lame and cannot walk, that is an evil since it is not the nature of a dog to be unable to walk. The former is an example of a negation, the absence of something, but not of something which it ought to have. The latter is a physical evil, or an evil in the natural world, since it is a deprivation of a good that ought to be there, such as blindness (*ST*, I, q. 48, a. 2, *ad* 1; a. 3; a 5, *ad* 1). The former is not an evil. The latter is. Not every absence of a good is evil; only the absence of a good that is a privation, of some good that ought to be present. For Aquinas, and in the classical tradition, no being is evil in itself. Rather evil is the absence of a good that ought to be there, a *privatio boni*.[35] Evil is a lack, closer to non-being if you will,

32. See Davies, *God and Evil*; Journet, *Meaning of Evil*; Turner, "How Could a Good God Allow Evil?," in *Mystery and Mystification*, 3–23.

33. Today there are many treatments on the forms of destructiveness that we find within nature itself. E.g., consider Johnson, *Ask the Beasts*, a theological reflection on varied facets of our knowledge of an evolutionary world view.

34. Meconi, *On Earth* is a collection of challenging and ecologically conscious essays. Edwards, *Partaking of God* approaches a theology of creation from an evolutionary and ecological perspective. Pope Francis's 2015 encyclical, *Laudato Si* (*On Care for Our Common Home*), focuses on the same concerns.

35. The expression "*privatio boni*" can easily be misunderstood. It is simply the denial that evil has a nature or being *in itself*. It was the subject of misunderstanding between Carl Jung and Viktor White, OP, which led them to part company. See Jung, *Memories*, 328–29; and Weldon, *Victor White*, with references to "*privatio boni*" in the indices.

the reality of which exists in the natural world itself apart from humankind. There is a special kind of evil, of course, in rational creatures, moral evil, among creatures who have free will (*ST*, I, q. 48, a. 5). Any discussion of evil needs to consider this distinction between physical evil, or evils we find in the natural world, and moral evil which we find only in creatures who are free. God is in no way the cause of moral evil, but indirectly is the cause of some physical evils in the sense that God creates a diversity of creatures, some of whom will die or suffer pain. Yet what God wills is the good of the universe and its plenitude.

Lest one think that Aquinas minimizes the reality of evil in the natural world, since he sees evil as lying between non-being and being, Aquinas clearly affirms that evil exists. It simply exists *as a privation* and not as a positive created thing in itself (q. 48, a. 2, *ad* 1–3; a. 3). It is not that there is no evil in God's creation. It is just that evil exists *in* something, not in itself, and *in* something *as* a lack or defect. The major problem with respect to evil, however, is not the existence of natural evil but the reality of human suffering, of the barbarous forms of evil in the human world, the inhumanity of the human species. While Aquinas recognizes the reality of evil, he also sees that it has its place in nature. The nature of corruptible creatures is that they corrupt; mortal beings die. That is part of their nature. In a way, the evils of nature are part of the plenitude of the universe itself, which is why Aquinas's discussion of evil in general comes within his discussion of the diversity of things within creation.

> As, therefore, the perfection of the universe requires that there should be not only beings incorruptible, but also corruptible beings; so the perfection of the universe requires that there should be some which can fail in goodness, and thence it follows that sometimes they do fail. Now it is in this that evil consists, namely, in the fact that a thing fails in goodness. Hence it is clear that evil is found in things, as corruption is also found; for corruption is itself an evil. (*ST*, I, q. 48, a. 2, *corpus*; also 49, a. 2)

For Aquinas it is better to be than not to be, even if one finds in a being the lack of a perfection. For Aquinas, the perfection of the universe requires a diversity of beings some of whom will lack the fullness of being. Living beings die. Some beings are food for others. That is in the nature of things. God not only permits it; he creates it. In that sense (we are not talking about moral evil here), a world with evil is a better world than a world without evil, as strange as that may sound, since a world without natural or physical evils would be a world without diversity. "Hence many good things would be taken away if God permitted no evil to exist." (*ST*, I, q. 48, a. 2, *ad* 3). Having sufficiently undermined any latent Manicheism, Aquinas is able to say that God is the cause of a certain kind of evil, namely that which is intrinsic to nature with respect to the diversity of its creatures, such as the corruption of that which is corruptible by nature (*ST*, I, q. 49, a. 2). It is as if God could not create a universe of such diverse beings without allowing a certain kind of evil into creation.[36]

However satisfactory or unsatisfactory one might find Aquinas's treatment of this question of evil at this point, one needs to recognize that we are dealing with one of the more challenging philosophical issues. Aquinas does not, however, want to minimize in any way evil's existentiality; he does however deny it substantiality. It is not something *in itself.* It *exists* but as a *privation.* As such, it lacks the desirability and intelligibility of the created order. The major dilemmas connected with the mystery of evil, of course, have to do with rational creatures, something to be considered in chapter 4. Even here in the *prima pars*, however, Aquinas cannot avoid referring to the human and moral realm which is such a significant part of the diversity of creation and its plenitude.

In Conclusion: What then are Thomas Aquinas's contributions to a theology of creation? In what does his theocentric cosmology consist? The universe not only is, but is created, is God's creation. It could not be, would not be, apart from God who gives it being and sustains it in its continuing to be. In other words, the universe is dependent on God for its being; it is contingent; it could not be. But it is because God is a Creator. Not only is creation dependent on God in order to be but it participates in being. The kind of being it has is being by participation. This principle of participation looms large in Aquinas's thought. Creation, creatures, participate not only in being (they are not Being Itself nor beings by themselves) but in the Truth and Goodness that God is. The created world, the cosmos, the universe, is intelligible, knowable, created to be known, and the universe is good, good in itself, with a participated goodness. As Aquinas puts it, there is one Goodness and many goodnesses, one Creator, many creatures. Aquinas's theology of creation is opposed to any form of Manicheism. God is good, and so is God's creation.

Creatures participate in the intelligibility and goodness that only God truly is because the universe is not without God's sustaining presence to it. God is omnipresent, present in *all* creatures, although there are

36. Note Aquinas's approach here and contrast it with that of Teilhard's in chapter 7.

degrees of presence, of participation. There is the cosmos, with its planets and stars, its oceans and mountains, but there are also living creatures, a multitude of diverse plants, and among the living creatures some that are sentient beings, that sense things, that move and have locomotion, that can swim or fly or climb or run. There is an incredible diversity in God's universe the beauty of which lay in this plenitude of being or beings. This principle of plenitude is as important to Aquinas's theology as is that of participation. Both disclose creation's ultimate relatedness to the Creator. This diversity is manifest not only in the world of corporeal creatures but also with incorporeal angelic beings. The existence of purely spiritual beings in the universe makes sense in a creation by a God who loves diversity. Aquinas is neither a materialist in the modern sense nor a Manichean. Corporeal creatures are good. Spiritual creatures also exist.

Within this universe of diverse creatures there is the human being who stands midway between the corporeal and the incorporeal as embodying both. Why would there not be such a creature? The human being in that sense is a central point in the created world, bridging if you will matter and spirit. What is significant is that Aquinas places his discussion of the nature of the human animal here within the *prima pars* of his *Summa* as a part of his theology of creation. In other words, man and woman are not apart from creation but are a part of the natural world. While unique, they find their proper place within nature itself, although many anthropologies or philosophies place humankind over against the natural world, but not Aquinas. There would be no complete theology of creation without it including the creation of man and woman, without an anthropology situated within it. Nor could there be a complete theology of creation apart from the Christ, apart from Christology, even though these require separate treatments. But Jesus Christ is also a human being and as such within creation.

The distinctive aspect about the human being is how like God we are. We are creatures, but created in God's very own image, created to become more and more like God. But we are God's image in our very makeup, in our nature, even if we are called to become more and more like God during our lives. Aquinas distinguishes image and likeness and finds these equally present in woman as well as in man. There is no inequality in our natures when it comes to being created in God's image.

Although not all creatures are created to image God as the human being does, nevertheless God is present in all creatures. For Aquinas this presence is a trace of God, not an image of God, yet important. God sustains a plenitude of diverse creatures in existence, which means that there is also in God's universe, inevitably, realities such as death and corruption, natural evils. These exist for the sake of the whole. We are not talking here about sin and moral evils, which are destructive of the perfection of the universe, but natural evils that contribute to its plenitude, while still being diminishment in human eyes. Existentially, evil does exist, and is not to be minimized; but evil lacks substantiality, having only the nature of a privation. The latter means that the power of evil is never as powerful as the power of the good. Such is Aquinas's theological appreciation of the universe that God has brought into being and continues to create and sustain.

There is a beauty to creation, reflecting God, a fullness or plenitude, which does not exclude the reality of evils within nature but sees these as within the whole or totality. There are gradations of being which are not so much inequalities as diversity. Creation is good for it participates in the goodness that God is. It is good to be. The universe is good because God is good, Goodness Itself. The human creature is in some ways a key that unlocks the mystery of creation. Aquinas's cosmology is the context and starting point for his anthropology.

3

Teilhard de Chardin's Cosmological Vision

WHAT MAY BE MOST notable about Teilhard at first glance is his cosmic sense, his feel for the universe, the cosmic scope of his vision. His first major essay,[1] written in 1916, while a stretcher bearer in World War I, was entitled "Cosmic Life."[2] As a young man, matter, the material universe, had an attraction for him. One of Teilhard's earliest memorable experiences was seeing iron rust. He was taken aback that it was not as solid a thing as he had thought. No one doubts that a major effort of his was to do cosmology in a new key, from within the context of an evolutionary world view. The cosmos is not yet done; it is unfinished; it is a cosmogenesis, a movement more than a finished product. God's creation must be understood as evolving. God creates the universe, yes, for sure, but God creates the universe evolutively. Evolution is God's creative act expressed in time. It is an ongoing act. It continues.

Teilhard is writing, and thinking, in a post-Copernican, post-Darwinian world. He did not engage to the same degree the paradoxes of quantum physics although he and Einstein were contemporaries.[3] We can be sure, however, that science did not frighten him but contributed

1. There was an earlier 1913 essay entitled "The Progress of Prehistory," *AP*, 11–24.

2. "Cosmic Life" (1916), *WW*, 13–71.

3. Einstein was born in Germany in 1879; Teilhard in France in 1881. Teilhard died on April 10, 1955; Einstein on April 18, 1955. Teilhard did make a reference to Einstein, *MPN* (1949), 34.

to his sense of the cosmic extent of things. The mystery of the universe would continue to fascinate him. In that first essay, "Cosmic Life," his life's work is already there, in an inchoate, clear, but not yet matured form. He speaks of an awakening to the cosmos, a vision, something deeply felt; of a communion with the earth, an earth community that includes but goes beyond the human community; a cosmic movement that has a *telos* or purpose. Cosmogenesis becomes biogenesis as the universe gives birth to life; and biogenesis becomes anthropogenesis, as in due time within the midst of the biosphere there emerges *Homo sapiens*. There are stages in the unfolding mystery of the universe. One's communion with the earth, in its ultimate depth, is also a communion with God. It is never, for Teilhard, God *or* the world but both God *and* the world. Their reconciliation is his life's work. Both God and the world, both creation and evolution, both faith and science. At its close "Cosmic Life" speaks of "communion with God through the earth," and cosmology becomes Christology.

If one were to contrast "Cosmic Life," his first significant essay, with a much later essay from 1950, "The Heart of Matter,"[4] one would find almost parallel outlines, indicating that much of Teilhard's thinking was there early on even if the details were to be filled in and refined over time. In "The Heart of Matter," Teilhard develops three chapters entitled respectively: (1) The Cosmic, or the Evolutive; (2) The Human, or the Convergent; and (3) The Christic, or the Centric. The outline of his earlier "Cosmic Life," comprised: (1) Awakening to the Cosmos; (2) Communion with the Earth; (3) Communion with God; and (4) Communion with God through the Earth. The cosmos, the cosmic sense, was always his starting point, perhaps understandably as a scientist, a geologist, and a paleontologist, one might say cosmologist. But that cosmos was never far removed from his Christic sense and the cosmic dimension of Christ—Christ in his fullness, or rather the cosmos in its wholeness, just as the *prima pars* of Aquinas's *Summa* and its *tertia pars* are parts of a whole, each essential to Aquinas's theological vision.

Thus, in "The Heart of Matter," he wrote: "When I look for my starting point, for a clue to lead the reader through these pages, for an axis that will give continuity to the whole . . . for want of a better name I shall call it the *Sense of Plenitude*.[5] The evolution of matter fascinated him. He was born in 1881. Darwin had published his "Origin of the Species"

4. *HM*, 14–79.

5. "The Heart of Matter" (1950), *HM*, 16. Emphasis in text.

in 1859 and his "Descent of Man" in 1871. Evolution was in the air. This was a seeming conflict for a man who saw the universe evolve but whose faith as taught at that time was unreceptive to the hypothesis of evolution, unable to see at that time how it might be reconciled with Christian faith. One of Teilhard's enduring contributions is that he reconciled evolution and creation in such a way that there ought no longer to be seen any intrinsic conflict between the two. God *creates* the universe *evolutively.* From the "outside" or "without,"[6] the universe evolves; one thing comes to be by way of birth from something that already is.[7] From the "inside" or "within," there is an energy of evolution that moves it. That energy ultimately is love, or God, the God of evolution, the God who makes creation evolve. The cosmos is a cosmogenesis, a coming to be that has a birth with time and unfolds in time.

Teilhard was at the opposite end of the spectrum from Manicheans as far as the material world is concerned, as we noted was also true for Aquinas. He wrote a hymn to matter.[8] He saw in matter the potential to become more than what it already was. This meant a deep reverence for the world, and so-called worldly things, the *saeculum*, and thus he could write in his major spiritual treatise, *The Divine Milieu*, that nothing is profane for the one who knows how to see.[9] As with Aquinas, there was a divine omnipresence in all things. The universe was a divine milieu, immersed in God.[10] But the cosmos is not a static reality, done from the beginning, but rather a genesis, having a beginning but also a continuous unfolding, with leaps along the way, from the lithosphere

6. The earlier translation, that of *The Phenomenon of Man*, trans. Bernard Wall, 53–54, translated "le Dedans des choses" and "le Dehors" as "the within" and "the without," while the later translation, *The Human Phenomenon*, trans. Sarah Appleton-Weber, 22, translates them as "inside" and "outside."

7. "One may say that the fundamental structural law . . . in a universe in a state of evolution, is that EVERYTHING IS BORN, that is to say that everything appears in the function of an antecedent (and, yet we must add, in the case of life, more or less *by way of addition*)." "The Phyletic Structure of the Human Group" (1951), *AM*, 136. Capitals and italics in text. In many ways this is Teilhard's definition of evolution, that everything that comes to be comes to be by way of birth from that which was there before.

8. "The Spiritual Power of Matter" (1919), *HU*, 57–71, esp. 68–71. Also see *DM*, 81–87.

9. *DM*, 35.

10. "Cosmic Life" (1916), *WW*, 60: "*through all nature I was immersed in God.*" Emphasis in text.

and stratosphere to the biosphere and noosphere.[11] Atoms, molecules, mega-molecular substances, and then *woof*, a cell, life. In hindsight we can see that cosmogenesis became biogenesis. The earth became alive. The pre-living world held on even after the birth of life, but its crowning achievement, its pride, was the living cell to which it had given birth. That cell multiplied and multicellular organisms emerged, and suddenly life itself had a sensibility of its own, sentient life. The rhinoceros was no longer a plant.

The theory, the reality, fascinates us even today. It also gives us a sense of the earth, to use one of Teilhard's expressions again, and the earth's rightful place in the scheme of things. Without planet earth, that which came to be would not have been. To return to an expression already quoted earlier—the sense of plenitude—the desire for wholeness, for seeing deeply, for there being an intelligibility in things, for Christ as a part of creation and not apart from creation, and for the human as also a part of creation and not apart from it, for seeing God in all things and all things in God: this was Teilhard's cosmic sense. He wrote an essay subsequently entitled "Man's Place in Nature."[12] The human phenomenon was never to be extracted from the natural world for the natural world is what gave humanity its birth.

To get a feel for his sense of things, we only need note the titles of some of his essays: "Christ in the World of Matter" (1916); "My Universe" (1918); "The Spiritual Power of Matter" (1919); "Mass on the World" (1923); "My Universe" (1924)[13]; "The Basis and the Foundation of the Idea of Evolution" (1926); "The Spirit of the Earth" (1931); "Man's Place in Nature" (1932); "The Mysticism of Science" (1939); "Man's Place in the Universe" (1942); "Evolution of the Idea of Evolution" (1950); "The Heart

11. "Noosphere" was a word coined by Teilhard to describe a layer of thought or reflective consciousness that encircles the earth with the coming of humankind, analogous to the biosphere. Already used in his 1923 essay, "Hominization," *VP*, 51–79. As an aid to understanding Teilhard's distinctive use of language and what words or expressions mean for him, see Cowell, *Teilhard Lexicon*.

12. "The Human Zoological Group, Evolutionary Structure and Directions" (1949), was Teilhard's own title for the work. In a later edition it was entitled "Man's Place in Nature." Teilhard considered this work to be an even more clear statement of his vision than *The Human Phenomenon*. See the preface to *AM*. There was an earlier 1932 essay entitled "Man's Place in Nature," *VP*, 175–82, not to be confused with the later 1949 work.

13. A different essay from the 1918 one although bearing the same name.

of Matter" (1950); "The Stuff of the Universe" (1953) and many others into which the cosmos as really real and as created is woven.

One will immediately note upon reading Teilhard that his language is not "scholastic" as is that of Aquinas, not even what one might think of as "scientific," at least for the most part, perhaps "speculative" but not even that in a strictly philosophical sense. It has been described as poetic,[14] yet is not poetry, except in several places. One's style, use of language to communicate, can incline one to enjoy and prefer the writings of Thomas Aquinas or not prefer them, apart from their content and depth. Likewise, for Teilhard. One may be drawn in, or driven away, by his way of expressing himself. How is one to interpret him? Whether it is Teilhard or Aquinas, how is one to have access to his thought and not blocked from going deeper? One could certainly describe Teilhard's work as a *mélange* or medley, which challenges as well as confuses. Aquinas too is theologian, philosopher, and poet, but it is more easily recognizable what a particular text might be. With Teilhard all three might be in any one essay. As I mentioned in the prologue, he is more like a juggler. It may be best to think of him as a mystic, a man attempting to communicate a vision, a conviction, an idea, an experience.

Many of his essays contain "mysticism" in their titles. Although he was professionally a scientist, and as a priest also a theologian, he will be remembered I think more as a mystic for whom language is always inadequate, more like straw as Aquinas eventually said, who was also a spiritual master and one for whom poetry was a means of communication. The scholastic method was not available to Teilhard and exclusively scientific writing too restrictive. He saw something new, and it needed a new style and at times new words. Teilhard invites us *to see*. He thus entitles the prologue to *The Human Phenomenon*, his most comprehensive work, "*Voir*" or "Seeing," where he writes, "These pages represent an effort *to see* . . . One could say that the whole of life lies in seeing—if not ultimately, at least essentially."[15] He said the same in that early essay, "Cosmic Life":

> To make men see and make them feel—that is my first aim: to make an impassioned profession of my faith in the richness and value of the world and so vindicate myself against those who smile and shake their heads when they hear talk of an ill-defined

14. See Appleton-Weber's excellent introduction to *The Human Phenomenon*, xvii–xxxi, esp. xxvi–xxviii.

15. *HP*, 3. Emphasis in text.

> nostalgia for something hidden within us which transcends and fulfills us—to win the day against them by showing them beyond all possible doubt that their self-sufficient individual personality is but a wisp of straw in the grip of forces they seek to shut their eyes to, forces that, when we speak of building up a temple to them, they dismiss as laughable. If man is to come up to his full measure, *he must become conscious of his infinite capacity for carrying himself still further*; he must realize the duties it involves, and he must feel its intoxicating wonder . . . I am not directly concerned with science, nor philosophy, nor apologetics. Primarily, I am concerned to express an impassioned vision.[16]

Precision of thought is not the strength of poetic or mystical writing while at the same time experiential wisdom cannot always be confined to the wineskins of philosophical theology. The differences are not primarily in the content, nor even in the different historical contexts out of which the two visionaries speak, but in their language—the one best described as the language of the schools, and the other the language of mystical experience. Each one sees, but each one expresses it differently, not that what they see is so different, or the One whom they see, but that which makes one see his writings but as straw makes the other search for words that also fall short. Yet each acknowledges the plenitude, the fullness, the richness of Being.

What are some theses central to Teilhard de Chardin's cosmology? (1) The universe evolves. (2) The universe is created. (3) God is Creator. (4) The evolving creation has a direction to it. (5) This creative evolutionary process has a center, is centered, is a process of centration. (6) This Center is both up above and up ahead. (7) God's creation evolves by stages, through metamorphoses, with emergent novelty along the way. (8) Evolution and centration are processes of unification, convergence, as well as unfolding. (9) Union differentiates. (10) There is an interiority as well as an exteriority to creation. We must now briefly give further attention to each of these convictions of Teilhard's. Some are grounded in fact, in science; others are extrapolations, intuitions; still others are grounded in Christian faith. Teilhard's endeavor is both a work of faith and a work of reason working in conjunction with each other: *fides et ratio.*[17]

16. "Comic Life" (1916), *WW*, 15–16. Emphasis in text. For references to "seeing," also *DM*, 15, 35.

17. The first line of Pope St. John Paul II's encyclical, *Fides et ratio*, is "Faith and reason are like two wings on which the human spirit rises to the contemplation of truth."

The universe evolves. Evolution is accepted today as a fact about our world and as intrinsic to a modern world view. The debates are not over whether biological species have evolved or over whether the concept of evolution can be applied in an analogous way beyond that of organic evolution alone, but more as to how this occurs, the mechanisms of evolution.[18] This was not always the case in the Catholic and wider religious world. Pope Pius XII in his encyclical, *Humani generis* (1950), was hesitant about the degree to which the teaching of evolution was compatible with Christian faith. However, in 1996, Pope St. John Paul II in an address to the Pontifical Academy of Sciences, stated:

> New scientific knowledge has led us to realize that the theory of evolution is no longer a mere hypothesis. It is indeed remarkable that this theory has been progressively accepted by researchers, following a series of discoveries in various fields of knowledge. The convergence, neither sought nor fabricated, of the results of work that was conducted independently is in itself a significant argument in favor of this theory.[19]

Catholic philosophers and theologians even much earlier argued that this convergence of knowledge from various fields favored the explanatory power of the theory of evolution even if placed within certain limits.[20]

The story of the struggles between science and religion are no secret.[21] All of Teilhard's writings (from 1913 through 1955) came before the Catholic Church's being reconciled with an evolutionary world view and they thus manifest an adventurous but committed spirit. As Thomas Aquinas's adventure with the philosophy of Aristotle at a time when Aristotle was not yet seen as amicable from the vantage point of Christian faith, so in a somewhat similar fashion a warning (*monitum*) about the writings of Pierre Teilhard de Chardin was issued in 1962 by the Vatican's Sacred Congregation of the Holy Office. Aquinas had died in 1274 and the story of the gradual acceptance of his thought following the 1277 condemnations is now well known.[22] Teilhard died in 1955. *Le phénomène humain* appeared shortly thereafter and was translated into English in 1959. His

18. E.g., see Ayala, *Darwin's Gift*, along with many of his other books.

19. Quoted in Ayala, *Darwin's Gift*, 164–65.

20. E.g., Nogar, *Wisdom of Evolution*.

21. E.g., see the writings of Ian G. Barbour on science and religion. His father was George B. Barbour, renowned geologist, who worked with Teilhard in China.

22. See among others Torrell, *Saint Thomas Aquinas*, 1:298–303; as well as Weisheipl, *Friar Thomas d'Aquino*, 331–50.

thought is widely accepted today.[23] Whatever the context within which Teilhard wrote, evolution is accepted today as an empirical fact but one which Teilhard at that time had to reconcile with his Christian faith. For him it was a starting point for his cosmology and from which he extrapolated to interpret widely his vision of the world. His challenge at that moment of history was to reconcile Christianity and evolution, the empirical evidence for evolution with the doctrine of creation.

The universe is created. However widely or however limited one applies the concept of evolution to one's understanding of the world, the question has been whether it is compatible with the theological doctrine of creation. Affirming the conviction that our universe evolves does not necessitate a denial of the role of God in creating our evolving world. For Teilhard, both statements are true: (1) Based on scientific evidence, the universe is evolving; (2) Based on Christian faith, the universe is created. It is not an either/or. It simply means that God creates the universe evolutively. The universe not only evolves but is itself also creative. From within nature itself there are forces and sources of creativity. There is the emergence of the new; there is novelty. Teilhard's own definition of evolution is that which comes to be comes to be by way of birth from that which already is.[24] Saying that evolution itself is creative, however, is not saying the same thing as that the universe is created.[25] "Being created" indicates something outside the evolutionary process itself that undergirds it, gives rise to it, accompanies it—something that transcends it.

Whether one is comfortable with the extent of Teilhard's extrapolation of the concept of evolution back to the very beginnings of the universe itself, Teilhard nevertheless recognizes two faces to evolution, its "outside" and its "inside." He writes of this bifacial structure in

23. He has been quoted by Pope Paul VI, Pope John Paul II, and Pope Benedict XVI. For these references see Francis, *Laudato Sí*, note 53. Many Roman Catholic theologians have written commentaries on his work, particularly Henri de Lubac, SJ, who wrote four books on Teilhard's thought, as well as Robert Faricy, SJ, Christopher Mooney, SJ, Robert North, SJ, Piet Smulders, SJ, Max Wildiers, OFM Cap., among many others. Bishop Sheen also highly praised Teilhard in *Footprints*, 69–82. de Lubac, *Religion of Teilhard*, is a thorough, sympathetic, yet critical presentation of the thought of Teilhard.

24. See n7 above.

25. "It [evolution] is certainly not 'creative', as science for a brief moment believed; but it is the expression of creation, for our experience, in time and space" From "Man's Place in the Universe" (1942), *VP*, 231.

Le phénomène humain: "*coextensive with its outside, everything has an inside*."[26] This helps us to reconcile further these two contrasting truths, one empirical, one meta-empirical, both compatible even if reached from a different kind of knowledge. If we look at the universe from the outside, as a phenomenon, scientifically investigable, we can affirm that the universe evolves. But if we look at the universe from the inside, from deep within where empirical investigations reach their limit and a metaphysical or theological investigation is required, the universe is created. This emphasis on creation is equally central to Teilhard's cosmic vision. Already in "Cosmic Life," he had written: "*The world is still being created, and it is Christ who is reaching his fulfillment in it.*"[27] In another early essay (1917), "Creative Union," he wrote of the force that creates the world as "extra-cosmic," operating "*ab extra*," and as "*real* and *transcendent*."[28] In the 1924 essay "My Universe," he wrote of "the creative influence of God, 'qui creat uniendo'—'who creates by uniting.'"[29] In "Man's Place in the Universe" (1942), he affirms that evolution "is the expression of creation, for our experience, in time and space."[30] Evolution is thus God's creative act expressed in time. Creation continues. God is continually creating. From our temporal vantage point, God created in the past, is still creating, and will continue to create. From the vantage point of God's eternal vision, God simply is Creator. God's creation is an evolving universe, and it is God who creates that universe.

God is Creator. In the Christian tradition God is both Creator and Redeemer. God *as Creator* is essential to Teilhard's cosmology. Creation implies a God who is Above, Beyond, Transcendent, not a part of creation although immanent within it, omnipresent. The created universe as a divine milieu immersed in God is central to Teilhard's cosmic vision. God and Christ are both omnipresent. The God who evolves the universe is both Alpha and Omega, the Beginning and the End (Rev 1:8), the One from whom all comes and to whom all returns, not dissimilar to the *exitus* and *reditus* theme in much of medieval thought including that of Thomas Aquinas. Some of Teilhard's emphases in his theology of creation are distinct from those of Aquinas. Teilhard put particular emphasis on

26. *HP*, 24. Emphasis in the original.

27. *WW*, 60. Emphasis in the original.

28. *WW*, 159. Emphasis in the original.

29. *SC*, 45.

30. *VP*, 231, originally an unpublished lecture given in Peking.

the conservational or continuing aspect of God's action more so than on God's initial act which he also affirmed. For Aquinas as well as for Teilhard, creation is a metaphysical reality and not a chronological "first" act. Creation *ex nihilo* places God outside the realm of what Aquinas would call secondary causes. Rather as First Cause, he is the Cause of causes.

In two unpublished essays from 1920, "On the Notion of Creative Transformation," and "Note on the Modes of Divine Action in the Universe,"[31] Teilhard affirms creation *ex nihilo* although his emphasis lies elsewhere. He understood scholasticism's emphasis on creation as distinct from conservation as disconnected, which is not how Aquinas would have understood them. Teilhard wished to emphasize the continuing transformative action of God and thus gives less attention to the initial creative action. First Cause and secondary causes are two different kinds of causality, but they act in harmony with each other, not in competition. Teilhard writes:

> There is not one moment when God creates, and one moment when the secondary causes develop. There is always only *one* creative action (identical with conservation) which continually raises creatures towards fuller being, *by means of* their secondary activity and their earlier advances. Understood in this way, creation is not a periodic intrusion of the First Cause; it is an act co-extensive with the whole duration of the universe. God *has been creating* ever since the beginning of time, and, *seen from within*, his creation . . . takes the form of a transformation. Participated being is not introduced *in batches* which are differentiated later as a result of a non-creative modification: God is continually breathing new being into us.[32]

Earlier in the same essay, he affirms "*creatio ex nihilo subjecti*" but is at pains to make the point that besides that, there needs to be that act which "*makes use* of a pre-existent created being and builds it up into a *completely* new being."[33] As we have seen, Aquinas would have no dispute with that. Teilhard acknowledges that "Where God is operating it is always possible for us . . . to see only the *works of nature*."[34] Teilhard is not a naturalist who

31. *CE*, 21–35.

32. "On the Notion of Creative Transformation" (1920), *CE*, 23. Emphasis in text.

33. "On the Notion of Creative Transformation" (1920), *CE*, 22. Emphasis in text.

34. "Note on the Modes of Divine Action in the Universe" (1920), *CE*, 27. Emphasis in text. On this theme of the mode of God's creative action, also see Schoonenberg, *God's World*, 25–35.

denies anything other than natural causes. He recognizes the First Cause. Nevertheless, how does the First Cause act once the initial action *ex nihilo* has produced finite being? "Properly speaking, God *does not make:* He *makes things make themselves.*"[35] As does evolution so does a theology of creation play a central role in the thought of Teilhard: a creation that evolves, an evolution that is being continually created and creative.

The evolving creation has a direction to it. In contrast to a Whiteheadian philosophical perspective and a common scientific assumption, Teilhard's evolving universe has a definite *telos* to it: Omega. God's creation is nothing other than an Omegalization. It is guided, directed, by God. From a purely scientific or empirical vantage point, this would not be possible to establish, although Teilhard sees a direction to evolution even scientifically. From the viewpoint of revelation, however, there can be no doubt. God has created us for himself, as the great text of St. Augustine affirmed: "You have made us for yourself, [Lord], and our heart is restless until it rests in you."[36] According to St. Paul, all of creation is in travail awaiting its own redemption (Rom 8:19–23). As in Aquinas, there is intricately interwoven in Teilhard's thought the homage due to both reason and revelation, both science and faith. Aquinas's use of Aristotle was grounded in Aristotle's due diligence toward the philosophy of nature. Revealed truth is something Teilhard takes for granted but scientific evidence is not to be theologically discounted. God will be all in all, as Teilhard's favorite text from St. Paul asserts (1 Cor 15:28).

From an empirical perspective, Teilhard sees in creation's evolution *both* a process of complexification *and* the emergence of consciousness, what he calls the law of complexity-consciousness.[37] Even looked at scientifically, from Teilhard's point of view, entropy does not have the last word, is not the bottom line, about evolution's future, although scientific materialism does not recognize this. Science, however, need not be equated with materialism. To deny the existence of anything beyond matter goes beyond science's own methodology. Teilhard seeks to engage scientists in a wider vision of things. We must look at things not only from outside but also from their inside. This is where a significance is given to the evolution of consciousness itself.

35. "Note on the Modes of Divine Action in the Universe" (1920), *CE*, 28. Emphasis in text.

36. Augustine, *Confessions*, 3 (ST I, 1).

37. *HP*, 16–21, 216–18.

One can see complexification simply by looking at creation from the outside. In a very rudimentary way, there are atoms, molecules, megamolecular substances, emergent living cells, multicellular organisms, plant life in all its variety, the biosphere, sentient life, mammals, advanced mammalian nervous systems, and the complexity of the human brain. Although there may be missing links, there are still links. Also, for Teilhard, empirically, there is the emergence of the phenomenon of consciousness, empirically apparent with the human phenomenon. With the evolution of humankind there appears something remarkably new, a psychic factor. If one allows what now appears on the outside to be traced to less perceptible prehuman forms, one sees in evolution a psychogenesis as well, however far back or forward one wishes to project it. This then is evolution's direction: increased complexification, increased consciousness. When Teilhard gives his words a feel for an unfolding universe—cosmogenesis, biogenesis, anthropogenesis, psychogenesis—it is only to give us an appreciation of a universe that is on the move, going somewhere. Each of those words have two connotations to them. They can refer to the moment of emergence as well as to the continuing unfolding: the emergence of the cosmos out of nothing and its lengthy process of cosmic evolution, the emergence of life with the birth of a cell and all organic evolution that follows in its footsteps, the emergence of a reflective consciousness and the continuing evolution of *Homo sapiens*. Whatever we observe or hypothesize with respect to the outside of things, creation has a purpose which is confirmed from the vantage point of revelation. It is being created by a God who is a God of all creation,[38] who draws all things to himself (Col 1:20; John 12:32). The Omega of evolution *is* the God of creation. Teilhard wrote in a brief 1953 essay, "The God of Evolution": "only a God who is functionally and totally 'Omega' can satisfy us."[39]

This creative evolutionary process has a center, is centered, is a process of centration. If creation is going somewhere, has a direction, has a purpose, as one can scientifically hypothesize or as a believer consider a fact, then there is a focus to it. There is something (or Someone) that constitutes its center, that from which it has come and to which it returns, even if one distinguishes that Center as Alpha from the Center as Omega. As Omega, that center lies up ahead. It is as much final cause as efficient

38. Note the prayer in the Roman Catholic Missal, where during the offering of the gifts at Mass, the priest addresses the God of all creation: "Blessed are you, Lord God of all creation, for through your goodness we have received the bread we offer you."

39. *CE*, 240.

cause. It exerts influence from what to us is the future. It pulls, attracts, undergirds, centers the differentiating evolving world that it draws to itself. There are different words that Teilhard will use to describe different facets of the evolutionary process, words like convergence, unification, spiritualization, and centration. Each gives an insight into what is going on.

The word "centration" (we might say "centering") helps Teilhard to picture a movement from that which is more dispersed to that which is more focused, from diverse multiplicity to an organic unity, from the many to the One, through a process moving inward, then outward, both forward and upward. Later in his anthropology we will see that the notion of centration operates in each of us individually, as we personally are called to be more and more centered; as well as collectively, as in any process of socialization in which a social organism takes shape around a point that brings about a unity. Here, however, centration is being considered cosmically, as a grand, unfinished, organic, and cosmic movement. It is descriptive of creation or cosmogenesis as a whole: an energizing magnetic-like pull towards the future—a still-to-come maturation point.[40]

The theme of centration was most developed in a then unpublished 1944 essay entitled "Centrology."[41] As in a variety of Teilhard's essays, his language can confuse as well as elucidate. Centricity exhibits degrees of deepening interiority made possible by degrees of complexity, as with the law of complexity-consciousness. Complexification—> interiorisation—> centration—> Omegalization. Evolution is a "*transition from a lower to a higher state of centro-complexity*" or a "*centered universe*."[42] The stages or degrees of centrogenesis, the process of creation's evolution becoming increasingly more and more centered, is not as important as it is to be aware that evolution is going somewhere and that the "where" is up above and up ahead. That's where its center lies. Teilhard was also aware of the distinction between the natural and supernatural orders, between omicron and Omega,[43] if you will, although in his later writings he does not see them as independent of each other.[44]

40. Cf., "Two Principles and a Corollary (Or a *Weltanschauung* in Three Stages)" (1948), *TF*, 148–61.

41. See *AE*, 99–127.

42. "Centrology" (1944), *AE*, 103, 102, emphasis in text.

43. E.g., see "My Universe" (1918), *HM*, 202–4.

44. See the introductory remarks to "The Soul of the World" (1918), *WW*, 177–78. There is an extensive bibliography in recent theology on the relationship between the

This Center is both up above and up ahead. In two essays, Teilhard emphasizes this direction: in a 1948 essay, "Two Principles and a Corollary (Or a *Weltanschauung* in Three Stages)," and a 1949 essay "The Heart of the Problem."[45] In both he speaks about evolution's trajectory not only being forward, horizontal, up ahead, but also a movement upward, higher, having a verticality to it.[46] They manifest for Teilhard two facets of his faith, namely in God and in the world: Christianity's ascensional drive upward towards the Transcendent as well as humanity's propulsion forward towards a more inclusive humanism. These two vectors are not a compromising middle but mutually reinforce each other within evolution's maturation. Teilhard writes of his Christian vision: "But let there be revealed to us the possibility of believing *at the same time and wholly* in God *and* the World, the one through the other"[47] The thrust of Teilhard's thought is toward what he calls a new humanism or a neo-humanism, to which we will return in part two. For Teilhard, as he had already pointed out in *The Divine Milieu*, it is not a question of Christianity or humanism, but of a Christian humanism, not God or the world, but both God and the world, not creation or evolution, but an evolving creation. Teilhard's drive toward a synthesis of his Christian faith and scientific facts is centered *both* Up Above *and* Up Ahead.

He wrote in his more autobiographical 1950 essay:

> The time had now come when I could see one thing: that, from the depths of the cosmic future as well as from the heights of Heaven, it was still God, it was *always the same God*, who was calling me. It was a *God of the Ahead* who had suddenly appeared athwart *the traditional God of the Above*, so that henceforth we can no longer *worship fully* unless we superimpose those two images so that they form *one*.[48]

Evolution becomes, for Teilhard, both a humanization and a christification, but this is to jump ahead of ourselves, to his anthropology and Christology.

---

natural and supernatural, to which debate Henri de Lubac, SJ, himself made a most significant contribution. See Healy, "Nature and Grace," 181–203; as well as de Lubac's own writings such as *Mystery of the Supernatural.*

45. "Two Principles and a Corollary" (1948), *TF*, 160; "The Heart of the Problem" (1949), *FM*, 269.

46. Teilhard diagrams this in the two essays "The Heart of the Problem" (1949), *FM*, 269 and "Two Principles and a Corollary" (1948), *TF*, 160.

47. "The Heart of the Problem" (1949), *FM*, 268–69. Emphasis in text.

48. "The Heart of Matter," *HM*, 53. Emphasis in text.

God's creation evolves by stages, through metamorphoses, with emergent novelty along the way. If one considers creation through an evolutionary lens, we see major stages along the way from its initial moment through cosmogenesis to biogenesis to anthropogenesis and continuing onward and upward. We will consider future stages later, but it has become apparent that evolution is ongoing. Creation continues. God's creative act is a continuing action from any temporal perspective. Just as there is the geological and paleontological past, so there is creation's future. In other words, an immediate corollary of evolution is that creation is unfinished.[49] This unfinishedness impacts how we see and understand our world and ourselves.

Some phases in the evolutionary process may seem to be minor. Others, however, manifest a tremendous leap forward, what Teilhard will describe variously as critical points or steps, something entirely new, a leap, a change of state, a discontinuity in continuity, a mutation from zero to everything, a threshold, a "transexperimental interval," a metamorphosis.[50] Again it depends upon what one observes at the level of the "outside" as science does its research, and what goes on deeply "inside," as perceived through the lens of faith. With these critical moments, there is more *being* than was there previously, which levels or stages require explanation beyond the merely phenomenal or scientific. In a footnote in *The Human Phenomenon*, Teilhard makes this point clear:

> Need I repeat once again that I restrict myself here to the phenomenon, that is, to the experimental relationships between consciousness and complexity, without prejudging in the least what action from deeper causes might be calling the play . . . But having said this, there is nothing to prevent the thinker adopting a spiritual explanation . . . from placing any "creative operation" or "special intervention" one might wish *under the phenomenal veil* of a revolutionary transformation.[51]

These evolutionary leaps, the emergence of real novelty, are to be probed by science, philosophy, and theology, by both reason and faith. From one vantage point, there was an evolution from the pre-living world to a living world and from there to a reflective world. From another vantage

49. In *DM*, he writes: "We may, perhaps, imagine that the Creation was finished long ago. But that would be quite wrong" (31).

50. Cf. *HP*, 42, 48, 49, 113–16, 153.

51. *HP*, 113–14. Emphasis in text.

point, God was creating life and human life. Psychogenesis was a consequence of both natural and one can say supernatural causes. God works from within the created order and creates from within the world that had already come to be. Hence Teilhard's definition of evolution as that which comes to be comes to be by way of birth from what already is.[52] God works through secondary causes and respects the autonomy of nature. There is as much diversity in Teilhard's universe as in that of Aquinas, even more given the knowledge of the universe's diversity made available by science. There is a natural hierarchy or a hierarchy within nature itself from cosmogenesis to biogenesis to anthropogenesis.

Evolution and centration are processes of unification, convergence, as well as unfolding. Teilhard places less emphasis on the ontological questions that emerge in considering a theology of an evolving creation than he does on an effort to enable us to see the significance of the evolutionary side of things. What are some of the dynamics that one might see within the evolutionary process? The theme of unity, or unification, emerges at the heart of matter. He writes: "*So far as we can see, to create is to condense*, concentrate, organize—*to unify.*"[53] We have seen that evolution has a direction, creation a purpose. It is going somewhere. It is creative due both to what its ongoing complexification makes possible and to what God's creative activity brings forth. At the level of the outside, we can see the increased complexity as well as a birth of consciousness, particularly with the birth of human consciousness. This happens due to an energy that brings things more elementary together into a deeper or more advanced and complex unity. Atoms unite to become molecules. Molecules unite to become more complex substances. Cells unite to become multicellular organisms. The human soul unites or configures all the elements of the human organism into being a human body. Teilhard sees within evolution a process of increasing unifications. This can also describe the direction toward which evolution moves.

In what Teilhard calls a metaphysics of union he maintains, "To be = to be united."[54] Or rather, to *become*, which is to evolve, is to be united. "To be more is to be more fully united with more" and "to be more is to more fully unite more" for God "creates by uniting."[55] Insofar as the evolving

52. See n7 above.

53. "The Struggle Against the Multitude" (1917), *WW*, 95. Emphasis in text.

54. "My Fundamental Vision" (1948), *TF*, 193. In pp. 192–99 he outlines the varied phases in his metaphysics.

55. "My Universe" (1924), *SC*, 45. Also see "Centrology" (1944), *AE*, 113.

universe is being created, creation itself, following upon the initial act *ex nihilo*, moves forward by God's uniting the material that has now been made available and bringing forth something new, infusing the material with more being. In other words, "Creation is brought about by an act of uniting; and true union cannot be effected except by creating. These are two correlative propositions."[56] God's and creation's activity bring forth more and more unity. God creates evolutively by uniting more and more into a deeper or higher synthesis. As Teilhard puts it, "Evolution = Rise of consciousness. Rise of consciousness = Effect of union."[57] Human consciousness becomes possible due to the increased complexity at the material level of the brain's formation which brings forth a transformation, or metamorphosis, at the level of the inside. A new species, *Homo sapiens*, emerges.

It is not that the human soul as such, to use philosophical and theological language, evolves, but that the material universe evolves (is being created) to the point where the matter is available for a human soul to be infused and bring forth creatively something new: the capacity for reflection.[58] The human soul is not simply the result of an organic evolution devoid of God's activity. There is a critical leap forward, but a leap made possible by the evolution that had preceded it. The evolving, creative, and created universe proceeds by way of increasing unification: "everything in the universe moves in the direction of unification."[59] A corollary of this is that union also differentiates.[60]

Union differentiates. Increased complexity does not mean increased disorganized multiplicity. The process of centration, of being gathered around a center, brings that which is more elementary into a higher synthesis or union but also a union that respects what it unites. Parts are united while remaining themselves. This will be particularly emphasized when we come to human evolution and its respect for both community and individuality but is true throughout the cosmos. As Teilhard puts it:

> Whatever the domain—whether it be the cells of the body, the members of society, or the elements of a spiritual

56. "Creative Union" (1917), *WW*, 156.

57. *HP*, 172.

58. A valuable study in this regard is North, *Creation of the Soul.*

59. "Centrology" (1944), *AE*, 115.

60. There are numerous references in Teilhard's writings to this axiom. Among them are *FM*, 55, 302n1; *HE*, 149, 152; *SC*, 184; *AE*, 116.

> synthesis—"*union differentiates.*" In every organized whole the parts perfect and fulfill themselves. By failing to grasp this universal law of union, so many kinds of pantheism have led us astray into the worship of a great Whole in which individuals were supposed to become lost like a drop of water, dissolved like a grain of salt, in the sea.[61]

> Let us observe any unification by *convergence* that operates in the field of our experience: a grouping of cells in a living body, a grouping of individuals and functions in a social organism, a grouping of souls under the influence of a great love. And we come to a factual conclusion that easily proves the theory. It is this: the phenomena of fusion or dissolution are in nature only the sign of a return to fragmentation in homogeneity. Union, the true upward union in the spirit, ends by establishing the elements it dominates in their own perfection. *Union differentiates.*[62]

True union is not the same as fusion. Ultimately the energy that underlies evolution, lies deeply inside evolution, which makes for a differentiating union, is for Teilhard, love. It is love which unites while respecting and differentiating that which it brings together.

> . . . if you consider the mutual fulfillment of two beings who love one another; if you analyze philosophically the effect of a center on the elements it gathers together, and note that it does not dissolve but inevitably completes them—in every case you will come to the conclusion that directly contradicts what first seemed to be indicated. True union does not run together the beings it joins. but rather differentiates them more fully.[63]

This theme as well as the role of love in creation will emerge again in Teilhard's anthropology and Christology. The lack of appreciation for a union that differentiates leads to a conformity or collectivization that disrespects the dignity of the human person. It leads to depersonalizing mass movements, to communism or national socialism, to the anthill rather than human brotherhood.[64] True union does not destroy that which it unites but brings the elements into a higher synthesis or way of

61. *HP*, 186. Emphasis in text.
62. "Human Energy" (1937), *HE*, 144. Emphasis in text.
63. "The Salvation of Mankind" (1936), *SC*, 136–37.
64. *HP*, 182.

being. They become more. To be united to more or from more is to be more: "*Plus esse est a* (or *ex*) *pluribus uniri.*"[65]

There is an interiority as well as an exteriority to creation. We can now recapitulate and bring our reflection on Teilhard's cosmology to a close. Creation and evolution express two sides of our finite and material universe. God's creative action and natural or secondary causes complement each other. They are not in an either/or relationship but manifest two different kinds and levels of causality. Early in *The Human Phenomenon*, in discussing the stuff of the universe, Teilhard affirms that "*coextensive with its outside, everything has an inside.*"[66] We can probe our material universe from the outside, chart its evolutionary unfolding, give due diligence to the laws of nature, hypothesize and theorize with respect to the mechanisms of this grand cosmogenesis, observe carefully what the sciences of geology, paleontology and evolutionary biology have to teach us. Our cosmos is evolving. It is unfinished. It is moving toward some goal, Omega. We can also probe our world from the inside, speculate on the kinds of energy that move it, see within it that which evolves it, that which creates it, that it is being created and being created evolutively. While this interior side is most evident, phenomenal, with the emergence of the human animal, once seen, one can see it earlier as well, even if only in rudimentary ways.

There is an analogy between Teilhard's postulation of this cosmic bifacial reality and Aristotle's hylomorphic theory. For Aristotle, every finite material being is a composite of "matter" and "form." Ultimately there is no such thing as "pure formless matter." Such would simply be pure potency. Everything that is actual has as a principle of its makeup that which makes it to be what it is: form. Form configures matter in such a way that it is this or that. The direction of evolution, for Teilhard, is not only cosmogenesis, biogenesis, unification, upward and forward. It is also a spiritualization. Matter and spirit form a whole, make a composite being, the "without" and the "within," or the "outside" and the "inside" of all that is. Teilhard is not speaking here of purely spiritual beings but of our material world. Even matter has a "spiritual" side to it. For the Thomistic tradition, there is no matter without form. For Teilhard there is no matter without spirit, even if that spiritual side is very rudimentary and only analogously spirit.

65. "Centrology" (1944), *AE*, 113.

66. *HP*, 24. Emphasis in text.

Teilhard's cosmology, or he might say "physics," yields to a "hyper-physics," which he affirms is not quite the same as a metaphysics, although the boundary line may be delicate.[67] It was Aristotle's own *Physics* which gave us two of the principles of finite material beings, matter and form, and it is Teilhard's physics which has given us two sides to the stuff of things, and ultimately two energies or kinds of energy operative, the physical or tangential energies that science studies, and a radial or spiritual energy at the heart of matter. That is to say, the more deeply we probe the *inside* of things, where the empirical and natural sciences reach their limit, the more we are aided by metaphysics or even more so by revelation. We cannot in the end understand matter itself apart from faith. As Owen Barfield once stated: "There will be a revival of Christianity when it becomes impossible to write a popular manual of science without referring to the incarnation of the Word."[68] This goes beyond where we are ready to go at this point, a point to which we must return, but the point to be made here is that we need both science and religion, both reason and faith, both human knowledge and revelation if we are to understand ourselves and our universe more completely, in all its plenitude.[69] There is no cosmos without God and God is the God of creation. This is simply to say that Teilhard de Chardin had a cosmic sense, a cosmic consciousness, a deep appreciation of creation, a call to incorporate the created universe more and more into our vision of the plenitude of God's creation and into our spiritual and moral lives. His theology of creation as a work of a God who loves sees that creation in its infinite unfolding and unfinished expansiveness. As with Aquinas, so with Teilhard, one can affirm with Gerard Manley Hopkins: "The world is charged with the grandeur of God."[70] And both Aquinas and Teilhard would relish the observation of Saint Albert the Great, patron of the natural sciences, "The whole world is theology for us, because the heavens proclaim the glory of God."[71]

67. See *HP*, 2.

68. Barfield, *Saving Appearances*, 164. Owen Barfield was a member of the "Inklings" who had a significant effect on both C. S. Lewis and J. R. R. Tolkien. He was a lifelong friend as well as protagonist of Lewis and played a role in Lewis's conversion from atheism.

69. Much has been written on the topic of faith and reason. E.g., see Gilson, *Reason and Revelation*. Also, John Paul II, "Fides et Ratio."

70. From Hopkins, "God's Grandeur," 66.

71. From Albert's commentary on the Gospel of Matthew. See Tugwell, *Albert and Thomas*, 29.

At this point there is little in Thomas or in Teilhard that would allow for major disagreements between the two. There is little in Aquinas's theology of creation with which Teilhard would disagree, even if Teilhard would choose to emphasize certain aspects of creation to bring out its evolutionary dimension. Aquinas's appreciation of creation in all its diversity and God's divine omnipresence within it, Teilhard would wholeheartedly affirm. Aquinas's creation theology readily opens the door to an evolutionary understanding which was itself unavailable to Aquinas but quite compatible with his thought. Teilhard brings out creation's evolutionary unfolding, its ongoing and unfinished nature, its emergence through time.[72] For both, God is Alpha and Omega. For both, there is a sense of plenitude about God's universe. For both there is the eternal and the temporal. Both would see hierarchy in nature itself. Both see creation has having a *telos*. Teilhard might not speak with Aquinas's more philosophical language and Aquinas might not talk about creation within the *Summa* with some of Teilhard's ecstatic outbursts. Both, however, saw the cosmos as a unity. Both saw the universe as created. Both saw the human creature as a part of nature and not apart from nature. Both saw the cosmos not as a part of God, but also not apart from God. Both saw God as transcendent and yet eminently immanent. Aquinas speaks more metaphysically about "being," but not in ways with which Teilhard would be uncomfortable for whom the universe itself participates in the very Being that God is. Teilhard emphasizes strongly that it is God *and* the world, which Aquinas's theology of creation can also affirm. In the end the two can be seen to complement each other, and enriched from dialogue with each other, each one challenging while at the same time appreciating the other. Each has his role to play in the evolution of consciousness.

72. A twentieth-century theologian, influenced by the thought of Teilhard, who has developed a significant evolutionary theology is John F. Haught. See *God After Darwin*; *God After Einstein*; *Making Sense*; *New Cosmic Story*; *Resting on the Future*.

4

Thomas Aquinas's Theological Anthropology

To SUMMARIZE AQUINAS'S MONUMENTAL anthropology briefly is an impossible task. It encompasses the second part of his *Summa*, which itself is divided into two parts, as well as portions of the first part. We would need to consider what human nature is, the role of law and the reality of sin, the life of grace, the powers of the soul or intellect and will, the virtues as the perfection of those powers, the nature of virtue in general as well as the moral and theological virtues along with the gifts of the Holy Spirit, in other words both the natural as well as the supernatural life of the human person. I am choosing here to highlight a few of Thomas's insights pertinent to the origin of sin, the necessity of grace, the theological virtues as the core of one's moral and spiritual life, along with comments on the human person's capacity to think, choose, and pray as basic to who we are.

Aquinas had already considered evil, both physical and moral, as a privation, in question forty-eight of the *prima pars.*[1] In the *secunda pars* he considers further the kind of evil which we find in creatures with free will. He has already taught that evil exists, is real, although it does not have a nature of its own. He also taught that human beings are created to God's image. Now that he begins the second part of his *Summa*, it remains for him to treat of the human person, created in that image, insofar

1. See the discussion in chapter 2.

as a human person "is the principle of his actions, as having free will . . ." (*ST*, I-II, prologue). Aquinas's approach will be teleological, considering the human species in light of our last end, to which specifically human or voluntary acts ought to be ordered, which is happiness, namely eternal happiness, or beatitude (*ST*, I-II, q. 1), which is to be found in God alone (*ST*, I-II, q. 2, a. 8), who is happiness itself (*ST*, I-II, q. 3, a. 1, *ad* 1). Eternal happiness consists in the vision of God's essence (*ST*, I-II, q. 3, a. 8). Aquinas's analysis of human acts is a centerpiece of his moral outlook. This takes him of course not only into a discussion of the will (*ST*, I-II, qq. 6–21) but also of the passions or emotions (*ST*, I-II, qq. 22–48, 59),[2] a finely tuned awareness of the role realities such as love and hate; sorrow, pain, and pleasure; hope and despair; fear and anger play in human life, all treatments of which contain valuable psychological insights. Given the challenges to human freedom and the role emotions can play for good or for ill, can there be a formation of the will to act in a habitual way for the good (*ST*, I-II, qq. 49–54)? Is it possible for us to develop good habits or virtues, ways of acting in a morally good way (*ST*, I-II, qq. 55–70), or by way of contrast, bad habits or vices (*ST*, I-II, q. 71)? The latter brings Aquinas to the subject of sin (*ST*, I-II, qq. 72–89); the role of law, eternal law, natural law, human law along with the Old Law and the New Law (*ST*, I-II, qq. 90–108); as well as grace (*ST*, I-II, qq. 109–14), with which the *prima secundae* concludes. All this is simply the content of the first part of the second part of his *Summa*. At the heart of it of course is the reality of sin and the correlative reality of grace. He inquires as to the origin of sin (*ST*, I-II, qq. 81–83). Human beings were created good, were "originally" good, but human beings also sin, which are voluntary acts offensive to God, actions contrary to God's eternal law (*ST*, I-II, q. 71, a. 6). These acts distort the relationship of the creature to the Creator. How could this have come to be? How could a human's will, or a human person created to God's image, have become so prone to sin?

The Origin of Sin. Aquinas is not considering the origin of sin within the context of an evolutionary perspective. In looking back to the origin of sin, his eye remains teleological, looking ahead to human destiny. For many, the teaching on original sin has become problematic, not only because it does not seem to fit an evolutionary understanding of human

2. There could be extended discussion of how best to translate Aquinas's use of the word *passio*. The English word "passion" is not a good fit and so it is often translated as "emotion," which is not always a good fit either depending on how these words are understood in varied contexts. See Lombardo, *Logic of Desire*.

origins but because it is often identified with a literal interpretation of the story of the Fall, of Adam and Eve, in the book of Genesis, even though today the story is not interpreted literally.[3] If there is any doctrine for which there is more than ample empirical evidence, it is the doctrine of original sin, as Cardinal Newman so aptly described.[4] Sin seems to reign in our world. About this there can be little dispute. We are talking here about the human condition or *peccatum originale originatum*, that which is called passive original sin or that which is handed on. If sin abounds, as St. Paul testified (Rom 5:12), how do we account for this sinful human condition? Sin has a history. God is not its cause. Its cause must lie within the human story itself, within human history. According to the teaching of the Church, sin is not only *malum* but also *peccatum*, not only evil but sin. Without denying its existential reality, we must trace it back to its beginning. Active original sin, *peccatum originale originans*, the source from which sin originated, is sin that goes back to the beginning of humanity. There are then two facets to original sin, the fallen human condition (passive original sin which we inherit as the situation into which we are born) and the history or origin of that fallen condition (active original sin). Original sin is not the same as our actual sins, to which we are prone, but rather that kind of sin which has been with us *ab origine*, from the beginning of human history. Even though our human origins may remain shrouded in mystery, and for Aquinas that would have been less the case, sin had to have a beginning and it began with the beginnings of humanity. That is where it had to start and that is where we pick up with Aquinas's take on it.

Setting aside the question of exactly *how* sin is transmitted,[5] namely by the mere fact of being born and not by imitation alone (*propagatione non imitatione*), Aquinas sees many explanations of this transmission insufficient (*ST*, I-II, q. 81, a. 1) and thus maintains:

3. There is much contemporary research on the doctrine of original sin and the story of Adam and Eve. E.g., James Alison, *Being Wrong*; André-Marie Dubarle, OP, *Biblical Doctrine*; Alan Jacobs, *Cultural History*; Karl Rahner, SJ, "Theological Reflections on Monogenism"; Piet Schoonenberg, SJ, *Man and Sin*; Raymund Schwalger, SJ, *Banished from Eden*; O'Sullivan, "Re-examining"; Bennett et. al., eds., *Evolution of Evil*; Madueme and Reeves, eds., *Adam*; and many others.

4. See the dramatic description by Newman of his appreciation of the reality of original sin. Newman, *Apologia*, part VII, 319–21.

5. An intriguing study of this in the light of contemporary insights is Schwager, *Banished from Eden*.

> "Therefore we must explain the matter otherwise by saying that all men born of Adam may be considered as one man, inasmuch as they have one common nature, which they receive from their first parents . . . Accordingly the multitude of men born of Adam are as so many members of one body . . . In this way, then, the disorder which is in this man born of Adam, is voluntary, not by his will, but by the will of his first parents . . . so original sin is not the sin of this person, except inasmuch as this person receives his nature from his first parent, for which reason it is called the *sin of nature*, according to Ephesians 2:3 . . . (*ST*, I-II, q. 81, a. 1, *corpus*)

In other words, for Aquinas, the sin that we inherit is not sin in the same way that actual sin is sin. We are all guilty of actual sin, true (except for Jesus Christ and Our Blessed Mother[6]), but the kind of guilt associated with original sin is not the kind of guilt that is ours through actual sin. The words "sin" and "guilt" here are being used analogously. Original sin is not my personal sin but rather a sin of nature, a nature that I inherit which is infected as it were, weakened, prone to sin. I inherit a fallen human nature. When I am born or conceived the history of humanity does not begin anew with me. My humanity is something that I share with all others and this humanity is not what God desires it to be. This is not my fault but a fault in which I do participate for we are all as it were one in Adam. As human, I bear the burden because I am a member of the body that was Adam but is now Christ as St. Paul teaches (Rom 5:12–17; 12:4–5; 1 Cor 12:12–13). Aquinas's understanding moves beyond an individualistic approach to human nature, of which I am one specimen, to an appreciation of our unity within one (fallen) human nature that we all share. Sin is not natural; it is not a part of human nature as such; it is rather a part of human nature as it comes to us given whatever the actual sin of our first almost still prehuman parents chose. Original sin then is a corporate kind of thing in contrast to its being my thing, a corporate kind of guilt in contrast to my personal guilt. Our human origins may lie in mystery but somewhere within that mystery is the origin of sin. We inherit a faulty nature through no fault of our own but nevertheless therein does lie a fault in which we participate. It is our common human nature, from which for Aquinas, only baptism can extricate us.

6. The Church teaches that the mother of Jesus was conceived without sin and remained sinless throughout her life. This does not mean that she did not inherit our common human nature but rather that she was free from the stain of sin due to a special grace given her.

This is Aquinas's introduction to the topic of original sin, in the first article of the first question on the topic (*ST*, I-II, q. 81, a. 1) and there are twelve more articles to go which we cannot consider here. Original sin is the absence of something that could have been there had our primitive ancestors set us on a different trajectory.[7] In many ways they themselves may not have been so much to blame, as Irenaeus suggests in his own approach to original sin[8] as distinct from an Augustinian approach which influenced Aquinas. For us today it is difficult to appreciate what it means for us to be "one in Adam" as we think of ourselves only as individuals. Owen Barfield picked up on this in discussing the evolution of consciousness when he wrote:

> For instance, a non-participating consciousness cannot avoid distinguishing abruptly between the concept of "man," or "mankind," or "men in general" on the one hand and that of "*a* man"—an individual human spirit—on the other. This difficulty did not arise to anything like the same extent as long as original participation survived. Therefore our predecessors were able, quite inwardly, to accept the sin of Adam as being *their* original sin. And therefore we are not—because, for us, Adam (if he existed) was after all—somebody else![9]

The sense of separateness in modern individualism prevents us from the deeper awareness of our entanglement with each other, of which we are beginning once again to become more aware, that we are in fact "one in

7. The condition of our ancestors before the Fall was known as original justice, and the essence of original sin was the loss of original justice, which was the loss of the gift of a supernatural grace that had been given, a gift that had made the condition of our first ancestors to be existentially more than that of what philosophically one might define as pure nature (*ST*, I-II, q. 82 a. 2).

8. Irenaeus considered our first parents to be more like children than like adults, and thus less aware of the consequences of their choice, which nevertheless was their choice, and which had its impact on the human history and nature we inherit. See *Against Heresies*, Book IV, chapter xxxviii; and *Proof of the Apostolic Preaching*, #12.

9. Barfield, *Saving Appearances*, 183. For Barfield, we in the modern world operate with a different kind of consciousness (non-participating consciousness) than did our ancestors whose consciousness was a participating one. Today we might think more in terms of solidarity, our solidarity in Adam and our solidarity in Christ. Barfield, for whose thought the evolution of consciousness was central, was one of the "Inklings," as well as being influenced by the thought of Rudolf Steiner. He had a significant influence on C. S. Lewis who dedicated his first major scholarly work, *The Allegory of Love*, to Owen Barfield. Yet Lewis and Barfield were intellectual antagonists. See Adey, *Great War*. Also n68 in the previous chapter.

Adam." Original sin in which we all participate as descendants of Adam, Jesus Christ and Our Blessed Mother being exceptions for different reasons (*ST*, I-II, q. 81, a. 3), is that "sin of the world" to which the Gospel of John (1:29) refers (*ST*, I-II, q. 82, a. 2). There is then in the story of sin not only our own personal actual sins but also a corporate condition which is also ours in which there is a loss of rectitude or a weakening of the will, an inclination toward sin (*ST*, I-II, q. 83, a. 3). But original sin is not sinful in the same way nor are we guilty in the same way as for personal sins.[10] Yet we all come into the world in need of redemption (*ST*, I-II, q. 81, a. 3). The story of human freedom is intermingled with this history of sin and only grace sets us free from this bondage.

The Reality of Grace. Aquinas's teaching on grace (*ST*, I-II, qq. 109–14) connects the two parts of the second part of his *Summa*. In the *prima secundae,* the story of sin and humanity under the law culminates in a treatise on grace, the life of which is the content of the *secunda secundae.* St. Paul had said (Rom 5:15–21) that although sin abounds, grace is even more abundant, which is true for Aquinas as well. Grace not only heals what sin had broken but offers us a new and even more elevated life. Aquinas discusses the necessity of grace (*ST*, I-II, q. 109), the essence of grace (*ST*, I-II, q. 110), various kinds of grace (*ST*, I-II, q. 111), the source or cause of grace (*ST*, I-II, q. 112), the effects of grace (*ST*, I-II, q. 113), and that in which merit consists (*ST*, I-II, q. 114). Before these questions, however, in his conclusion to the treatise on law in which Aquinas talks about the New Law, he points to grace as being the content of the New Law:

> Now that which is preponderant in the law of the New Testament, and whereon all its efficacy is based, is the grace of the Holy Spirit, which is given through faith in Christ. Consequently, the New Law is chiefly the grace itself of the Holy Spirit, which is given to those who believe in Christ. (*ST*, I-II, q. 106, a. 1, *corpus*).[11]

One can thus see that Thomas's treatment of grace in the *secunda pars* connects itself back to his treatment of the Holy Spirit in the *prima pars* (*ST*, I, qq. 36–38). The treatise on grace is also connected to what St. Thomas had to say about predestination in the *prima pars* (*ST*, I, q. 23)

10. See Schoonenberg, *Man and Sin*, 168–77, for a summary of doctrinal statements pertinent to original sin.

11. I have translated "Spiritus Sanctus" as "Holy Spirit" where the original English translation used the words "Holy Ghost."

as well as to his consideration of the grace of Christ in the *tertia pars* (*ST*, III, q. 7), manifesting how interconnected all the parts of the *Summa* are. To understand Aquinas fully on the topic of grace one needs to go beyond the explicit questions in the *prima secundae*.[12]

Given the human condition, Aquinas sees the aid that grace offers as necessary.

> But in the state of corrupt nature, man falls short of what he could do by his nature [if it had not been corrupted by sin], so that he is unable to fulfill it by his own natural powers. Yet because human nature is not altogether corrupted by sin . . . even in the state of corrupted nature, it can, by virtue of its natural endowments, work some particular good, as to build dwellings, plant vineyards and the like; yet it cannot do all the good natural to it . . . (*ST*, I-II, q. 109, a. 2, *corpus*)

Human nature is not destroyed by sin. We still retain the natural human powers of intellect and will, even if our wills have been seriously weakened and our capacity for correct reasoning clouded, yet we remain free and rational beings. There are good things that we can do without grace, but grace is needed "in the state of corrupt nature . . . in order to be healed, and furthermore in order to carry out works of supernatural virtue" (*ST*, I-II, q. 109, a. 2). Aquinas points to the two major effects of grace, that it heals, and that it elevates our nature to a new level, which will be particularly prominent for Aquinas, that we might live a supernatural life. Aquinas will always make a distinction between what we could do if there had been no history of sin and our human nature had not been distorted, and the present fallen human condition with which we must existentially concern ourselves. For Aquinas humanity had in fact never actually existed as purely natural, in a purely natural state, even before Adam had sinned.[13] In the present situation, however, human beings need grace. They cannot

12. Vincent B. Dávila, OP, in a paper on "Grace in Romans," submitted as a doctoral student at the University of Notre Dame, made me aware that to do justice to Aquinas's teaching on grace, one needs to consider not only the discussion within the *Summa* but must also take into consideration his commentary on the Letter to the Romans which is an important treatment of the doctrine of grace as well.

13. The question of the relationship between nature and grace, and whether there is in Aquinas a concept of pure nature, has become a disputed question and the literature extensive. Henri de Lubac, SJ, initiated the contemporary discussion with his return to the texts of Aquinas with a reading different from that of Aquinas's early commentators. See Kerr, *After Aquinas*; de Lubac, *Mystery of the Supernatural*; de Lubac, *Augustinianism*; Healy, "Nature and Grace." By way of contrast to those who have favored the interpretation of de Lubac, is Feingold, *Natural Desire*.

even prepare themselves for grace without grace (*ST*, I-II, q. 109, a. 6). Aquinas is as opposed to Pelagianism as was Augustine.

But what is grace? It is not the same thing as virtue (*ST*, I-II, q. 110, a. 3) for a life of supernatural virtue presupposes grace (*ST*, I-II, q. 110, a. 3, *ad* 3; a 4). Rather grace transforms the soul itself, giving us something like a second nature, acting more like a formal cause than an efficient one (*ST*, I-II, q. 110, a. 2, *ad* 1), not of course changing the soul substantially as the soul remains a human soul (*ST*, I-II, q. 110, a. 2, *ad* 2), but rather it re-forms or transforms the soul and thus enhances the powers of the soul. Grace then is understood by Aquinas to be a gift (*ST*, I-II, q. 110, a. 2), a participation in the divine nature (*ST*, I-II, q. 110, a. 3; q. 112, a. 1), whereby we are born again as daughters and sons of God (*ST*, I-II, q. 110, a. 3), and are thus deified, becoming in some way like God (*ST*, I-II, q. 112, a. 1), in one sense gods by participation (*ST*, I-II, q. 3, a. 1, *ad* 1).[14] Essential to the notion of grace is that it is freely given, *gratis*, and given in varied ways.

The first distinction that Aquinas makes with respect to grace is that between habitual or sanctifying grace and other gratuitous or charismatic graces (*ST*, I-II, q. 111, a. 1), the former being *gratia gratum faciens* (grace that makes one pleasing to God) and the latter *gratiae gratis datae* (graces freely given). The most common term for the former in Aquinas is habitual grace, since it endures, although it can be lost, but once given puts the human person in a different relationship with God, unites her to God and truly deifies the person, making her more and more like unto God. The expression sanctifying grace became more common later for that same reality, the human soul's transformation. All grace is freely given, but those designated specifically as such are today more often spoken of as charismatic graces or gifts such as St. Paul delineates in 1 Corinthians, chapter 12. These are distributed variously, do not necessarily make one holy, but are given for the common good, the good of others, such as the gifts of prophecy, tongues, discernment, healing, administration and so on. The former (habitual grace) transforms the person who is then no longer in the state in which the history of sin had put one whereas the latter (charismatic graces) are for the sake of the community.

A second distinction is that between operating and co-operating grace (*ST*, I-II, q. 111, a. 2). In the former, an act is attributed to God

14. Much is written on the topic of deification. A strong emphasis on our being "gods by participation" can be found in Arintero, *Mystical Evolution*. For other references see n95 in chapter 2. Also, Christianson, "Thomistic Model."

alone; in the latter cooperation is involved, even though that cooperation remains a graced act, but one in which we participate, in which our wills or freedom are involved about which we will say more shortly. Operating grace heals and brings justification, but cooperating grace allows us to participate for "God does not justify us without ourselves" (*ST*, I-II, q. 111, a. 2, *ad* 2), as Aquinas and Augustine both affirmed. Co-operating grace, in allowing the human will a role, allows one to speak about one's role in terms of merit (although merit is always itself an effect of grace) and denotes our lack of resistance to the help that God has given (*ST*, I-II, q. 114). Some graces, which we call actual, are really helps (*auxilia*)[15] that God gives; they are not the same as that grace which makes us holy, for they do not perdure but assist us in particular circumstances. All grace of course is always to be traced back to God alone who is its principal cause (*ST*, I-II, q. 112, a. 1, *ad* 1–2).[16]

In question 111, article three, Aquinas spoke about five effects of grace: (1) it heals the soul; (2) enables us to desire the good; (3) enables us to carry into effect the good proposed; (4) enables us to persevere in the good; and (5) empowers us to reach the state of glory. The power of sin is broken. In question 113 he speaks about an effect of grace as being justification, a complex subject into which we cannot go here.[17] Justification and its concomitant remission of guilt as an effect of grace, however, means that, through grace alone, not discounting our human role that can be meritorious, we are made just, holy, pleasing to God: we are now in a right relationship with him. God alone, and yet our free wills also have a part to play. The question may have emerged already: Grace alone, but human freedom also?

The reality of grace, involving God's action and presence in our lives, does not compete with human nature. It is not grace *or* free will, but *both* free will *and* grace. In fact, it is grace that makes us free, given that our human wills are severely weakened due to sin. Grace really sets us free

15. The question of grace as an aid, and particularly actual graces, and how grace operated, became the subject of the *De Auxiliis* controversy in the late sixteenth and early seventeenth centuries, a dispute between Dominican theologians (particularly Bañez) and Jesuit theologians (particularly L. de Molina) as the post-Reformation church attempted to steer a middle course between Calvinism and Pelagianism.

16. A distinction commonly made, that between sufficient grace and efficacious grace, is not found in Thomas himself but rather among later Thomists. See Most, *Grace*, 469–70, 486, one of the more trustworthy treatments of Thomas on predestination.

17. A valuable study of justification is Küng, *Justification*.

even though human freedom was never completely destroyed by original sin, but severely damaged. This ultimately goes back to a fundamental principle for St. Thomas, namely that grace does not destroy nature but perfects it (*Cum enim gratia non tollat naturam, sed perficiat . . . ST* I, q. 1, a. 8, *ad* 2). God's action is that of a First Cause and a principal cause and a different kind of causality than that of a secondary cause, which we are. The causality of one does not hinder the workings of the other.

> Free-will is the cause of its own movement, because by free-will one moves oneself to act. But it does not of necessity belong to liberty that what is free should be the first cause of itself, as neither for one thing to be the cause of another need it be the first cause. God, therefore, is the first cause, who moves causes both natural and voluntary. And just as by moving natural causes God does not prevent their acts being natural, so by moving voluntary causes God does not deprive their actions of being voluntary: but rather is God the cause of this very thing in them; for God operates in each thing according to its own nature. (*ST*, I, q. 83, a. 1, *ad* 3)

In other words, God as the cause of grace respects nature and its natural causes, and in this case the nature of voluntary creatures. God respects human freedom.

Without grace we would be far less free. As St. Paul had written to the Galatians: "For freedom, Christ has set us free; stand fast therefore, and do not submit again to a yoke of slavery" (5:1). Situated within the history of sin, we are in bondage, with diminished freedom, but grace enables us to be truly free. Other texts make the same point:

> Now God moves everything in its own manner . . . Hence God moves man to justice according to the condition of his human nature. But it is man's proper nature to have free will. Hence in him who has the use of reason, God's motion to justice does not take place without a movement of the free-will; but he so infuses the gift of justifying grace that at the same time he moves the free-will to accept the gift of grace, in such as are capable of being moved thus. (*ST*, I-II, q. 113, a. 3, *corpus*)

Although we are not able to do good without grace, we can of our own accord refuse or resist the grace God offers. We retain the freedom to resist the grace that enables us to choose the good.

> To settle this difficulty, we ought to consider that, although one may neither merit in advance nor call forth divine grace by a movement of free choice, he is able to prevent himself from receiving this grace . . . And since this ability to impede or not to impede the reception of divine grace is within the scope of free choice, not undeservedly is responsibility for the fault imputed to him who offers an impediment to the reception of grace. In fact, as far as God is concerned, God is ready to give grace to all; "indeed He wills all men to be saved, and to come to the knowledge of the truth" as is said in 1 Timothy (2:4). But those alone are deprived of grace who offer an obstacle within themselves to grace; just as, while the sun is shining on the world, the man who keeps his eyes closed is held responsible for his fault, if as a result some evil follows, even though he could not see unless he were provided in advance with light from the sun. (*SCG*, Book 3, Part 2, chapter 159, #2)

In a human person's being justified, sanctified, deified, *both* the infusion of grace *and* free will are necessary (*ST*, I-II, q. 113, a. 6). Aquinas has thus contemplated human nature, fallen human nature due to the history and reality of sin, and human nature redeemed or graced. Our actual lives are lived at this intersection of sin, grace, and human freedom.

With grace, that is with God's help, we are able to live not only natural lives but supernatural lives, and this supernatural life is the life of virtue, the cornerstone of Aquinas's moral theology, which takes us to the second part of the second part of his *Summa*.[18] The bulk of this part of the *Summa* goes into detail concerning the life of virtue, the three theological virtues (faith, hope, charity), the four cardinal moral virtues (prudence, justice, fortitude, temperance), along with all those virtues which are daughters of these or annexed to them in some way. Here we will only give some consideration to the theological virtues.[19]

Faith. The Christian life, a life of grace, is fundamentally a life of faith, hope, and love. "And now faith, hope, and love abide, these three,

18. Aquinas's approach to ethics is often referred to as virtue ethics, for which there is an extensive bibliography. See works by Alasdair MacIntyre, Servais Pinckaers, OP, and Jean Porter.

19. Josef Pieper has written excellent reflections on both the moral and the theological virtues, individual essays later collected into a single volume. Pieper, *Faith, Hope, Love*; *Four Cardinal Virtues*. In the *prima secundae*, Aquinas also discusses the intellectual virtues, *ST* I-II, qq. 57–58, of which prudence is also one but considered under a different aspect.

and the greatest of these is love" (1 Cor 13:13).[20] The Christian life is grounded in the theological virtue of faith, a supernatural virtue, an infused virtue, a gift, which opens Aquinas's discussions in the second part of the second part of his *Summa* (*ST*, II-II, qq. 1–16). For Aquinas there is no dichotomy between the moral life and the spiritual life, or between the ascetic life and the mystical life, or between theology as such and spirituality: all comprise the Christian life. These are not separated out in the *Summa* into separate sections. It is all *sacra doctrina*, the holy teaching (*ST*, I, q. 1).[21] Life in the Spirit, life in Christ, the Christian life begins as a life of faith (*ST*, II-II, q. 4, a. 7). Faith has to do with what God has revealed to us (*ST*, II-II, q. 1, a. 1). It is an assent to that which is to be believed (*ST*, II-II, q. 1, a. 4). The act of faith itself can be distinguished as (1) *credere Deum*, (2), *credere Deo*, and (3) *credere in Deum* (*ST*, II-II, q. 2, a. 2). The first is the simplest act of faith, to believe that there is a God. The second is to believe God, to believe what God has revealed. The third is the highest or deepest or most lively faith, to believe from within God, an affective as well as cognitive faith, a faith infused with love or a faith formed by charity (*ST*, II-II, q. 4, a. 3). Faith can be further distinguished between a living faith, one formed by charity, and a lifeless or dead faith unformed by charity (*ST*, II-II, q. 4, a. 4), the latter still being true faith insofar as it is an act of the intellect as an intellectual assent (*ST*, II-II, q. 4, a. 2; q. 1, a. 4). Living faith pertains to the will as well and thus to the life of charity (*ST*, II-II, q. 4, a. 4). One can simply believe, or one can believe in a way whereby one's life is informed or transformed by love. Faith as a theological virtue is a gift from God (*ST*, II-II, q. 6, a. 1); even lifeless faith is a gift, even though it is a faith lacking in the perfection of Christian love (*ST*, II-II, q. 6, a. 2).

Another important distinction for Aquinas is that between explicit faith and implicit faith. Aquinas held that faith is necessary for salvation (Heb 11:6). However, it is not necessary that one believe *explicitly* everything contained in the profession of faith (*ST*, II-II, q. 2, a. 5). The

20. In his commentary on 1 Cor 13:13, Aquinas writes, "The reason he does not mention all the gifts but only three is that these three join to God; the others do not join to God except through the mediation of these three. . . . Hence, too, only those three, namely, faith, hope and charity, are called theological virtues, because they have God for their immediate object." Aquinas, *Corinthians*, 304 (#805).

21. The very first article in the first part of Thomas's *Summa* is on *sacra doctrina* or the holy teaching. On the unity between theology and spirituality, see Torrell, *Saint Thomas Aquinas*, 2:1–21. For Thomas, as well as among the Fathers in the patristic period, theology was spirituality. All theology was spiritual.

distinction is important as it will later impact European evangelization in the new world.[22] The question, not uniformly answered by Aquinas, is in what implicit faith consists. Aquinas describes it in various ways. Is it necessary to believe at least implicitly in the mystery of Christ (*ST*, II-II, q. 2, a. 7)? Is it necessary to believe in the doctrine of the Trinity (*ST*, II-II, q. 2, a. 8)? Aquinas is careful and discriminating but does write:

> If, however, some were saved [e.g., Gentiles] without receiving any revelation, they were not saved without faith in a Mediator, for, though they did not believe in him explicitly, they did, nevertheless, have implicit faith through believing in Divine providence, since they believed that God would deliver humankind in whatever way was pleasing to Him. (*ST*, II-II, q. 2, a. 7, *ad* 3)

The topic will come up again in the *tertia pars* when Aquinas discusses the necessity of baptism for salvation and the distinction between baptism of water and that of desire. Aquinas firmly believes that faith is necessary for salvation, yet he wants to make allowances for those who do not know Christ explicitly. The teaching of the Church has since developed in this area both in the documents of Vatican II and the writings of Pope St. John Paul II.[23] Yet Aquinas needs to be credited with giving the Church an important distinction even if it would require further clarification with respect to salvation outside the Church.

Aquinas sees the gifts of the Holy Spirit as in some way complementing or completing acts of virtue. With each virtue (theological as well as moral) there is an aligned gift of the Holy Spirit. With respect to faith the gifts of the Spirit that accompany it are those of understanding (*intellectus*) and knowledge (*scientia*).[24] The gifts are distinct from the

22. Of note is the mutual relationship between the theology of the school of Salamanca and the experience of missionaries in the "new world," such as one finds in the thinking of Francisco de Vitoria and Bartolomé de las Casas in the sixteenth century. For an excellent and detailed reflection on las Casas see Gutiérrez, *Las Casas*.

23. See Flannery, *Vatican Council II*, "Declaration on the Relation of the Church to Non-Christian Religions (*Nostra aetate*)," #2; "Dogmatic Constitution on the Church (*Lumen gentium*)," #16; "Decree on the Church's Missionary Activity (*Ad gentes*)," ##3, 7, 9, 11. See also John Paul II, "*Dominum et vivificantem*," #53; "*Redemptoris missio*," ##4, 28; "*Ut Unum Sint*," #3.1; "*Fides et ratio*," #72. A thorough exploration of the question of the relationship between Christian theology and non-Christian religious traditions is Dupuis, *Religious Pluralism*.

24. Hope is accompanied by the gift of fear of the Lord (*ST*, II-II, q. 19); charity by the gift of wisdom (*ST*, II-II, q. 45); prudence by the gift of counsel (*ST*, II-II, q. 52); justice by the gift of piety (*ST*, II-II, q. 121); fortitude by the gift of courage (*ST*, II-II,

virtues but are aids to living the life of virtue which takes on a facilitated or more "inspired" character through the action of the gifts. One becomes more docile to the working of the Holy Spirit through the action of the gifts (*ST*, I-II, q. 68, a. 1). Aquinas notes that in the text of Isaiah 11:2 referring to the gifts, that they are not referred to as gifts but rather as *spirits*, the spirit of wisdom, of understanding, etc. Thus, in addition to the gift of rationality which is part of our nature, the gifts manifest a more direct or directive action of the Holy Spirit in our lives which are given to us with the gift of the Holy Spirit itself. Aquinas sees the gifts as necessary in our spiritual lives (*ST*, I-II, q. 68, a. 2). He treats of the gifts in general in the *prima secundae* (q. 68) which is followed by his reflection on the beatitudes in general (*ST*, I-II, q. 69). Although the gifts excel in some respects the virtues due to their *modus operandi*, or way of operating or interacting, they are not more perfect than the virtue of charity (*ST*, I-II, q. 68, aa. 5, 8) which is the supreme goal of the Christian life.

Hope. Aquinas gives a beautiful twist to his understanding of hope when he describes it as leaning on God (*ST*, II-II, q. 17, aa. 1, 2). That for which we hope, as a theological virtue, *is* God, or eternal happiness which consists in enjoying God (*ST*, II-II, q. 17, aa. 2, 5). In his brief and unfinished *Compendium of Theology*,[25] Thomas discusses hope in the context of a reflection on the Lord's Prayer, for we pray for what we hope for, and our ultimate hope is for union with God. Our hope is for the coming reign of God in which we hope to participate. "Thy kingdom come." Our hope is not for ourselves alone (*ST*, II-II, q. 17, a. 3). That for which we hope is not something to be easily attained but rather "something arduous" or difficult to attain (*ST*, II-II, q. 17, a. 3). As St. Paul had put it in the Letter to the Romans (8:24–25): "Now hope that is seen is not hope. For who hopes for what is seen? But if we hope for what we do not see, we wait for it with patience."

We commonly think, and rightly so, that virtue can be understood as a mean between two extremes, as Aristotle presented it.[26] This is only applicable to the moral virtues where one can go to an extreme either by excess of something or by a deficiency of it. It is possible to be too courageous or foolhardy, also possible to be cowardly. The virtue of courage or

q. 139); and temperance as well by the gift of the fear of the Lord. See Goergen, *Fire of Love*, 128–50; and Kiesling, "Seven *Quiet* Gifts." For an excellent discussion on the Holy Spirit, also see Levering, *Engaging the Doctrine*.

25. Aquinas, *Compendium of Theology*, 313–43.

26. See Aristotle, *Nicomachean Ethics*, 303–4; also Book II, chs. 6–9.

fortitude lies between these two extremes. One can seek pleasure to an excess, as an end in itself, or one can disdain its value as a good thing. The virtue of temperance lies between these two extremes. The same, however, cannot be said about the theological virtues. One cannot have an excess of faith, hope, or love.

> Now a moral virtue is concerned with things ruled by reason, and these things are its proper object; wherefore it is proper for it to follow the mean as regards its proper object. On the other hand, a theological virtue is concerned with the First Rule not ruled by another rule, and that Rule is its proper object. Wherefore it is not proper for a theological virtue, with regard to its proper object, to follow the mean . . . Thus faith can have no mean or extremes in the point of trusting to the First Truth, in which it is impossible to trust too much . . . So too, hope has no mean or extremes, as regards its principal object, since it is impossible to trust too much in the Divine assistance. (*ST* II-II, q. 17, a. 5, *ad* 2)

We cannot trust in God's assistance too much. Nevertheless, we can sin against hope in two ways, by way of presumption or of despair (*ST*, II-II, qq. 20–21).

The virtue of hope does give us a degree of assurance, however, for God keeps his promises. Hope does not give us absolute certitude with respect to eternal salvation, but it does carry with it the certitude of faith, and whoever has faith is certain of God's mercy (*ST*, II-II, q. 18, a. 4, *ad* 2, 3). Presumption can be either relying on oneself when something is beyond one's own power or taking God's mercy for granted, whereas despair is unwilling to trust in God's mercy.

As the virtue of faith is aligned with the Holy Spirit's gifts of knowledge and of understanding, so the virtue of hope is aided by the gift of fear. This is not a servile fear which turns to God only out of fear of punishment, but a filial fear concerned about offending God, as someone would not want to offend someone whom one loves (*ST*, II-II, q. 19, aa. 2, 4, 9). Some contemporary usage in the church, especially in relationship to the sacrament of Confirmation, speaks of the gifts of awe or wonder (the fear of the Lord); reverence or devotion (piety); courage or strength (fortitude); consultation or collaboration (counsel); learning or love of sacred truth (knowledge); insight or vision (understanding); as well as the gift of wisdom for which there is no need for any change in contemporary usage.

Charity. We come now to the heart of a Christian's moral and spiritual life. As St. Paul wrote to the Corinthians (1 Cor 12:31; 13:13), its goal is love, which Aquinas also affirms: "the perfection of the Christian life consists radically in charity" (*ST*, II-II, q. 184, a. 1). Charity is not only the most excellent of the virtues (*ST*, II-II, q. 23, a. 6), but no virtue at all is possible without it (*ST*, II-II, q. 23, a. 7.) Charity or love informs all the virtues as it directs the acts of all other virtues to their last end (*ST*, II-II, q. 23, a. 8) which is enjoying God (*ST*, II-II, q. 23, a. 2, *sed contra*), which we saw when we noted that charity informs the virtue of faith and makes it living faith (*ST*, II-II, q. 4, aa. 3–4).

Latin offers Aquinas several words for love (*amor*): *caritas*, *dilectio*, *amicitia*, or charity, love, and friendship, all of which assist Aquinas in his treatise on charity (*ST*, II-II, qq. 23–46). For Aquinas charity (*caritas*) is friendship (*amicitia*) with God (*ST*, II-II, q. 23, aa. 1, 5). Charity of course, as was true for St. Augustine,[27] comprises both love of God and love of neighbor. Aristotle had delineated different kinds of friendship: those that are directed toward delight, use, or virtue.[28] Friendship, for Aquinas, is love that is benevolent (wishing good for the other), mutual, and founded on communication (*ST*, II-II, q. 23, a. 1). Charity is this kind of friendship, which love does not exclude one's enemies, since our friendship for someone we love includes those whom our friend loves (*ST*, II-II, q. 23, a. 1, *ad* 2, 3). God is our friend. God is love. God is charity (1 John 4:16). Charity is closely associated with the Holy Spirit but not to be equated as such with the Holy Spirit (*ST*, II-II, q. 23, a. 2). God's love is poured into our hearts through the Holy Spirit who is given to us (Rom 5:5). Charity is more of a participation in the Holy Spirit (*ST*, II-II, q. 23, a. 3, *ad* 3) whose proper names are Love and Gift (*ST*, I, qq. 37–38).

After offering his definition of charity as friendship with God, Aquinas goes on to show that acts of charity reside in the will (*ST*, II-II, q. 24, a. 1) as acts of faith were related to the intellect (*ST*, II-II, q. 1, a. 4; q. 4, a. 1), although here Aquinas makes a distinction less familiar to us, namely between *voluntas* and *liberum arbitrium*, between "will" and "free will" or "choice," (*ST*, II-II, q. 24, a. 1, *ad* 3; I, q. 83, a. 4).[29] Both

27. Augustine, *Teaching Christianity*, 114–19 (Book I, sections 20–30).

28. Aristotle, *Nicomachean Ethics*, 166–69 (Book VIII, chap. 3).

29. Aquinas explains, as we indicated above in chapter 2, that although the intellect as a power of the soul is one power, nevertheless it has two dimensions to it, namely those of *intellectus* and *ratio*, so likewise the appetitive power has two dimensions as well, namely *voluntas* and *liberum arbitrium*. The former is simply the appetitive

intellect and will are powers of the human soul. Free will is not a power distinct from that of will itself but rather the capacity to make choices, *to choose the good.* Choice is directed towards a specific end or the means towards an end, whereas the will as such seeks or desires the good in general. Charity resides in the will (*voluntas*) and not as such in choice. Throughout one's life one can grow in charity (*ST*, II-II, q. 24, a. 4), and in fact there is no limit to its increase as it is a participation or sharing in the infinite charity which is the Holy Spirit (*ST*, II-II, q. 24, a. 7). Aquinas describes this growth according to three degrees, namely that of beginners which is concerned with avoiding sin; the proficient who make progress in strengthening charity; and the third whose chief aim is union with and enjoyment of God (*ST*, II-II, q. 24, a. 9). These later became associated with a common way of speaking about the unfolding development of one's spiritual life, depicted as purgative, illuminative and unitive stages.[30] Charity, however, can be lost by placing an obstacle in its path, an obstacle to the outpouring of God's love into the soul, by preferring sin to friendship with God (*ST*, II-II, q. 24, aa. 11–12).

As mentioned earlier, charity includes love of neighbor within one's love of God (*ST*, II-II, q. 25, a. 1), and not only our neighbor but also ourselves (*ST*, II-II, q. 25, a. 4), which includes respect for our bodies as well since our bodies have been created by God (*ST*, II-II, q. 25, aa. 5, 12). All this contrasts with the teaching of the Manicheans. All, insofar as we are speaking about charity or friendship with God, is done for God's sake, out of love for God, as is true of love of enemies.

> For since man loves his neighbor, out of charity, for God's sake, the more he loves God, the more does he put enmities aside and show love towards his neighbor: thus if we loved a certain man very much, we would love his children though they were unfriendly toward us. (*ST*, II-II, q. 25, a. 8, *corpus*)

---

power as desiring the good, that is a movement of the soul towards the good, whereas the latter carries the connotation of choice. There is a movement in the soul towards the good, but free will or choice (*liberum arbitrium*) determines means towards that end. Although it is not a distinction so familiar to us in Anglo-American philosophy, Aquinas distinguishes between *volo*, *velle* (to will) and *eligo*, *eligere* (to choose). *ST*, I-II, q. 83. For many in the English-speaking world "to will" and "to choose" are practically synonymous.

30. See Arintero, *Mystical Evolution*, vol. 2; Garrigou-Lagrange, *Three Ages*; Garrigou-Lagrange, *Christian Perfection*.

Charity, as Augustine had already taught,[31] also extends to angels (*ST*, II-II, q. 25, a. 10), who are neighbors to us as much as any other creature. God, however, has a primacy within charity (*ST*, II-II, q. 26, aa. 1, 2), for God "is loved as the cause of happiness, whereas our neighbor is loved as receiving together with us a share of happiness from God" (*ST*, II-II, q. 26, a. 2); and also because we have received from God two goods, that of our human nature as well as that of grace (*ST*, II-II, q. 26, a. 3).

The proper act of charity is simply to love (*dilectio*). It is more proper to love than to be loved, whether this be in the love of friendship or of a mother for her child. This does not imply that it is unimportant to be receptive to love, but by the virtue of charity one actively loves (*ST*, II-II, q. 27, a. 1). *Amor* is a more generic word for love, which can also refer to love as a passion or emotion (*ST*, I-II, qq. 26–28). Insofar as love resides in the will (in contrast to its being an emotion or *passio*) and is directed towards God, others, and self, it is *caritas* which is also *amicitia* because it carries with it the qualities that accompany friendship. Hence *caritas* is *amicitia* with God, a supernatural and infused virtue. It is also *dilectio* reflecting a willed aspect that makes it truly human. Thus, ordinarily, *amor* is a more generic expression comprising *caritas*, *amicitia*, *dilectio*, and also *passio*. There is a richness in the appreciation of the facets of love. While *caritas* is always *amor*, not every kind of *amor* is necessarily *caritas*. Nor is every expression of *amicitia* necessarily *caritas* unless it is grounded in one's friendship with God. Aquinas carefully distinguishes *amor* and *dilectio* (*ST*, I-II, q. 26, a. 3). While I might love my pet rabbit, only rational creatures show *dilectio* towards God, neighbor, self, and enemy.[32]

In the *prima secundae* Aquinas had discussed love as an emotion. He also discussed its effects, such as: (1) the union of lover and beloved, as when a friend is called one's other self or considered half one's soul; (2) an intimacy or mutual indwelling whereby love makes the beloved to be in the lover and vice-versa; (3) a certain kind of ecstasy as in friendship when one is taken outside one's self while wishing good for one's friend; (4) a zealousness whereby one comes to the defense of one's friend, along with other effects (*ST*, I-II, q. 28, aa. 1–6). Now in the *secunda secundae* where he is discussing the infused supernatural virtue of love or charity, these same effects are found, but there are also three additional interior effects of the virtue, namely joy, peace, and mercy (*ST*, II-II, qq. 28–30).

31. *Teaching Christianity*, 119–21 (Book I, sections 31–33).

32. For further reflection on the richness of the Latin vocabulary as it was especially used in the twelfth century, see Casey, *Thirst for God*, esp. 88–110.

The joy of which Aquinas speaks is not a separate virtue but rather an effect of the virtue of charity (*ST*, II-II, q. 28, a. 4). As Aquinas had said when speaking about love as one of the passions or emotions, joy follows upon love either through the presence of the one loved or through good that comes to the beloved even though he or she be absent (*ST*, I-II, q. 28, aa. 1–6). Charity, however, is love of God, who is in those who love him by a mutual indwelling as the beloved is in the lover, giving rise to a spiritual joy (*ST*, II-II, q. 28, a. 1). Yet in this life our joy can never be complete, only in the life to come.

> But as long as we are in this world, the movement of desire does not cease in us, because it still remains possible for us to approach nearer to God by grace . . . When once, however, perfect happiness has been attained, nothing will remain to be desired, because then there will be full enjoyment of God. (*ST*, II-II, q. 28, a. 3)

The same is true for peace. It is also not a virtue separate from charity but rather an effect of friendship with God (*ST*, II-II, q. 29, a. 4) which remains imperfect in this life (*ST*, II-II, q. 29, a. 3, *ad* 2).

Mercy is another matter. On the one hand, Aquinas considers it like joy and peace as an effect of charity (*ST*, II-II, q. 28, prologue). On the other hand, he also speaks of it as a virtue in itself (*ST*, II-II, q. 30, a. 3), and in one sense the greatest! (*ST*, II-II, q. 30, a. 4). Aquinas approaches it first etymologically. The Latin word *misericordia* implies one who has a heart for the wretched or sorrowful, one who has compassion for those in distress, one who has a heavy heart due to another's misfortune (*ST*, II-II, q. 30, aa. 1–2). So *misericordia* is both an effect of love but also a virtue in that it brings another dimension to love, namely the misfortune or condition of the one with whom one sympathizes (*ST*, II-II, q. 30, a. 3, *ad* 3). As a virtue, however, it is not a theological virtue but rather a moral one (*ST*, II-II, q. 30, a. 3, *ad* 4). Mercy then is considered the greatest of the moral virtues. It is biblically attested as the fundamental attribute of God.

> In itself, mercy takes precedence of other virtues, for it belongs to mercy to be bountiful to others . . . Hence mercy is accounted as being proper to God: and therein his omnipotence is declared to be chiefly manifested . . . as regards man, who has God above him, charity which unites him to God, is greater than mercy . . . But of all the virtues which relate to our neighbor, mercy is the greatest . . . (*ST*, II-II, q. 30, a. 4, *corpus*)

Mercy is a manifestation of God's love. Among us, however, nothing surpasses charity or friendship with God. With respect to our neighbor, however, there is no greater virtue than mercy. In reply to an objection in the same question Aquinas states:

> The sum total of the Christian religion consists in mercy, as regards external works: but the inward love of charity, whereby we are united to God preponderates over both love and mercy for our neighbor. (*ST*, II-II, q. 30, a. 4, *ad* 2)

Mercy is a significant theme for Aquinas.[33] It is strongly attested biblically which is always important for Aquinas. He already discusses it in the *prima pars* (*ST*, I, q. 21) in the question following upon his discussion of God's love (*ST*, I, q. 20), and in relation to God's justice, where he had stated that mercy in particular is an attribute of God (*ST*, I, q. 21, a. 3). Mercy is a theme that manifests the interrelatedness of the parts of the *Summa*, as was true for grace. With respect to who God is, mercy appears in the first part of the *Summa*. As a virtue, and in one sense the greatest and in another sense not, it appears in the second part. And it will appear again in the third part when Aquinas considers why Christ became incarnate and the meaning of the cross. Mercy is also an example of Aquinas's way of speaking: "*In one sense*" and "*On the other hand.*"

What remains in our consideration of charity is the gift of the Holy Spirit that corresponds with it, namely wisdom (*sapientia*), which is the highest of all the gifts of the Spirit as charity is the greatest of all the virtues. The gifts as we have said are considered by Aquinas to be a perfection of the virtues. Does that mean that wisdom has a more noble place in Christian life than charity? Yet charity is the summit of the moral and spiritual life. How *caritas* and *sapientia* intertwine is considered in question forty-five of the *secunda secundae*. The gifts of knowledge and understanding accompanied the virtue of faith. The gift of wisdom presupposes faith, but it belongs to wisdom to consider all things from the vantage point of their highest cause, namely God—to know God insofar as God can be known and to be able to consider things from that vantage point (*ST*, II-II, q. 45, a. 1). This wisdom is the gift, not the acquired intellectual virtue (*ST*, II-II, q. 45, a. 1, *ad* 2).[34] With both charity and wisdom

33. See Kasper, *Mercy*, esp. 23, 51, 90, 98, 100, 137.

34. Aquinas considers the intellectual virtues, as distinct from the moral and theological virtues, in the *prima secundae*, *ST* I-II, qq. 57–58. The virtues are divided into intellectual, moral, and theological; theological virtues being infused, moral virtues being both acquired or natural and also as infused; intellectual virtues being acquired habits.

one has a connaturality or sympathy with the divine. It is charity that unites us to God, however, and thus is presupposed by wisdom, which pertains more to the intellect than the will which is the basis for charity (*ST*, II-II, q. 45, aa. 2, 4). In the interplay between the two, both the intellect and the will reach the perfection of which each is capable in this life. The wise person is one who loves God with his whole mind and the charitable person is someone who loves God with his whole heart and in this mix, we cannot have one without the other. The wise person loves God in all things and the loving person is wise as we will see in considering the contemplative life shortly, for Christian contemplation and wisdom are also closely connected. Aquinas even considers theology, or rather *sacra doctrina*, the holy teaching, as a sapiential form of knowledge (*ST*, I, q. 1, a. 6).[35] Love unites us to God from which there flows a mutual indwelling. Wisdom, a deepened appreciation of God's own way of knowing, allows one then to see from God's perspective.

Prayer. Christian life, a life of grace, expressed through acts of faith, hope, love and mercy, also summons one to pray. It is in prayer that our love for God manifests itself and the personal character of God comes through. For Aquinas, the most proper name for God is the tetragrammaton, the One Who Is, the name revealed to Moses at the bush (Exod 3:13–14), *Qui est*, He-Who-Is, or Being Itself (*ST*, I, q. 13, a. 11). While this is the most proper name for God, it does not capture the full degree of God's involvement with his people. He is also the God of Abraham, Isaac, and Jacob (Gen 50:24; Exod 3:15; Matt 22:32; Acts 7:32). We don't pray to Being Itself. While God *is* Isness, Being, *Esse*, First Cause, God is also the One-Who-Is-With-Us—*Immanuel* (Isa 7:14; Matt 1:23).[36] This is what led Eleonore Stump to maintain that, for Aquinas, God is both Being and also *a* Being, both *esse* and *ens* or an *id quod est*.[37] Prayer is a personal encounter with God, insofar as human nature assisted by grace is able to do so.

35. *Sacra doctrina*, or holy teaching, is the topic of Aquinas's very first article in his *Summa*. It is not simply doctrine as such, nor theology, but the Church's teaching widely considered, namely revealed truth, both demonstrable and contemplative, thus wisdom about God, or better a participation in God's wisdom. It is what Thomas sees himself as exploring in the *Summa*.

36. See Goergen, *Jesus, Son of God*, 40–53.

37. Stump, "God of the Bible," 80–97; Stump, "God's Simplicity;" Stump, "Simplicity and Aquinas's Quantum Metaphysics."

I have considered here only the theological virtues and not the four cardinal virtues and the daughters of those virtues or others connected with them. Aquinas deals most explicitly with the topic of prayer, however, as part of the virtue of justice. "The essential character of justice consists in rendering to another his due according to equality." (*ST*, II-II, q. 80, a. 1; q. 58, a. 11). Among the virtues annexed to justice is the virtue of religion (*ST*, II-II, q. 80, a. 1) which denotes a proper relation with God or giving God his due (*ST*, II-II, q. 81, aa. 1, 2). The two interior acts of religion are devotion and prayer (*ST*, II-II, qq. 82–83). Aquinas discusses prayer (*oratio*) in seventeen articles (*ST*, II-II, q. 83) although what we consider prayer is broader than his usage,[38] and includes adoration which Aquinas considers as an external act of religion in a later question (*ST*, II-II, q. 84). It is becoming for rational creatures to pray (*ST*, II-II, q. 83, aa. 2, 10), not to change God but in order that we may become more aligned with God (*ST*, II-II, q. 83, a. 2). *Homo sapiens* is not only a rational animal but also an animal that prays, *homo orans.* In these articles Aquinas sees prayer as particularly petitionary, whereby we pray for something specific, even a temporal good, whether for ourselves or for others, including our enemies, petitions such as we find in the Lord's Prayer (*ST*, II-II, q. 83, a. 9). Prayer can be common prayer or personal prayer, vocal prayer or silent prayer, with one's mind and with one's body (*ST*, II-II, q. 83, a. 12). Aquinas endorses the idea of continuous prayer as mentioned by St. Paul in his first letter to the Thessalonians (5:17): Pray always, which may well simply be a case of continuing desire, for even the desire to pray is a prayer (*ST*, II-II, q. 83, a. 14). Although prayer is always approaching God, raising up one's mind to God, prayer is not only intercessory but also thanksgiving, praise, or sorrow for one's sins (*ST*, II-II, q. 83, a. 17). Aquinas offers many further reflections on the topic of prayer within these articles as well as elsewhere, such as in the *tertia pars* where he considers the prayer of Christ for whom it was also fitting to pray and whose practice of prayer is given testimony in the Scriptures (*ST*, III, q. 21).

In question 82, prior to the question in which Aquinas considers prayer more explicitly, he considers the topic of devotion, which we ourselves might simply put within the topic of prayer, and with devotion he asks a question about meditation and contemplation (*ST*, II-II, q. 82, a. 3). Although today we tend to distinguish those two words, the former being more discursive and the latter more receptive, Aquinas does not

38. See Goergen, "Prayer."

emphasize here the distinctiveness of each, although aware of it, but rather that they are supportive of the devout life and expressive of our need to lean on God. Yet in other contexts Aquinas does consider the topic of contemplation without giving it a precise definition. Contemplation presupposes sanctifying grace (*gratia gratum faciens*) and the indwelling of the Holy Spirit, which have as supernatural gifts elevated us above what we might do by nature and brings about a connaturality with God. In his commentary on Boethius, Thomas compares contemplation to play. We enjoy playing, an activity done for its own sake, no purpose beyond itself, and such is contemplation.[39] In the *Summa contra Gentiles*, Thomas emphasizes that happiness or the ultimate end of the human person consists in the contemplation of truth, which would be the First Truth, or God (*SCG*, Bk 3, 37, #1).

> Therefore, the last and perfect happiness [*beatitudo*], which we await in the life to come, consists entirely in contemplation. But imperfect happiness, such as can be had here, consists first and principally in contemplation, but secondarily, in an operation of the practical intellect directing human actions and passions. (*ST*, I-II, q. 3, a. 5, *corpus*)

In question 180 of the *secunda secundae*, Thomas considers the contemplative life. Although contemplation is focused on contemplating the truth (*ST*, II-II, q. 180, aa. 1, 3, 4), it is also related to the affective life, for it produces delight and makes our love of God and neighbor more intense (*ST*, II-II, q. 180, aa. 1, 7; *ST*, I-II, q. 3, a. 4).

> Wherefore Gregory [the Great] makes the contemplative life to consist in the *love of God*, inasmuch as through loving God we are aflame to gaze on his beauty. And since everyone delights when he obtains what he loves, it follows that the contemplative life terminates in delight, which is seated in the affective power, the result being that love also becomes more intense. (*ST*, II-II, q. 180, a. 1, *corpus*).

Contemplation resides primarily in the intellect, as an act of knowing, but is a kind of affective knowing. Thomas is very favorable to Gregory the Great on this topic for whom love itself is a kind of knowledge. *Amor ipse notitia est.*[40] As Josef Pieper has written:

39. See Tugwell, *Albert and Thomas*, 279–90, for further development of this observation.

40. Michael Casey writes: "The Gregorian axiom, *amor ipse notitia est*, was taken seriously by the monastic authors of the twelfth century, to the extent that it was

> Contemplation is a form of knowing arrived at not by thinking but by seeing, intuition. It is not co-ordinate with the *ratio*, with the power of discursive thinking, but with the *intellectus*, with the capacity for "simple intuition." Intuition is without doubt the perfect form of knowing.[41]

As we had stated earlier in our discussion within the *prima pars*,

> Intellect and reason differ as to their manner of knowing; because the intellect (*intellectus*) knows by simple intuition, while reason (*ratio*) knows by a process of discursion from one thing to another. (*ST*, I, q. 59, a. 1, *ad* 1)

In our present lives we are not able to see God as we will in the life to come, although St. Paul in his experience of rapture manifests a degree of contemplation that exceeds what we ordinarily find (*ST*, II-II, q. 180, a. 5; q. 175, aa. 3–6).

Thomas's discussion of contemplative and active life sees symbolism in the two wives of Jacob as well as with Mary and Martha (*ST*, II-II, qq. 179–82). It is not surprising that Thomas shows himself grounded in his Dominican life with his opinion that, within religious life, the more excellent way of life is a mixture of the two, and for Thomas one that is directed to teaching and preaching (*ST*, II-II, q. 188, a. 6), without denying the excellence of the contemplative life in accord with the tradition before him (*ST*, II-II, q. 182).[42] When it comes to religious life, we find a statement in Thomas which the Order of Preachers later chose as one of its mottoes: *contemplari et contemplata aliis tradere*. "For even as it is better to enlighten than merely to shine, so is it better to give to others the fruits of one's contemplation than merely to contemplate" (*ST*, II-II, q. 188, a. 6).

As Thomas began his discourse on the Christian life with the human person's quest for happiness, cognizant of a history of sin which had

---

generally taken for granted that love was not without cognitive effect, on the one hand, and, on the other, that perfect knowledge was impossible without love" (*Thirst*, 100). Casey is a student of the mysticism of Bernard of Clairvaux to whom Thomas also refers although Thomas relies more heavily on Gregory, *ST*, II-II, q. 180, aa. 4–5.

41. Pieper, *Happiness and Contemplation*, 73–74, an excellent study of Aquinas on contemplation.

42. Interestingly Meister Eckhart, a century later, interpreted the Lucan story of Martha and Mary as Martha being the more spiritually mature. See Goergen, *Fire of Love*, 197–99. For Eckhart's sermon to this effect, see Eckhart, *Sermons and Treatises*, I:79–90. Also translated in Eckhart, *Teacher and Preacher*, 338–45.

originated with the first human beings, and appreciative of how God has come to our aid with varied gifts of grace allowing us to lead virtuous and even superhuman or supernatural lives, as manifest in *caritas*, *sapientia*, *misericordia*, and *contemplatio*, so the human person, that rational creature, created toward God's image, is *capax Dei*, called to be a member of the body of Christ, to which we will turn in chapter 6.

5

The Human Phenomenon in Teilhard de Chardin

As cosmic in scope as is Teilhard's vision, central to that vision is the human person. He entitled his most extensive work *Le phénomène humain.* His cosmology is both cosmocentric and biocentric. At the forefront of the evolving universe was the emergence and evolution of life. Cosmogenesis gave rise to biogenesis. And at the heart of biogenesis was the emergence of the human phenomenon. Teilhard's cosmology is not only biocentric but also anthropocentric. At the core of the story of life lies reflective life. This is the direction that God's evolving creation has taken. Cosmocentricity and anthropocentricity are not in opposition: no "either/or." Anthropology cannot be seen apart from cosmology nor vice-versa. We cannot see ourselves apart from the universe but rather as a part of the universe, evolving and unfinished.

Anthropocentricity can be understood in varied ways. There is an anthropocentric perspective that sees humanity not only central to the universe but as apart from the universe, not a part of the universe—a kind of "us against them," or better said a "we against it" anthropocentrism, allowing us to dominate the universe however we wish. This is a distorted or pathological anthropocentrism. Another kind of anthropocentricity, at the heart of evolution, recognizes that the emergence of the human phenomenon, namely reflective consciousness, is a pinnacle at which evolution arrived. Nature is itself anthropocentric. Humanity is now a part of the cosmos. The cosmos is inclusive of us. We are in the universe and the universe is in us. At the heart of the universe, of time's arrow, is humankind. There is no necessary tension between being cosmocentric and anthropocentric. No cosmos, no *anthropos*. No *anthropos*, a far more unfinished universe. As has often been said, we *are* evolution become conscious of itself. One can be *both* cosmocentric *and* anthropocentric simultaneously.

Cosmogenesis was pushed toward, or guided toward, or found itself moving toward life as a supreme manifestation of its evolutionary momentum. Evolution gave birth to life, and this was no small accomplishment. The web of life is an amazing achievement. Even now we search to find life elsewhere in the universe beyond planet earth. Biogenesis, however, was also pushed or pulled or stumbled upon a dramatically new form of life—reflective life, intelligent life, human life. This too was an accomplishment. Biogenesis became anthropocentric, pointing to the human phenomenon as its crowning achievement. As evolution unfolded, there was an increase in value with the emergence of the human. If that were not the case, what increase in value was there with the emergence of life itself? This flat universe would suggest that there is no more "being" in a tulip than in a rock, nothing more of value in a gazelle than in a cabbage patch, and nothing more in Socrates than in a zebra or chimpanzee. In saying this, we are not demeaning in any way the zebra or tulip or polished stone, but we are saying how good it is that evolution did not stop there along the way.

At least for Teilhard, we must add, just as cosmogenesis culminates in a biosphere, and biogenesis in a noosphere, so anthropogenesis recognizes another momentous moment in its history with the coming to be of Jesus Christ, for anthropogenesis found its own crowning achievement in christogenesis. Evolution is cosmocentric, biocentric, anthropocentric, christocentric, and theocentric all at the same time. We do not have one without the other in the present state of our evolving universe. Cosmology and Christology are two sides of a coin. As Teilhard realized, our Christology needs to take on cosmic proportions, as the age-old concept of the cosmic Christ suggests, and our cosmology needs to take on Christic proportions if it is to be true to itself. There is no cosmos without the Christ and no Christ without the cosmos. This is something to be developed at greater length in chapter 7, but it is important for us to see that evolution, while having given birth to the human, does not stop with the human alone, but moves on to an even deeper integration of the human and the divine in the Christian doctrines of Incarnation and deification. The universe itself is anthropocentric. That's the way it is, or that's the way it happened. Being anthropocentric, however, need not mean the destruction of the cosmos by humankind. That would be a consequence of sin. The human person is an achievement of which evolution can be rightly proud. It is to Teilhard's understanding of the human person, his anthropology, to which we now turn as a complement to Aquinas's *Summa*'s *secunda pars*. From Teilhard's evolutionary perspective, we find ourselves engulfed in a set of words which we need to explore in order to appreciate his phenomenological and theological anthropology: hominization, anthropogenesis, psychogenesis, noogeneis, noosphere, personalization, socialization, spiritualization, excentration, affectionization, and amorization. They all say something about how Teilhard understood the *humanum* and creation's *telos*. In this, the emphases in Teilhard's anthropology are distinct from those in Thomas's, while the former need not exclude the latter.

Hominization and Anthropogenesis. In 1923 Teilhard wrote from China: "I am a pilgrim of the future on my way back from a journey made entirely in the past."[1] As a paleontologist and geologist, it was the past that drew his scientific attention. Nevertheless, he was more concerned about the future of humanity. Just as biogenesis was a critical leap forward for evolution from the realm of the pre-living to that of a world swarming with life, so anthropogenesis was another metamorphosis in evolution's trek. What was so distinctive about the emergence of the human was the appearance of *psyche* as a phenomenon, an evolutionary advance that can be described as psychogenesis, or to use a word that Teilhard himself coined to connote the collective nature of this reflective advance, noogenesis. As "biosphere" refers to a layer of life encompassing and surrounding the planet earth, a consequence of biogenesis, so "noosphere" refers to a conscious, thinking, reflective layer, consequent upon noogenesis or hominization.[2] Humanity was that phenomenon through which psychism or spirit broke through in a phenomenal, that is empirical, way. With humankind one can no longer deny that there are two sides to matter, its "outside," and its "inside." What appears at one point in evolution has had a prehistory, and so likewise does psychism or

1. *LT*, 101.

2. The word "noogenesis" was first used in Teilhard's essay, "Hominization" (1925), *VP*, 51–79. See n11 in chapter 3.

consciousness. There is this pan-psychic element in Teilhard even though prior to humanity's appearance it may have been there only in rudimentary, virtual, or potential ways. But there is no question about evolution's achievement in having given birth to reflective consciousness's ability to look at itself. Evolution had become conscious.

The emergence of this new "phylum" in evolution's trajectory does not diminish the layers on which it had been built. The whole cosmos is essential for the future of life. Cosmogenesis continues even as biogenesis enters the scene. Plants and animals continue to proliferate and evolve as the ancestors of *Homo sapiens* emerge, and some of those ancestors were ones in whose discovery Teilhard played a leading role.[3] There is no denying that there was something new here, as evolution disclosed the other side of matter. Teilhard then explored the role of socialization, the structure of personality, the meaning of human sexuality, the significance of evolution for morality, the interconnectedness of the human family, the phenomenon of spirituality, human energy in both its reflective and affective dimensions, for all of these were impacted by the genesis of the human.

Teilhard had given the law, or directionality, that evolution manifests when he spoke about it as one of complexity-consciousness. The evolution of consciousness is coextensive with evolution's complexification on its material "outside" face. The complex human brain was required for reflexive consciousness to emerge. Another descriptive law for Teilhard was "Union differentiates." The union of a man and woman in love perfects each, individualizes each, enables each to reach the acme of what the personal can achieve. It does not destroy but completes. The psychic energy that underlay this is that of love, along the lines of St. Paul in 1 Corinthians. Human evolution is a phenomenon, and what the human does with evolution is vital to its future. We may be more evolved than our ancestors but not necessarily more moral.[4] There has been progress at the level of the "outside": in agriculture, medicine, technology, etc., and consciousness itself has evolved within the life span of humankind. The reality remains, however, that we can do more good than ever before in history, and more harm. Agriculture has developed to a point where we could feed the population of the world if we had the will to do so, yet the

3. E.g., *Sinanthropus pekinensis*. See chapter 1.

4. "A Note on Progress" (1920), *FM*, 17–18.

exploration of atomic energy has left us insecure even though its merits are significant.

The Personal and the Social. With the emergence of the human phenomenon, of reflective consciousness, and the hominization of evolution, a new creation emerges from within the pre-hominid world and prepares the way for a metamorphosis of the cosmos and the biosphere. Biogenesis has become anthropogenesis. The universe is still the same and yet radically new. There is continuity for sure, but a discontinuity within it. What are we to make of this novelty, this anthropogenesis? We can judge from where it has come, its prehistory, even if we cannot trace its lineage completely, but what lay ahead? Life forms had spread, diversified, evolved, and even become extinct. Within the biosphere we discover a noosphere—a realm or layer of thought or "thinking" surrounding the planet. Thinking is a part of the universe, not apart from the universe, but manifests the universe as having become conscious. That which is new is not only the bodily and cranial structures that support a leap forward on the "outside" of creation's evolution, but also new is what was happening on the "inside." Now there is not only the interdependence of the elements of the universe; there is the interdependence of humanity. There is now not only a complexification on the plane of matter, but a psychogenesis within which we are all entangled. My very individuality is transformed while preserved: union differentiates.

In a less well-known essay of Teilhard's, "What Exactly Is the Human Body?" he prepares the way for us to see our interrelatedness, not only with all others but with the cosmos as well.[5] Each of us has a cosmic body. Each of us is a member, at least potentially,[6] of the mystical body of Christ. We can see here again Teilhard's respect for St. Paul. When we think of our bodies, we ordinarily think of our biological bodies, with their spatial boundaries, this flesh and these bones. For Teilhard my true body is not just this flesh and these bones. It comprises others who are a part of who I am. I am literally the center of a network of relationships. The "other" is as much a part of me, from a psychological or spiritual point of view, as the biological parts are. Teilhard wrote often about "the other."[7] This relational or social body (family, friends, community, faith community) has not only a social but a universal dimension to it. All

5. "What Exactly Is the Human Body?" (1919), *SC*, 11–13.

6. This is true for Thomas Aquinas as well. See *ST*, III, q. 8, a. 3; q. 48, a. 1.

7. E.g., "The Rise of the Other," (1942), *AE*, 59–75.

others are a part of who I am. My "extendedness" or "spatiality" does not stop but is cosmic in scope.[8]

Although we are familiar with St. Paul's emphasis on the body of Christ in 1 Corinthians, chapter 12, where he states that each of us is a member of Christ's body, in the Letter to the Romans Paul states that we are members one of another (12:5): "So we, who are many, are one body in Christ, and individually we are members one of another." I am not who I am apart from others who are a part of me. If I were forced to make a choice between having a finger amputated and losing someone, friend, or spouse, about whom I care most deeply, most of us would sacrifice the so-called part of our body because at a certain psychic level we realize that the other is as much or more me than the biological part. As Augustine had put it, and Horace before him, "A friend is half my soul."[9] Thus Teilhard writes in his essay on the human body:

> My own body is not these cells or those cells that *belong exclusively* to me: it is *what*, in these cells *and* in the rest of the world feels my influence and reacts against me. My matter is not a *part* of the universe that I possess *totaliter*: it is the *totality* of the Universe possessed by me *partialiter*."[10]

Each of us is an individual, a center. Each of us needs to be grounded, centered, integrated, but our center also needs to move outside ourselves. The direction of a person's growth becomes an excentration, a movement outward that incorporates others.

Centration and Excentration. Teilhard's *Divine Milieu* is a spiritual or mystical treatise as well as an effort to present a Christian humanism in contrast to the atheistic humanisms of his day. In *The Divine Milieu*, he speaks of our divinization as well as our humanization, of the sanctification of human endeavor and the humanization of Christian endeavors.[11] Christianity and humanism are not mutually exclusive. In fact, they complement each other. In *The Divine Milieu*, Teilhard wrote about the importance of *both* attachment *and* detachment:

8. Alfred North Whitehead wrote: "The unity of man and his body is taken for granted. Where does my body end and the external world begin? . . . The body is that portion of nature with which each moment of human experience intimately cooperates." *Modes of Thought*, 155, 157.

9. Augustine, *Confessions* (Book IV, vi), 59.

10. "What Exactly Is the Human Body?" (1919), *SC*, 13. Emphasis in text.

11. *DM*, 33–40.

> Why separate and contrast the two natural phases of a single effort? Your essential duty and desire is to be united with God. But in order to be united, you must first of all *be*—be yourself as completely as possible. And so you must develop yourself and take possession of the world *in order to be*. Once this has been accomplished, then is the time to think about renunciation: then is the time to accept diminishment for the sake of *being in another*. Such is the sole and twofold precept of complete Christian asceticism.[12]

First, according to Teilhard, Christianity says: develop yourself, quoting an ancient axiom: *Nemo dat quod non habet.*[13] No one gives what she does not have.

Teilhard approaches the human person as a process of personalization. If we begin with the image or metaphor of "centering," the human person is an embodied center of consciousness in the universe whose direction of development involves centration (self-development), excentration (a movement out toward "the other" and finding one's self outside one's self), and supercentration (finding one's center ultimately Above, or Beyond, in a process of increasing spiritualization and divinization). Individuality and sociality are being woven together, neither of which can be understood apart from the other. An individual is always an individual *in* a community. I am distinct from others but not separable from others. Personalization is an integration of individualization and socialization. These two processes are neither exclusive of each other nor opposed to each other.

In *The Divine* Milieu (1927) Teilhard wrote that "each man, though enveloped within the same universe as all other men, presents an independent center of perspective and activity for the universe."[14] In "Sketch of a Personalistic Universe" (1936) he asks: "Isn't it an essential duty to perfect within oneself the individuality entrusted to one?"[15] In "The Grand Option" (1939), he wrote: "Thus socialization, whose hour seems to have sounded for Mankind, does not by any means signify the end of the Era of the Individual upon earth, but far more its beginning."[16]

12. *DM*, 70. Emphasis in text. Also "The Concept of Christian Perfection" (1942), *TF*, 105.

13. *DM*, 69. Also see 69–76.

14. *DM*, 122.

15. *HE*, 62.

16. *FM*, 54.

Teilhard describes the individual variously as a personal molecule, the incommunicable singularity of being which each of us possesses, those inexpressible enchanting characteristics that determine our individuality.[17] Again from *The Divine Milieu*: "each one of us constitutes a particular center of divinization," and ". . . the total divine milieu is formed by the confluence of our individual divine milieux."[18]

This process of individualization, of our selves coming to be, is accompanied by a process of socialization. "The end of ourselves and the culmination of our originality is not in our individuality, but in our person; and according to the evolutionary structure of the world, the only way we can find our person is by uniting with one another"[19] One becomes a person, or more and more becomes the person one is to become, through a process of socialization or excentration. Personalization = individualization + socialization, or centration + excentration. One's "self" or "personhood" evolves, unfolds, develops, comes to be. In a convergent universe, each individual element achieves completeness, not in a separate consummation, but by incorporation into a higher pole of consciousness within which it enters into contact with all others. By an inward turn towards the other, one's growth culminates in an act of giving and in excentration.[20] Teilhard's socialization is not a depersonalization. Societies are "mysterious associations of *free* metazoa."[21]

> False and contrary to nature is the egocentric ideal of a future reserved for those who have known egotistically how to reach the extremes of "everyone for himself." No element can move or grow unless with and by means of all the others as well as itself.[22]

"The human being can have no hope of an evolutionary future except in association with all the rest."[23]

This perspective on becoming a "person" is grounded in Teilhard's cosmology in which unification is a law of the universe and true union differentiates. One becomes a person "*in and through personalization.*"[24]

17. *HE*, 60; *FM*, 194, *WW*, 45.
18. *DM*, 122, 123.
19. *HP*, 187.
20. "The Grand Option" (1939), *FM*, 55–56.
21. *HP*, 64. Emphasis mine.
22. *HP*, 173.
23. *HP* 174.
24. *HP*, 116. Emphasis in original.

Individuality and sociality are the two poles of personality growth. Neither one can dominate to the exclusion of the other. For a healthy society, each individual must be both healthily self-centered as well as decentered,[25] lest one affirm an individualism wherein there are those "who seek to grow by excluding or diminishing their fellows, individually, nationally or racially."[26] In an essay, "The New Spirit" (1942): "Life has an objective; and that objective is a summit; and this summit, towards which all our striving must be directed, can only be attained by our drawing together, all of us, more and more closely and in every sense—individually, socially, nationally, racially."[27] Neither individualism nor collectivism but an evolutionary personalism. How does this happen? Love. Evolution is a process of amorization.

Amorization. For Teilhard, love is an energy at the core of the universe.[28] It is an energy, noted early in *The Human Phenomenon*, a radial energy, an energy on the "inside" of things, which undergirds both the unification and the differentiation that guide the universe in its evolutionary unfolding. Within anthropogenesis, love is the basis for an individual's personalization as well as the personalization of the universe. Here I will be attentive more to the former without taking time to develop the correlative relationship between personalization and universalization. Neither the personal nor the universal are mutually exclusive but rather enhance each other. Such is the nature of love. The universe, as well as the human person, is in the process of being brought to completion, to a fullness, by love. At the personal level, this involves an *affective* dimension intrinsic to hominization.

> The human mass will only become thoroughly unified under the influence of some form of *affective* energy which will place the human particles in the happy position of being unable to love and fulfill themselves individually except by contributing in some degree to the love and fulfillment of all.[29]

Love is an energy by means of which evolution, whether at the personal level or the cosmic level, is continually innovative: "Love alone is capable

25. Teilhard at times also used the word "decentration," *WW*, 42.

26. "Some Reflections on Progress" (1941), *FM*, 72.

27. "The New Spirit" (1942), *FM*, 91.

28. See "The Heart of Matter" (1950), *HM*, 50–52; *HP*, 188–91; "Human Energy" (1937), *HE*, 145–60.

29. "Human Unanimisation" (1950), *FM*, 284. Emphasis in original.

of completing our beings in themselves as it unites them, for the good reason that love alone takes them and joins them by their very depths."[30]

> It is through love and within love that we must look for the deepening of our deepest self, in the life giving coming together of humankind. Love is the free and imaginative outpouring of the spirit over all unexplored paths. It links those who love in bonds that unite but do not confound, causing them to discover in their mutual contact an exaltation capable, incomparably more than any arrogance of solitude, of arousing in the heart of their being all that they possess of uniqueness and creative power.[31]

> Only union *through* love and *in* love (using the word "love" in its widest and most real sense of "mutual internal affinity"), because it brings individuals together, not superficially and tangentially but center to center, can physically possess the property of not merely differentiating but also personalizing the elements which comprise it.[32]

At the heart of excentration, socialization, and personalization is not only the energy of love but sexual love. In his essay "Sketch of a Personalistic Universe" (1936), Teilhard writes: "The mutual attraction of the sexes is so fundamental that any explanation of the world (biological, philosophical, or religious) that does not succeed in finding it a *structurally essential* place in its system is virtually condemned."[33] Sexuality is a structure underlying the relationality of the human person. Sexual love implies an affective pull or push toward another. It is not only a force of attraction but an energy.

Evolution implies the emergence of discontinuity *within* continuity. What does this mean with respect to the evolution of sexuality? the evolution of chastity?[34] In other words, what is *hominized* sexuality, not simply sexuality as it existed in the prehuman world, with which it is in continuity, while at the same time having crossed a threshold, a metamorphosis? What happens to sexuality when it crosses that critical threshold of hominization? Precisely because it is evolutionary, it "undergoes metamorphosis at the passage to reflection. And from there

30. *HP*, 189. Also see 188–91.

31. "The Grand Option" (1939), *FM*, 55.

32. "The Directions and Conditions of the Future" (1948), *FM*, 235. Emphasis in text.

33. *HE*, 72. Emphasis in text. Also see *LTF*, 207, 209.

34. "The Evolution of Chastity" (1934), *TF*, 60–87.

it sets out again, enriched with new possibilities, new colors, and new fruitfulness. In some sense remaining the same thing. But also becoming entirely different."[35] Hominization opens the door to new possibilities for sexuality. "'Hominized' love is distinct from all other love, because the 'spectrum' of its warmth and penetrating light is marvelously enriched."[36] Hominized sexuality cannot be restricted to a procreative role which was the primary function in the animal world. *Human* sexuality, *hominized* sexuality, is not the human person's lower nature but constitutive of one's *human* nature.

> In its initial forms, and up to a very high stage in life, sexuality seems identified with propagation . . . That the dominant function of sexuality was at first to assure the preservation of the species is indisputable . . . But from the critical moment of hominization, another more essential role was developed for love, a role of which we are seemingly only just beginning to feel the importance.[37]

Hominized love becomes distinct little by little although "still *confused* for a very long time with the simple function of reproduction."[38]

Love, like thought, is still evolving in the noosphere. The excess of its growing energies over the diminishing needs for human propagation has become more manifest. Love is therefore tending, in a purely hominized form, to fill a larger function than the simple need for reproduction. "Between man and woman, a specific and mutual power of spiritual sensitization and fertilization is probably still slumbering."[39] Love, like evolution itself, seeks union. "Hence it is no longer strictly correct to say that the mesh of the universe is, in our experience, the thinking monad. The complete human molecule is . . . a duality, comprising masculine and feminine together"[40] Friendship emerges as a specifically human form of sexual love. "We are now discovering the possibility and glimpsing the outline of a *second fundamental affective component of the world*; the love of mutual linkage above the love of attraction, elements drawing together

35. *HP*, 122.

36. "The Spirit of the Earth" (1931), *HE*, 33.

37. "Sketch of a Personalistic Universe" (1936), *HE*, 73. Emphasis in original.

38. "The Spirit of the Earth" (1931), *HE*, 33. Emphasis in text.

39. "Human Energy" (1937), *HE*, 129. Also see "The Spirit of the Earth," *HE*, 33–34; "Creative Union" *WW*, 170.

40. "Sketch of a Personalistic Universe" 1936), *HE*, 74.

to achieve union."[41] "Great friendships are formed in the pursuit of an ideal, in defense of a cause, in the ups-and-downs of research."[42] What emerges with *human* sexuality is a capacity for friendship.[43] This is not, however, the creation of a two-person universe. Love by its nature does not exclude.

> When two beings between whom a great love is possible manage to meet among a swarm of other beings, they tend immediately to enclose themselves in the jealous possession of their mutual gain. Impelled by the fulfillment that has engulfed them, they try instinctively to shut themselves into one another, to the exclusion of the rest. And even if they succeed in overcoming the voluptuous temptations of absorption and repose, they attempt to reserve the promise of the future for their mutual discovery, as if they constituted a *two-person universe.*[44]

To close ourselves off would be a dead end, just as to close oneself off would go against the evolutionary impulse. It is in the direction of universalization that true love goes. This is not to deny the important intimate nature of the friendship but rather to indicate that friendships themselves cannot close themselves off into a world of their own.

The specifically human purpose of sexuality, not to the denial or diminishment of its procreative function, is nevertheless the affectionization of the universe. The "human" is a synthesis of the "reflective" and the "affective," or of our thinking processes and feeling processes, of thought and of emotion. Essential for personalization is "the development of the *affective* energies which are the ultimate generators of union: a sublimated sense of sex and a generalized sense of man."[45] Humanity "will only become thoroughly unified under the influence of some form of *affective* energy which will place the human particles in the happy position of being unable to love and fulfill themselves individually except by contributing in some degree to the love and fulfillment of all."[46] "It can only be done, in the last resort, through the meeting, *center to center*, of human

41. "The Spirit of the Earth" (1931), *HE*, 36. Emphasis in original.

42. "Sketch of a Personalistic Universe" (1936), *HE*, 79.

43. An insightful exploration of the theme of friendship, very compatible with the thought of Teilhard, as well as that of St. Thomas, is that by Mark Vernon, *Meaning of Friendship*.

44. "Sketch of a Personalistic Universe" (1936), *HE*, 75. Emphasis in original.

45. "The Sense of the Species in Man" (1949), *AE*, 203.

46. "Human Unanimisation" (1950), *FM*, 284. Emphasis in original.

units, such as can only be realized in a universal, mutual love."[47] "It is not a *tête-à-tête* or a *corps-à-corps* that we need; it is a heart to heart."[48]

Socialization becomes, if one does not curtail it, universalization. As stated previously, my body is not just this flesh and these bones but the space throughout which my person radiates its influence—my spatiality. "The Body is the very Universality of things."[49] My "bodiliness" and "personhood" extend out into the world. To have a body is to be rooted in the cosmos. "In the domain external to our flesh, our *real and whole body* is continuing to take shape."[50] It is shaped by what we do and what is done to us, a concern in many of Teilhard's writings and particularly in his spiritual treatise, *The Divine Milieu*. We are not just spectators in an evolutionary process but free agents. With the arrival of *Homo sapiens* evolution has become conscious of itself and with that reflective dimension comes a new degree of freedom. Human freedom is at the heart of Teilhard's universe. "*Evolution, by the very mechanism of its syntheses, charges itself with an ever-growing measure of freedom.*"[51]

Reflections for Moral Theology. Teilhard's emphasis on the dignity of the human person grounds three principles for him: (1) the individual's duty toward society;[52] (2) the responsibility of society toward the individual,[53] and (3) respect for human freedom.[54] With respect to the latter he states: "Every limitation imposed on the autonomy of the element by the power of the group must, if it is to be justified, operate only in conformity with the free internal structure of the element."[55] And, "unification through coercion leads only to a superficial pseudo unity."[56] Human

47. "Some Reflections on Progress," (1941), *FM*, 75. Emphasis in original.

48. "Some Reflections on Progress," (1941), *FM*, 75.

49. "What Exactly Is the Human Body?" (1919) *SC*, 12.

50. "A Note on Progress" (1920), *FM*, 17. Emphasis in text.

51. "Some Reflections on Progress" (1941), *FM*, 72. Emphasis in text.

52. Teilhard speaks of "the absolute duty of the individual to develop his own personality," and "upon his individual perfection depends the perfection of all his fellows." "Some Reflections of the Rights of Man" (1947), *FM*, 195.

53. Teilhard speaks of "the relative right of the individual to be placed in circumstances as favorable as possible to his personal development." "Some Reflections of the Rights of Man" (1947), *FM*, 195.

54. "In no circumstances, and for no reason, must the forces of collectivity compel the individual to deform or falsify himself." "Some Reflections of the Rights of Man" (1947), *FM*, 195.

55. "Some Reflections of the Rights of Man" (1947), *FM*, 195.

56. "Some Reflections on Progress" (1941), *FM*, 74.

freedom pertains not only to an individual's freedom, however, but has a social dimension as well. "The man of today acts in the knowledge that the choice he makes will have its repercussions through countless centuries and upon countless human beings."[57] Freedom carries with it, as we all know, responsibility. Hence the call to a moral life is essential to what it means to be human. "From man onwards, the universe is constructed of moral magnitudes."[58]

As with Aquinas, there can be no effort here to delineate all Teilhard's contributions to moral philosophy and theology. We can indicate, however, several insights that follow upon his understanding of an evolving, continuing, unfinished, personalizing universe in which we are called upon to be co-creators of the future.

> Life has made us conscious collaborators in a Creation which is still going on in us, in order to lead us, it would appear, to a goal (even on earth) much more lofty and distant than we imagined. We must, therefore, help God with all our strength, and handle matter as though our salvation depended solely upon our industry."[59]

The human species itself is evolving, but this does not mean that we are more moral than our ancestors.[60] We may, indeed, be less moral. We are not more moral than they, but we are capable of more than they. This makes moral questions even more urgent. Both the potentiality for harm as well as for growth are real. The ever deepening and expanding noosphere relies on us. Humanity's moral sensibility is not only one of individual responsibility, which it is, but of a sense of the future, where we are going together. Our *telos* is human unity.

Teilhard writes that: "being is good . . . that it is better to be than not to be; and that it is better to be more than to be less . . . that it is better to be conscious than not to be conscious; that it is better to be more conscious than less conscious."[61] Evolution is not only the birth and rise of consciousness but the evolution of consciousness. Our moral consciousness also evolves, unfolds, develops. Humanity cannot be content with a static approach to a morality based primarily on rules as Aquinas's

57. "A Note on Progress" (1920), *FM*, 18.

58. "Sketch of a Personalistic Universe" (1936), *HE*, 71.

59. "Science and Christ" (1921), *SC*, 32.

60. See "A Note on Progress" (1920), *FM*, 17.

61. "My Universe" (1924), *SC*, 39–40.

ethics itself was also not organized around the concept of duty but rather growth in virtue. Teilhard writes: "Morality and religion (like the entire social order) *have ceased to be for us static: if they are to appeal to us, and save us, they must be dynamic*."[62] He contrasts a closed morality with an open morality, a morality of regulation with a morality of conquest, a morality of balance with a morality of movement, the most common expression being that of a morality of movement, a morality that respects creation as evolving.[63] "A morality of movement necessarily inclines towards the future, in pursuit of a God."[64] The moral theologian is not a jurist but more akin to an engineer who is attentive to the spiritual energies of the universe.[65] Among the functions of morality is that of building the earth.[66] Three pillars upon which morality is to be grounded are: the personal, the universal, and the future.[67] Morality has its eye on the future and its increased unity and spiritualization.[68] Humanity's aim is toward a more spiritual universe. Morality and spirituality form an integral whole within evolution's unfolding hominization.

Morality is concerned with channeling human energy toward a better world and the full development of the human person. Spiritual energies comprise affective, intellectual, and volitional dimensions, or values like friendship, research, and democratic life.[69] A morality of movement is less focused on order than it is on growth, particularly spiritual growth. "Many things seemed allowed by the morality of balance which we find to be forbidden by the morality of movement," and "Many things seem to be forbidden by the morality of balance which become virtually permitted

62. "Christianity in the World" (1933), *SC*, 103. Emphasis in original.

63. "The Phenomenon of Spirituality" (1937), *HE*, 105–10; "Christianity in the World" (1933), *SC*, 103.

64. "The Phenomenon of Spirituality" (1937), *HE*, 109.

65. "The Phenomenon of Spirituality" (1937), *HE*, 106.

66. Among other references, see "Mastery of the World and the Kingdom of God" (1916), *WW*, 88.

67. "The Salvation of Mankind" (1936), *SC*, 137.

68. "I cannot conceive of any such morality outside belief in the existence of a transformation which will bring the universe from the material to the spiritual state," "The Phenomenon of Spirituality" (1937), *HE*, 112.

69. See "Human Energy" (1937), *HE*, esp. 136–37; "Sketch of a Personalistic Universe" (1936), *HE*, esp. 71–84; "The Religious Value of Research" (1947), *SC*, 199–205; "Research, Work, and Worship" (1955), *SC*, 214–20; "The Essence of the Democratic Idea" (1949), *FM*, 238–43.

or even obligatory by the morality of movement."[70] Moral understanding can, has, and will change. The distinction between "natural" and "artificial" also breaks down, fails to appreciate the human person's place in nature, for the "artificial" can be the "hominized natural." The products of human energy are still products of nature, of human nature. They can serve the good or they can do harm, but products of human labor or art are not intrinsically less natural in the noosphere. "What is, in fact, from a profound biological point of view, the difference between the machine formed by a limb and the machine obtained by the artificial extension of that limb, between a bird's wing and an airplane's?"[71]

Humanity cannot shirk its role in evolution. We have the obligation to discover, to explore, not to hold back out of fear, to advance, but in the right direction. This will raise delicate and complex moral questions but questions which are our duty to address.[72] Morality aims at the highest possible development of the human person, which means also human society. Morality, like personality, is also social. There is no personal morality that is not a social morality and vice-versa. Both personalism and universalism underlie Teilhard's morality of movement. A person's respect for the common good and the state's respect for the rights of an individual go hand in hand.[73] Teilhard by no means presents us with a complete moral philosophy. He nevertheless makes valuable contributions, offers insights to be explored and refined, challenges a

70. "The Phenomenon of Spirituality" (1937), *HE*, 107.

71. "Human Energy" (1937), *HE*,116. Also see "Hominization" (1923), *VP*, 56–66; "The Place of Technology" (1947), *AE*, 159.

72. See "The Phenomenon of Spirituality" (1937), *HE*, 108, "Human Energy" (1937), *HE*, 126; *DM*, 137–38. Teilhard manifests an adventurous, courageous, and even risky spirit. Our efforts and trials are to be understood within some limits. There are pages in "Human Energy" that could cause alarm, e.g., 131–37, but one must realize that he is saying we ought not be afraid to raise the questions and face the possibilities. His questions are not suggestions but questions from which we cannot run. Teilhard clearly rejects racism and excessive nationalism in any form: *HP*, 173, 174; *FM*, 72, 73, 91; *HE*, 37; *LT*, 103, 133. In the light of these references, articles by John P. Slattery are disingenuous and misinformed. See John Haught, "Trashing Teilhard," 7–9. Cuénot, *Teilhard de Chardin*, 300–303, addresses the question as well. As Aquinas raised questions which were *au courant* in his day but not in ours, so the questions Teilhard raises are real questions that his period of history, and ours, face. When he uses a word like "totalitarian" or "totalization" he is not thinking in terms of totalitarian regimes which he readily condemns but rather in the sense of an awareness of "totality," the whole. In this regard, Douglas Farrow also misrepresents Teilhard's thought in "Problem with Teilhard."

73. "The Essence of the Democratic Idea" (1949), *FM*, 242–43.

pre-evolutionary way of seeing things. Humanity cannot back away from its obligation to think and rethink things. Just as society has a moral obligation toward the rights of an individual and an individual towards the rights of a social group, so morality values the rights of the earth, whose future takes precedence over the rights of any one nation.

Good and evil then are not two categories of human actions but rather two directions for human growth. "That which is good, sanctifying, and spiritual for my brother below or beside me on the mountain-side, can be material, misleading or bad for me. What I rightly allowed myself yesterday, I must perhaps deny myself today."[74] The principle of growth introduces a certain kind of relativity into morality without being relativism. Growth demands some fluidity, flexibility, consciousness of stages of life or stages in the development of nations. Growth becomes a value, something to be reckoned with. Moral theology may find it difficult to take development into consideration but development, both personal and societal, is a fundamental principle and value in human life. Although it may appear as if Teilhard's reflections on the moral life might challenge traditional Christian morality, which in some areas they do, nevertheless in a morality based on growth and movement, the virtues, as in a virtue ethic, acquire renewed meaning and increased emphasis. Faith, hope, and charity become vital if the universe is to advance. The supreme function of the Christian religion is hope, Teilhard emphasizes.[75] However, "Charity is the force that stops beings from shutting themselves up in a self-centered folding-in of their energies, and makes them 'unbutton', open themselves and surrender themselves to one another: it makes them *find a center outside themselves* and so enhance a higher center of association."[76] Moral perspectives and challenges themselves evolve but their direction is that of further hominization, personalization, unification, and spiritualization. In an evolving universe the spiritual life becomes the cutting edge for evolution. Excentration will require super-centration—a focus on something deeper and other than ourselves alone.

Morality and Spirituality. There are four terms that can be used almost interchangeably although with different connotations: spiritualization, omegalization, divinization, and christification. They are all facets of super-centration. Spiritualization denotes a process of increased

74. *DM*, 84.

75. *DM*, 114–18, 134–36.

76. "Creative Union" (1917), *WW*, 172. Emphasis in text. Also see "Human Energy" (1937), *HE*, 153.

unification and integration, a movement toward an ultimate unity or Omega. In a theistic context this is also seen as divinization—the human person's and all of creation's becoming one with God. The more deeply one is one with God, and one with all in God, the more one has come, or society or the world has come, to that which it is called to be. In a Christian context this means coming to God through Christ who is Omega, as St. Paul suggests in Teilhard's favorite biblical text, 1 Corinthians, chapter 15, verses 26 to 28. Spiritualization does not, for Teilhard, imply any rejection of the bodily or material, nothing Manichean, for we have already seen how he sees spiritual power in matter. Spiritualization simply denotes the direction of matter's future. Spiritualization does not mean de-materialization but a more highly organized, unified, form of matter. Spirit and matter are not exclusive but rather the "inside" and the "outside" of our world. Spirit is the direction that matter takes,[77] but it is always both spirit *and* matter, both God and the world, both sanctification and humanization, both sacred and profane. One does not think in terms of "pure matter" or "pure spirit" but rather in terms of "spirit-matter." As Teilhard wrote, "By virtue of the Creation and sill more, of the Incarnation, *nothing* here below is *profane* for those who know how to see."[78]

A Christian's life involves a way of seeing, particularly in the case of anyone grasped by Teilhard's vision, which "consists in seeing how . . . we can reconcile, and provide mutual nourishment for, the love of God and a healthy love of the world, a striving towards detachment and a striving towards development."[79] Or as a theologian coming at the same question but not as such from a Teilhardian perspective wrote:

> The sacred and the secular are, therefore, not two things placed side by side; they are one thing seen under two aspects. Something is sacred, precisely in its relationship to God. Since everything is related to God, everything is radically sacred. The secular, the profane, is that which is *seen* by man apart from, even in opposition to, the divine. Since everything can be seen apart from the divine, even though in its own radical being it is related to the divine, everything can be secularized or profaned, except the divine by definition. Thus, if the sacred and secular

77. "From Cosmos to Cosmogenesis" (1951), *AE*, 258–59. *DM*, 81–87.

78. *DM*, 35.

79. *DM*, 21. Note Teilhard's emphasis in the beginning of his *HP*, where the Prologue is simply entitled "Voir."

> appear as opposed spheres in man's life, this opposition says more about the moral conditions of man than it says about the structure of reality.[80]

Spiritualization involves the same upward and forward movement that all of evolution takes—toward the Father, in the Son, through the Spirit—creation's movement as a divine milieu in which God and the human cooperate bringing God's evolving creation to its ultimate fulfillment.

Teilhard wrote many essays pertinent to the topic of the spiritual life,[81] the most extensive being *The Divine Milieu*.[82] We cannot outline here the contents of that work, but we can mention the primary concerns he addresses, which have emerged for us already:

- The Christian problem of the sanctification of action, the divinization of one's activities, how to reconcile love of God with a love for the world, or the sanctification of human endeavors along with the humanization of religious life. How does one see spiritual value in one's worldly activities?
- The problem of the divinization of passivities, not what we do but what happens to us, especially those that seem to diminish us, natural failings, physical health, limitations on life, old age, death, all of which involve providence and the struggle with and transfiguration of evil.
- The two phases of Christian asceticism, attachment and detachment are not mutually exclusive, but like breathing in and breathing out, the rhythm of a spiritual life as one desires union with God and copes with the reality of the cross.
- The divine milieu or God-soaked creation, not as in pantheism which identifies God and the universe and fails to differentiate them, but rather in that of a theocentric theosphere or Christocentric Christosphere, the divine omnipresence about which we will speak later, through which we progress individually and collectively as a communion of saints in expectation of a final Parousia.

The personalization of an individual is a lifelong process that reaches its own critical moment with the reality of death as one of the

80. Kiesling, "Paschal Mystery," 102–3. Emphasis in text.

81. E.g., "The Mystical Milieu" (1917), *WW*, 117–49; "The Mass on the World" (1923), *HM*, 119–34; "The Phenomenon of Spirituality" (1937), *HE*, 93–112; "Introduction to the Christian Life" (1944), *CE*, 151–72.

82. Also see Savary, *Divine Milieu*.

diminishments in life. Just as there is an "outside" and "inside" to the universe, so here there is the outside of our lives which culminate in death, and the inside which is resurrection. Death and resurrection are like two sides of a coin. Death is but a change of state, one of evolution's critical metamorphoses.[83] Although death is often accompanied by apprehensiveness, bewilderment, fear,[84]nevertheless, "Death becomes a resurrection."[85] Death brings a definitive close to our earthly way of being in the world but is also transformation to a new way of being. Given that we are body-soul unities, that is embodied souls or besouled bodies, psychosomatic units, what is left behind as a corpse is the materiality that is unnecessary for an embodied risen life, very much in accord with St. Paul' descriptions in 1 Corinthians, chapter 15. Death is not the end of life but the beginning of something new, with a discontinuity in the embrace of a continuity which longs for one's completion in Christ-Omega.

Death and resurrection mirror the relationship between matter and spirit that lay at the heart of Teilhard's perspective. He wrote in *The Divine Milieu*:

> The full truth of our situation is that, here below, and by virtue of our immersion in the universe, we are each one of us placed within its layers, or on its slopes, at a specific point defined by the present moment in the history of the world, the locality of our birth, and our individual vocation. And *from that starting point*, variously situated at different levels, the task assigned to us is to climb towards the light, passing through, so as to attain God, a *given series of created things* which are not exactly obstacles but rather foot-holds, intermediaries to be made use of . . . matter falls into two distinct zones, differentiated according to our effort: the zone already left behind or arrived at, to which we should not return, or at which we should not pause, lest we fall back—this is the zone of matter *in the material and carnal sense*; and the zone offered to our renewed efforts towards progress, search, conquest and "divinization," the zone of matter *taken-in the spiritual sense*; and the frontier between these two zones is essentially relative and shifting. That which is good, sanctifying, and spiritual for my brother below or beside me on the mountain side, can be material, misleading or bad for me. What

83. See "Sketch of a Personalistic Universe" (1936), *HE*, 87–88; "Creative Union" (1917), *WW*, 173.

84. *MM*,144–46.

85. *DM*, 91.

> I rightly allowed myself yesterday, I must perhaps deny myself today . . . In other words, the soul can only rejoin God after having traversed *a specific path* through matter—which path can be seen as the distance which separates, but it can also be seen as the road which links.[86]

Although Teilhard's insights may raise for us questions, we can see that his understanding of the human person is central to his cosmic vision; that the human phenomenon is a key to understanding the world in which we find ourselves; that his *Weltanschauung* or world view is both cosmocentric and anthropocentric; that it is person-centered and that the person is a social being as well as a moral and spiritual being; that the human person is in process both individually and collectively; that there is both an affective as well as reflective component to personalization and noogenesis; and that while the human emerges from within the evolutionary process, what emerges is something new that is a consequence of both natural or secondary causes as well as God's creative action. We find ourselves as pivotal amid a creation that is evolving and unfinished while being divinized, a universe that is person-centered but persons who are being universalized, persons who are becoming themselves while becoming more and other than themselves. This requires a Center beyond our selves, up Above and up Ahead, the Christ of evolution, to which we turn in chapter 7.

The contrast at this point between Teilhard and Thomas is not so much in what they say, although there are significant differences there, but in how they let their thought unfold. Thomas is systematic, thematic. His anthropology moves from human nature as rational and free, to the story and history of sin, grace, and the life of virtue which it undergirds, along with the gifts of the Holy Spirit. None of this does Teilhard deny. He speaks of faith, hope, and love. He sees the moral life and spiritual life as integrally one, not as separable but as the life of Christian perfection, as does Aquinas. His moral questions, however, as well as understanding of "the human" is deeply impacted by an ongoing, developmental, evolutionary perspective in which humanity itself is unfinished.[87] Human nature is what it is but is not static. Although Teilhard does not treat the doctrine of grace systematically, he sees his universe and the human person as graced. In the preface to *The Divine Milieu*, he writes:

86. *DM*, 83–84. Emphasis in text.

87. See "The Heart of Matter" (1950), *HM*, 36: "hominization is still going on."

> Nor should the fact arouse concern that the action of grace is not referred to or invoked more explicitly. The subject under consideration is actual, concrete "supernaturlized" man . . . although the terms may be absent, the thing is everywhere taken for granted. Not only in the sense of a theoretically accepted entity, but also in the sense of a living reality, the notion of grace impregnates the whole atmosphere of my book.[88]

Sin, grace, and virtue are all there in Teilhard. We can be grateful for Thomas's extended philosophical, theological, and unsurpassed systematic treatment of them. We can also be grateful for Teilhard's situating them in the context of a universe undergoing a process of hominization. What questions are raised when we look at these realities through the lens of an evolving universe? How does our cosmic awareness impact an understanding of these same realities? Both the universe and individual human persons are in the process of coming to be. They are, yes, but they are also not yet all that they are called to be. This developmental, evolutionary structure of God's creative act has implications for how grace operates, how we grow in virtue, and how we mature morally and spiritually. These are questions Thomas could not have asked but which he would have welcomed.

88. *DM*, 12.

6

Thomas Aquinas's Christology

As with Aquinas's theology of creation, and even more so with his anthropology, there is no way in which one can do justice to his Christology in one chapter. We need to consider the motive or purpose for the Incarnation; the nature of the hypostatic union, the true divinity and real humanity of Christ; the conception, birth, ministry, death, and resurrection of Christ; the theology of redemption; the grace of Christ, particularly as Head of the mystical body; and how to speak properly about the *mysterium Christi* insofar as we can speak of it at all. Aquinas will give his highest allegiance to the Scriptures and after that to the Fathers of the Church and the teachings of the Councils. In his Christology, Aquinas's theology of creation and theological anthropology come to completion, for the Word made flesh is not apart from creation but a part of creation, although not only a human being, yet uniquely human. So let us proceed with some of the questions to which Aquinas offers us insight.

Why did God choose to become incarnate among us? In the very first articles of the *tertia pars*, wherein we find his Christology, Aquinas takes up the classic question: *Cur deus homo*? There are three things of which to take notice: (1) It was not, strictly speaking, absolutely necessary for God to become incarnate in order to save us (*ST*, III, q. 1, a. 2). Aquinas differs from the emphasis within the more classic Anselmian theology of atonement.[1] For Aquinas, given God's omnipotence, God could have chosen to

1. For a critique of Anselm's theology of atonement, see Stump, *Atonement*, 71–114.

save us in other ways. (2) Nevertheless, although not necessary as such, it was fitting (*conveniens*) that God become incarnate (*ST*, III, q. 1, a. 1).[2] Arguments from fittingness play an important role in Aquinas's thought, especially when it comes to Christology where we deal with many contingent facts. God did in fact become incarnate. It was not necessary that he do so. How explain this fact then? There was something extremely fitting about it, one might even say necessary in a certain sense, in order to produce the effect that God wanted. Aquinas gives five reasons why the Incarnation was most fitting (*ST*, III, q. 1, a. 2). (3) Although fitting, but not absolutely necessary, why then did God choose to become incarnate? In one way we are unable to answer this question since particularly in matters contingent we cannot know the mind of God.

However, the question gets shifted, or expanded, rephrased: Would God have become incarnate if humanity had not sinned (*ST*, III, q. 1, a. 3)? Would that have also been fitting? There have been two primary paths that theology has taken in response to this question. Even if humanity had not sinned, God could have and would have chosen to become incarnate among us. It would have been a fitting crown or culmination to God's creation. On the other hand, and this is Aquinas's opinion in the *Summa Theologiae*, he states that "seemingly our assent ought rather to be given" to the opinion that if Adam had not sinned, the Son of God would not have become incarnate. In this latter opinion, Aquinas himself had changed his mind from the opinion he had held earlier when composing his commentary on the Sentences of Peter Lombard. What would have led Aquinas to change his mind? In changing his mind, he was then expressing an opinion different from what his mentor, Albert the Great, held. What would lead him to disagree with his former teacher and change his mind on this question?[3]

Earlier Aquinas had maintained that God not only could have but probably would have become incarnate even if humanity had not had a history of sin. In the *Summa*, however, he maintains that God could have but we cannot say that God would have become incarnate if humanity had not fallen. Aquinas changes his mind because, when it comes to what God would have done, we are dealing with something speculative, and we can then only base our response on what we know from Scripture,

See index under "atonement, Anselmian interpretation of" for further references.

2. See Turner, *Julian of Norwich*, 38–51, for a discussion of the meaning and use of "fittingness" (*conveniens*) in theology.

3. Cf. Goergen, "Incarnation."

what God has revealed. And the testimony of Scripture suggests that the motive for the Incarnation was a redemptive one (Luke 19:10; 1 Tim 1:15). This shows an aspect of Aquinas's method. When both opinions are reasonable, the mature Aquinas will come down on the side of what Scripture says. Aquinas in the end was always a biblical theologian as well as a philosophical one. Scripture wins the day. He spent his academic life as someone commenting on the Scriptures, not teaching speculative theology as such. It also shows that Aquinas is quite able to change his mind. He thinks carefully if one looks for the nuance.

> For such things as spring from God's will, and beyond the creature's due, can be made known to us only through being revealed in the Sacred Scripture, in which the Divine Will is made known to us. Hence, since everywhere in the Sacred Scripture the sin of the first man is assigned as the reason of the Incarnation, it is more in accordance with this to say that the work of the Incarnation was ordained by God as a remedy for sin; so that, had sin not existed, the Incarnation would not have been. And yet the power of God is not limited to this; even had sin not existed, God could have become incarnate (*ST*, III, q. 1, a. 3, *corpus*).

Aquinas is quite aware that God may have become incarnate no matter what, but given the human condition, God's primary motive was to save us. In an earlier section of the *Summa*, Thomas had even written, "before the state of sin, man believed explicitly in Christ's Incarnation, in so far as it was intended for the consummation of glory, but not as it was intended to deliver man from sin by the Passion and Resurrection, since man had no foreknowledge of his future sin. He does, however, seem to have had foreknowledge of the Incarnation of Christ" (*ST*, II-II, q. 2, a. 7). Bonaventure agreed with Aquinas although later John Duns Scotus maintained an opinion closer to what Albert the Great held and what Thomas had previously held. For Aquinas, what was also cogent was the fact that the redemptive motive more readily and fittingly revealed the mercy of God (*ST*, III, q. 46, a. 1, *ad* 3). A redemptive Incarnation reveals God as mercy.[4]

In what kind of union did this Incarnation of the Word consist? It seems to go against reason to think that one concrete existing being might subsist or exist *in two natures*. We are certainly dealing here with something unique. Aquinas moves from the question of the purpose of

4. See Kasper, *Mercy*, esp. 83–89, 97–102. In this regard also see Eckhart, *Sermons and Treatises*, II:189 (#72). Also see Thomas's emphasis on mercy as a virtue in chapter 4.

the Incarnation to the kind of union, a hypostatic union, or a union in the *hypostasis* (the underlying subsisting reality or personhood) of the Word, and puts his philosophical acumen to work (*ST*, III, q. 2).[5] Jesus Christ, or the Word *as incarnate*, is only one being even though that one being subsists in two natures. Here the language becomes technical, but one can nevertheless understand what Aquinas is trying to say. We have to do with one being, or one Person (*person* is the ordinary way in which the word *hypostasis* gets translated) but two distinct natures, one divine, which is the nature of the pre-incarnate or eternal Word, and one human, the nature that the Word assumes in the Incarnation. It is in the *hypostasis* or the "person," the underlying reality that the Word of God is, that the union of the two natures takes place (*ST*, III, q. 2, aa. 2–3). There is not a "third nature," some combination of the two. Rather each nature remains intact. The Word is *both* divine, and after the Incarnation, *also* human, really human, but still truly divine. The Word, the Second Person of the Trinity, now subsists in two natures. Jesus Christ remains *one* Person, one substantial being, but one person subsisting in two natures (*ST*, III, q. 2, a. 4). God, while remaining God, becomes human while remaining a Divine Being (*ST*, III, q. 2, a. 6, *ad* 4). This union of the two natures in the personhood of the Word is, vis-a-vis the human nature, a gift of God, (*ST*, III, q. 2, a. 10) and thus this hypostatic union is sometimes called the grace of union (*ST*, III, q. 2, a. 12). There were no preexisting merits on the part of the human nature prior to its being created as the Word's human nature (*ST*, III, q. 2, a. 11), for Jesus Christ was not first a man (*ST*, III, q. 4, a. 3) who then became one with God, as adoptionists[6] maintain, for Jesus Christ was not an adopted son of God but truly God from the moment of his conception.

For Aquinas, this incarnation of the Word was genuinely unique, one of its kind (*ST*, III, q. 2, a. 9), revealed for Aquinas once again in Scripture, particularly in the Gospel of John. Yet, from a speculative point of view, showing Aquinas's openness to philosophical questions, he held that there could in theory be or have been more than one incarnation of

5. For a more thorough discussion, see Goergen, *Jesus of History*, 206–31; and Thomas Joseph White, *Incarnate Lord*, 73–125.

6. "Adoptionism" is recognized as a heresy that maintains Jesus was not the natural Son of God but rather an adopted son, thus not God in Person. It does not do justice to the full divinity of Christ by asserting that Christ was a man before being adopted by God. As a formal heresy, it emerged in the eighth century. In the 19th century it began to be applied to early strains of thought such as the Ebionites for whom Christ was not truly God.

this sort (*ST*, III, q. 3, a. 7). To deny such would be to deny the omnipotence of God. On the other hand, if such were to be the case, although the two humans would be numerically distinct, they would be the same Person, as they would be two distinct human natures of the one Person of the Word if that union were truly a hypostatic union. For the Incarnate Word to have two distinct natures, however, one human, one divine, will not one predominate? Will the divine nature not overwhelm or diminish the humanity of Christ, the humanity of the Word?

Jesus Christ is really, truly, fully human. For classical christologies, those that begin "from above," that is with the doctrine of the Trinity and the Son of God becoming human, as is the case with Aquinas, the danger is that one's Christology could become docetic or monophysitic, as indeed has happened in history.[7] Yet Aquinas carefully steers a delicate balance and follows the teaching of the Council of Chalcedon in that each nature remains intact, real, unconfused. One of the marks of Aquinas's Christology is his commitment to the humanity of Christ. The Son of God assumed a true earthly body (*ST*, III, q. 5, aa. 1–2) as opposed to the opinion of docetists, as well as a complete human soul (*ST*, III, q. 5, aa. 3–4), as opposed to the opinion of Apollinarians,[8] grounding his theology of the humanity of Christ on the patristic principle that "what was not assumed is not curable" (*ST*, III, q. 5, a. 4). One can see in Thomas's Christology as elsewhere in his theology the intent to refute the Manicheans for whom a carnal, earthly embodiment would be unfitting the Son of God.

Thomas's respect for the full humanness of Jesus is manifest in his desire to give to Jesus everything that belongs to human nature, except for sin, which does not belong to human nature as such but only to the human condition as it has unfolded since Adam. As both the Letter to

7. "Docetism" is the heretical tendency, in contrast to that of adoptionism, which does not do justice to the humanity of Jesus, maintaining that Jesus did not assume a truly human body but only seemed to do so, appeared to do so (Gk *dokéo* means "to seem"). It is not a formal heresy but reflective of early tendencies to explain Jesus, associated later especially with the Gnostics. "Monophysitism" was a heresy, following upon the Council of Chalcedon, that maintained there was only one nature in Christ, that being the divine nature, thus also not doing full justice to the humanity of Christ, associated particularly with Eutyches and then the post-Chalcedonian monophysite churches.

8. "Apollinarianism," condemned by the First Council of Constantinople in 381 AD, and flowing from the teaching of Apollinaris of Laodicea, maintained that Jesus did not have a fully human soul, thus not doing justice to Jesus's full humanity. The *Logos* became *sarx* or flesh, thus had a truly human body, but lacked a fully human psychology as the functions of the soul were replaced by the divine Word.

the Hebrews (4:15) states as well as the Council of Chalcedon (451 AD) in quoting it, Christ is like us in all things but sin. Thus for Aquinas, even though there is in Christ the grace of the union, there is also habitual grace (*ST*, III, q. 7, a. 1) in Christ's human soul (what Aquinas also refers to as *gratia gratum faciens*, or the grace that makes one pleasing to God) and thus Christ's human soul is divine by participation (*ST*, III, q. 7, a. 1, *ad* 1) as is ours if we live in that grace which makes one holy. The grace of the union overflows into Christ's soul as impacted by its union with the Divine Word (*ST*, III, q. 7, a. 1) while at the same time the soul remains distinct from the Word's divine nature. In Christ there were thus the infused virtues as well as the gifts of the Spirit, and to a preeminent degree (*ST*, III, q. 7, aa. 2, 5). Aquinas discusses at length the grace of Christ because habitual or sanctifying grace is a perfection of Christ's human nature and thus a manifestation of the humanity of Christ, which Aquinas sees as an instrument of Christ's divinity (*ST*, III, q. 7, a. 1, *ad* 3).

Thomas's exploration of the nature of Christ's humanity leads him to discuss several questions which are disputed today and were also disputed in Aquinas's day, namely the question of whether there was the theological virtue of faith in Christ (*ST*, III, q. 7, a. 3), in what Christ's human knowledge consisted, given his divine knowledge as Son of God (*ST*, III, qq. 9–12), and whether Christ was omnipotent (*ST*, III, q. 13). Given his divine nature, did his human nature experience any defects at all (*ST*, III, qq. 14–15)? How perfect was it?

As Son of God, Christ had access to divine knowledge within his divine nature. The question for Aquinas was then whether he had any human knowledge other than the divine (*ST*, III, q. 9, a. 1), which Christ did have according to Aquinas. "And therefore, it was necessary that there should be another knowledge in Christ besides the Divine knowledge, otherwise the soul of Christ would have been more imperfect than the souls of the rest of men" (*ST*, III, q. 9, a. 1). In what then did the human knowledge in the human mind of Christ consist? For Aquinas there are three kinds of knowledge that human beings can have: (1) acquired knowledge, what we learn over time, how to walk, how to problem solve, how to think logically; (2) infused knowledge that we do not acquire, but comes to us, which is given to us like inspirations or intuitions, knowledge that we simply receive; and (3) beatific knowledge, or that of the vision of God which saints in heaven have through which they see God, which might at times be approximated on earth but the permanence of which is reserved to the blessed. For Aquinas, Christ had all three kinds of *human* knowledge (*ST*, III, q. 9, aa. 2–4).

Thomas attributes all three kinds of human knowledge to Christ on earth, to Christ as *viator* or a wayfarer, because he wants all that is human to be Christ's. For many moderns the question has been whether Christ had any knowledge besides the human. For medievals, the question was whether Christ had any knowledge other than the divine. Hugh of St. Victor (d. 1142) held the position of absolute omniscience in Christ. Peter Lombard (ca. 1100–1160) modified that position and postulated two kinds of wisdom in Christ, pertaining to the two natures, distinguishing the intensiveness of Christ's human knowledge which was not as intensive as the divine knowledge, and the extent of Christ's human knowledge which was co-extensive with the divine knowledge. Lombard's opinion prevailed. Aquinas, however, went further by attributing acquired knowledge to Christ, which was not a common opinion at the time, but which strongly affirms Christ's human ways of knowing and thus the fullness of his humanity.

The dispute today is whether Christ would have had beatific knowledge or the beatific vision while on earth. For Aquinas the question was whether Christ needed to *acquire* knowledge, which is what he maintains in the *Summa* where he also acknowledges it as an opinion on which he had changed his mind from what he had held when writing the Sentences (*ST*, III, q. 9, a. 4).[9] For Aquinas Christ on earth was both a pilgrim like the rest of us but also one who already possessed heavenly beatitude given the uniqueness of the hypostatic union, hence he was both *viator* and *comprehensor* (*ST*, III, q. 15, a. 10; also q. 7, a. 8). Christ was divine by nature; we become divine by grace. He *was* the Son of God; we are daughters and sons of God by adoption. Aquinas thus also held, given Christ's beatific knowledge, that Christ had no need for the virtue of faith since he *saw* God's essence while on earth (*ST*, III, q. 7, a. 3). This today has become a debated question. On the other hand, Aquinas did not maintain that the human Christ, that is the human soul of Christ, was omnipotent since Christ was a creature, not as God, but as a human being. Aquinas of course makes significant distinctions when discussing the powers of Christ's soul (*ST*, III, q. 13).

Aquinas steers a middle course between doing justice to the impact of the hypostatic union on Christ's human nature and that human nature

9. For three varied approaches to these questions, see Gaine, *Did the Saviour*; Gorgen, *Jesus Son of God*, 74–93; and Maritain, *On Grace*, 47–144.

being credible. On the one hand, if one takes the uniqueness of a human nature united to the Person of the Word, Aquinas considers it fitting for Christ's humanity to be as perfect as a human being can be. Hence the fullness of habitual grace as well as the three kinds of human knowledge attributed to Christ as well as the power of his will. On the other hand, Christ did not assume some abstract human nature but the concrete humanity we all share as children of Adam and Eve, the human nature that we existentially inherit, hence he also considers the so-called defects in that human nature which make Christ human as we are except for sin, things assumed along with his assumption of a human nature (the *co-assumpta* considered in *ST* III, qq. 7–15).[10] Aquinas considers both bodily defects and those that pertain more to the human soul (*ST*, III, qq. 14–15). These latter highlight a kenotic aspect to the Incarnation which instantiate the Word's incarnate presence among us as both the humanity of God's Word and as one who shares our humanity with us, as both Son of God and son of Mary. Christ's uniqueness cannot be compromised by his freely chosen identity with us, but neither can his being one of us be compromised by his uniqueness and divinity. Aquinas writes that "the union of the two natures in the Person of Christ took place in such a way that the properties of both natures remained unconfused" (*ST*, III, q. 10, a. 1).

Among the bodily "defects" in human nature that Christ assumed are death, hunger, thirst, and the capacity to suffer (*ST*, III, q. 14). If the Son of God had assumed a human nature without these defects, it would seem that he was not a true human being, and that he did not have true but only imaginary flesh, as the Manicheans held (*ST*, III, q. 14, a. 1). Thomas here also quotes Scripture once again upon which he always relies: "For because he himself has suffered and been tempted, he is able to help those who are tempted" (Heb 2:18, quoted in *ST* III, q. 14, a. 1, *sed contra*). In considering the defects or limitations that pertain more to Christ's soul (*ST*, III, q. 15), he attributes to Christ neither sin nor ignorance (*ST*, III, q. 15, aa. 1–3) but does attribute to him human emotions (*ST*, III, q. 15, a. 4). Here he quotes Augustine: "The one who had the true body of a man, and the true spirit of a man, did not have counterfeit human feelings" (*ST*, III, q. 15, a. 4).[11] Christ experienced genuine pain (*ST*, III, q. 15, a. 5); sadness (*ST*, III, q. 15, a. 6); fear (*ST*, III, q. 15, a. 7); wonder (*ST*, III, q. 15, a. 8); and anger (*ST*, III, q. 15, a. 9). In these

10. See Walsh, introduction to *Summa theologiae*, for more on the *co-assumpta*.

11. This translation of the text of St. Augustine (*City of God*, 14, 9) in Aquinas comes from *Summa Theologiae* (New York: McGraw Hill, 1974), vol. 49:203.

texts Thomas also quotes Scripture. These emphases emerge again when Thomas considers Christ's passion (*ST*, III, q. 46).

In considering Christ's humanity, does Aquinas give any consideration to the so-called historical Jesus? Yes, but not in the sense of the nineteenth and twentieth centuries search for Jesus. For Aquinas there would have been no difference between the earthly, historical Jesus of Palestine and the Jesus of the New Testament, as many contemporary exegetes today would also maintain. According to the Gospel of John, Jesus is Son of God, the enfleshment of God's preexistent Word. And according to the Synoptic Gospels, Jesus was virginally conceived, baptized by John, preached, taught, healed, drove out demons, and worked miracles. According to St. Paul, as well as the Gospels, Jesus suffered, died, and rose from the dead. This biblical Jesus *is* the historical Jesus, granted the need for refinements that come from biblical interpretation to which Aquinas would not have been opposed, and indeed would have endorsed as a theologian for whom Scripture was paramount. Aquinas's approach to Scripture was both literal and figurative, finding meaning in a fact, which factuality a contemporary exegete might sometimes question. As a theologian who also had changed his mind over the course of his own life,[12] Aquinas would have been open to the developments in biblical criticism with a discerning heart.

It is in this vein, following upon Aquinas's emphasis on the humanity of Christ, that he devotes thirty questions, comprising 162 articles, to the conception (*ST*, III, qq. 30–34), birth (*ST*, III, qq. 35–36), circumcision (*ST*, III, q. 37), baptism (*ST*, III, qq. 38–39), life (*ST*, III, qq. 40–41), ministry and miracles (*ST*, III, qq. 42–44), transfiguration (*ST*, III, q. 45), passion and death (*ST*, III, qq. 46–52), resurrection (*ST*, III, qq. 53–56), and ascension of Christ (*ST*, III, qq. 57–59). It is this Jesus of history, the Jesus of the Scriptures, who is the Incarnate One. Aquinas had placed the Incarnation on a firm foundation in his philosophical theology of the hypostatic union. He can now consider that concrete historical existence from both a biblical and theological perspective. Prior to this discussion of Jesus' life, death and resurrection, Aquinas had also given attention to its preparation by considering the conception and virginity of his Blessed Mother (*ST*, III, qq. 27–29). With respect to his treatise on "the life of Christ," we can only highlight certain insights, giving more attention to Aquinas's theology of the death and resurrection.

12. See Goergen, *Jesus of History*, 74–77.

Aquinas taught: the virginal conception of Christ (*ST*, III, q. 28, a. 1);[13] the perpetual virginity of Mary (*ST*, III, q. 28, aa. 2–3); Christ as a true son of Adam, having assumed a human nature and human flesh that derived from Adam (*ST*, III, q. 31, a. 1); that Christ's conception was effected primarily by the Holy Spirit (*ST*, III, q. 32, aa. 1–2); that the Blessed Mother can be called both the mother of Christ with respect to his temporal birth (*ST*, III, q. 35, a. 3) but also the Mother of God since the human nature of Christ was assumed into the personhood or *hypostasis* of the Word, the Second Person of the Trinity (*ST*, III, q. 35, a. 4). Christ, as indicated previously, is truly the Son of God and the son of Mary. Although it was fitting that Christ be baptized by John (*ST*, III, q. 39, aa. 1–2), John's baptism, while being from God (*ST*, III, q. 38, a. 2), was not effective in the way that Christ's baptism would be for it did not grant grace which comes only through Christ (*ST*, III, q. 38, a. 3). It was fitting that Christ himself be baptized, and by the baptism of John, not that he needed to be cleansed of any taint of sin but to cleanse the water with which others would later be baptized (*ST*, III, q. 39, a. 1). Aquinas accepts the factuality of Jesus' baptism by John, about which there can be no question for Aquinas, and thus attempts to see theological meaning in the fact, which at times someone could find contrived but at other times something which contains great insight. Exegetes today do not contest Jesus' being baptized by John. For Aquinas, Jesus sets an example in submitting himself to the baptism of John. It was fitting that, when Christ himself was baptized, that the Holy Spirit descended upon him, even though the Spirit had been with him from the moment of his conception, for the Spirit is symbolic of the kind of baptism, namely that of Christ, by which we are baptized. For John baptized with water, but Jesus baptized with water *and* the Holy Spirit (*ST*, III, q. 39, aa. 2, 6; also see Matt 3:11; Mark 1:8; Luke 3:16; John 3:5).

As an example of some of the insights that Aquinas brings to his appreciation of the historical Jesus, or we might simply say the human Christ, he discusses among other topics the manner of Christ's life (*ST*, III, q. 40). We see him emphasize that Christ wished to make his Godhead known through his human nature (*ST*, III, q. 40, a. 1, *ad* 1); that his earthly life modeled an active life in which someone by preaching and teaching hands on to others the fruits of a contemplative life (*ST*, III, q. 40, a. 1, *ad* 2; also *ST* II-II, q. 188, a. 6); that Christ himself modeled

13. See Brown, *Virginal Conception* for more recent biblical interpretations of these themes.

what a good preacher ought to do, at times withdraw from preaching for the sake of the ministry itself and seek solitude (*ST*, III, q. 40, a. 1, *ad* 3); that a life of poverty was fitting for Christ as it was in keeping with his ministry of preaching that required freedom from worldly possessions (*ST*, III, q. 40, a. 3; also *ST* II-II, q. 186, a. 3)); and that it was fitting that Christ be tempted (*ST*, III, q. 41, a. 1). All these emphases connect with the principle that Christ's humanity needed to be both credible but also exemplary. In an interesting way, Aquinas also raised the question whether Christ the Teacher ought to have submitted his teaching to writing, which he did not do (*ST*, III, q. 42, a. 4). One can see how Aquinas takes facts biblically attested and ponders the meaning in those facts, the fittingness of the way of salvation. Neither Pythagoras nor Socrates submitted their teachings to writing, he says, and it would be good to contrast the reasons Aquinas gives with those which Plato offers pertinent to putting one's doctrine in a circumscribed form which can ossify it and to which profound teaching cannot be confined.[14]

For Aquinas, Christ not only was preacher and teacher but also performed miracles, which he did not question as contemporary historical critics might. His preaching had a healing effect, and his healings were a form of preaching. His life was all a piece. While in Christ there were two natures, in the miracles it is the divine that showed forth, since it is only through divine power that Aquinas considered true miracles possible (*ST*, III, q. 43, a. 2). While his earthly life for the most part proved the credibility and reality of his human nature, at the same time the impact of the hypostatic union could not be downplayed. Both natures become manifest. In his treatment of miracles Aquinas is consistent with traditional approaches to apologetics for he sees the miracles of Christ as proof of his divinity (*ST*, III, q. 43, a. 4).

When it comes to the manifestation of Christ's divinity *par excellence* in the Transfiguration, as Christ approaches closer and closer to his passion and death, Aquinas asks how the body of Christ that is made manifest in the Transfiguration contrasts with the glorified resurrection body (*ST*, III, q. 45, a. 2), the latter being incapable of further suffering which Christ is about to undergo. For Aquinas, the clarity of Christ's bodiliness, which was manifested in his transfiguration, was essentially the same as that of the glorified risen body, but not exactly, not as to its mode of being, which mode was still Christ's earthly sojourn and thus

14. See Plato's seventh letter, in *Phaedrus*, esp. pp. 131–42, or ##338–45.

lacking the permanent quality of the risen body. In theory, strictly speaking, Christ could have always moved about with a glorified body while on earth. Hilary of Poitiers considered the glorified body to be Christ's ordinary mode of being while on earth, but that he held back from making that manifest, a particular form of kenoticism. Aquinas is aware of this, but again does not want to diminish in any way Christ's humanity as being like ours. He writes:

> . . . the clarity of Christ's body in his transfiguration was derived from his Godhead, as Damascene says, and from the glory of his soul. That the glory of his soul did not overflow into his body from the first moment of Christ's conception was due to a certain divine dispensation, that . . . he might fulfill the mysteries of our redemption, in a passible body. (*ST*, III, q. 45, a. 2, *corpus*)

When the qualities of the risen glorified body are discussed by Aquinas in the supplement to his *Summa* (qq. 82–85), he notes that those qualities are clarity, agility, subtlety, and impassibility. In the Transfiguration, Christ's body had the clarity of any risen body but lacked the impassibility. It still had the capacity to suffer. The Transfiguration was prelude to the Passion.

As one approaches the death of Christ and the passion narratives in the Scriptures, what are the emphases in Aquinas's theology of redemption? Since Aquinas considered redemption as the primary reason for the Incarnation, as we have said, in what does his understanding of redemption, grounded in the death of Christ, consist? Clearly the theology of redemption is important for him. It must be emphasized that for Aquinas it was not necessary that Christ suffer and die to save us, although he makes a distinction as is often the case. Just as it was not necessary that God become incarnate to save us, so it was not necessary that Christ suffer and die (*ST*, III, q. 46). It was not necessary but nevertheless fitting (*ST*, III, q. 46, a. 3). The word "necessary" can be understood in various ways. The death of Christ was not absolutely necessary (*ST*, III, q. 46, aa. 1–2; q. 1, a. 2), not necessary in the way we ordinarily understand the word, not necessary in the sense that it could not have been otherwise. But it was necessary in another way; in the sense that it was fitting, as Aquinas had already spoken in the first question of the *tertia pars*, "when the end is attained better and more conveniently, as a horse is necessary for a journey" (*ST*, III, q. 1, a. 2).

There was something about the death of Christ that makes it fitting from God's point of view, one might say necessary relatively speaking, relative to other ways in which God could have saved us. What is it that made the passion of Christ so suitable a way for saving humankind? As Aquinas's thought unfolds, there are many reasons, but already in his first question discussing the Passion of Christ, in its third article, Aquinas gives five reasons why it was more fitting "that we should be delivered by Christ's Passion than simply by God's good-will" (*ST*, III, q. 46, a. 3). Among these: (1) We know how much God loves us, given the extent to which Christ was willing to go for our sake; (2) Christ sets for us an example of obedience and humility as well as other virtues; (3) and also merits for us the grace of justification; (4) and by which we are more motivated to refrain from sin ourselves; and (5) humankind, given Jesus' true humanity, participates in redemption, restoring dignity to the human race. To whatever degree we appreciate each of these facets of Christ's suffering and dying, they are all grounded in biblical texts to which Aquinas refers and show that there are both objective and subjective aspects to our redemption. Our redemption was not simply God's decree but was worked out amid human history and still unfolds in our responses today.

The classical theology of atonement is much discussed and critiqued today. One critique pertains to a theology in which the Father required his Son to suffer and die.[15] Although for Aquinas there are two aspects to this question, in such a way that his response is *both/and*, he made the point first that Jesus Christ "laid down his life . . . voluntarily" (*ST*, III, q. 47, a. 1). His death was *both* voluntary *and* obedient (*ST*, III, q. 47, a. 3), for these are not mutually exclusive. Scripture again comes to the foreground in Aquinas's discussion. Christ became obedient even unto death (Phil 2:8). But also, "I have power to lay it [my life] down, and I have power to take it up again" (John 10:18). There is a certain beauty, a certain fittingness, in Christ's submission to death being both his free act and an obedient one. God the Father did not "require" that his Son suffer and die, but nevertheless the Father and Son were united in mind and will in this regard, the coming together of Christ's human will with the divine will (*ST*, III, q. 47, a. 3, *ad* 2). God the Father did not spare his Son

15. Recent explorations on the atonement include Finlan, *Problems with Atonement*; and *Options on Atonement*; Lombardo, *Father's Will*; Stump, *Atonement*; and Thomas Joseph White, *Incarnate Lord*, 277–464, among many others. Approaching the subject from a different perspective is that of Anatolios, *Deification*. I will say more about both Anatolios and Stump in chapter 10.

(Rom 8:32) but asked him to bear the burden of sin for all of us (*ST*, Isa 53:6, 10), giving Christ the grace and love to bear the burden, and thus not shielding Christ from his Passion, not preventing it (*ST*, III, q. 47, a. 3). The end of Christ's earthly sojourn with its suffering and death comprises a complex of factors, historical and theological, contained within the mind of God, involving the Father's will, Jesus' human act, Judas's betrayal, Peter's denial, Caiaphas's role, and Pilate's fear. In contrast to aspects of Aquinas's opinion (*ST*, III, q. 47, aa. 4–5), within which he does make important distinctions, today the church understands that the Jewish people themselves held no responsibility for the death of Christ.[16]

Aquinas's understanding of the atonement, the sacrificial act of Christ, Jesus' death on the cross, is biblical, traditional, and robust. He asks about the effects of Christ's suffering and death (*ST*, III, q. 48) which were many, presented by words which we tend to conflate but which for Aquinas have distinct significance: merit (q. 48, a. 1), satisfaction, (q. 48, a. 2), sacrifice (q. 48, a. 3), ransom or redemption (q. 48, aa. 4, 5), salvation (q. 48, a. 6). No previous understanding of redemption is left out. It is true that Christ had earned salvation for us simply by being conceived and becoming one of us, and thus that his passion and death were not strictly speaking necessary, but on our side, obstacles had to be overcome for us to share in the work of Christ, so that we too might merit the salvation Christ had won for us. Christ freely chose to suffer for us out of love and obedience, but in doing so clearly did more than was necessary to atone for the history of human sin. His passion and death were over and above anything required, an act of superabundant love on Christ's part, revelatory of God's love while at the same time compensating for our offenses. This was not a payment of a debt that God required of Christ but an example that Christ chose in order to break through our hearts of stone. In this sense Christ's passion was a true sacrifice pleasing to God

16. For some discussion of how difficult it is to place blame with respect to the death of Christ, and whether we ought to even raise the question, see Goergen, *Death and Resurrection*, 20–22. In *ST*, III, q. 47, a. 4, *ad* 3, Aquinas places responsibility primarily with the Romans. In a. 5, he nuances various degrees of responsibility among the Jews, that of the elders in contrast to others, but does not exonerate them. He bases his discussion on their not being excused due to ignorance of his being the Son of God, whereas today we are aware of how unlikely it was that even some of his disciples would have been aware of his divinity. Likewise, in a. 6, he does not allow ignorance as an excuse and thus the Jews were more responsible than the Gentiles. Aquinas's approach to this question had to do with the question of culpable ignorance. The question is significant for post-Holocaust Christian theology about which there is much written. For a readable history of anti-Semitism, see Carroll, *Constantine's Sword*.

as it was done out of love for God and for us. It was a freely chosen self-offering for our sake on Christ's part. He did it *for us.*

One cannot appreciate any theology of redemption without first having analyzed or diagnosed the human condition, which for Aquinas went awry from the beginning. On the one hand, we have been in bondage to sin, so easily verifiable however we seek the cause, and on the other hand we have deeply offended God. Such is the nature of sin. In some way then we needed to be "ransomed" or "rescued" or freed or saved from this bondage while at the same time make some response to the offense that sin is. Here the traditional language of ransom and satisfaction take on a particular character for Aquinas. Nothing was owed the devil (*ST*, III, q. 48, a. 4, *ad* 2 & 3) but something is owed God. Through the sacrifice of Christ, humanity has once again been made pleasing to God due to Christ's superabundant love. By his wounds we have been healed (Isa 53:5; 1 Pet 2:21–25). God himself is of course the principal cause of our salvation. But as Christ's humanity is the instrument of the Godhead (*ST*, III, q. 43, a. 2; q. 48, a. 6), so his human life, death, and resurrection remain the instrument of our salvation. Christ's obedience and love, objectively speaking, atones for our disobedience and lack of charity while at the same time opening the door for us, subjectively, to be transformed and merit the salvation Christ won for us.

Thomas's doctrine of atonement is unique and yet traditional. Its central role in the history of Christian thought is challenged in our own day. This makes pondering the doctrine even more necessary, even though it will always remain a mystery, the richness of which can never be fully captured, and yet a mystery that is at the core of the Scriptures, especially in the theology of St. Paul. Christ died for us. There will always be more to the mystery than our minds may be able to fully grasp, but that does not mean we let go of the effort. There is much in Aquinas's treatment of the passion of Christ that I have necessarily left untouched. Here as much as anywhere theology becomes faith seeking to understand. We stand before the cross facing a risen Christ. Christ's death and resurrection go hand in hand. Yet as we look back at the insights Aquinas offers, one catches a good glimpse among the reasons he offers as to whether it was fitting for Christ to have suffered on the cross. The sixth of the seven reasons he gives pertains to Christ as Teacher. The cross is Jesus' teaching, as a teacher *par excellence*; the cross is his teacher's podium or professor's chair. He quotes St. Augustine to that effect: "Not without purpose did he choose this class of death, that he might be a teacher . . . The tree upon which were fixed the members of him dying was even the chair of the Master teaching" (*ST*, III, q. 46, a. 4).[17]

What does it mean to say that Christ has been raised from the dead? As one reads Aquinas carefully, one will note that he asks many questions, one following logically upon the other, questions that we would not be inclined to ask today. In his discussion of the resurrection of Christ, he clearly believes that Christ has been raised from the dead, in a bodily way, and that the tomb was empty, following upon his resurrection. Each detail of the biblical account has some significance. For example, it was fitting for Christ to rise from the dead on the third day because this signifies the third epoch in the history of salvation. The first epoch was before the giving of the Law, the second that under the Law. The third was the coming of Christ and the epoch of grace (*ST*, III, q. 53, a. 2). Although Christ rose from the dead bodily with a true body (*ST*, III, q. 54, a. 1), he rose with a glorified body (*ST*, III, q. 54, a. 2), which meant that he had the power to be seen or not to be seen as he wished (*ST*, III, q. 54, a. 1, *ad* 2 & 3), for such is a quality of a glorified body as we mentioned previously in the discussion of Jesus' transfiguration. Indicative of the kind of detail that Aquinas considers, he maintains that the blood one finds in relics of Christ, relics of the precious blood, are not the actual blood of Christ but rather true blood that came miraculously from an image of Christ (*ST*, III, q. 54, a. 3, *ad* 3). And given the medieval perception of women, who were not allowed to teach publicly in church, Aquinas sees meaning in the fact that Christ appeared first to women because the women's "love for our Lord was more persistent" (*ST*, III, q. 55, a. 1, *ad* 3). There is no facet of the biblical resurrection accounts that Aquinas leaves unexamined.

There is an intrinsic connection between Christ's resurrection and our own. St. Paul had already maintained that if there is no resurrection of the dead then Christ has not been raised, and if Christ has not been raised then our preaching and our faith are in vain (1 Cor 15:12–13). Likewise for Aquinas, Christ's resurrection is the cause of our own resurrections. God is of course the first cause, but Christ's resurrection is a secondary, instrumental, efficient and exemplar cause (*ST*, III, q. 56, a. 1, *ad* 2–3). We are all interconnected in that our bodies have an intrinsic

17. Lest there be confusion, in *ST*, III, q. 46, a. 4, Aquinas gives *seven* reasons *why it was fitting* for Christ to die on the cross, even if it was not necessary as such; whereas in q. 46, a. 3, he gives *five* reasons, but along the lines of means suitable to the end that God wished to accomplish. All these, however, pertain to the suitability of Christ's passion and death with respect to our salvation.

relationship to Christ's risen body. As Saint Paul had also maintained, we are one body in Christ (1 Cor 12; Rom 12:4–5). This relationship is also manifest in Christ's ascension into heaven (*ST*, III, q. 57), for Christ ascended into heaven as God *with* his human nature (*ST*, III, q. 57, a. 2; q. 58, a. 3), and in doing so, took us with him, given the common human nature we share, the "Head with whom the members must be united" (*ST*, III, q. 57, a. 6, *ad* 2). Unless we separate ourselves from him, we are united with him even in his ascension and he is the cause of our salvation (*ST*, III, q. 57, a. 6).

Christ as Head of the Church. When discussing the grace of Christ (*ST*, III, qq. 7–8), following upon the union of the two natures, Aquinas discussed the grace of Christ as an individual (q. 7) and then as head of the church (q. 8). Following upon the grace of the hypostatic union, there was the overflowing effect of that union into Christ's human soul, namely the fullness of habitual or sanctifying grace as we mentioned previously. But that same fullness of habitual grace that flowed into Christ's soul is the same grace that flows out from Christ into the members of his body, the church (*ST*, III, q. 8, a. 5). Aquinas does not treat ecclesiology apart from his Christology, for his ecclesiology is grounded in his theology of Christ as Head.

> As the whole Church is termed one mystic body from its likeness to the natural body of a man, which in diverse members has diverse acts . . . so likewise Christ is called the Head of the Church from a likeness with the human head . . . (*ST*, III, q. 8, a. 1, *corpus*)

As head of the church, the habitual grace that is Christ's own in his human nature is also the source of grace in us, his members, since Christ's humanity is an instrument of his Godhead (*ST*, III, q. 8, a. 1, *ad* 1). Christ gives us the gift of the Holy Spirit, who is the heart of the church (*ST*, III, q. 8, a. 1, *ad* 3) *as God* but *as human* is the source of grace in us which is but a participation in the grace of Christ (*ST*, III, q. 8, a. 1, *ad* 1). Christ is, however, not only the head of those who are baptized but of all, for all are members of the church at least potentially (*ST*, III, q. 8, a. 3, *corpus* and *ad* 1). Christ is the head of all of humanity, but diversely so: those who are united to him as are the blessed in heaven, those who are united to him given their lives of charity, those who are united to him through faith, those who are united to him potentially and will be united to him actually, and those united to him potentially who will not become united actually (*ST*, III, q. 8, a. 3). Christ is the head of all but particularly of the baptized.

Christ's role as head emerges again following upon Aquinas's treatment of the death and resurrection of Christ, particularly his death, for it is his death that merits for us our salvation. "Grace was bestowed upon Christ, not only as an individual but inasmuch as he is the Head of the Church, so that it might overflow into his members . . . Consequently, Christ by His Passion merited salvation not only for himself, but likewise for all his members" (*ST*, III, q. 48, a. 1), who form one mystic person with Christ (*ST*, III, q. 48, a. 2, *ad* 1). The grace of Christ earned by his passion was superabundant. The church is his body. He is the head. The Holy Spirit is its heart or soul. Christ is the head of his body, the church, and the grace of Christ the head (the capital grace of Christ, *gratia Christi capitis*) comes to all his members through the sacraments of the church.

The risen Christ is present in the sacraments of the church. I will not go here into the nature of a sacrament as a visible sign of an invisible grace (*ST*, III, q. 60), nor of their necessity for salvation (*ST*, III, q. 61), but rather emphasize the sacraments as the source of grace (*ST*, III, q. 62), the two principal sacraments being Baptism and Eucharist (*ST*, III, q. 62, a. 5). Although God is the principal cause of grace, which is a participation in the divine nature, the sacraments of the church are instrumental causes instituted by God for the purpose of conferring grace (*ST*, III, q. 62, aa. 1, 3). Their power comes principally from the passion of Christ through which forgiveness of sin was merited (*ST*, III, q. 62, a. 5) but which comes to us through the risen Christ in whom we live the new life of grace (*ST*, III, q. 62, a. 5, *ad* 3; q. 69, a. 5). Although the sacraments of the New Law cause grace according to the dispensation ordained by God, it is also true that "God did not bind his power to the sacraments, so as to be unable to bestow the sacramental effect without conferring the sacrament" (*ST*, III, q. 64, a. 7), for God "did not confine his power to those that are baptized, as neither did he to the sacraments" (*ST*, III, q. 67, a. 5, *ad* 2).

The reality (the *res*) with which sacraments are concerned is our incorporation into Christ raised from the dead, or the interior life of sanctifying grace (*ST*, III, q. 66, a. 1). Although, as sacrament (*sacramentum*), we speak about being baptized by water (*ST*, III, q. 66, a. 3) in the name of the Father, and of the Son, and of the Holy Spirit (*ST*, III, q. 66, a. 5), there is also a baptism in blood as well as of desire (*ST*, III, q. 66, aa. 11, 12; q. 68, a. 2). The latter two are not sacraments strictly speaking since they lack the visible sign although not the invisible grace (*ST*, III, q. 66, a. 11, *ad* 2). Access to grace is not too quickly to be confined. Even circumcision as a "sacrament" in the Old Law conferred sanctifying grace, although not as grace is conferred in baptism, another opinion on which Aquinas had changed his mind over time (*ST*, III, q. 70, a. 4; q. 61, aa. 3, 4). Baptism is a channel instituted by Christ for the grace merited by Christ's passion and death to be freely given to us as a gift (*gratia gratum faciens*). Baptism gives us access to the Eucharist, what the Second Vatican Council described as "the source and summit of the Christian life."[18] Baptism is "the door of the sacraments; whereas the Eucharist is, as it were, the consummation of the spiritual life, and the end of all the sacraments" (*ST*, III, q .73, a. 3). And "just as for the spiritual life there had to be Baptism, which is spiritual generation; and Confirmation, which is spiritual growth; so there needed to be the sacrament of the Eucharist, which is spiritual food" (*ST*, III, q. 73, a. 1).

That which is contained in the sacrament of the Eucharist, that which is symbolized by it, the reality (*res tantum*) to which it points and which it effects is "the unity of the mystical body" (*ST*, III, q. 73, a. 3) and the life giving sanctifying grace in the soul (*ST*, III, q. 73, a. 6; q. 79, a. 1).[19] In this sacrament the bread and wine are that which signifies (the *sacramentum* or *signum: significant*) and the life of grace shared by the mystical body of Christ is that which is signified (the *res, significatum*). That which is both signified and signifies is the actual and real presence of the risen Christ (the *res et sacramentum*) who is both signified by the bread and wine but is also truly and bodily present (*ST*, III, q. 75, a. 1). This real presence "cannot be detected by sense, nor understanding, but by faith alone (*ST*, III, q. 75, a. 1), something accomplished supernaturally by divine power which change "can be called *transubstantiation*" (*ST*, III, q. 75, a. 4).[20] Thus Christ, the Incarnate Word, was visibly present among us historically, and continues to be present with us today—invisibly, but sacramentally, particularly in the Eucharist. The risen Christ comes to be with us in the sacraments of the Church which is his body. The Eucharist is the summit of the history of God coming to be present with his people as he gathers us into the body of his Beloved Son.[21]

18. *Lumen gentium*, no. 11, in Flannery, *Vatican Council II*; *Catechism of the Catholic Church*, no. 1324.

19. See *ST*, III, q. 73, a. 1, *ad* 2 on the role of the Holy Spirit. For contemporary discussions of the role of the Holy Spirit within the epicleses of the Eucharistic prayer, see e.g., McKenna, *Eucharistic Epiclesis*.

20. For an exploration of this concept of transubstantiation, see Schillebeeckx, *Eucharist*.

21. See Congar, *Mystery*.

Aquinas's Eucharistic theology and devotion are not only present in his more philosophical theology but also in his poetry. Having been requested to compose the liturgical prayers for the Feast of Corpus Christi, the prayers give witness to Thomas's own Eucharistic devotion. His *Pange lingua* as well as *Adoro te devote* express poetically and prayerfully his Eucharistic theology, stanzas of which remain to this day a part of Eucharistic adoration.[22]

Tantum ergo sacramentum
veneremur cernui,
et antiquum documentum
novo cedat ritui,
praestet fides supplementum
sensuum defectui.

Genitori genitoque
laus et jubilatio,
salus, honor, virtus quoque
sit et benedictio,
procedentis ab utroque
compar sit laudatio.

Therefore, we, before him bending,
this great Sacrament revere;
types and shadows have their ending,
for the newer rite is here;
faith, our outward sense befriending,
makes our inward vision clear.

Glory, let us give, and blessing
to the Father and the Son,
honor, might, and praise addressing
while eternal ages run;
ever, too, his love confessing,
who, from both, with both is one.[23]

God is present among us as the Word Incarnate. How are we able to speak of such a mystery? As we move closer to concluding our reflection on Aquinas's tripartite *Summa*, what is apparent, particularly within the christological portion of the *tertia pars*, is Aquinas's sensitivity as a

22. See Murray, *Aquinas at Prayer*, 159–259; and Torrell, *Saint Thomas Aquinas*, 1:129–36.

23. Text from the *Pange lingua*. Translation from Murray, *Aquinas at Prayer*, 191–92.

preacher and teacher to language. Although a spiritual master, as evidenced in his theological writings, most especially in his treatment of the moral and theological virtues along with the gifts of the Holy Spirit, and a mystic, evidenced in his poetry, the precision in Thomas's speaking about God and Christ is what comes through as a contribution to philosophical theology. This is one of Aquinas's strengths. Although never having formulated a distinct treatise on analogy itself,[24] already in his talk about God in the *prima pars* Aquinas is careful to note what can and cannot be said, or how language works. This desire for clarity in one's theological speech underlay his treatment of christological language in question 16 of the *tertia pars* where he outlines the principles of what is known as the *communicatio idiomatum*, how to speak without confusion about Christ as one Person in two natures.

How do we speak about such a mystery, for a right way of speaking manifests a correct understanding?[25] For instance, one cannot say that the divine nature suffered but one can say that the Son of God did. A property or attribute of one nature could be attributed to the Person of Christ (the *hypostasis*) but not to the other nature. For Aquinas, christological language is technical, requiring precision. The two natures are not to be confused. Even if the Person is the subject of the predication or attribution but qualified to refer to only one of the two natures, one cannot attribute that predicate to the other nature. Predication of attributes of either nature can take place only when the subject of the predication is clearly the Person. This applies of course to affirmative statements and not negative ones. Something that can be denied of one nature cannot be denied of the Person because the Person subsists in two natures. One can say that the divine nature does not die but one cannot say that Christ did not die. All twelve articles of question 16 of the *tertia pars* exemplify the importance Aquinas gives to theological speech[26] and the importance of not speaking in a way that would be misleading or connote heresy. It is not a question of semantics, but of how to preserve the faith. How we say something expresses what the church believes. This same concern for precision is also manifest in Aquinas's commentaries on Scripture, remembering that Aquinas was primarily a biblically grounded theologian.

24. I talk more about analogical speech in chapter 8.

25. For a brief reflection on the *communicatio idiomatum*, see Goergen, *Jesus of History*, 223–27.

26. This is also manifest in *ST*, III, q. 46, a. 12, as well as throughout many places in *ST*.

His basic Christology can also be found in his commentary on the prologue to the Gospel of John.[27]

The act of creation is a unique kind of causation, *ex nihilo*, whereby something comes to be. The Incarnation is likewise a unique act of God in which God assumes a human nature. There are not two preexisting realities which at a moment in time are united. There is only one, the preexistent and pre-incarnate eternal Word who takes to himself a particular human nature, which human nature is the humanity of the Word. Neither adoptionism nor docetism but a real and true incarnation of the Son of God. As important as this event in history was, and as important as it is for our salvation, so it deserves care in our way of speaking about it, as is true for Aquinas's theology of creation as well as for his theology of the Eucharist. What is at stake for Aquinas is our redemption and who Jesus of Nazareth truly is and why he chose to come among us. Language must be a servant of truth.

27. Aquinas, *Commentary on John*, 23–106.

7

Teilhard de Chardin's Christocentrism

We have not been able to discuss Teilhard's cosmology or his anthropology without mentioning Jesus Christ. Each is incomplete without the others. His cosmology is anthropocentric; his anthropology is Christocentric. Cosmogenesis gives rise to anthropogenesis which gives rise to christogenesis with the birth of Christ. This is the direction that evolution has taken which, for Teilhard, is a fact of faith but also justified from a more phenomenological point of view. Within the noosphere, at a certain moment in human history, and at a certain place within the space-time continuum, Jesus of Nazareth is born. He writes in *The Divine Milieu*: "If you suppress the historical reality of Christ, the divine omnipresence which intoxicates us . . . [lacks] the decisive experimental verification by which to impose itself on our minds, and without the moral directives to assimilate our lives into it."[1]

Teilhard was not so interested, however, as is much contemporary research, in the historical data about Jesus of Nazareth as he is in the mystical Christ. "Across the immensity of time and the disconcerting multiplicity of individuals, one single operation is taking place: the annexation to Christ of his chosen; one single thing is being made: the Mystical Body of Christ."[2] Nevertheless, "However far we may be drawn into the divine spaces opened up to us by Christian mysticism, we never depart from the

1. *DM*, 94.

2. *DM*, 124.

Jesus of the Gospels."[3] The Incarnation, the Cross, the Resurrection are important for Teilhard but what is most important is their meta-historical implications. Yet it is necessary that Jesus be born in time, that there be a foundation in history, that he comes to be from within the evolutionary process itself. There could be no evolution of life without the first cell, no human evolution without the first human beings, and no cosmic Christ without the historical Jesus. There needs to be "an historical center . . . transmitted along a traditional and solidly defined axis."[4] But our understanding of the Incarnation ought not be confined to the moment of Jesus' conception and birth; nor our appreciation of the resurrection to its impact on Jesus alone; nor our faith in Jesus's first coming neglect his second coming or the future of the Christ. "The Israelites were constantly expectant, and the first Christians too. Christmas, which might have been thought to turn our gaze towards the past, has only fixed it further in the future."[5] There is the Jesus born in Bethlehem and there is Christ-Omega and the evolution that takes place between those two critical points. It is to the story of that Jesus, that Christ, that we now turn, a story not only of Jesus' Epiphany, but of God's diaphany or transparency within the universe,[6] not only of Jesus' historicity but of his cosmicity. For Jesus born in history, as the Word Incarnate, breaks through the confines of history in his meta-historical or meta-historiographical resurrection from the dead.[7] The story of the earthly Jesus is incomplete without the story of the whole Christ, the *totus Christus*, to use Saint Augustine's expression. For Teilhard, the totality of Christ embraces the whole cosmos.

THE COSMIC CHRIST

Central to Teilhard's Christology is the cosmic "nature" of Christ, not to disregard Christ's human nature, nor his divine nature, nor to consider the cosmic "nature" to be a nature in any traditional christological sense, but rather to emphasize Christ's relationship to all of creation. Just as there

3. *DM*, 95.

4. *DM*, 94. Emphasis in text.

5. *DM*, 134.

6. *DM*, 108–12. In his later more autobiographical essay, "The Heart of Matter" (1950), *HM*, 16, he speaks in a similar way of "the Diaphany of the Divine at the heart of a glowing Universe."

7. On the historical and historiographical aspects of the Resurrection, see Goergen, *Death and Resurrection*, 155–59, 188–203.

is the historical human biological body of Christ, and the risen body, that selfsame body as raised from the dead, so there is the mystical body comprising the Head and all its members,[8] but also Christ's embodiment within all of creation—the omnipresence of Christ. Strongly present in the Christian tradition is the reality of Christ understood as incorporative of those who are a part of Christ—going back to St. Paul's image of our being members of the body of Christ in 1 Corinthians, chapter 12; to St. Augustine's emphasis on the "total Christ" or the "whole Christ"; with Aquinas's reflection on all of humanity being at least potentially members of Christ; up to and beyond Pius XII's encyclical *Mystici Corporis*. The theme was central to the teaching of the Greek Fathers, among whom was an emphasis on the cosmic ramifications of Christ's embodiment in the created world.[9]

What is the relationship between Christ and the whole of creation, between creation and the Incarnation? For Teilhard, Christ is in some way the fulfillment of creation, that for which the created order itself yearns. According to St. Paul, creation itself waits with eager longing to be set free from bondage: "the whole creation has been groaning in labor pains" (Rom 8:18–23). The wider universe itself finds its ultimate finality in Christ who, again according to St. Paul, hands it over to the Father "so that God may be all in all" (1 Cor 15:28). Christ, at Omega, as Omega, is the completion or culmination of evolution. He is the universal Christ. This universal Christ, this cosmic Christ, is Jesus of Nazareth come to his full stature. "The mystical Christ, the universal Christ of St. Paul, has neither meaning nor value in our eyes except as an expansion of the Christ who was born of Mary and who died on the Cross. The former essentially draws his fundamental quality of undeniability and concreteness from the latter. However far we may be drawn into the divine spaces opened to us by Christian mysticism, we never depart from the Jesus of the Gospels."[10] This universal Christ, the cosmic Christ, the total Christ, the

8. Teilhard writes in "Cosmic Life" (1916), *WW*, 51: "The mystical Body of Christ should, in fact, be conceived as a physical Reality, *in the strongest sense the words can bear.*" Emphasis in text. See 49–53, 57–59.

9. See Maloney, *Cosmic Christ* for his treatment of this theme in St. Paul, St. John, Irenaeus, Clement of Alexandra, Origen, Athanasius, Gregory of Nazianzen, Gregory of Nyssa, Cyril of Alexandria, Maximus the Confessor, as well as Teilhard. Also Lyons, *Cosmic Christ*.

10. *DM*, 95. Also see "Forma Christi" (1918), *WW*, 252: "Men are called to form one single Body, in an intensely intimate divinization; and Christ's humanity was chosen to serve as the instrument of this unification in which the unraveled skein of all

super-Christ, all varied expressions used by Teilhard is the same Jesus of Nazareth who by his resurrection becomes co-extensive with the physical expanse of space-time.[11]

If Jesus Christ is understood to be the fulfillment of that for which creation yearns, it can also be said, although it may seem strange, that the universe brings fulfillment to Christ. The universe itself assumes a great importance when we realize that it gains something for Christ. This may seem easier to grasp if we think first of the relationship between Christ and humanity, of the relationship between Head and the members of his body, between *caput* and *corpus*. Pope Pius XII himself wrote in *Mystici Corporis* that "marvelous though it may seem: Christ has need of his members."[12] Pius XII is speaking here, of course, of the human portion of creation that has been grafted into Christ—of Christ in his fullness, the Pleroma. For Teilhard this pleroma helps "to perfect Christ in his mystical totality."[13] In his last essay before he died, "The Christic," Teilhard writes that Christ consummates while being consummated.[14] Christ has not yet attained his fullness.[15] There is a certain mutuality, not equality, between Christ and creation. In the present order of things, as willed by God, there is a complementarity between Christ and creation, between God and the world. "God did not will individually . . . the sun, the earth, plants, or Man. He willed his Christ—and in order to have his Christ, he had to create the spiritual world, and man in particular, upon which Christ might germinate—and to have man, he had to launch the

---

the fibers of the universe is woven into one. In Scripture Christ is essentially revealed as invested with the power of giving the world, in his own person, its definitive form. He is consecrated for a cosmic function. And since that function is not only moral but also (in the most real sense of the word) physical, it presupposes a physical basis in its humano-divine subject."

11. "Super-Humanity, Super-Christ, Super-Charity" (1943), *SC*, 164–67.

12. Pius XII, "Mystici Corporis Christi," 45, par. 44. Pope Saint Leo the Great, in one of his sermons, also noted, "The head cannot be separated from the members, nor the members from the head" (Roman Breviary, *Liturgy of the Hours*, Office of Readings, Wednesday, Second Week of Easter). Also see Isaac of Stella (Roman Breviary, *Liturgy of the Hours*, Office of Readings, Friday, Fifth Week of Easter): "And so, according to this well-known reading of Scripture, neither the body without the head, nor the head without the body, nor the head and body without God make the whole Christ."

13. *DM*, 31.

14. "The Christic" (1955), *HM*, 90–96. In his early essay, "Cosmic Life" (1916), *WW*, 62, he had already noted that, in the present order of things, Christ is incomplete apart from creation.

15. "Cosmic Life" (1916), *WW*, 59.

vast process of organic life . . . and the birth of that organic life called for the entire cosmic turbulence."[16]

As Robert Faricy, SJ, phrased it: "God, therefore, by his own free willing of a total plan of creation that includes his Incarnation, has freely immersed himself in his creation, has freely willed a real mutual complementarity between himself and the world."[17] This so-called third "nature" of Jesus Christ, his cosmic extendedness, his universal scope, his omnipresence, his coming to "completion" by creation itself, is freely chosen on Christ's part. God freely chose to create. Christ freely chose to become incarnate. God so loved the world that what might seem like a dependency of Christ on creation for his own completion is something that Christ chose out of love. The universalization of Christ accompanies the still-to-be-completed-universe-in-the-process-of-being-formed. In bringing his evolving creation to completion within himself, Christ himself comes to completion as Christ-Omega. For Teilhard, in the end, there is only one center for the universe, and not one that is natural and one supernatural. The natural world itself finds it meaning and fulfillment in Christ. Cosmogenesis is directed toward building up the body of Christ.

> There is only *one single center* in the universe; it is at once natural and supernatural; it impels the whole of creation along one and the same line, first towards the fullest development of consciousness, and later towards the highest degree of holiness: in other words, towards Christ Jesus, personal and cosmic.[18]

> And since Christ was born, and ceased to grow, and died, everything has continued in motion because he has not yet attained the fullness of his form . . . The mystical Christ has not reached the peak of his growth—nor, therefore, has the cosmic Christ. Of both we may say that they are and at the same time are becoming . . . By the Incarnation, which redeemed man, the very Becoming of the Universe, too, has been transformed. Christ is the term of even the natural evolution of living beings; evolution is holy.[19]

Teilhard is interested in affirming the primacy of Christ over all creation and at the same time dispelling the notion of the arbitrariness of creation once God has freely chosen to create a universe. The christified

16. "My Universe" (1924), *SC*, 79.
17. Faricy, *Teilhard's Theology*, 116.
18. "Forma Christi" (1918), *WW*, 256. Emphasis in text.
19. "Cosmic Life" (1916), *WW*, 59. Emphasis in text.

universe or universalized Christ is the telos of creation and the plenitude of Christ. We must remind ourselves, however, that unification is not identification, that union differentiates, and thus not confuse Christ and his body. In a 1950 letter, he wrote: "The last essay of all is now finished—on 'two inverse forms of the spirit'—spirit of identification and spirit of unification. I felt the need to write this in order to have an exact text to give to anyone who raised the matter with me in conversation."[20] Teilhard's vision of creative union does not destroy the identifiable distinctiveness of the cosmos, nor of humankind, nor of Christ: "the mysterious Pleroma, in which the substantial One and the created many fuse without confusion in a whole which, without adding anything essential to God, will nevertheless be a sort of triumph."[21] And, "The Christian who is animated by cosmic consciousness, must hold above all else that God, the only Absolute, is essentially distinct from creation."[22]

Teilhard chose to be bold in his expressions which he defends as doing more justice to Scripture and the Greek Fathers.[23] Yet his Christology remains traditional while being situated in an evolutionary world view. In "The Christic," he spoke about three characteristics of the Christian's Incarnate God: (1) his experiential tangibility due to his historical birth into the process of evolution; (2) his universal expansibility due to his resurrection; and (3) his power to integrate into a single body the totality of humanity.[24]

THE INCARNATION

Teilhard speaks frequently of the Incarnation. His spirituality is deeply incarnational. God has immersed himself in the world. Toward the close of *The Human Phenomenon* he writes that evolution is in a sense "an enormous biological operation: that of the redemptive Incarnation."[25] Teilhard's interest, however, was not so much in the metaphysical aspects

20. *LT*, 302. See the later "A Clarification: Reflections on Two Converse Forms of Spirit" (1950), *AE*, 215–27.

21. *DM*, 100. Emphasis in text. At Omega, the Parousia or Pleroma will be a triumph for being itself, when God will be all in all.

22. "The Universal Element" (1920), *WW*, 294.

23. See "Cosmic Life" (1916), *WW*, 49–53; "My Universe" (1924), *SC*, 54–56; "Super-Humanity, Super-Christ, Super-Charity" (1943), *SC*, 165–67.

24. *HM*, 89.

25. *HP*, 211.

of the Incarnation, the philosophy that undergirds the theology of the hypostatic union, nor even the biblical stories that are revelatory of the Jesus of history, both of which Aquinas dealt with extensively, but rather with the continuing impact of the reality that God has become incarnate, really present, enfleshed in our world. Teilhard's emphasis, however, is on the Incarnation as a continuing reality. It is not something that was accomplished once and for all. It too remains unfinished.[26]

Just as words like cosmogenesis, biogenesis, and anthropogenesis have a twofold sense to them in that they indicate both a moment of emergence as well as a continuing process, such as the birth of life, the living cell, as well as the ongoing process of organic or biological evolution, and as anthropogenesis can refer to the emergence of the first human beings as well as the continuing evolution of humankind, so christogenesis refers to the conception and birth of Christ but also to Christ's ongoing embodiment. There is of course the unfolding of Jesus, the Incarnate Word, in the womb of Mary, throughout his childhood, as a prophetic preacher and teacher following upon his baptism by John, though his death on the cross. Theologians today do speak about the Incarnation continuing through the cross and resurrection. It was not simply something done instantaneously once and for all, although it was that, but it was also more. It was the life, death, and resurrection of Jesus. But this does not stop with the resurrection of Christ. Christ's body is not yet fully formed if we truly see ourselves as members of his body, not in a figurative sense but in the realistic way in which St. Paul speaks of it. It is this Pauline perspective that intrigues Teilhard—Christ's own unfinishedness as his incarnation in the world continues to take shape. Christ-Omega is the selfsame Jesus that was born in Bethlehem, but that same Jesus come to his pleromic completion. It is the importance of this that Teilhard emphasizes.

Others before Teilhard have spoken about a threefold birth of Christ: eternally within the Trinity itself as the Only Begotten One, historically from the womb of Mary as the Incarnate One, and his birth in us today. The Dominican mystic Johannes Tauler emphasized the significance of the latter without which the historical birth would remain incomplete: "The third birth is effected when God is born within a just soul every day and every hour truly and spiritually, by grace and out of love," and "In

26. *DM*, 30, already speaks about the Incarnation as incomplete. Also consider the discussions pertinent to what some contemporary theologians refer to as "deep Incarnation." See Gregersen, *Incarnation*.

eternity, he was born without a mother, and in time he was born without a father. 'Mary,' so Saint Augustine tells us, 'was more blessed because God was born spiritually in her soul than because he was born from her in the flesh.'"[27] It is the christification of the individual and of the whole universe that is pivotal for Teilhard and which occupies his attention, not to the denial or exclusion of other aspects of the Incarnation about which much had previously been written, but rather for the sake of a Christology that would be fitting for the world in which we now find ourselves.

Expressions of Teilhard thus take on their most profound meaning when manifesting a mystical quality: "a directed and realized omnipresence"[28]; "a 'pan-Christic' mysticism"[29]; a "total amorization."[30] Christian love or Christian charity, through which the Incarnation continues, is an effective power of pan-amorization.[31] "The Incarnation is a making new, a restoration, of all the universe's forces and powers; Christ is the Instrument, the Center, the End of the whole of animate and material creation; though him, everything is created, sanctified, and vivified."[32] The divinity, the historicity, and the cosmicity of Christ are all central to the Incarnation: the three births if you will.

> For God to be incarnate in a world in evolution means *to be born in it* . . . Even today abandonment of the historical character of Christ (that is, the divinity of the historic Christ) would mean the instant dismissal into the unreal of all the mystical energy accumulated in the Christian phylum during the last two thousand years. Christ born of the Virgin, and Christ risen from the dead: the two are one inseparable whole.[33]

THE RESURRECTION

As Teilhard stated, the resurrection of Christ is inseparable from the Incarnation. They go hand in hand, the resurrection being impossible

27. Tauler, *Sermons*, 35, 39.
28. "The Heart of Matter" (1950), *HM*, 47. Emphasis in text.
29. "The Heart of Matter" (1950), *HM*, 47.
30. "The Heart of Matter" (1950), *HM*, 50. Emphasis in text. Also see "The Christic" (1955), *HM*, 82–83.
31. "The Christic" (1955), *HM*, 88.
32. "Cosmic Life" (1916), *WW*, 58.
33. "Introduction to the Christian Life" (1944), *CE*, 158–59. Emphasis in text.

without Christ's historic insertion into the human phylum, and the Incarnation being incomplete without Christ's resurrection from the dead. Although he may write less about the resurrection, he by no means sees it as insignificant. The whole process of Omegalization depends on it—Christ's historical existence transformed into another way of being in relation to space-time. Without the resurrection, the christified universe and the universalized Christ become impossible.

Teilhard is less concerned than modern exegetes with the historical character of this trans-historical event. He does not deny its factuality nor its miraculous nature. He is more concerned with its implications, with its theological significance, with the importance it has for God's ongoing evolving creation. Few events if any could have more of an impact on the future of evolution and thus the future of humanity. It is an event that assumes an importance proportionate to the initial creative action *ex nihilo* and the incarnation of the Word within the cosmos. As already mentioned, the resurrection allows for the expansibility of the Christ, for his universalization, something that his immersion into history alone would not make possible. The resurrection of Christ is both a historic event (in the sense that it happened within history, within the created order) while being meta-historiographical (not accessible in all its facets to historical research as the event transcends history as we know it or knew it),[34] but for Teilhard what is significant is that it was a cosmic event. It is not only where history meets what transcends history but where the deeper meaning of the cosmos itself becomes clearer. Through the power of the resurrection, Christ the Evolver opens the door to re-creation, to the new heavens and the new earth (Rev 21:1).[35]

For Teilhard, the resurrection is "Christ's transition from his individual state to his 'cosmic' state as center of evolution."[36] There is something "unrepresentable" and "inexpressible" about this cosmic leap, which cannot be subjected "to a scientific criticism" but would

34. See n7 above.

35. "Christ the Evolver" (1942), *CE*, 145.

36. "Introduction to the Christians Life" (1944), *CE*, 162. Cuénot, *Teilhard de Chardin*, wrote: "Since Christ before his death was an integral part of the cosmos, organically included in the stuff of the universe, then the risen Christ, who can have been nowise less that he had been before his death, became the organic center of the cosmos . . . By the resurrection, the body of Christ became coextensive with the cosmos, to which it had already been organically bound by the Incarnation; and the Pantocrator of the ancient Byzantine churches was revealed as the organic center of the universe and the motive power of evolution" (122–23).

nevertheless be "disastrous to reject," since "this would be to rob Christogenesis of its trans-experiential essence."[37] In its prolongation of the Incarnation and its transformation of the biological individual that Jesus was, it was another one of evolution's critical moments for now more clearly "all might be one" (John 17:21). The risen Jesus, the Risen Christ, now becomes the super-center towards which all humanity, all creation, will converge. Centration had given way to ex-centration which now gives way to a super-centration in Christ up Above and up Ahead. There can be only one Omega,[38] one Christ, the humano-divine Jesus of Nazareth come to full form. The risen Christ is the Jesus of Nazareth conceived in the womb of his Blessed Mother, within the womb of the world; and the cosmic Christ is this selfsame risen Christ in its full stature, co-extensive with the cosmos itself which has its being *in Christo*.

> In these circumstances, there is nothing to prevent a human individual nature from having been so chosen, and its omni-influence having been so elevated, that from being "*una inter pares*" it has become "*prima super omnes*." Just as in living bodies a cell, at first similar to the other cells, can gradually come to be preponderant in the organism, so the particular humanity of Christ was able (at least at the Resurrection) to take on, to acquire, a universal morphological function.[39]

Such were the super-human powers with which Christ's resurrection was endowed, as he states in the celebrated text of The Mass on the World,[40] which was a testimony to the role of the Eucharist within an evolving universe in Teilhard's thought.

THE EUCHARIST

The "extension" of the Incarnation, the universalization of Christ, due principally to the risen Christ and the power of the Holy Spirit, is manifest in and accomplished through the Eucharist. The emphasis in Teilhard's writings is on this relationship between the cosmic body of Christ or the universal Christ and the sacramental or Eucharistic body of Christ,

37. "Introduction to the Christian Life" (1944), *CE*, 162.

38. "Centrology" (1944), *AE*, 127.

39. "Fall, Redemption, and Geocentrism" (1920), *CE*, 41.

40. "The Mass on the World" (1923), *HM*, 131. Also see "Introduction to the Christian Life" (1944), *CE*, 165–67.

for each is indeed Christ's body. What we celebrate in the Eucharist is also happening in the world. The *"Hoc est corpus meum"* ("This is my body") and the *"Ite, missa est"* ("Go, the Mass is ended") are of equal importance. "Let the creation repeat to itself again today, and tomorrow, and until the end of time, so long as the transformation has not run its full course, the divine saying: 'This is my body.'"[41] The Incarnation, like creation itself, continues to unfold, to evolve, and it is especially through the Eucharist that the christification of the universe takes place.[42] The body of Christ extends beyond that of the consecrated bread and the wine. Yet the Blessed Sacrament is the center from which Christ expands his presence in the world.

> If we are worthily to interpret the fundamental place the Eucharist does in fact hold in the economy of the world; if we are to meet the legitimate demands of those who, because they love Christ, cannot bear to be for one moment excluded from him, then I believe we must accord an important place in Christian thought and prayer to the real, and physical, extensions of the Eucharistic Presence . . . we must say that the initial Body of Christ, his *primary body*, is confined to the species of bread and wine. Can Christ, however, remain contained in this primary Body? Clearly, he cannot . . . The Host is like a blazing hearth from which flames spread their radiance.[43]

The bread and wine, the Eucharistic real presence, are now in the present order of things the center for Christ's universalization and the universe's divinization. His Body extends beyond the host and yet the host is the center from which it extends. Teilhard does not hesitate to use the word "transubstantiation," and sees that word figuratively helpful in describing the whole process of what is going on in the world.

> And then there appears to the dazzled eyes of the believer the eucharistic mystery itself, extended infinitely into a veritable universal transubstantiation, in which the words of the Consecration are applied not only to the sacrificial bread and wine but,

41. "The Priest" (1918), *WW*, 207. "The Priest," along with "The Mass on the World" (1923), *HM*, 119–34, a later reworking of "The Priest"; and "Christ in the World of Matter" (1916), *HU*, 42–55, speak in a mystical fashion about the Mass.

42. "My Universe" (1924), *SC*, 60–66.

43. "My Universe" (1924), *SC*, 64–65. Emphasis in text.

> mark you, to the whole mass of joys and sufferings produced by the Convergence of the World as it progresses.[44]

The universe itself is becoming the Body of Christ in a very real way. "The transubstantiation . . . extends to the whole universe."[45]

> Thus when the phrase "Hoc est corpus meum" is pronounced, "hoc" means "primario" the bread; but "secundario," in a second phase occurring in nature, the matter of the sacrament is the world, throughout which there spreads, so as to complete itself, the superhuman presence of the universal Christ . . . Since all time a single word and a single act have been filling the universality of things: "Hoc est corpus meum."[46]

Teilhard expressed it thus in *The Divine Milieu*:

> When the priest says the words *Hoc est Corpus meum*, his words fall directly on to the bread and directly transform it into the individual reality of Christ. But the great sacramental operation does not cease at that local and momentary event . . . from the beginning of the Messianic preparation, up till the Parousia, passing through the historic manifestation of Jesus and the phases of growth of his church, a single event has been developing in the world: the Incarnation, realized, in each individual, through the Eucharist.[47]

What we see in Teilhard is this intrinsic, distinguishable but inseparable, connectedness between creation and Incarnation, between Incarnation and Eucharist, and thus between the Eucharist as sacrament and creation itself, the Eucharist as center of the omnipresence of christification, of the ongoing evolution of the universe. Through the Eucharistic presence of Christ, the universe itself continues its transformation that is not yet finished.

REDEMPTION

Rethinking Christology in the light of an expansive, evolving, and unfinished universe is challenged when it comes to the theology of

44. "The Christic" (1955), *HM*, 94.
45. "The Priest" (1918), *WW*, 207.
46. "My Universe" (1924), SC, 65–66.
47. *DM*, 102.

redemption.[48] Christ, the evolver, yes; Christ, the redeemer, also yes; but in what does redemption consist? Here we must come to grips with sin, the origin of sin, the cross, the mystery of evil itself and what the death of Christ accomplished. Teilhard's emphases do not deny the doctrine of an atoning death although his challenge lay elsewhere. It is in this area that he took some of his greatest risks. It is in this area that theologians have ever since struggled as well. His earliest essay touching upon these topics, "Fall, Redemption, and Geocentrism" dates to 1920[49]—over a hundred years ago and long before the Second Vatican Council grappled with the church and the modern world. Here we can only touch the surface of what Teilhard had to contribute, whose thoughts were simply exploratory, suggestive.

The Nature and Origin of Sin: We must distinguish between evil, what is often considered physical evil that we find in the natural world prior to the emergence of *Homo sapiens*, and moral evil that is consequent upon human freedom with its concomitant responsibility for actions offensive to God. There was no moral evil prior to anthropogenesis. Moral evil has a long history—the history of sin in the world. We are not who we ought to be, whom God created us to be. We fall short of our destiny. The history of sin takes us back to prehistory. The Christian conviction is that God is not the author of sin; we are. Sin has its origin with the coming of humankind and can be traced backwards to that origin; it was with us from the beginning, *ab origine*. The coming of the first humans carried great promise with it, a huge leap forward, but was also accompanied by setbacks that became catastrophic. It was into this universe that was both evolving and "fallen" that Jesus was born. Our first parents (whether one or many) manifested an evolutionary advance—the rise of consciousness. They also opened a door to a darker side. We are capable of doing more good than was ever possible before. We are also capable of more harm. We have evolved beyond the state in which our first ancestors found themselves, but we are not necessarily more moral than they.[50] Evolution has not only become conscious; we have become co-responsible for its future.

48. "It is impossible to think of Christ as 'evolver' without at the same time having to re-think the whole of Christology" ("The Stuff of the Universe" [1953], *AE*, 382).

49. "Fall, Redemption, and Geocentrism" (1920), *CE*, 36–44.

50. "A Note on Progress" (1920), *FM*, 17–18.

Yet, for Teilhard, it is difficult to accept the traditional interpretation of the Fall which seems to be contradicted by paleontology.[51] Our first humans emerged, to be sure, from within the prehuman biosphere, one might say "from the dust of the earth" (Gen 2:7), but an interpretation of the creation of Adam as found in the Genesis accounts cannot be taken literally as it is not by biblical exegetes today. What is central to the doctrine of original sin, among other things, is sin's universality, which Teilhard strongly emphasizes.[52] Evolutionary biologists can admit to a true unity to the human race, but they have difficulty with the traditional doctrine of monogenism. Still less would an evolutionary world view have a place for an historical earthly paradise. There needs to be new ways of conceiving original sin.[53] "Original sin is a static solution of the problem of evil," Teilhard writes.[54] The traditional idea of a Fall, and the Augustinian interpretation of original sin, were an attempt to explain evil within a fixed universe that came forth finished from the hands of God. But creation was not and is not finished.[55] Death also predates the emergence of the first humans.[56] St. Paul's understanding in the Letter to the Romans is understood today in the light of more recent exegesis. Teilhard chose to place the origin and history of sin within the broader context of an unfinished universe in which there was already "evil" prior to the emergence of *Homo sapiens*, not moral evil but nevertheless genuine corruption that was not a consequence of human sinfulness. Teilhard was not able to do full justice to the doctrine of original sin itself, but his reflections have challenged theology to think further about the reality of evil in an evolving creation.

The Mystery of Evil: Teilhard's suggestions are both significant but also tentative. Some of his convictions include: (1) Creation itself was not an instantaneously fully accomplished act. (2) An evolving and unfinished

51. "Introduction to the Christian Life" (1944), *CE*, 162–63.

52. "Fall, Redemption, and Geocentrism" (1920), *CE*, 36–39.

53. "Note on Some Possible Historical Representations of Original Sin" (1922), *CE*, 45–55. This early essay was hesitantly suggestive and not published but the ideas contained therein were the source of early suspicions about his thought. Also see "Reflections on Original Sin" (1947), *CE*, 187–98.

54. "Christology and Evolution" (1933), *CE*, 80. Emphasis in text. In "The Sense of Man" (1929), *TF*, 34, he writes: "Original sin is very gradually becoming, is it not, something more in the nature of a tough beginning than a fall?"

55. "Christology and Evolution" (1933), *CE*, 80.

56. "Fall, Redemption, and Geocentrism" (1920), *CE*, 39.

universe carried with it the high probability of evil; one might even say "statistical" necessity. (3) The reality and tragedy of moral evil must be understood within the context of "this other side" of creation. (4) Given this darker side of evolution and sin's exacerbating it in geometric proportions, God's redemptive work becomes necessary. The "twofold notion of statistical evil and evolutionary redemption" complements the traditional notions of a catastrophic original sin and reparatory expiation.[57]

Could God have created the universe "done" from the beginning? Could he have created it at Alpha as it will be at Omega? Why did God choose to create the universe evolutively? Could God have done otherwise? Teilhard is convinced that creation cannot be an instantaneous act,[58] not however due to impotence on God's part.[59] Thomas Aquinas had written, "There does not fall under the scope of God's omnipotence anything that implies a contradiction."[60] Teilhard surmises, "No one has ever thought it remarkable that God cannot make a square circle or perform an evil act. Why should we restrict the field of impossible contradiction only to those cases? There are certainly *physical* equivalents to the infallible laws of moral science and geometry."[61] One of these physical impossibilities for Teilhard would be an instantaneously consummated creation.

"God can proceed to creation *in only one way*: he must arrange, and, under his magnetic influence . . . gradually unify an immense multitude of elements . . . then they gradually become fewer, more complex, and ultimately endowed with reflection."[62] There is then an inevitable counterpart to this. Evil is the other side of the coin of cosmogenesis, for "evil appears in the wake of evolution . . . by the structure of the system."[63] Could God have created a universe without evil? Creation does not proceed toward unity without disunity and disorder along the way. "So we find physical

57. "The Stuff of the Universe" (1953), *AE*, 382.

58. "Christology and Evolution" (1933), *CE*, 82–83; "How I Believe" (1934), *CE*, 132; "Christianity and Evolution: Suggestions for a New Theology" (1945); *CE*, 178–79; "The God of Evolution" (1953), *CE*, 239.

59. "Some General Views on the Essence of Christianity" (1939), *CE*, 134–35. From a different perspective, David Meconi, SJ, in exploring St. Augustine's theology of atonement, speaks of creation's incompleteness (*Self-Harm*, 46–57).

60. *ST*, I, q. 25, a. 4.

61. "Note on the Modes of Divine Action in the Universe" (1920), *CE*, 33. Emphasis in text.

62. "My Fundamental Vision" (1948), *TF*, 197. Emphasis in text.

63. *HP*, 225. Also see "Some General Views on the Essence of Christianity" (1939), *CE*, 134–35.

discords or decompositions in the pre-living; suffering in the living; sin in the domain of freedom. There can be no *order in the process of formation* which does not at every stage imply *some disorder*."[64] Evil emerges, as Teilhard would say, as highly probable, through "statistical necessity," which denies neither God's freedom nor human freedom but merely refers to an interplay of large numbers in terms of probability theory. I can say that it is inevitable that someone will have an accident on a particular holiday weekend which does not mean that anyone in particular is determined to have an accident but rather that, statistically, chances are that someone will. "Evil is thus a *secondary* effect, an inevitable *by*-product of the progress of a universe in evolution."[65] Although "God cannot ordain that the elements of a world in the course of growth—or at least of a fallen world in the process of rising again—should avoid shocks and diminishments, even moral ones . . . God will make it good . . . by making evil itself serve the higher good of his faithful, the very evil which the present state of creation does not allow him to suppress immediately."[66] This latter text from *The Divine Milieu* takes us into the mystery of the cross, for ultimately a mystery it is. "The problem of evil, that is to say the reconciling of our failures, even the purely physical ones, with creative goodness and creative power, will always remain one of the most disturbing mysteries of the universe for both our hearts and our minds."[67]

Given the reality of evil, we must make a distinction, not only between physical "evil," which preexisted as well as continues throughout human evolution, and moral evil or sin as a dimension of humanity's history, but also between evil which is a consequence or presupposition of the unfinishedness of the universe into which humankind was born, and that which has gone against the upward and forward direction of evolution due to human freedom's tragic history. This latter requires God's redemptive activity. Teilhard's emphasis will be on God in Christ building up creation's advance, not to the exclusion however of an atonement or expiation to which Aquinas's theology gave significant attention.[68] Not only Christ the Evolver, but also Christ the Redeemer is essential to creation's progress.

64. "My Fundamental Vision" (1948), *TF*, 197. Emphasis in text.

65. "From Cosmos to Cosmogenesis" (1951), *AE*, 260. Emphasis in text.

66. *DM*, 58.

67. *DM*, 57.

68. Teilhard's tendency to downplay the expiatory nature of redemption can be seen in "Christology and Evolution" (1933), *CE*, 79–86.

If original sin is the resistant side of creation's advance, its shadow side, then redemption is God's commitment to reverse that or counteract it.[69]

> In one sense, if to create is to unite (evolutively, gradually) then God cannot create without evil appearing as a shadow—evil which has to be atoned for and overcome . . . This, incidentally, broadens, without distorting, the "meaning of the cross" to a remarkable degree. The Cross is the symbol and significant act of Christ raising up the world with all its burden of inertia, but with all its inherent drive, too; an act of expiation but also one of breakthrough and conquest . . . From this it follows that, understood in their full sense, creation, incarnation, and redemption are not facts which can be *localized* at a given point in time and space; they are true dimensions of the world . . . It is nevertheless true that all three [creation, incarnation, redemption] can take the form of particular *expressive* facts, such as the historical appearance of the human type (creation), the birth of Christ (incarnation), his death (redemption). These historical facts, however, are only a specially heightened expression of a process which is "cosmic" in dimensions.[70]

In the doctrine of redemption, even traditionally according to Teilhard, there was the primary emphasis on its expiatory role but also a secondary consideration of a cosmic dimension, the new heavens and the new earth, the new creation. Teilhard's suggestion for our times is to reverse these two emphases, not to the exclusion of the first but neither to have it hold primacy within the doctrine. The redemptive work of Christ thus becomes primarily the consummation of creation itself. "No longer *first* to expiate, and then *in addition* to restore; but *first* to create (or supercreate) and, in order to do so . . . pay for evil."[71]

The Cross of Our Lord Jesus Christ: The reality of evil and the tragedy of moral evil are counteracted, outweighed, by God's redemptive action in the world. God redeems or saves what at first sight he seems "unable" to prevent. In what does God's redemptive action consist, and what does the cross of Christ symbolize and accomplish? In Teilhard's spiritual

69. "Fall, Redemption, and Geocentrism" (1920), *CE*, 39–41.

70. "Some General Views on the Essence of Christianity" (1939), *CE*, 134–35. Emphasis in text.

71. "Christ the Evolver" (1942), *CE*, 146. Emphasis in text.

theology as outlined in *The Divine Milieu*, he gives a significant place to the cross. Before going there, however, let me quote from another essay.

> Christianity is pledged to the Cross, and dominated by the sign of the Cross . . . But what exactly is the essence—what is *the true* meaning of the Cross? . . .
>
> If the Cross is to reign over an earth that has suddenly awoken to consciousness of a biological movement drawing it ahead, then at all costs and as soon as possible it must . . . present itself to us as a sign, not merely of "escape," but of progress . . .
>
> Can the Cross be so transformed, *without distortion*? My answer is an emphatic "Yes"; it can, and it must, if we get right down to the root of the problem, be transformed by what is most traditional in the Christian spirit . . .
>
> . . . Is not the God of evolution—the God for whom our neo-humanism is looking—precisely and simply, taken in the fullest sense of the words and in a generalized form, the very God of expiation? And this because, if we consider the matter carefully, "to bear the sins of the guilty world" means precisely, *translated and transposed into terms of cosmogenesis*, "to bear the weight of a world in a state of evolution."[72]

Teilhard wrestles with expanding and understanding the cross, the death of Christ, the theology of redemption from within an evolutionary understanding of the world, not to the exclusion of more traditional emphases associated with theories of atonement, but to see the wood of the cross as bearing the full weight of evolution itself in its movement upwards and forwards. It is in that spirit that the cross takes its place within Teilhard's christocentric humanist spirituality.

It is there, in his theology of the cross, that Teilhard emphasizes the important role and value of human action and effort, essential to a world not yet done, in which we are participants. It is there that he discusses all that we must endure in our struggle against evil, in which struggle we cannot remain passive, even if in the end transformation through true resignation is part of the rhythm of life. It is there, within his remarks on Christian asceticism, that the cross acquires its deepest meaning: "The royal road of the Cross is no more nor less than the road of human endeavor supernaturally righted and prolonged. Once we have fully grasped the meaning of the Cross, we are no longer in danger of finding life sad

72. "What the World Is Looking For from the Church of God at this Moment: A Generalizing and Deepening of the Meaning of the Cross" (1952), *CE*, 216–19. Emphasis in the text.

and ugly. We shall simply have become more attentive to its incomprehensible gravity."[73] God acts not only in creating the universe but also in redeeming it. Both facets of the divine action reveal the value God places on his evolving universe and, with his redemptive Incarnation, the extent to which he will go to save it from destruction. A greater love there could not be than the act of creation itself, for a God who does not need us to freely choose to share his life with us. But greater yet is the love manifest in the Incarnation itself, whereby God chooses to become one with us in our mystical journey toward the Omega of evolution and not remain an outside observer. But greater love indeed is the extent to which God is willing to share the burden of this journey in his death, even a death on the cross. Creative love, incarnate love, redemptive love, a God of love at the heart of the universe in the process of its amorization.

The Redemptive Value of Suffering: It is worthwhile to place the mystery of human suffering within the context of an evolving world because Teilhard offers us a valuable image. He was not immune to suffering himself and his choice for a more optimistic perspective was not naive, but rather faith filled, more hope than optimism.[74] In *The Divine Milieu* Teilhard speaks about ways in which God can providentially bring forth good from evil, through "the progressive destruction of our egoism" and thus the "gradual spiritualization of our desires and ambitions," although in the end there are situations that "utterly disconcert our wisdom."[75] Physical evils are a source of deep pain and sadness but moral evils have the character of the tragic about them because they are avoidable given human freedom. Original sin is that teaching which instructs us that, in our present condition, we cannot easily distinguish between what could not have been avoided and what could have been, since there is such a long history now of human irresponsibility. Noogenesis faces inevitable but also morally indefensible setbacks. Original sin is a complex doctrine based upon a natural distance between the Creator and his evolving creation, but a distance aggravated to the point of alienation by human history, an alienation insurmountable without God's redemptive Incarnation.

The helpful image Teilhard gives us comes from his brief reflection on the death of his sister as he writes in "The Significance and Positive Value of Suffering." He offers us the comparison between a tree and a

73. *DM*, 78–79.

74. "The Grand Option" (1939), *FM*, 37–40.

75. *DM*, 59–60.

bunch of hand-picked flowers, contrasting a universe in the process of growth and a more static universe that was seemingly finished.

> In a bunch [of flowers]one would be surprised to see imperfect or "sickly" flowers because the constituents have been gathered one by one, and artificially put together. On a tree, on the other hand, which has had to fight against inner accidents in its development and the external accidents of bad weather, broken branches, torn leaves, parched, sickly or wilted flowers are "in place": they express the more or less difficult conditions of growth encountered by the trunk that bears them.
>
> Similarly, in a universe where each creature forms a little whole enclosed and desired for its own sake and theoretically transposable at will, we should have some difficulty in mentally justifying the presence of individuals sadly arrested in their possibilities of ascent. Why this arbitrary inequality, these gratuitous restrictions? On the other hand, if the world in fact represents a work of achievement at present taking place; if at birth we are really thrown into the midst of battle, we can see that, for the success of the universal effort of which we are at the same time the participators and the stake, it is inevitable that there shall be pain. The world, seen by experience at our level, is an immense groping, an immense search, an immense attack; its progress can take place only at the expense of many failures, or many wounds. Sufferers of whatever species are the expression of this stern but noble condition. They are not useless and dwarfed. They are simply paying for the forward march and triumph of all. They are the casualties, fallen on the field of honor.[76]

Undoubtedly the image comes to Teilhard as he served as a stretcher-bearer during the First World War which was for him a kind of baptism into the reality of evil in the world and how one can humanly cope with it. His appreciation of the universe as a work in progress was of help to him. In a "static" or more or less "finished" universe, handed to us as if "done," it is more difficult to situate the reality of evil. In a universe whose inner structure, however, is one of growth, unfolding, "evils" find their place as the universe advances, struggles with its setbacks. There is no growth without suffering: a lesson Teilhard learned as a stretcher-bearer in the war.

76. "The Significance and Positive Value of Suffering" (1933), *HE*, 49–50. See also "The Spiritual Energy of Suffering" (1950), *AE*, 247–49.

> More than ever, perhaps, during those days, I felt that I was living in another world, superimposed on the surface of the other, shaping it, and yet so different!—It was still roads, fields, ripening corn.—And still—what irony!—in front of us, menacing and impregnable, arose the wooded ridge on which last October I used to walk. But the whole wore a different face, compounded of horror and something super-human. You'd have taken it for a place where what lies before death was *in the very act of passing into* what lies beyond death. The relative proportions of things, the normal scale of their values, were altered, ceased to apply. All the time I felt, very strongly, that my own turn to die might come—a thing that never happened to me at the beginning of the war.[77]

CHRIST-OMEGA

The Christocentric character of evolution, the christification of the universe, the universalization of Christ, christogenesis at the heart of the cosmos may strike one as narrowing one's perspective on the cosmic process, but it is rather a widening of our understanding of Christ. Teilhard saw creation as having a purpose. It is moving—upward and forward. There is an Omega point or point of ultimate convergence.[78] Teilhard's project of integrating religion, his Christian faith, with science is grounded in both a cosmology and a Christology, seeing their complementarity given the present order of things. The freely chosen creative act of God finds its meaning in creation's ultimate fulfillment in God. Relying again on his interpretation of St. Paul, everything will be handed over to the Father who will be all in all (1 Cor 15:28). It is through the mediation of Christ that this is accomplished. At the heart of the noosphere is the Christosphere, a realm of love surrounding the universe, a realm of love that radiates from and through the Person of Christ, as embodied and

77. *MM*, 219–20. Emphasis in text.

78. Teilhard speaks about this Omega Point in many essays. In "My Fundamental Vision" (1948), *TF*, 185, he writes: "I shall continue here to use the term 'Omega Point' in the sense I have long attributed to it: an ultimate and self-subsistent pole of consciousness, so involved in the world as to be able to gather into itself, by union, the cosmic elements that have been brought by technical arrangement to the extreme limit of their centration—and yet, by reason of its supra-evolutive (that is to say, transcendent) nature, enabled to be immune from that fatal regression which is, structurally, a threat to every edifice whose stuff exists in space and time. In itself, and by definition, such a center is not directly apprehensible by us."

symbolized in the cross of Christ, though whose life, death and resurrection love will triumph.

At the close of Teilhard's major work, *The Human Phenomenon*, he added an epilogue to complete it, which he entitled "The Christian Phenomenon." God's evolving creation is not complete apart from Christianity. We can turn to that epilogue to bring Teilhard's Christology to a close.[79] Evolution requires "a higher pole of attraction," an "extra-human energy," a "Center of centers," the "uncompromising affirmation of a personal God . . . who is Providence, guiding the universe with loving and attentive care, and God who is a Revealer, communicating himself to the human." For Teilhard, "Omega already exists *and is at work right here and now* in the deepest part of the thinking mass." Creator, Revealer, Redeemer. It is Christ, both personal and universal, not being one without being the other, "who is the principle of universal vitality," who "has sprung up as man among us," and who "has put himself in the position of, and forever has been, actively curving beneath him, purifying, directing, and superanimating the general rise of consciousness into which he has inserted himself." What has the Christ inserted into the noosphere? Christian love: "something incomprehensible . . . that the infinite and the intangible can be lovable, that the human heart can beat in true charity for its neighbor. . . ." Yet it is a fact that "for twenty centuries thousands of mystics have drawn such burning passion from its [Christian love] flame that their brilliance and purity far outstrip the impulses and devotion of any kind of human love . . ." and "other thousands of men and women daily renounce all ambition and joy except for the joy of laboriously abandoning themselves to it more and more."

Evolution infuses "new blood into Christian perspectives." At the same time Christian faith is prepared to save evolution and move it forward. Teilhard, whose perspective must be placed today within the continuing discussion of inter-religious dialogues,[80] nevertheless believed that "Christianity represents the only current of thought bold and progressive enough to embrace the world practically and effectively, in a complete and indefinitely perfectible act where faith and hope are consummated in charity." Teilhard's vision does not diminish the role of Christ but enlarges it. "The more vast the world becomes and the more

79. *HP*, 209–15. Texts in quotes in the following paragraphs are from that epilogue unless a particular text has a footnote of its own. Emphases are in the original.

80. See Ursula King, *Eastern Religions*, for the most thorough discussion of Teilhard's approach to Eastern religious traditions.

organic its interior connections, the more the perspectives of the Incarnation will triumph." Christ-Omega is the center. "The Christogenesis found in Saint Paul and Saint John is no more nor less than both the expected and the unhoped-for prolongation of the noogenesis in which cosmogenesis culminates for our experience. Christ is organically clothed in the very majesty of his creation." What Christ mediates to and through creation is the power of love. As Teilhard wrote in an essay on the evolution of chastity "The day will come when, after harnessing the ether, the winds, the tides, gravitation, we shall harness for God the energies of love. And, on that day, for the second time in the history of the world, man will have discovered fire."[81]

81. "The Evolution of Chastity" (1934), *TF*, 86–87. If Teilhard were writing today, he would probably refer to "space" rather than to "ether."

8

Two Cosmotheanthropic Visions

We have looked at both Thomas's and Teilhard's cosmologies, anthropologies, and Christologies. It remains for something to be said about their approaches to God.

THOMAS'S THEOLOGY OF THE ONE TRIUNE GOD

In chapter 2 we considered Thomas's theology of God *as* Creator and that it is the Trinity who creates. Thomas's extensive treatise on the Trinity (*ST*, I, qq. 27–43) is as masterful as Augustine's *De Trinitate*. Together they have shaped Catholic teaching. It is question 43, the last in his discussion of the Trinity, that forms the link between his theology of the Trinity and his theology of creation, on the missions of the divine persons, or the economic Trinity as it has come to be called.[1] Mission implies being sent (Latin *mittere*, to send). With respect to the one to whom a divine person is sent, mission implies being there in some way in which he was not there before (*ST*, I, q. 43, a. 1). Hence the Father sends the Son into the world in a new way, for the Son was already in the world, but invisibly so. Whereas words associated with the theology of the Trinity, like procession, generation, and spiration, signify something eternal, the

1. Karl Rahner's *The Trinity* made prominent the distinction between the immanent Trinity and the economic Trinity.

word "mission" has a temporal significance. It speaks of the Trinity in a relationship *ad extra* (*ST*, I, q. 43, a. 2). The sending or mission of a divine person pertains to the gift of sanctifying grace.

> For God is in all things by his essence, power, and presence, according to his one common mode, as the cause existing in the effects which participate in his goodness. Above and beyond this common mode, however, there is one special mode belonging to the rational creature wherein God is said to be present as the object known is in the knower, and the beloved in the lover. And since the rational creature by its operation of knowledge and love attains to God himself, according to this special mode God is said not only to exist in the rational creature, but also to dwell therein as in his own temple. So no other effect can be put down as the reason why the divine person is in the rational creature in a new mode, except sanctifying grace. (*ST*, I, q. 43, a. 3)

We spoke of God's omnipresence of immensity when discussing creation in chapter 2. Thomas also mentioned there a special mode of presence in the rational creature (*ST*, I, q. 8, a. 3, *ad* 4). That special mode, grace, was then discussed in the *prima secundae*. Sanctifying grace is the consequence of an invisible mission on the part of both the Son and the Spirit.

> But that a divine person be sent to anyone by invisible grace signifies both that this person dwells in a new way within him and that he has his origin from another. Hence, since both to the Son and to the Holy Spirit it belongs to dwell in the soul by grace, and to be from another, it therefore belongs to both of them to be invisibly sent. As to the Father, though he dwells in us by grace, still it does not belong to him to be from another, and consequently he is not sent. (*ST*, I, q. 43, a. 5)

The whole Trinity indwells the human soul (*ST*, I, q. 43, a. 5) but the Father is not *sent* (*ST*, I, q. 43, a. 4). Therefore, one only speaks of mission in relationship to the Son and Spirit. But one can speak not only of the invisible missions but also the visible ones, such as the Son being sent into the world as incarnate, or the Spirit on Pentecost or at the baptism of Jesus (*ST*, I, q. 43, a. 7 and *ad* 6). The processions within the Trinity are made manifest in missions *ad extra*. As the Son manifests and reveals the Father, the Spirit manifests the Son (*ST*, I, q. 43, a. 7, *ad* 6). The Son is the image of the invisible God (Col 1:15; *ST*, I, q. 35), and the Spirit, whose proper names are Love and Gift (*ST*, I, qq. 37–38), is the bond of unity between them (*ST*, I, q. 36, a. 4, *ad* 1). The invisible and visible missions of the Trinity connect the eternal tri-personal God to the universe as its Creator.

Prior to Aquinas's discussion of the Trinity, he had taken up the divine nature that the three *hypostases* (persons)[2] share, attributes such as simplicity, goodness, infinity, eternity, unity, as well as God's knowledge, freedom, love, justice, mercy, and power (*ST*, I, qq. 3–26). But before this Thomas makes an astounding and important observation which everything that follows must take into consideration. He says that when the existence of a thing has been ascertained, for example here when God's existence has been demonstrated (*ST*, I, q. 2), one proceeds to determine what it is, its essence. One goes from whether something is (*an sit*) to what it is (*quid est*). In the case of God, however, Thomas writes: "Now, because we cannot know what God is, but rather what he is not, we have no means for considering how God is, but rather how he is not" (*ST*, I, q. 3, prologue). So we cannot know who or what God is! Thomas continues then: "Therefore, we must consider (1) How he is not; (2) How he is known by us; (3) How he is named." Can we speak about God at all? Of course, in addition to that which can (not) be known by reason there is revelation. Clearly Aquinas thinks that we can talk about God, for he goes on to discuss God, but we must keep in mind that he is often talking about what God is *not*, not who God is. God remains shrouded in incomprehensible mystery no matter what we say. Aquinas protects the mystery. In the end we cannot know fully who or what God is. This does not mean we can say nothing. Yet Thomas's starting point is apophatic. He had alluded to this even earlier in the first question of the *prima pars* on the nature of *sacra doctrina:* "For what he [God] is not is clearer to us than what he is" (*ST*, I, q. 1, a. 9, *ad* 3).[3]

How then can we know or name God? For this, one must turn to questions twelve and thirteen of the *prima pars*. Even though Aquinas had demonstrated that God is, or that something is which people tend to call God, whether that be a first Mover, a first Cause, or "that without which nothing else would be," for Aquinas, creation does not contain

2. The Greek word "hypostasis" is translated into Latin as "persona" and into English as "person." What "person" in English connotes, however, is not the same as what "hypostasis" means in Greek, and in some ways is better left untranslated. In English, "person" can connote an "individual," and thus three persons can almost mean three gods. In the Greek one is talking about a subsistent reality, or subsisting relation, which Aquinas discusses in *ST*, I, q. 29.

3. See Victor White, *God the Unknown*, 16–34. Denys Turner, "'One with God as to the Unknown': Prayer and the Darkness of God," in *Mystery and Mystification*, 25–43.

within itself its own reason for being. His demonstrations only indicate that there is an unknowable X or mystery at the source of all there is (*ST*, I, q. 2). So how is the incomprehensible God knowable to us (*ST*, I, q. 12)? How does a finite mind grasp what is infinite and beyond its grasp? Aquinas's approach should keep us humble but not timid about what we say of God.

> God . . . is in himself supremely knowable. But what is supremely knowable in itself, may not be knowable to a particular intellect, on account of the excess of the intelligible object above the intellect; as, for example, the sun, which is supremely visible, cannot be seen by the bat by reason of its excess of light. (*ST*, I, q. 12, a. 1)

God in himself is supremely knowable, but not to us. The blessed in heaven do see God, not as God sees himself, but nevertheless, they do attain to the essence of God due to a strengthening of their intellects by the light of glory (*lumen gloriae*), that is with a glorified intellect (*ST*, I, q. 12, aa. 2, 4, 5). In this life, however, God cannot be known as he is in himself, but "it does not follow that he cannot be known at all, but that he exceeds every kind of knowledge, which means that he is not comprehended" (*ST*, I, q. 12, a. 1, *ad* 3).

On the one hand, God cannot be known as God is, due to the infinite distance between what God is and our finite intellects; on the other hand, this does not mean that God is not knowable at all in any way. God remains incomprehensible (*ST*, I, q. 12, aa. 7, 11) but in some way still knowable, even in this life. A basic principle for Thomas is that a thing is only known according to the mode of the knower (*ST*, I, q. 12, aa. 4, 11). How therefore do we in this life know God in our human natures with the natural power of our human reason? We can come to some knowledge of God from a knowledge of his effects: "We can be led from them [his effects] so far as to know of God *whether he exists*, and to know of him what must necessarily belong to him, as the first cause of all things, exceeding all things caused by him" (*ST*, I, q. 12, a. 12). In other words, a knowledge of creation does enable us to say *something* about its Creator. In addition to this kind of knowledge (from effects to cause) which we can have by natural reason, there is also revelation. Still, however, even in this life, by revelation:

> We cannot know of God *what he is*, and thus are united to him as to one unknown; still we know him more fully according as many and more excellent of his effects are demonstrated to us,

> and according as we attribute to him some things known by divine revelation, to which natural reason cannot reach, as, for instance, that God is Three and One. (*ST*, I, q. 12, a. 13, *ad* 1).

In this life we are united to God as to one unknown, yet not completely unknowable, due to a knowledge we can have from the visible effects of God in the universe (Rom 1:20) and to revealed knowledge (*ST*, I, q. 1, a. 1). Given then the limitations placed on us by our human nature vis à vis God, how do we proceed? Thomas responds to this in question 13 of the first part of his *Summa*.

We can say that God is good. We can say that God is our Creator and Savior. We can say that God is a rock. And we can say that God is Being Itself. Let us comment on these four ways of talking about God.

The most proper name for God is The-One-Who-Is (*qui est*), the tetragrammaton, the name that God revealed to Moses at the burning of the bush and recorded in the book of Exodus, chapter 3, verse 14 (*ST*, I, q. 13, a. 11).

There are other words that we use to talk about God which are not, properly speaking, names for God at all. They speak of God in a metaphorical way (*ST*, I, q. 13, a. 3, *ad* 1). Metaphors have a richness, however, and do communicate. God is not literally a rock, but the metaphor does tell us that God is someone on whom we can lean, that God is the source of our strength. "There is no rock like our God" (1 Sam 2:2). The word "rock" is used over twenty times in the Psalms to refer to God (Ps 18:1–2; 31:2–3). Names applied metaphorically to God *primarily* refer to the creature however (*ST*, I, q. 13, a. 6). In the very first question of the *Summa*, article 9, Aquinas asked whether it was fitting that Scripture use metaphors to communicate truth and defends their use. In this same vein one can speak about God as fatherly or motherly as do the Scriptures. Jesus teaches us to pray to God as our Father (Matt 6:9; Luke 11:2) and Isaiah the prophet spoke about God as mother (*ST*, Isa 49:15; 66:13). There is more to these latter names, however, than metaphor alone.

There are other names for God that derive from God's relationship with creatures (*ST*, I, q. 13, a. 7). Creator is such a name, as is Savior. They speak not of God as God is eternally but rather of God in relationship to time, from a temporal point of view. Were there no creatures, God would not be called Creator. Such would be the same in calling God Father. We cannot go into the whole philosophy of relationship here, but there are names that derive from the relationship between God and creation. The relationship, for Aquinas, is on our side. We are dependent on God simply in order to be. These relationships do not imply any change in God, for God is immutable for Aquinas.[4] Names such as these have reference to God acting *ad extra*.

We now move to those names which most properly describe God, while yet cognizant of God's incomprehensibility, those names which substantially name God. God *is* Goodness. God *is* Truth. God *is* Being. Even these names, however, although they can be predicated of God's essence, still fall short of our knowing God's essence in this life. The words do not signify exactly the same thing when applied to creatures, from whom we get our knowledge, and when applied to God (*ST*, I, q. 13, aa. 1, 2). How then can they be predicated of God at all? In three ways, which *triplex via* can be traced back to the Pseudo-Dionysius's treatment of God in his *On Divine Names*. As has already been said, we ourselves only know God from creatures, with God as their cause. The first way is thus that of causality. There is something in the effect that says something about the cause, and thus God can be named "yet not so that the name which signifies God expresses the divine essence in itself" (*ST*, I, q. 13, a. 1). Besides the approach through causality, however, there are two other methodological approaches or steps to naming God in this way, namely remotion or negation and excellence or eminence (*ST*, I, a. 13, a. 1). This is to say that God *is* good, but *not* in the ways we think of creatures as being good. Rather God *is* good in a super-eminent way that surpasses anything we understand by goodness as we find it in creatures. Yet it can be meaningfully said that God *is* good even if "his essence is above all that we understand about God and signify in word" (*ST*, I, q. 13, a. 1, *ad* 1).

These names or words, which denote absolute perfections and do not connote within them any imperfection as such, can be applied to God's very substance if we remember that they still fall short (*ST*, I, q. 13, a. 2). We understand what they mean but we do not know fully what they mean when applied to God for they only signify God imperfectly (*ST*, I, q. 13, a. 2, *ad* 1).

> So when we say, *God is good*, the meaning is not, *God is the cause of goodness*, or, *God is not evil*; but the meaning is, *Whatever*

4. "Now a relation of God to creatures is not a reality in God, but in the creature . . ." *ST*, I, q. 6, a. 2, *ad* 1. This is a statement often misunderstood. It is not saying that creatures make no difference to God but that they are not God's reality, that God does not depend on creatures, but rather that creatures depend on God and have their very being from God. On God's immutability, see *ST*, I, q. 9.

> *good we attribute to creatures, pre-exists in God*, and in a more excellent and higher way. Hence it does not follow that God is good because he causes goodness; but rather, on the contrary, he causes goodness in things because he is good. (*ST*, I, q .13, a. 2)

God is Goodness, Truth, and Being Itself, as well as Wisdom and Beauty, both as the cause of them in creatures, but not as we find them in creatures in an imperfect and finite way, but rather in a more eminent way than we can fully understand. Yet the statements are not meaningless.

This threefold way of getting at meaningful speech about God as ineffable leads to Aquinas's teaching on analogous speech. We must continue to keep in mind, however, Aquinas's cautions and what St. Augustine himself had once said in his *De Doctrina Christiana*:

> On the contrary, all I feel I have done is to wish to say something; but if I have said anything, it is not what I wished to say. How do I know this? I know it because God is inexpressible; and if what has been said by me were inexpressible, it would not have been said. And from this if it follows that God is not to be called inexpressible, because when even this is said about him, something is being expressed. And we are involved in heaven knows what kind of battle of words, since on the one hand what cannot be said is inexpressible, and on the other, what can even be called inexpressible is thereby shown to be not inexpressible. This battle of words should be avoided by keeping silent, rather than resolved by the use of speech.[5]

The concept of analogy is fundamental to Thomas's way of thinking. At the same time, as David Burrell once commented, "Aquinas is perhaps best known for his theory of analogy. On closer inspection it turns out that he never had one."[6] Here we need not go into the complexities and developments within Thomas's own thinking. Thomas clearly states, "Univocal predication is impossible between God and creatures" (*ST*, I, q. 13, a. 5). Univocal predication means that a word is applied to two different subjects in the same way with the same meaning. This would not safeguard the infinite distance between God and God's creation and no longer respect God's incomprehensibility. The names we give God do not have exactly the same meaning as they do when we predicate them of creatures.

5. Augustine, *Teaching Christianity*, Bk. I, #6, p. 108.

6. Burrell, *God and Action*, 55. There are a variety of works on Aquinas's approach to analogy, e.g., Clarke, *One and Many*; McInerny, *Aquinas and Analogy*; Wippel, *Metaphysical Thought*, 65–131; along with many others.

God's goodness is not the same as the ontological goodness that is ours, which is a *participation* in God's goodness (*ST*, I, q. 6, aa. 3, 4).

At the same time: "Neither, on the other hand, are names applied to God and creatures in a purely equivocal sense." (*ST*, I, q. 13, a. 5). If this were so, we could not speak meaningfully about God at all. Equivocal predication implies that the same word is applied to two different subjects but without anything in common in their meaning, e.g., the bark of a dog or bark on a tree. There must be something between univocal predication and equivocation. "Therefore it must be said that these names are said of God and creatures in an analogous sense" (*ST*, I, q. 13, a. 5). There are different kinds of analogy into which we cannot go here.[7] Analogy means that a name or word is applied to God in somewhat the same sense as we have derived its meaning from creatures but not completely so. There remains the infinite distance between God and God's creation, even though that creation participates in the being, goodness, and intelligibility that is primarily God's.

Some names for God refer primarily to creatures. Such are all metaphorical names. Others apply primarily to God and only secondarily to creatures, such as goodness (*ST*, I, q. 13, a. 6). Only God *is* Goodness. Only God truly *is*. All creatures fall short of that and fall short to different degrees, depending on the degree of their participation. Thomas remains committed to the fact that we cannot know what God is, but rather what he is not (*ST*, I, q. 3, prologue). We do not know God's essence in this life. That does not mean, however, that we are unable to make meaningful statements about God with the help of the *via negativa* and analogous language. What we say is true, even more true than we fully understand. Thomas even raises the question whether the word "God" can properly be a name for God as it has wider usage (*ST*, I, q. 13, aa. 8, 9). Even here we have analogical predication for we are gods by participation, but only he is God (*ST*, I, q. 13, a. 10). The bottom line for Thomas is that we cannot know the divine nature in itself, but we can approach it by way of causality, negation, and eminence (*ST*, I, q. 13, a. 8, *ad* 2). Thomas is *both* apophatic *and* cataphatic if we are to use those terms. We can speak truth about God and meaningfully so, but we must always remember that whatever we say falls far short of the divine mystery. There is much more that could be said about what Thomas says about God, but if so, we

7. Distinctions could be made between analogies of attribution—intrinsic and extrinsic, and analogies of proportionality—proper and improper, etc., about which there is not always consensus. Also see *SCG*, Bk I, 30–35.

would have to say as the evangelist does at the close of the Gospel of John: "if every one of them were written down, I suppose that the world itself could not contain the books that would be written" (John 21:25).

TEILHARD DE CHARDIN'S GOD OF EVOLUTION: ALPHA AND OMEGA

There is very little if anything that Aquinas says about God with which Teilhard would disagree. Teilhard does not write about the utter incomprehensibility of God although he clearly sees God as Mystery.[8] Teilhard does not articulate how our language about God can be best predicated, such as in analogical speech,[9] although his own way of speaking is often poetic. Teilhard does not attempt to probe the inner mystery of the Trinity by talking about the divine relationships among the Persons, but clearly believes what the church teaches about the triune God. Teilhard's emphases lay elsewhere. God is the God of creation and therefore the God of evolution. God is Alpha and Omega.

In *The Human Phenomenon*, what Teilhard considered his *magnum opus*, he clearly expresses his faith in the God of Jesus Christ. Nevertheless, out of respect for the limitations that had been placed on him as a writer, he presented the work as scientific and not as an expression of his faith.

> To be properly understood, the book I present here must not be read as a metaphysical work, still less as some kind of theological essay, but solely and exclusively as a scientific study. The very choice of title makes this clear. It is a study of nothing but the phenomenon; but also, the whole of the phenomenon.[10]

Nevertheless, the whole of the phenomenon, from Teilhard's point of view, could not exclude Christ, and thus he both attempts to avoid religious language and at the same time must use it. He thus becomes more explicit in the epilogue to the work where he acknowledges the Christian

8. He does share some reflections on how God is knowable to us in an early essay, "The Modes of Divine Action in the Universe," (1920), in *CE*, 26–30. In the same essay he shares his thoughts about divine omnipotence, 30–35.

9. He does suggest that there is a certain kind of analogous language very fitting to an evolving universe, in which that which comes later has an analogue in what came before ("Mastery of the World and the Kingdom of God," [1916], in *WW*, 83). In another context he refers to analogy ("Pantheism and Evolution," [1923], in *CE*, 67). Henri de Lubac, SJ, discusses Teilhard's use of analogy in *Eternal Feminine*, 66–84.

10. The very first lines of the book, *HP*, 1.

phenomenon as intrinsic to the human phenomenon. He speaks about an Omega Center, an extra-human energy, the Great Presence, which exists and is at work right here and now.[11] This Omega is "a personal God" who providentially guides the universe with loving and attentive care, "who is Revealer, communicating himself to the human at the level and through the modes of intelligence."[12] Teilhard wants to avoid a theology of God, and of the world governed by God, as understood in a juridical fashion. For Teilhard the relationship between God and the world is more organic, along the lines of the vision of St. Paul in 1 Corinthians where God, the Center of centers, will be all in all.[13] The vision is Pauline, not pantheistic,[14] although Teilhard had frequently to defend himself against the suspicion of pantheism. Today one could use the word "panentheism" to describe the Pauline theology but the word was not available to Teilhard and even today the word is used descriptively of various theologies that are not compatible.[15] He struggled to use other words to describe what he saw as St. Paul's vision, such as "Pan-Christism."[16] A personal God and a love of God were crucial to Teilhard's cosmic vision and to the future of evolution.[17]

> To be able literally to say to God that we love him, not only with our whole body, our whole heart, and our whole soul, but with the whole universe in process of unification—is a prayer that can only be made in space-time.[18]

11. *HP*, 209.

12. *HP*, 210.

13. *HP*, 211. He frequently refers to St. Paul's vision of God being "all in all" (1 Cor 15:28), e.g., "Some Notes on the Mystical Sense," (1951), in *TF*, 210.

14. *HP*, 211, 223. Also see *DM*, 93–94. Also "Pantheism and Christianity" (1923), in *CE*, 56–65; "Introduction to the Christian Life" (1944), in *CE*, 171–72.

15. The word "panentheism" is more often associated with a Whiteheadian version of process thought. To my knowledge the word was coined by K. C. F. Krause in 1828 but entered contemporary usage through the writings of Charles Hartshorne for whom God himself is in process. The expression, however, can extend beyond that more limited association.

16. "The Heart of Matter" (1950), in *HM*, 55.

17. *HP*, 212.

18. *HP*, 213.

This supreme Someone, this spiritual, transcendent, and preexistent reality, so essential to religion in the future, is for Teilhard none other than the God incarnate in Jesus Christ.[19]

This God is made more explicit in many of Teilhard's other essays, but particularly in his spiritual treatise, *The Divine Milieu*, whose pages one might say are soaked in his personal God. We have spoken of this essay previously and so ought not devote too much attention to it here. The essay is an attempt to teach us "to see God everywhere," that is "the true God, the Christian God," who "waits for us in things," reminiscent of Aquinas's own questions about the presence of God in things (*ST*, I, q. 8), as well as St. Ignatius's way of finding God in all things,[20] for the world is "full of God,"[21] is indeed a "divine milieu,"[22] formed by the divine omnipresence,[23] in which God shines through, is diaphanous, for the one who sees.[24] Teilhard's is a spirituality that attempts to reconcile "the love of God and a healthy love of the world."[25] Each of us exists "for God,"[26] in whom we are to immerse ourselves,[27] and whom we can find even in death,[28] for all things work unto good for those who love God as St. Paul maintained in his letter to the Romans (8:28).[29] It is God whom we seek in everything.[30] *The Divine Milieu* is permeated with prayers to the living God.

> *Yes, O my God . . . It is You Yourself whom I find, You who make me participate in Your being, You who mould me . . . O God, whose call precedes the very first of our movements, grant me the desire to desire being—that, by means of that divine thirst which is Your gift . . . I am not one of those who say Lord, Lord! with their lips only . . . I shall respond by taking great care never to stifle nor distort nor waste my power to love and to do . . . O God, that at all times You may find me as You desire me and where You would*

19. *HP*, 214, 223.
20. Ignatius, *Spiritual Exercises*, e.g., 235–36 (#39).
21. *DM*, 15, 16, 94.
22. *DM*, especially 89–131. Also see "The Heart of Matter" (1950), in *HM*, 46–47.
23. *DM*, 99.
24. *DM*, 108–12, 14–15; "The Heart of Matter" (1950), in *HM*, 16.
25. *DM*, 21.
26. *DM*, 25, 84.
27. *DM*, 35.
28. *DM*, 54.
29. *DM*, 55, 58.
30. *DM*, 112–21.

> *have me be, that You may lay hold on me fully, both by the Within and the Without of myself . . .*[31]

This passionate love of God (and of the world) is manifest in many of his prayers: "Lord, lock me up within you."[32] It is this God, *both* personal *and* transcendent, who is the basis of Teilhard's optimism, or perhaps better said, of his hope.[33] What is important in Teilhard's approach to a theology of God is that it is not God *or* the world, but rather God *and* the world. This theme runs through many of his essays.[34] Charles Taylor, in *A Secular Age*[35] to which we will give more attention in the next chapter, analyzed the emergence of unbelief in modern times. This is something to which Teilhard, as a scientist, was very attuned, the tendency to set aside religion as not having value within the scientific world view. Already in 1931, in his essay, "The Spirit of the Earth," he writes about humanity's contemporary tendency to sense no need for religion and its exclusion of a personal and transcendent God.[36] On the contrary, however, Teilhard maintained, based on his study of evolution, that God emerges as more necessary than ever.[37] It is true that religion can become an opium, he maintains, but its true function is to spur on the progress of life, to sustain us in our hope.[38]

Although Christianity has lost its appeal for many, since for them the Christian God "looks like a great landowner administering his estates," the truth about Christianity is that it "is neither more nor less than a belief in the unification of the world in God by the Incarnation."[39] We can look later at the critiques of religion and the Christian faith, but this is the context in which Teilhard, and we also, find ourselves. It is thus that Teilhard emphasizes a God of love,[40] not only based on his Christian faith,

31. *DM*, 50–51. Italics in the text.

32. "The Mass on the World" (1923), in *HU*, 34.

33. See "The Grand Option," (1939) in *FM*, 43–44; "Some Reflections on Progress," (1941), in *FM*, 72, 78–79; *DM*, 133–38.

34. E.g., *DM*; "Some Reflections on Progress," (1941), in *FM*, 61–81; "The Heart of the Problem" (1949), in *FM*, 260–69; "Suggestions for a New Theology" (1945), in *CE*, 174–76; and many others.

35. Taylor, *A Secular Age*.

36. "The Spirit of the Earth" (1931), in *HE*, 43.

37. "The Spirit of the Earth," *HE*, 43.

38. "The Spirit of the Earth," *HE*, 44.

39. "Sketch of a Personalistic Universe" (1936), in *HE*, 91.

40. There are a multitude of references in Teilhard to God as love, e.g., "Human Energy" (1937), in *HE*, 157.

but also based on his phenomenology of evolution. "Beneath a surface pessimism, individualism, or juridicism, Christ the King is *already worshipped today as the God of progress and evolution.*"[41] This early way of phrasing it, in contrast to a juridical understanding of Christianity, states as clearly as anything how Teilhard saw God—as the God of evolution.[42] Just as one sees the universe as evolving, so one sees God as creating that universe evolutively. God is immersed not in a static creation but in an evolving one. There is no evolution without God, but also no Creator God who is not immersed in evolution, although God himself does not evolve for God transcends the world he creates. God is "the indispensable 'mover,'"[43] the evolver who transcends the universe but acts from within the "inside" of the universe.

Here one must stop and take notice of a controversial statement in Teilhard, as he notes the role of love in human evolution and one's mystical communion with God. In referring to what we have to offer God, he writes of us: "Whether he [the Christian] lives or dies, *by* his life and *by* his death, he in some sense completes his God, and is at the same time mastered by him."[44] Note that he says, "in some sense." He is not saying that God is lacking in something without us. Yet he wants to affirm that we, the world, creation, are not matters of complete indifference to God. We bring something to God who is not indifferent to the future of creation. This again refers to his favored text from St. Paul's First Letter to the Corinthians in which Jesus hands all over to the Father who is then all in all. We have already stressed this in our discussion of the mystical body of Christ, the intimate relation between the Head and members. As I have said elsewhere,[45] God is perfect without his creation; God in no way needed to create. Creation is a completely free act of God's love. All this Teilhard affirms. Yet, in freely choosing to create, God also chose in that act to desire *in some sense* the response of the beloved and thus in some sense to be incomplete without us, not out of any deficiency on God's part. Whether we speak about creation's bringing some "completion" to God, or "satisfaction," or "giving God glory," we are emphasizing God's investment in creation. The infinitely perfect One chose out of perfect love to be vulnerable *for our sakes*. This is a supreme manifestation of

41. "Sketch of a Personalistic Universe," *HE*, 92. Italics in the original text.

42. See in particular, "The God of Evolution" (1953), in *CE*, 237–43.

43. "The Phenomenon of Spirituality" (1937), in *HE*, 109.

44. "Human Energy" (1937), in *HE*, 155.

45. Goergen, *Power of Love*, 192–213.

God's love, of God *as* love. How we can articulate this mystery remains a challenge, but one that we cannot afford to avoid.

Teilhard returns to this dilemma in several places. In a later essay (1945), Teilhard takes this up again in which he sees the dilemma as insoluble at present but nevertheless a pressing concern for theologians.[46] In one of his last and most autobiographical essays, "The Heart of Matter" (1950), he spoke about God "in the process of 'changing,'" placing the word 'changing' in quotation marks,[47] indicating his continued struggle how best to put the relationship between God and the world in such a way that God does not change and yet in some sense is impacted by creation. God as Omega is not God as God will be at the end of the evolution of things, but rather preexists as a force of attraction for evolution. Nevertheless, God as Alpha and Omega, while being the same God, have different connotations. This is a challenge to classical metaphysics for Teilhard sees in some way that creation must bring some "completion" or "fulfillment" to Absolute Being which is immutable and yet from our point of view awaiting the Pleroma.[48] How best to express this "fulfillment"? Although God himself does not evolve, the God of cosmogenesis, who is "complete" in relation to himself, does possess the power to "grow greater," and *for us* "is continually being born."[49] For Teilhard one cannot allow the fate or future of creation to be a matter of indifference to God who is always Love.

Besides the expression "God of evolution," another Teilhardian way of speaking is the way he talks about the kingdom or reign of God. Contemporary theology and particularly biblical exegesis have placed great emphasis on the importance of eschatology, especially in relationship to the teaching of Jesus, for whom the expression "reign of God" was typical of his way of speaking about God.[50] God, or God's reign, is both here and now. Yet there is still more to come, placing an emphasis on the

46. "Suggestions for a New Theology" (1945), in *CE*, 176–83.

47. "The Heart of Matter" (1950), in *HM*, 53.

48. "The Heart of Matter," in *HM*, 54.

49. "The Heart of Matter," in *HM*, 57–58. In this same essay Teilhard speaks about creation bringing some completion to God and at the same time in the same essay speaks about God complete in himself. He also speaks about God as "evolver" and "evolving" (58), but it is God as evolver that most represents Teilhard's understanding of God. Yet he struggles to find the best way to express that in some way creation brings something to God himself.

50. See Goergen, *Mission of Jesus*, 218–48.

future as well. Teilhard makes reference to the reign of God frequently in his essays, even in titles.[51] Not more common, but more Teilhardian as a way of speaking, however, is the expression "theosphere."[52] We have become familiar with how Teilhard speaks about the universe, with its biosphere, noosphere, Christic sphere, and so all is in the end a theocentric theosphere in which again, according to St. Paul (1 Cor 15:28), God will be all in all. The reign of God is a theosphere, a divine milieu, already realized, especially following upon the Incarnation, but still unfolding, or evolving toward that final consummation, the Pleroma, the Parousia, Omega. For Teilhard God, as well as Christ, is both Alpha and Omega, the beginning and the end, the prime mover, and the final reality. "God, the personal and loving Infinite, is the Source, the motive Force and the End of the Universe."[53] There may be no difference *in* God between Alpha and Omega but there is a significant difference *for* God as we all await the final consummation of all things.

> Cannot a further and final metamorphosis have been in progress since the birth of love in Christianity: the coming to consciousness of an "Omega" in the heart of the noosphere—the circles' motion towards their common center: *the appearance of the "Theosphere"?*[54]

God, for Teilhard, is not only personal and transcendent, but also immanent—the one in whom we live and move and have our being.[55] As we have emphasized often enough, "God is everywhere."[56] Teilhard early, while still a stretcher bearer in the war, describes a deeper realization of this: "I looked around and I saw, as though in an ecstasy, that *through all nature I was immersed in God*," and "The deeper I descend into myself, the more I find God at the heart of my being."[57] At the same time that Teilhard finds God "within" the universe,[58] he also realizes that

51. E.g., "Mastery of the World and the Kingdom of God" (1916), in *WW*, 73–91. Also see "Cosmic Life" (1916), in *WW*, 62; "The Mystical Milieu" (1917), in *WW*, 137.

52. "Human Energy" (1937), in *HE*, 160.

53. "Mastery of the World and the Kingdom of God" (1916), in *WW*, 81. In a similar vein, see "Operative Faith" (1918), in *WW*, 243.

54. "Human Energy" (1937), in *HE*, 160. Emphasis in text.

55. "Cosmic Life" (1916), in *WW*, 47.

56. "Cosmic Life," in *WW*, 60.

57. "Cosmic Life," in *WW*, 60, 61. Italics in original text.

58. "Introduction to the Christian Life" (1944), in *CE*, 160.

the world "does not hold together 'from below' but 'from above.'"[59] God is always transcendent and always immanent, always transcendent and always personal.

> God, I am quite certain, does not hide himself so that we shall have to look for him—any more than he allows us to suffer in order to increase our merit. On the contrary, reaching out to the creation, which is making its way up to him, he works with all his strength to beautify and illuminate it. Like a mother, he watches over his latest-born. But my eyes cannot yet see him.[60]

Although Teilhard's emphasis and concern is on God the Creator, God the Evolver, as Alpha and Omega, God is always the triune God. As I have said, Teilhard does not develop any theology on the inner life of the Trinity but does talk about the missions of the Son and the Spirit in the world, to use traditional language. He is emphatic about the importance of the Trinity.

> In reality, if the concept of the Trinity is properly understood, it can only *strengthen* our idea of divine oneness . . . If God were not "triune" (if, that is, he contained no inner self-distinction) we could not conceive the possibility of his subsisting in himself, independently . . . of his creating (and in consequence being incarnate) without totally immersing himself in the world he brings into being.[61]

In other words, it is the Trinity that grounds and preserves both God's transcendence and God's immanence. In his "Mass on the World," he speaks about the Trinity as Power, Word, and Fire.[62] Teilhard often tends to speak with images. It is quite clear that there is an essential role in Teilhard's vision for the Second Person of the Trinity, the Only Begotten One, Jesus Christ. His vision is christocentric. Christogenesis is like a phylum emergent within the noosphere. Christ is Omega in accord with St. Paul's vision of things. Although it is the cosmic Christ, the total Christ, that is of most interest to Teilhard, he realizes that the total or universal Christ requires the historic Christ, the man Jesus, that Christ

59. "How I Believe" (1934), in *CE*, 113.

60. "How I Believe," in *CE*, 132.

61. "Introduction to the Christian Life" (1944), in *CE*, 157–58. Italics in the original.

62. "The Mass on the World" (1923), in *HM*, 121–22.

"*be born*"[63] into the world. This historic Christ, or Incarnate Word, the child of Bethlehem, is divine.[64] The mission of the Word looms large within an evolutionary world in which the Incarnation is a leap forward.

Teilhard may speak less often, less explicitly, about the Spirit, but the Spirit's mission is equally important. As with St. Paul, he speaks at times almost interchangeably about Christ and the Spirit who is at work in the world. "In very truth, it is God, and God alone whose Spirit stirs up the whole mass of the universe in ferment."[65] In that same early text from the time of the war, the image of fire emerges. Referring to himself, he writes: "The mystic was looking for the devouring fire," the "fire that comes down upon earth," whose descent he awaits.[66] Fire is a particularly strong image in "The Mass on the World": "Blazing Spirit, Fire."[67] As he prays, "Lord Jesus," he passionately continues, "How strange, my God, are the processes your Spirit initiates!" and then returning to "Glorious Lord Christ," referencing the "furnace of fire" which can also connote his devotion to the Sacred Heart of Christ.[68]

There was something deeply traditional about Teilhard, and something radically new. His spirituality was profoundly Ignatian and yet sculpted for a new age. So likewise, his understanding of God. God is clearly the Triune God of Christian faith although he wrote little about the Trinity itself in an explicit way. As with the Christ, God is also Omega—the ultimate center that pulled the universe upward and forward due to its attractive power. Yet this Omega is not impersonal, but very much the personal Lord of history. Teilhard had to struggle to pull together the God with whom he had grown up and the God of evolution that he had discovered along the way. As much as Jesus of Nazareth emphasized in his teaching and preaching the coming reign of God, with the coming of the theosphere that reign had begun. The theosphere is not the birth and evolution of God but rather the culminating state of creation. And it was God who propelled it all along, who provided its energy and moved it.

Yet, although it is not a question of God's evolution in the sense of an objective genitive, as if God is the object of evolution, evolution

63. "Introduction to the Christian Life" (1944), in *CE*, 158. Italics in the original. See *DM*, 94–95.

64. "Introduction to the Christian Life," in *CE*, 158–59.

65. "The Mystical Milieu" (1917), in *WW*, 130.

66. "The Mystical Milieu," in *WW*, 129, 142, 143.

67. "The Mass on the World" (1923), in *HM*, 122.

68. "The Mass on the World," in *HM*, 130–34.

does bring something vitally important to God which Teilhard did not always find easy to express. Creation and its future are not something about which God is indifferent. God has a vital interest in it. He has accompanied it on its way. He wants to bring it home. Yet he allows it to be free. In the semi-autobiographical and quite philosophical essay, written in 1950 towards the end of his life, at almost seventy years of age, he boldly asserts:

> The time had now come when I could see one thing: that, from the depths of the cosmic future as well as from the heights of Heaven, it was still God, it was *always the same God*, who was calling me. It was a *God of the Ahead* who had suddenly appeared athwart *the traditional God of the Above*, so that henceforth we can no longer *worship fully* unless we superimpose those two images so that they form *one*.[69]

This is Teilhard at his most mature, his most free, his most grounded, having suffered much personally as well as at the hands of the church, having forged more carefully his vision, seeing now even more clearly God and the universe at one, not pantheistically but in that deep union which is the culmination based on the evolutionary principle that union differentiates. God now has his universe, and the universe now has its God—which paradoxically was true from the beginning. But we see the struggle that had been there. It *is* the same God, the God of his youth, the God of his ancestors, but this same God we now know as also the God of evolution, not just the God of the universe but of an evolving universe, the God who evolves that universe while not evolving with it. Just as evolution moves *both* upward *and* forward, so God is *both* above *and* ahead of us. Evolution does not flow only in a forward horizontal direction, according to some theory of progress, or along some Marxist line, although Teilhard's worldly vision provided much food for dialogue between Christianity and Marxism,[70] but evolution also ascends as it moves. Omega is *both* Above *and* Ahead. The same God, but now one whom we see more expansively and thus can worship even more fully. There is a God. There is one God. And God is *both* Alpha *and* Omega.

Teilhard treads metaphysical and theological ground. But it is the intuition to which he has come, what he has come to see. This is not a repudiation of classical metaphysics but its development—the

69. "The Heart of Matter" (1950), in *HM*, 53. Emphasis in text.

70. E.g., see Roger Garaudy, *From Anathema to Dialogue*.

incorporation of another insight that needed to be woven into the picture. In other words, creation does not come forth "finished" from God's hands, whereby God is seen primarily as an efficient cause, and creation seen as apart from God: God and the world seen not only as distinguishable but separable. He contemplates the meaning of an evolving creation grounded in the principle of creative union. There is something in the *union* between God and his creation. Classically all of creation participates in God. Creation's very structure is that of participated being, as Aquinas had so strongly emphasized. But there is a new dimension to this participation brought out by the contemplation of the universe *as* evolving, *as* having been created unfinished, *as* still being created evolutively, but an evolution that has a spiritual side to it, an inside all along the way. Yes, creation *is* the effect of God's creative efficient causality, but this causality is not understood now to separate things from God but to bring them more deeply into oneness with him.

TWO COSMOTHEANTHROPIC VISIONS

We have explored, however briefly, the thought of St. Thomas and that of Teilhard de Chardin. Both were, in their own ways, and in their own times, visionaries. Each had a vision of the whole. Each vision could also be described, to coin a word, cosmotheanthropic.[71]

We emphasized Aquinas's anti-Manichean theology of creation in the first part of his *Summa Theologiae*. His theology has been called creation centered. Likewise, Pierre Teilhard de Chardin's vision was cosmocentric. His cosmic sense and respect for the world of matter loom large and is also at the opposite pole of any Manichean tendency. Both recognize God's omnipresence throughout creation. Already in question eight of the *prima pars*, Aquinas asserts the extent and varying degrees of God's presence in the world. One of Teilhard's earliest essays (1916) was entitled "Cosmic Life," written during his years as a stretcher-bearer in the First World War. For Aquinas there is a hierarchy of being. Living

71. The word "theandric," well known in mystical theology, coined by St. Dionysius the Areopagite, referred to the joint interaction between the human and divine natures, particularly in reference to Jesus Christ. Raimon Panikkar, *Cosmotheandric Experience*, in the twentieth century, coined the words "cosmotheandric" and "theanthropocosmic" to express an unconfused unity among the divine, the human and the material. I prefer the word "cosmotheanthropic" to express the distinguishable but inseparable, interconnectedness of these three.

beings have more being than inanimate beings. A sentient soul *is* more (or configures more) than a vegetative soul. A rational animal surpasses pre-rational animals in their participation in being and thus are creatures not only in whom we find traces of the divine but in fact are created to the image of God (*ST*, I, q. 93). Teilhard de Chardin would not disagree with this natural hierarchy within the created order as it unfolds evolutively.

In that same question 8 of the *prima pars* (a. 3, *ad* 4), Aquinas acknowledged not only that human nature surpassed all other created natures by its capacity for thought and free action but that it also surpassed other creatures by the way in which grace builds upon that nature.

> No other perfection, except grace, added to substance, renders God present in anything as the object known and loved; therefore, only grace constitutes a special mode of God's existence in things.

Intellect, will, and supernatural grace make God's creation and Aquinas's thought not only creation centered but also anthropocentric. Within creation there is that unique creature which attracts our attention, what Teilhard called *le phénomène humain*. Both Thomas's vision and Teilhard's vision are cosmic, cosmocentric, grounded in the created order, and at the same time cognizant that the human creature surpasses all other creatures in what or who we *are*. The visions are *both* cosmic *and* anthropic.[72] Of immense importance to each is also the role of Jesus Christ.

In that same question 8 of the *prima pars* (a. 3, *ad* 4), Aquinas continues: "There is, however, another special mode of God's existence in man, by union, which will be treated of in its own place," namely in the *tertia pars* where he discusses the grace of union, or the hypostatic union, by means of which grace Jesus Christ is a Divine Person incarnate in history as a human being. The three parts of Aquinas's *Summa* structure his vision accordingly: (1) God's presence in all of creation; (2) God's unique presence in the human creature through grace and the human being's capacity therefore to live a truly humane life of virtue; and (3) God's presence in the humanity of Jesus Christ through which grace flows out to others in his body. For Teilhard this structure is simply that of (1) cosmogenesis; (2) anthropogenesis or noogenesis; and (3) christogenesis. Creation itself is christocentric, which is how Aquinas's thought unfolds and

72. I am not speaking here of the cosmological anthropic principle as such. See Dodds, *Divine Action*, 72–77. In whatever way the anthropic principle may be operative in God's evolving universe, for Teilhard God is involved in that universe both as efficient and as final cause.

Teilhard's understanding of evolution envisions it. The whole structure of the universe (whether from a Thomistic or Teilhardian perspective) is that of an *exitus* and *reditus*. All comes from God; all returns to God. All exists in and through Christ who turns all creation upon its completion over to his heavenly Father (1 Cor 15:28).

> Christ has been raised from the dead, the first fruits of those who have died. For since death came through a human being, the resurrection of the dead has also come through a human being; for as all die in Adam, so all will be made alive in Christ. But each in his own order: Christ the first fruits, then at his coming those who belong to Christ. Then comes the end, when he [Christ] hands over the kingdom to God the Father, after he has destroyed every ruler and every authority and power. For he [Christ] must reign until he has put all his enemies under his feet. The last enemy to be destroyed is death. For "God has put all things in subjection under his [Christ's] feet." But when it says, "All things are put in subjection," it is plain that this does not include the one who put all things in subjection under him. When all things are subjected to him, then the Son himself will also be subjected to the one who put all things in subjection under him, so that God may be all in all. (1 Cor 15:20–28)

Teilhard de Chardin and Thomas Aquinas are both visionaries. Both visions are cosmotheanthropic: creation centered, at the core of which is the human phenomenon, grounded in God's presence in Christ. Christ is Alpha and Omega. All comes from God through the eternal Word; all returns to God through the incarnate Word (John 1:3, 14, 16). One becomes aware of the differentiated but inseparable unity of the natural world, the human world, and the divine world. "In Christ all the fullness of God was pleased to dwell, and through him God was pleased to reconcile to himself all things, whether on earth or in heaven, by making peace through the blood of his cross" (Col 1:19–20).

PART TWO

Toward a Renewed Humanism

9

Humanism in an Age of Unbelief

We have pondered all too briefly two innovative thinkers. Their theologies are not incompatible. Neither do they simply overlap. What is important is the challenge they are to each other, and to us, to think through how to respond to today's concerns while remaining grounded in the tradition that has been handed on to us. What I wish to do in the next two chapters is consider the contribution of each to a Christian humanism that can meet the challenges of our secular age, a Christian humanism as a component of a renewed evangelization, a Christian humanism that incarnates the gospel in our world today. Humanism is concerned with the question, what does it mean to be human? Christianity is concerned with the question: what does it mean to live in Christ? How different are these questions? The word "humanism" itself can refer to a variety of ways of understanding what it means to be human; in other words, it is used analogously.[1] The following reflections manifest the desire to move beyond ideologies within which we confine ourselves and to build bridges across what may seem at times unbridgeable divides. We have here two visionaries. What is it they saw? Where do those visions coalesce? Whether they do or not, each has a contribution to make. It is up to us to ensure that each contribution is not lost. As the Gospel of Matthew put it, as I have previously said: "Every scribe who has been

1. R. W. Southern also distinguishes varied understandings of the world "humanism." *Medieval Humanism*, 29–33; *Scholastic Humanism*, 1:17–22.

trained for the kingdom of heaven is like the master of a household who brings out of his treasure what is new and what is old" (13:52).

My conviction is that we need a renewed emphasis on Christian humanism, at the heart of which will be Christianity's mystical tradition. Teilhard himself saw the need for both, as have several twentieth century interpreters of St. Thomas. At the same time, when engaging significant critical questions, we need to hear other interlocutors as well. Let us begin, however, with Thomas and Teilhard, and then attune ourselves to an awareness of context, culture, and dialogue. By way of example in the final chapter, we will ponder three current challenges to the Christian vision.

THOMAS AND TEILHARD RECONSIDERED

Anyone genuinely attentive to Aquinas cannot help but be impressed with the beauty and profundity of his thinking. They may not find pleasure in his style, its scholastic character, but they must acknowledge that he has given us an incredible synthesis, coherent, consistent, and open ended. For some who followed him, it may have become a closed system, but Aquinas himself never stopped thinking and was never afraid to change his mind.[2] One might disagree with some insight or conclusion of his but not with the wisdom contained in the whole. It is no wonder that Aquinas has been a beacon for the centuries that followed. His *Summa* is, as he himself understood it, a holy teaching, *sacra doctrina*, a graced outpouring of wisdom, and at the same time mere straw in comparison to the real thing. Although he lived after the close of the patristic age, he was in touch with the thinking of the Fathers, whom he greatly respected and who had great influence on him, especially Saint Augustine. He was also more than familiar with the perennial philosophical questions and the efforts there had been to ponder them. Yet he was quite capable of forming opinions of his own.

At the same time, granted Thomas's genius, he lived in a century removed from our own. His questions are not always ours; and not all of ours were his. As Thomas was grounded in the natural philosophy and natural science of Aristotle, our day requires being attuned, not

2. For example, he changed his mind as his thought developed on topics like the motive of the Incarnation (*ST*, III, 1, 3), whether Christ on earth had acquired knowledge (*ST*, III, 9, 4; 12, 2), and whether there was one *esse* or two in Christ (*ST*, III, 17), as mentioned in chapter 6, as well as on other questions as well. He would say, "although I wrote differently, it must be said that . . ." (*ST*, III, 9, 4).

uncritically of course, to the philosophies and sciences of nature as they have continued to unfold.[3] Looking at Aquinas through the lens of modern and contemporary thought discloses not weaknesses or disagreements as such, granted there will be those, but rather the need for supplemental insights, new emphases, even some revision. There is little in the theology of Aquinas that is to be set aside, but it is nevertheless a theology that must remain in conversation with modern and post-modern currents of thought in order to be helpful.

Aquinas's insights into the unknowable but Self-revealing Trinitarian God; his appreciation of the universe as a creation of that God, which creation is both intelligible and genuinely good, rich in diversity, all having come from God and returning to God; the tremendous significance of the creation of intellectual beings, those purely spiritual and those embodied who were created in God's image; the reality of evil, the story of sin, and creation's not only natural dependency on God but also, in the light of sin's history, its need for something redemptive from beyond itself; the freely given gift of grace, its variety, along with the affirmation of human freedom and the challenges to living a life of moral virtue; the theological virtues with assistance from the gifts of the Holy Spirit; the grace of Christ as Head of the church, that same Christ, fully human, God's Word Incarnate, who was born of Mary, died and rose from the dead, whose death merited the grace that overflows through the sacramental life of the church to all who believe, whether explicitly or implicitly; the *mysterium Christi* in which we are participants in our pilgrimage back to God—all this Aquinas unfolds for us in great detail and with great precision of thought.

We might still inquire further what Aquinas's major strengths are, what the gifts are. We can name, in particular, the gift of his faith, in troubled times, his total commitment to the truth of the Catholic faith and the need to defend and explicate it; his commitment to Truth, his Order's *Veritas*, that was his guiding light, as well as to *Caritas*, for he

3. Feser, *Aristotle's Revenge* is a robust defense of the continued relevance of Aristotelian science. He writes, however: "That certain key aspects of Aristotelian physics have been falsified is not in dispute. However, . . . the moderns have been all too quick to throw the Aristotelian metaphysical baby out with the physical bathwater . . . Geocentrism, the ancient theory of the elements, and the notion that objects have specific places to which they naturally move, are examples of Aristotelian ideas in physics that have been decisively superseded. But the theory of actuality and potentiality, the doctrine of the four causes, and the hylemorphic analysis of material objects . . . have . . . abiding value as elements of a sound philosophy of nature" (222).

knew as well as any of faith, hope, and love and that the greatest of these is love, which was manifest in both his respect for all interlocutors, even those not of his faith, as well as in his polemics; his capacity for speculative thought, manifest in the precision of his language, his concern for such precision, as in his ability to make distinctions before drawing conclusions, seeking wisdom from all sources and thus often a both/and appreciation of how truth is best articulated, along with a willingness to change his mind and acknowledge it so; his respect for the Bible as the source and arbiter of theological disputes, and a careful reading and exposition of those texts which was his life task; and thus a spirituality focused on the Word of God: all these and many other qualities mark him as a *Magister regens* still.

As we know, however, a person's strengths can also be the source of his or her weaknesses. Aquinas's gift for precision in language can produce that which is satisfying to the mind but may fail to stir the heart, as his poetry does. Questions disputed today, an openness to which Aquinas himself would be hospitable, include among others how best to understand the Fall in the light of creation's evolution; God's desire that all be saved through faith in Christ alongside religious traditions other than those that are Christian; moral questions due to newly acquired knowledge and possibilities; the nature of the glorified, spiritual, risen body; and God's action in the universe, especially through the sacraments: with all of these Aquinas would desire to be engaged. He himself would affirm that it is not so much what he thought but what he sought that is important. Even if one disagrees with Aquinas's opinion on any one of the myriad topics that he addressed, this will not constitute as such a weakness on Aquinas's part but rather an appreciation of the continually developing character of the theological enterprise to which each generation must give itself as a highly valued and responsible task.

Following upon Aquinas's death, there was strong opposition to his teaching as well as robust support.[4] We have spoken previously of the condemnation of 219 propositions on March 7, 1277, by Stephen Tempier, the Bishop of Paris, which involved some of Thomas's opinions although he was in no way directly implicated; also a similar condemnation by Robert Kilwardby, the Dominican Archbishop of Canterbury, on March 18 of that same year, more clearly aimed at some of the teachings of Thomas; followed by similar condemnations by Kilwardby's successor as Archbishop

4. For further details see chapter 1, as well as Torrell, *Saint Thomas Aquinas*, 1:296–326; and Weisheipl, *Friar Thomas d'Aquino*, 331–50.

of Canterbury, John Pecham, a Franciscan, manifesting Franciscan opposition to what was considered the overly Aristotelian teachings of Aquinas; as well as an effort around 1279 by William de la Mare, also a Franciscan, to correct and refute some of Thomas's errors. Although there were efforts to try and block Thomas's canonization in 1323, the Order of Preachers came to his defense. All this only indicates how Thomas's creative theological enterprise did not go unchallenged and was vigorously disputed within the first half century after Thomas died.

No thinker simply repeats borrowed thoughts.[5] New thoughts, however, risk resistance. They push against gravity. The more novel, the more profound, the more untested by time, the stronger the resistance. Who are you to think differently than we have always thought! Aquinas himself faced this very challenge. As a wise sage, he went into the deeper recesses of his mind and brought out something old and something new (Matt 13:52).[6] Faithful to tradition, highly respectful of it, he was also innovative. A new and brilliant synthesis was born. It is to be expected that it would be resisted. But if we ask, what was Aquinas's strength, his real gift, what is it that he has passed on to generations to come, it would be that he gave us a coherent vision of all things in the light of Christ. Revelation complemented reason which benefited from it. Reason understood itself as open to inspiration from beyond itself and thus reached new heights. Wisdom from above was channeled into forms that made it accessible. A new starting point was made for future reflection on the cosmos, on humanity, on God, a starting point that later thinkers would have to carefully tread upon and beyond. No greater synthesis has yet been given us even if the test of time reveals a need for its further development. Modern science offered a new mode of thought. Whatever the limitations to Thomas's synthesis may be, they are not so much on his thoughts as such but on the period of history from which he speaks to us. We have access to information he did not have and questions he did not ask.

As with Aquinas, so with Teilhard de Chardin. After Teilhard's death, there was strong opposition to his teaching as well as robust support. As with Aquinas, Teilhard's creative enterprise did not go unchallenged and

5. Kühlewind, *Normal to Healthy*, 29, asks the question: "When was the last time you had a new thought?"

6. Emerson offers a comparable image, that of a staircase: "There are stairs below us, which we seem to have ascended," and "stairs above us" or stairs still to be climbed. Or as others have put it, we stand on the shoulders of those who have gone before us. "Experience," in *Essential Writings*, 307.

was also disputed. His writings, largely published posthumously, were the object of an official warning (*monitum*) by the Vatican's Holy Office, now known as the Congregation for the Doctrine of the Faith, in June of 1962, seven years after Teilhard's death and the publication in French of *Le phénomène humain*, which warning about ambiguities and errors in the writings of Teilhard was reaffirmed in 1981. In 2017 the Vatican's Pontifical Council for Culture formally requested that Pope Francis lift the disclaimer against the writings. All the popes since the Vatican Council have quoted Father Teilhard affirmatively, and it is generally understood that Teilhard's thought had an influence on Pope John XXIII and the Second Vatican Council's Decree on the Church in the Modern World. The number of secondary sources—biographies, commentaries, expositions of aspects of Teilhard's thought—that appeared within a decade of Teilhard's death, and since, testify as well to robust support.[7]

The evolving nature of God's creation, which has a purpose, a direction which lay up ahead as well as up above, in other words having both immanent as well as transcendent dimensions, unfolding and continuing to unfold in stages with an interplay of unification and differentiation; at the center of which creation is the human phenomenon, having crossed the threshold into hominization, the continuing evolution of which undergirds both personal and social processes of increased individualization or personalization, excentration or socialization; within which human sexuality takes on new meanings, morality faces new challenges, and death is recognized as a change of state. This evolving creation in which moral and spiritual life take on cosmic dimensions and address the needs of this world as well as its transcendent future, this creation for one who has eyes to see becomes a divine milieu. Into this cosmos's noosphere, Christ is born, and evolution takes another leap. The cosmos finds its ultimate fulfillment in a Christ through whom God and the world become one as St. Paul envisioned it. No creation apart from Christ, and in the present order no Christ without creation, as Christ's redemptive Incarnation takes place amid a world pulled and pushed towards something, towards Someone, who is here now sacramentally and yet awaits us eschatologically. All these emphases can speak to the modern mind.

This may be the time to say something about how to read Teilhard in contrast to how one reads Aquinas whose language is scholastic,

7. Works by Barbour, Chauchard, Cuénot, de Lubac, Faricy, King, Mooney, North, Raven, Rideau, Schoonenberg, Smulders, Speaight, Wilders would be only some of the names that could number in the hundreds.

philosophical, precise, delightful to the mind. Teilhard's language often tends to be poetic, exuberant but less able to be pinned down, at times the language of science stretched beyond what science itself can say, raising philosophical questions without attempting to resolve them completely but rather enticing one to ponder something further, struggling to help us to see what perhaps cannot be said, hence having a mystical quality. One must sift it to see what is being said.[8] Teilhard uses language to help us *see*;[9] Aquinas in order to help us *understand*. Aquinas's language signifies; Teilhard's language evokes. Aquinas communicates with great care the vision he has of God. Teilhard finds language at times a constraint. He struggles to break through its limits. Aquinas speaks of God with analogy; Teilhard with ecstasy,[10] although at times Teilhard clearly takes the role of theologian or philosopher and Aquinas that of poet and mystic.[11] Different styles predominate at different times for each, even if one style has prominence more often for one than for the other. Alfred North Whitehead had once written: "Philosophy begins in wonder. And, at the end, when philosophic thought has done its best, the wonder remains."[12]

One can also raise the question for whom each wrote. Did Thomas indeed write his *Summa* as an introductory text for his fellow Dominicans? Teilhard had in mind unbelievers who were often his associates. As he began *The Divine Milieu*, he wrote:

> This book is not specifically addressed to Christians who are firmly established in their faith and have nothing more to learn about its beliefs. It is written for the waverers, both inside and outside; that is to say for those who, instead of giving themselves wholly to the Church, either hesitate on its threshold or turn away in the hope of surpassing it.[13]

8. This quality of Teilhard's writings has been noted by Cuénot, *Teilhard de Chardin*, 40–42; Rideau, *Thought of Teilhard*, 273–76; de Lubac, *Eternal Feminine*; Sarah Appleton-Weber, "Teilhard's Transforming Thought: Editor-Translator's Introduction" to Teilhard's *Human Phenomenon*, xxvi–xxviii, xxxi.

9. Recall Teilhard's prologue to *The Human Phenomenon*: "These pages represent an effort *to see*" (*HP*, 3).

10. On Teilhard and analogy see the previous chapter, as well as de Lubac, *Eternal Feminine*, 66–76.

11. E.g., see Murray, *Aquinas at Prayer*.

12. *Modes of Thought*, 232.

13. *DM*, 11. He mentions this again on p. 14.

At the same time, *The Divine Milieu* was his major spiritual treatise, containing a matured reflection on the Christian life. In a later essay, "The Zest for Living," while speaking about the evolutionary role for religion, he did not see atheism itself as the major challenge, but rather an unsatisfied theism.

> We are surrounded by a certain sort of pessimists who continually tell us that our world is foundering in atheism. But should we not rather say that what it is suffering from is *unsatisfied theism*? Men, you say, no longer want God; but are you quite sure that what they are rejecting is not simply the image of a God who is too insignificant to nourish in us this concern to survive and super-live to which the need to worship may ultimately be reduced?[14]

Today of course atheism is a different kind of challenge than when Teilhard wrote those words in 1950. Yet Teilhard does not see an evolutionary framework meaning the demise of religion. Teilhard's concern, however, differs from that of Thomas who introduced his *Summa* thus:

> Because the Master of Catholic Truth ought not only to teach the proficient, but also to instruct beginners . . . we propose in this book to treat of whatever belongs to the Christian Religion, in such a way as may tend to the instruction of beginners.[15]

We see in Thomas the concerns of a teacher who desires to present his material systematically. We also see the concerns of someone writing 700 years before Teilhard in an age of belief in contrast to Teilhard writing in an age of unbelief.

What did Teilhard himself think of Thomas? In a 1929 essay, he recognizes the intellectual foundation on which we are to build, namely that of Plato, Aristotle, and St. Thomas. Thomas was someone on whose shoulders we stand but also someone on whom to build. Teilhard wrote: "Although Aristotle, Plato, and St. Thomas may well have been, individually, more powerful thinkers than any we could name today, yet not one of them saw the world as we now see it."[16] The Thomism with which Teilhard was most familiar, however, would have been a neo-scholastic version prior to the resurgence of historical studies of Thomas with the *ressourcement* following the Second Vatican Council. At the same time, he

14. "The Zest for Living" (1950), *AE*, 239–40. Emphasis in text.
15. See the "Prologue" to *ST*.
16. "The Sense of Man" (1929), *TF*, 14.

was drawn toward the openness in the Thomism manifest in the thought and writings of Antonin Sertillanges, OP, to whom he wrote in 1934:

> I have just been reading your excellent little book, *Dieu ou Rien*, which has just landed on our distant shores. Let me tell you how delighted I have been with it. You are beginning at last, and in a tone so measured and authoritative, to make people hear the word that for so long I have dreamt of hearing echoing openly through the church.[17]

In the work, *St. Thomas Aquinas and His Work*, Sertillanges had expressed his own desire for an approach to the thought of St. Thomas that would have resonated with that of Teilhard. Sertillanges saw Thomas as "a humanist in the best sense of the word," as "a genius in his treatment of the mystic life." He continued: "It is not enough to re-edit Thomism and defend it vigorously: we must rejuvenate it"; and with some hyperbole, "We need a Thomism that will be to S. Thomas' work what the New Testament is to the Old."[18] For Teilhard, Thomas helps us to clarify our thinking but does not confine it. The sage goes into the storeroom and brings out something old and something new, the age-old truths of the Catholic faith in dialogue with the discoveries of modern science.

Aquinas's philosophical theology has had centuries for refinement, refutation, reformulation, revision, and contemplation. It has met the test of time while at the same time its long history is being revisited. What of Teilhard's insights will remain, indeed how they will have been reconceived 750 years from now, remains to be seen. He himself would assume that what he presents will continue to unfold and evolve. Nevertheless, questions are asked of Teilhard's vision. Is it naively optimistic, utopian, embedded in some discredited theory of progress?[19] Does he take evil

17. See de Lubac, *Religion of Teilhard*, 97. On Sertillanges, see O'Meara and Philibert, *Scanning the Signs*, 1–16. For another translation of the above text, see pp. 9–10. Reference to Sertillanges is also found in Smulders, *Design of Teilhard*, 56.

18. Sertillanges, *St. Thomas Aquinas*, 65, 86, 143, 150 for the references in the text.

19. Some have seen an overly optimistic or utopian flavor in Teilhard's vision. At its base, however, is a theology of hope. He certainly realized that the future for evolution is not something guaranteed, even if the movement forward is irreversible. "For example, no factor in evolution known to our experience can make it clear that our human race *was bound to* succeed: nor is there any guarantee, immanent in progress, that can insure mankind for the future against any irrational cataclysm" ("Creative Union" [1917], *WW*, 160–61). On evolution's irreversibility, see "How I Believe," (1939), *CE*, 108–13; "My Fundamental Vision" (1948), *TF*, 185–88; "The Heart of Matter" (1950), *HM*, 38. Teilhard distinguishes his understanding from "the nineteenth century's often childish worship of progress" ("The Sense of Man" [1929], *TF*, 21) while at the same

seriously and personal redemption as important?[20] Is Teilhard's view of history, that is of evolution, open to an apocalyptic interpretation?[21] The cosmos, according to Teilhard, is blessed by the God of creation. The human person has a dignity beyond every other prehuman creature; the moment of hominization is transformative. The interconnectedness of all creation is made manifest. Christ takes his place within creation and not apart from it as all creation yearns for its fulfillment in him. Yet is Omegalization faithful to the biblical picture of "the End"?[22] How do time and eternity intersect in Teilhard's thought, an eternal realm that knows not time and therefore evolution? How do we live "in time" and yet "in eternity" simultaneously? These are only some of the questions that are bound to come to mind.

THEOLOGY, CULTURE, AND DIALOGUE

One question, for both Teilhard and Thomas, is how to see the Christian message in relationship to the culture in which one finds oneself. The interaction between faith and culture was an important theological topic for Pope St. John Paul II.[23] In the interaction between the gospel and

time holding firmly to a "*belief in human progress*" ("Cosmic Life" [1916], *WW*, 380), grounded in his faith in the Transcendent as a basis for hope: "Having clarified our ideas, let us see what action they require of us. If progress is to continue, it will not do so of its own accord. *Evolution by the very mechanism of its syntheses, charges itself with an ever-growing measure of freedom.* If indeed an almost limitless field of action lies open to us in the future, what shall our moral dispositions be, as we contemplate this march ahead? I can think of two, which may be summarized in six words: *a great hope held in common*" ("Some Reflections on Progress" [1941], *FM*, 72). In other words, our faith in a future for humanity involves a choice, or choices, we must make. See "Some Reflections on Progress," 74–81; and "The Grand Option" (1945), *FM*, 37–60.

20. In chapter 7 we discussed Teilhard's approach to the mystery of evil and redemption and will discuss again shortly his theology of atonement.

21. On the apocalyptic strain in Christian eschatology, and its contrast to a more prophetic eschatology, see Goergen, *Mission of Jesus*, 68–83, 177–204. We do not know how the final end will come. Neither an apocalyptic vision nor any theory of progress can tell us. The *Catechism of the Catholic Church*, #675, does teach a final trial *for the Church* before the Second Coming of Christ.

22. This is a question to which Jacques Maritain was particularly sensitive and on which point he was critical of Teilhard, to which we shall come later in this chapter.

23. See Pope John Paul II's encyclicals, *Slavorum Apostoli*, ##21–22; *Redemptoris Missio*, ##31–40, 52, 57; *Centesimus Annus*, ##44–52; *Fides et Ratio*, ##36–42, 64–79; along with many other references among his talks, such as his message for the World Day of Peace.

culture, does one view Christianity in tension with culture, as beyond culture, as interactive to the mutual benefit of each? How would Thomas and Teilhard understand this relationship? This topic was given attention by H. Richard Niebuhr in his *Christ and Culture*.[24] Niebuhr organized varied theological approaches into five categories: (1) Christianity as over against culture, in opposition to each other, in an either/or way, such as may have been the situation for early Christians in a time of persecution or even the path of early monasticism as we find it in the desert father, St. Antony; (2) Christianity and culture in a paradoxical relationship, where they are not mutually exclusive but neither are they easily reconciled, less dualistic than the first category but nevertheless still in tension, perhaps as we find in the anguished existentialism of Kierkegaard or even earlier in the thought of St. Paul; (3) Christianity as transformative of culture, thus the relationship being seen in a more positive way, slightly different from the second category, but still conscious of the dualism of sin and grace, perhaps as in St. Augustine; (4) Christianity being above culture, but not outside it, where grace builds on nature and does not destroy it, where faith and reason have respect for each other, where one renders unto Caesar what is Caesar's and unto God what is God's (Matt 20:21), a both/and approach which the previous two categories are as well but to different degrees; and (5) a Christ of culture, where Christianity gives way to culture, accommodates culture to the detriment of the gospel, such as we find in civil religion and in some forms of liberal Protestantism, in which the offensiveness of the cross of Christ is put to the side, the opposite of the first category with Christianity here being compromised, the religion of a Thomas Jefferson or of the Enlightenment.

We know that such efforts to categorize responses of faith to culture have limitations. Yet Niebuhr's schema can highlight some important questions. What is the relationship between faith and reason, grace and nature, redemption and creation? How polemic, how irenic, is a Christian to be vis-a-vis the society in which one finds oneself? What is the difference between a Tertullian and a Clement of Alexandria? Do we participate in the political life of a secular nation or absent ourselves from it? What is the relationship between church and state? What does Athens have to do with Jerusalem? How world affirming or how world rejecting must we be? What ought our attitude to "the world" be? Answers to these questions change over time and depend on the socio-cultural context in

24. Niebuhr, *Christ and Culture*.

which one finds oneself. The response of St. Benedict to the world was not the same as that of St. Dominic, nor the response of Karl Rahner the same as that of Karl Barth. How do we see the God of Jesus Christ in relationship to the socio-cultural context in which we find ourselves? Context is important, as is the case with Aquinas's medieval world and Teilhard's modern world. What does it mean to *be* church in the *modern* world? The response may also vary depending on whether we are speaking more theoretically and theologically about the relationship or in terms of Christian praxis. Even in the Bible we find varied responses to our questions. We see this even within the Johannine corpus. "For God so loved the world that he gave his only Son . . . For God sent the Son into the world, not to condemn the world, but that the world might be saved through him" (John 3:16–17). "Do not love the world or the things in the world. If anyone loves the world, love for the Father is not in him" (1 John 1:15).

Much of the Catholic intellectual tradition is at home along the lines of Niebuhr's fourth category above. This would be true of both Aquinas and Teilhard. This is not to say that such a category does justice to a Dorothy Day, an Oscar Romero, a Franz Jägerstätter, a Saint Perpetua or a Saint Lawrence, or the Vietnamese martyrs of the eighteenth and nineteenth centuries. Catholic life thrives in different cultures and across different eras. Hence there is the need for social, cultural, and contextual analysis. Yet, going back to the great theologians of Alexandria, Antioch, and Cappadocia we see a respect for philosophy, reason, nature as well as revelation, faith, and grace. These realities are not opposed to each other but complement each other, each recognizing its limits. Aquinas struggled to make the truth of the Catholic faith recognized as reasonable even if not something to which reason by itself could attain. His was a world abounding with new learning. Teilhard recognized the role and the limits of science in a world that had weathered the scientific age whose new learning was here to stay. Both, in other words, were on the side of faith *and* reason, religion *and* science, God *and* the world, transcendence *and* immanence. These seeming polarities are compatible and do not contradict each other. Both Aquinas and Teilhard engaged wholeheartedly with the culture or world in which they found themselves. One thing that differentiates them, however, is the world of which each was a part. Each wanted to make sense of the data of Christian faith. Each needs to be read contextually.

A lacuna in the syntheses of both Thomas and Teilhard, because they are syntheses and present the big picture, is an inability at times to be as attentive to the existentiality of human life. Thomas's cosmological, metaphysical, and theological vision cover the gamut of God, the world, and the human person's quest for happiness, but even his perspicacious and still relevant theology of virtue cannot always do justice to the individuality of human experience in *angst* before the living God. Likewise, Teilhard's cosmic and scientific perspective, committed as it is to the centrality of the human phenomenon and the mystery of Christ, is wide in scope. For Teilhard, even a historical perspective is narrow within an expansive Christ-centered cosmos. He does give witness to existential pain in his letters and his plea for hope within *The Divine Milieu*, yet both thinkers can be complemented by reading Christian existentialists. Teilhard and Gabriel Marcel interacted on various occasions in varied formats and did not agree. It would be refreshing to have been privy to their interactions.[25] Teilhard was aware for sure of pathos in the human story, but Dostoyevsky delivers it. One can only ask so much of any visionary, however.

One of my motivations for writing this book has been the promotion of dialogue between tradition and modernity, between religion and science, between faith and reason, with the goal of building bridges among those searching for truth. In a time when the human being could as easily be described as an irrational animal as much as a rational animal, I consider it important to promote conversation among views that at first glance may seem irreconcilably different. I chose Aquinas and Teilhard because they are the two thinkers about whom I am most knowledgeable, because I have learned much from each of them, because I have been challenged by each of them, and because each has been held in his own way in high esteem. Although they differ in many respects, they also agree in many, and in what may be considered most important for our period of history. Each of them has a contribution to make to a renewed Christian humanism.

Jonathan Sacks, an Orthodox Rabbi who served as the Chief Rabbi of the United Hebrew Congregations of the British Commonwealth from 1991 to 2013, in a still highly relevant book, *The Dignity of Difference: How To Avoid the Clash of Civilizations*, wrote in 2002: "Conversation, the heartbeat of democratic politics, is dying and with it our chances of

25. Cuénot, *Teilhard de Chardin*, 251–53, 258, 260–61.

civic, let alone global peace."[26] He also wrote, in response to the question of how we can live with different moral perspectives and yet sustain an overarching sense of community:

> The answer . . . is *conversation*—not mere debate but the disciplined act of communicating (making my views intelligible to someone who does not share them) and listening (entering into the inner world of someone whose views are opposed to my own). Each is a genuine form of respect, of paying attention to the other, of conferring value on his or her opinions even though they are not mine. In a debate one side wins, the other loses, but both are the same as before. In a conversation neither side loses, and both are changed, because they now know what reality looks like from a different perspective. That is not to say that either gives up its previous convictions. That is not what conversation is about. It does mean, however, that I may now realize that I must make space for another deeply held belief, and if my own case has been compelling, the other side may understand that it too must make space for mine.[27]

What would a conversation look like between an unsurpassed medieval theologian whose philosophical acumen was extraordinary and a twentieth century geologist and paleontologist whose commitment to scientific truth was as important to him as his unsurpassed commitment to Christian faith, whose primary dialogue partners were often non-believers? How often have we not emphasized the need for dialogue? How often are we able to achieve it?[28] The bibliography on dialogue is extensive. Scott Steinkerchner, OP, in *Beyond Agreement*, approaches the topic from the perspective of interreligious dialogue, but his approach is applicable elsewhere. In a separate article, using the analogy of a riverbed that changes over time and yet remains the same riverbed, he wrote about dialogue that does not seek agreement on all fronts but nevertheless is impacted by the dialogue itself. We are changed even if we remain the same.

> A riverbed guides the water in the river, governing its flow. In the same way our thinking is guided by what we already know. In time, the riverbed of thoughts shifts and changes as new

26. Sacks, *Dignity of Difference*, 3.

27. Sacks, *Dignity of Difference*, 83. Emphasis in text.

28. Another prolific Jewish author for whom dialogue remained significant was Martin Buber. See *I and Thou*; the recent biography, Mendes-Flohr, *Martin Buber*; and its review by Patrick Jordan.

> ideas are carried by the current and deposited while other ideas are washed away. What was once a guide to our thinking can at other times become an object of our thought. Like the rocks of the riverbed, particular beliefs and dogmas are held in place by what surrounds them. Some might appear to be bedrock, but over time, erosion can dramatically change the contours of the river and even wear through bedrock. Through all these changes, the river remains, defined by its ever-changing bed—our system of thought.[29]

Without seeking complete agreement, through deepened understanding, our own current of thought or synthesis can be impacted for the good by openness to conversation with others. Dialogue among varied theological perspectives will be important to the witness that the Christian faith offers the world. It will also be important if we are to offer a genuinely Christian humanism to our twenty-first century.

CHRISTIAN HUMANISM REVISITED

The Christian Churches today are called upon to demonstrate that their message is humane, more humane than that of secular humanisms, and that a theistic humanism is the only truly humane humanism there is. They need to show Christianity's human face, just as God chose to manifest himself among us through his humanity. The Gospel with its emphasis on both God and neighbor has recognized that there can be no true knowledge of God that does not manifest itself in love of neighbor, whether one goes back to the Hebrew prophets or up to St. Paul and St. John (Gal 5:14; 1 John 3:17–18, 4:20–21). The Catholic Church has a long tradition of corporal works of mercy and institutions of charity—the Church with a human face. How Christian faith's humanistic dimension became blurred while secularism arose is something to which we will turn shortly. At the core of Teilhard de Chardin's teaching, as well as that of Aquinas, it is not Christianity *or* humanism, but Christianity *and* humanism. A theistic humanism is not only a viable humanism but a preferable one. There cannot be a profound philosophical humanism that is not grounded in the transcendent. An atheistic humanism is a false humanism. No evangelical witness to the Christian faith can downplay God's love for the human, or fail to communicate God's desire that

29. Steinkerchner, "Exploring Other Rivers," 10–11.

humanity flourish, or that God desires nothing but good for those created in God's image. The search for God and the search for the human is one search. One cannot be found without the other. It is to a renewed humanism that both Aquinas and Teilhard have something to contribute.[30] It is a renewal in that it accepts the challenges of the modern and post-modern world views. Teilhard diagnosed part of the problem in 1927 when he wrote: "The great objection brought against Christianity in our time . . . is the suspicion that our religion makes its adherents *inhuman*."[31] Timothy Radcliffe, OP, more recently, in his book *Alive in God*, shows that this continues to remain a challenge for us. He writes, "The argument of this book is that we are most likely to excite people with our faith if Christianity is grasped as the invitation to live fully."[32]

Many names witness to this search for the renewal of a humanism that is grounded in the search for God as well as in a respect for the advances of modern science. Dominique Dubarle, OP (1907–1987), with whom Teilhard himself had interacted, acknowledged the need for both God *and* science in any authentic humanism. In varied essays that were collected in a little volume entitled *Scientific Humanism and Christian Thought*,[33] he asked, pondering the text in Genesis 2:17 about not eating of the tree of knowledge of good and evil: "Does this mean that a desire for knowledge independent of any relation to God constitutes what we might call the root of man's sin?"[34] In a different essay in the same volume he had written:

30. With respect to medieval humanism and particularly that of Thomas Aquinas, see Southern, *Scholastic Humanism*; also Southern, *Medieval Humanism*.

31. *DM*, 37, emphasis in text. See a similar reference in "Mastery of the World and the Kingdom of God" (1916), *WW*, 90: "Never again, please God, may we be able to say of religion that its influence has made men more indolent, more unenterprising, *less human*; never again may its attitude lie open to the damning suspicion that it seeks to replace science by theology, effort by prayer, battle by resignation, and that its dogmas may well debase the value of the world by limiting in advance the scope of enquiry and the sphere of energy. Never, again, I pray, may anyone dare to complain of Rome that it is afraid of anything that moves and thinks." Emphasis in text. Teilhard is here aware of the effects of the Church's condemnation of modernism.

32. Radcliffe, *Alive in God*, 259.

33. Dominique Dubarle, *Scientific Humanism*, a collection of five essays published at various times from 1950–952.

34. From an essay entitled "The Attitude of Christianity to Scientific Progress" (1951) in *Scientific Humanism*, 114.

> We now have a clear picture of the evolution of the manifold forms in which life unfolds itself . . . We have, broadly speaking, unraveled the history of the earth and our thought is dominated by the concepts of biological evolution. That the latter is a fact we have no doubt . . . that evolution is a successful undertaking there can be no question . . . All this implies a new view of the human situation. Man is, in a certain sense, a mere episode if we consider the vast sidereal expanses which envelop the tiny space in which we have our earthly abode, or if we think of those immense aeons of time of which our historic millennia are a mere minute fraction.[35]

The religious quest and the scientist's vocation have complementary goals. It is not a question of one or the other, either the physical or the metaphysical, but of each respecting the domain of the other if a deeply humane humanism is to be attained. Many names could be added to the list of those who have reflected on this quest for human flourishing in our times, from Jacques Maritain's theocentric humanism in his *Integral Humanism* published in 1936,[36] to Henri de Lubac's *The Drama of Atheist Humanism* published in 1944,[37] as well as Martin Buber's "believing humanism."[38] Pope Francis in both *Laudato Sí* (#141) and *Fratelli Tutti* (#86) has spoken of the need for thinking further about Christian humanism.[39] However, at this point, it is to Charles Taylor's *A Secular Age* that I would like to turn.

Charles Taylor, in *A Secular Age*, asked the question: "Why was it virtually impossible not to believe in God in, say, 1500 in our Western society, while in 2000 many of us find this not only easy, but even inescapable?"[40] In the Western world we have moved from a social con-

35. From an essay entitled "The Universe of Science and Philosophy" (1952) in *Scientific Humanism*, 69–70.

36. Jacques Maritain, *Integral Humanism*.

37. Lubac, *Atheist Humanism*. On de Lubac's critique of atheist humanism, see Gardner, "Inhuman Humanism," 225–46.

38. Mendes-Flohr, *Martin Buber*, 290.

39. He also writes: "Now is the time for a new Nehemiah project, a new humanism that can harness the eruption of fraternity, to put an end to the globalization of indifference and the hyperinflation of the individual" (*Let Us Dream*, 46–47).

40. Taylor, *A Secular Age*, 25. For Taylor secularity can be understood in various ways (1–22), such as for societies in which there is a separation of church and state which does not exclude believing in God but only religion's access to public spaces; or the decline of religious beliefs and practices. Taylor, however, is using the word secularity to refer to a social context in which belief becomes one option among many alternatives and thus unbelief becomes plausible.

text in which it was difficult not to believe in God to a situation in which it has become plausible, even commonplace. We now have alternatives to belief—forms of humanism, secular humanisms—for which belief is unnecessary or even undesirable. With a humanism that sees human fulfillment as exclusively immanent, here on earth, one can now be fully human without belief in God. Taylor traces the trajectory of how we have come to be where we are. Social changes, along with the rise of the modern sciences, have created a world in which we no longer live in the premodern enchanted world open to extra-human influences, in which one's "self"[41] and identity were socially embedded and bound up with collective belief, in which a hierarchical complementarity among various states of life was a basis for social order, and in which there was such a thing as sacred time which had a vertical dimension to it and was open to God's involvement in history. All that was needed was the emergence of a humanism that was not dependent on a sense of the transcendent. Belief in God as foundational for a society can no longer be taken for granted. Taylor tells the complicated story of the erosion of belief.

Taylor does not accept an interpretation of the rise of secularity as an inevitable linear move forward from premodern to medieval to modern times in which the role of religion gradually declined and eventually disappears. His account follows a zigzag course, many steps of which were filled with unintended consequences in which deism, Calvinism, Cartesianism, modern individualism and many other actors played significant roles. In the modern world society exists for the sake of the individual. The political order is intended to safeguard an individual's rights and freedom. An egalitarian society can no longer be hierarchical but becomes "horizontal" without any "verticality" open to a transcendent order. How did a humanism that excludes the transcendent become an option, Taylor asks.[42] Deism, in which God's providential presence to the universe became reduced, impersonal, and disengaged, was an intermediate stage on the way to our secular age. An anthropological shift, particularly in the eighteenth century, witnessed the demise of a sense of transcendent purpose for the universe. God's plan for us was reduced to our happiness and the need for grace replaced by that goal of happiness apart from any need for God. The fading of a sense of mystery was accompanied by reason's being understood as sufficient to probe the laws of nature. The Christian aspiration to

41. Charles Taylor's earlier work was devoted to the emergence of the modern concept of "self." *Sources of Self.*

42. *A Secular Age*, 221.

transcend human flourishing with thoughts such as our being partakers of the divine nature was rejected. There was a gradual eclipse of the need for God. A secular or exclusively immanent humanism became plausible, and religion became more and more associated with superstition or fanaticism or mere enthusiasm. We will return to the Enlightenment's critique of religion but with deism God became impersonal and indifferent and we were halfway to our secular age.

A new moral sensibility entered the scene as well. Taylor writes: "The slide to Deism was not just the result of 'reason' and 'science,' but reflected a deep-seated moral distaste for the old religion that sees God as an agent in history."[43] Theistic traditions had seen human fulfillment in a relationship with God grounded in virtue. Utilitarian and post-Kantian ethics saw the moral life in terms of duty and rules. The path to Descartes's understanding of a human being as a "thinking thing"[44] was zig followed by zag, in which the theology of Aquinas was lost through the path of late scholasticism, nominalism, Occam, Cajetan, Suarez and Descartes. The path to contemporary secularity followed three stages: (1) the emergence of new humanist alternatives to Christian faith; (2) critiques of orthodox religion and a further diversification of humanist options; and (3) a widening throughout society, beyond simply that of the elites, of the impact of the emerging pluralism such that there is, for those seeking a spiritual path, no need to belong to a church.[45] Thus we have a move, not in a linear fashion, but nevertheless, from theism—> deism—> a non-religious humanism—> pluralism—> belief as optional—> unbelief as seemingly more reasonable. The challenge is thus not simply a debate between belief and unbelief, or a defense of religion, but the gamut of alternatives to belief, an expanding universe of unbelief, and pluralism as our contemporary context.

What then will make Christian faith a viable option at all? Although Taylor does not mention Teilhard de Chardin, a response to that question was one of Teilhard's primary concerns. It was also the concern of

43. *A Secular Age*, 274.

44. See here the essay as well as the semiotic project. Smith, "Replacing Descartes," 143–204. This is not the place to pursue John Deely's and semiotics' contributions to a move forward beyond the Enlightenment, but see Deely, *Four Ages*; and *Basics of Semiotics*.

45. *A Secular Age*, 299–321. I have chosen not to ordinarily note the precise pages in *A Secular Age* to which my summary remarks refer or there would be notes at the end of each sentence.

Jacques Maritain's Thomistic humanism. As does Taylor, both Maritain and Teilhard recognized a new context in which we have found ourselves, for Teilhard that of a vast and evolving universe no longer fixed from its beginning. For Taylor the shift in world view and the zigzag path to the present comprised ethical considerations as much as scientific ones. Science does not provide all the meaning that our lives seek. One also seeks an ethical perspective that goes beyond one's childhood faith. Is Christian ethics up to the challenge? The path to contemporary secularity was complex and multifaceted. In the nineteenth century there was a critique of the Enlightenment but not a return to religion. Ethical concerns focused on the relief of suffering, the value of equality, and the seeking of a just social order. With Nietzsche to the contrary on some of these, nevertheless: "A race of humans has arisen which has managed to experience its world entirely as immanent. In some respects, we may judge this achievement as a victory for darkness, but it is a remarkable achievement nonetheless."[46] Taylor does not see modernity as all bad. He attempts to understand it and the challenge it presents.

There has been at times a resurgence of belief, such as among Evangelicals.[47] A faith freed of the supernatural, however, such as that to which Ralph Waldo Emerson came after his early involvement with Unitarianism, made traditional Christianity less satisfying and even inferior to humanism.[48] "Christianity offers extrinsic rewards for altruism in the hereafter, whereas humanism makes benevolence its own reward."[49] The emergence of humanism as a viable alternative to Christianity had been established by the end of the eighteenth century and the process of its pluralization continued throughout the nineteenth up until our own times. Religion had come to be seen as false by science, irrelevant with the rise of modern medicine, and authoritarian. Taylor quotes Jeffrey Cox with respect to the view of Victorian churchgoers: "Society would fall apart without morality, morality was impossible without religion, and religion would disappear without the churches."[50] I am drawn to this

46. *A Secular Age*, 376.

47. In the nineteenth century, evangelical revivals contributed to a resurgence of a religious sensibility. Since then, however, in the latter half of twentieth century, evangelicalism became transformed. See Du Mez, *Jesus and John Wayne*.

48. Richardson, *Emerson*.

49. *A Secular Age*, 398.

50. Cox, *English Churches*, 271, quoted in *A Secular Age*, 471. Cox's research supports Taylor's theses about the decline of religion's not simply being an inevitable

point of view myself but to how many is it convincing? Religion itself is being held up to a new moral standard.

Taylor's analysis goes much deeper and with greater detail than I can present here. The last half of the twentieth century witnessed a revolution, an age of authenticity, expressive individualism, "I've gotta be me," emphasis on choice, a youth culture, a new consciousness, new gender roles, homosexuality as a legitimate option, and on and on. Affluence, consumerism, geographic mobility, new family patterns, suburbanization, television, and the more recent technologies, all have played their role. But they are here to stay. They go beyond anything that Maritain or Teilhard may have experienced. "For many people today, to set aside their own path in order to conform to some external authority just doesn't seem comprehensible as a form of spiritual life."[51] Spirituality divorced from religion has become an option, as the modern humanisms became in earlier centuries.

Are we, however, as closed to the transcendent as many academics lead us to believe? It is not necessarily an exclusive immanentism *or* openness to the transcendent. Many find themselves between the Scylla of atheistic materialism and Charybdis of orthodox religion. It is perhaps for these that a renewed evangelization is opportune, but one that recognizes the plurality of options available in our contemporary world. I have said enough for my purposes here. Taylor's analysis can be extremely helpful in an appreciation of our secular, but not necessarily non-religious, certainly not non-spiritual, age.

The Christian faith, and the Catholic tradition to which I belong, must come to terms not only with the context in which it finds itself, but also with its history and its blind spots.[52] What valid critique does the

---

consequence of "a process of secularization." He sees, as well, the important role of pluralism: The churches had to adapt to the fact of competition (Cox, 265–76). Will Durant, a historian of philosophy, a devout Catholic who moved away from belief in God, wrote, "There is no significant example in history, before our time, of a society successfully maintaining moral life without the aid of religion" (Durant, *Lessons of History*, 51, quoted in Sacks, *Morality*, 277). Also see Sacks's chapter on religion (*Morality*, 276–92).

51. *A Secular Age*, 489.

52. For some of Teilhard's own critique of religion and Christianity, see "Mastery of the World and the Kingdom of God" (1916), *WW*, 84–91; "Notes on the Presentation of the Gospel" (1919), *HM*, 210–22; "The Sense of Man" (1929), *TF*, 25–37; "Some Reflexions on the Conversion of the World" (1936), *SC*, 126–27. These essays and others can give one a sense of Teilhard's passionate concern about the future of Christianity. Owen Barfield wrote about blind spots: "When we look back on past periods

modern world pose for us? Does religion have a future? Where do we go from here? Taylor does not accept a theory of secularization in which religion and faith eventually disappear.[53] Nevertheless it is important to take note of the challenges to Catholic theology, catechesis, and evangelization. I mention three here by way of example. All are challenges which have been taken up, however, with which theologians, preachers, and pastors continue to wrestle, and to which I will return in the next chapter.

First, how do we understand predestination, grace, and the redemptive sacrifice of Christ? How these truths of the Catholic faith are explicated can make the Christian religion appear appealing or appalling from a humanistic perspective. How they may have been presented or understood in the past is not necessarily how the church understands them today. Taylor mentions several times the doctrine of the damnation of the majority of human beings or that of double predestination that fail to give the Christian faith a human face.[54] He writes, "I mention this [doctrine] here because the hegemony of this juridical-penal model plays an important role in the later rise of unbelief, both in repelling people from the faith, and in modifying it in the direction of Deism."[55] The church's teaching on atonement, damnation, and predestination are subject to critical studies today to which we shall return in the next chapter. The objectionable side of these doctrines and how they have often been

---

of history, we are often confronted with inconsistencies and blind spots in human thinking which to us are so palpable that we are almost astonished out of belief . . . Such are the Athenian emphasis on liberty—with the system of slavery accepted as a matter of course . . . the Calvinist doctrine of pre-election to eternal damnation . . . I believe that the blind spot which posterity will find most startling in the last hundred years or so of Western civilization, is, that it had, on the one hand, a religion which differed from all others in its acceptance of time, and of a particular point in time, as a cardinal element in its faith; that it had, on the other hand, a picture in its mind of the history of the earth and man as an evolutionary process: and that it neither saw nor supposed any connection whatever between the two" (*Saving Appearances*, 167). A fascinating study on the mystical element in Christianity, heavily influenced by Owen Barfield, is Vernon, *Secret History*.

53. Nor did Teilhard. See "The Zest for Living" (1950), *AE*, 238–43, referred to above.

54. *A Secular Age*, 78, 105, 262, 651–52.

55. *A Secular Age*, 78–79. The penal substitution theory of atonement maintains that Jesus suffered the penalty for humanity's sins based on the idea that divine forgiveness must satisfy divine justice, namely that God is not willing or able to forgive sin without first requiring a penalty for it. Aquinas is not a proponent of it. See Eleonore Stump's critique of it as well (*Atonement*, 76–78), about whose approach I will say more in the next chapter.

popularly understood was never the teaching of Thomas Aquinas whose own thought frequently became misinterpreted in the modern period. Nevertheless, what the church has to say about original sin, hell, and salvation can make these teachings credible or offensive.

Secondly, there are not only doctrinal questions but moral ones. What about the Christian faith's moral teaching needs to be revisited? We are not speaking about denying anything that is revealed but rather the need to return to the contents of what has been revealed and its development over the centuries. An important area, among others, such as the social doctrine of the church, is that of human sexuality. Taylor highlights this area of Christian teaching and a drift toward "excarnation" which poses a dilemma.[56] Christianity as an incarnational religion ought to resist excarnation. The Christian faith is alone among the religions of the world to be deeply incarnational, yet we have become uncomfortable with embodiment as sexual and social beings. We have moved in the Cartesian direction of living more in our heads than in our bodies. Even liturgy and ritual can come to reside more and more in the head.[57] I think here of James Joyce's description of a Mr. Duffy: "He lived a little distance from his body,"[58] and of Graham Greene's comment in *The End of the Affair*: "It's a strange thing to discover and to believe that you are loved, when you know that there is nothing in you for anybody but a parent or a God to love."[59] Love is meant to be embodied.

If the Christian tradition is to re-own embodiment and retrieve the sensual side of its faith, this has implications for one's appreciation of human sexuality and how we understand its purpose. Taylor writes:

> The repression and marginalization of one such facet is the process that I've been referring to here as "excarnation," the steady disembodying of spiritual life, so that it is less and less carried in deeply meaningful bodily forms, and lies more and more "in the head" . . . Excarnation is also connected to a fear and therefore repression of sexuality, and hence an avoidance, or too timid treatment of questions of sexual identity.[60]

56. *A Secular Age*, 288, 554, 613–15, 741, 746, 751, 766. "Excarnation" here could also be described as "de-incarnation," removing oneself from the embodiment dimension of human existence.

57. *A Secular Age*, 613.

58. Joyce, "A Painful Case," 96.

59. Greene, *The Affair*, 92.

60. *A Secular Age*, 771. Also see 503 for a critical statement to the same effect, also 496, 499, 502.

These questions of course can become the target of our culture wars but as Christians we ought to address them for the sake of the future. We need to have continued conversations about them.

Thirdly, there is the question of religious pluralism itself. Not only has there been a pluralization of humanisms but a greater cognizance of the plurality of religious options. What is the attitude of the Christian traditions, of the Catholic faith, toward the other religions of the world? Taylor gives less emphasis to this topic, but it is clearly related to questions about salvation and how the traditional teaching of salvation outside the church is to be understood. Much research has been given to this, but it too remains a disputed question although the Catholic Church since the Second Vatican Council clearly teaches that there is salvation beyond the institutional church, which is again something that Thomas Aquinas had always accepted.[61] Unfortunately we are not able to say more about this topic here. The Second Vatican Council and its theologians saw a need to present the truth of the Catholic faith as well as the church with a human face if we were to reflect the human face of Christ who became incarnate among us.[62]

The preceding questions are not the only challenges we face. These disputed questions have been taken seriously by Christian and Catholic theologians and were so taken by Teilhard de Chardin even before the Second Vatican Council. Nor do many misunderstood responses to these questions portray accurately the teaching of Thomas Aquinas. His teaching on predestination and grace, on human sensuality, and on salvation by a God who is not bound by the sacraments God has instituted are often significantly different from what one might suppose. I mention these concerns as examples reflected in the mirror within which secular humanisms see us. The question is whether there can be a Christian humanism as edifying for our age as are some of the secular ones, and whether the human face of the Catholic faith can shine forth to make belief truly desirable, without compromising the profundity and truth in the Catholic faith.

As I have said, Taylor does not see the rise of secularity as indicative of the demise of religion. Many still find a spiritual home in the religions.[63] It does mean, however, that religion must find its place in a world

61. On this question see Dupuis, *Religious Pluralism*; Sullivan, *Salvation Outside the Church*; Aquinas, *ST*, III, q. 8, a. 3.

62. Among other works by Edward Schillebeeckx, OP, see *The Church*.

63. *A Secular Age*, 515–16.

of unbelief where it will remain an option and not always perceived a reasonable one. There are signs of discontent with an exclusively immanentist humanism and an openness to, even thirst for, transcendence,[64] as we continue to search for meaning.[65] The Christian faith is committed to both immanent and transcendent dimensions of life, to both horizontality and verticality, or as Teilhard would put it, the Forward and the Upward. It can satisfy the yearning for each with its realized and its future eschatology, but it needs to acknowledge the blind spots of its history. As incarnational it needs to counteract the tendency toward excarnation and a disincarnate God and present Christianity's full beauty.[66] It is not just Christianity's dogmatic truth as contained in propositional knowledge but the Christian narrative,[67] interwoven as it is with the lives of those who have and continue to witness to its meaning. Unbelief has become an appealing and reasonable option, but a life of faith can be even more appealing and reasonable with the witness of heroic lives as well as of ordinary Christian lives. Pope St. Paul VI had written that "the first means of evangelization is the witness of an authentically Christian life."[68] Many Christians continue to live inspiring lives. Taylor, for example, remains moved by the life of Francis of Assisi,[69] as I have been by the life of St. Dominic.[70] Taylor also mentions the deep conversions to Catholicism in our own time, like Evelyn Waugh, Charles Péguy, and Thomas Merton.[71] We may all have our own list of the great cloud of witnesses (Heb 12:1).

The case against Christianity is that it hampers human fulfillment.[72] The "adversarial picture of the relation of faith to modernity is not an invention of unbelievers. It is matched and encouraged by a strand of

64. *A Secular* Age, 530.

65. E.g., see the works of Viktor Frankl, especially *Search for Meaning*. The whole question of "meaning" is much discussed in twentieth century existentialist literature.

66. Here it is worth pursuing an emerging emphasis on "deep incarnation." See the essays in Gregersen, *Incarnation*. The work of Sarah Coakley also deserves consideration, e.g., *God, Sexuality, and Self*.

67. The eminent Thomistic scholar Eleonore Stump recognizes the important role of narrative in the pursuit of truth. See her *Wandering in Darkness*, esp. 23–81. There is also lengthy literature on the role of narrative.

68. Paul VI, *Evangelii nuntiandi*, #41.

69. *A Secular Age*, 436.

70. Goergen, *Preaching Friar*.

71. *A Secular Age*, 728–72.

72. *A Secular Age*, 623.

Christian hostility to the humanist world."[73] Is a truly Christian humanism not desirable for meeting some of the demands of modernity? Jacques Maritain and Teilhard de Chardin both offered responses to this demand. Maritain, a significant twentieth century interpreter of the thought of Aquinas, lacked appreciation for the thought of Teilhard of whom he was a critic. Teilhard's call for dialogue between science and religion presented its own vision of a Christian humanism. Let us consider each of these for a moment.

In 1936, before the Second World War, Jacques Maritain published *Humanisme Intégral*, an expanded version of six previously given lectures in which he drew a contrast between an exclusively anthropocentric humanism and a theocentric humanism, or between atheistic humanisms in contrast to Christian humanism.[74] Is a theocentric or Christian humanism possible in our modern and post-modern world? Is such desirable from the vantage point of the Christian faith? Are humanism and Christianity compatible?[75] Jacques Maritain saw the importance of these questions as he explored the relationship between Western humanism and religion. Is a religious humanism a contradiction in terms? It would not seem so, but they have not always been seen as integral one to the other. What is impressive though is that Maritain himself saw the need to approach the topic of humanism and give it philosophical reflection, as well as his naming Christian or Catholic humanism "integral."[76]

Maritain's starting point is the thought of Thomas Aquinas. What ought the relationship between the Christian and the world be, or between the spiritual and the temporal?[77] He writes that the spiritual must

73. *A Secular Age*, 569. Pope St. Pius IX's *Syllabus of Errors* is but one example.

74. Maritain, *Integral Humanism*.

75. Karl Rahner, SJ, as well as many others, takes up this same question. See Rahner's "Christian Humanism," in *Theological Investigations*, 9:187–204. His opening words are: "Perhaps a question-mark ought to be put after this title, for as it stands it leads one to expect that a theologian is going to clarify and give reasons as to how Christianity and humanism form a unity, how humanism, when it is genuine, full-blooded and is really being itself, is actually Christianity."

76. The word "integral" can carry with it varied nuances. The Indian guru, Sri Aurobindo, spoke of his synthesis of yoga as integral yoga (*Integral Yoga*). Ken Wilbur described his approach to spirituality as integral (*Integral Spirituality*). On the other hand, Thomas Crean and Alan Fimister's "integralism" is reactionary (Crean and Fimister, *Integralism*). Also see Trouter, "New Integralists," 32–37.

77. Maritain, *Integral Humanism*, 95–126. See also Rahner, n75 above. This was also the concern of the Second Vatican Council's document, *Gaudium et spes* (On the Church in the Modern World).

vivify the temporal. "Christianity must inform, or, rather, transpenetrate the world." This "new humanism" requires a "new style of sanctity."[78] Maritain may have been optimistic about the possibility of a truly Christian culture, but he sees the problem. What is the relationship between the kingdom of God and the world?[79]

Maritain singles out three *erroneous* responses to that question: (1) The world is where Satan reigns. This world and God's kingdom are antithetically opposed. (2) The world here on earth is to be God's kingdom, which position fails to distinguish the temporal and spiritual orders. (3) A world of pure nature, or naturalism, in which there is no relationship between the natural and the supernatural, such as in varied forms of utopia. These also reflect to some degree the varied possible relationships between theology and culture as outlined by H. Richard Niebuhr. Each of these carries its grain of truth but lacks the ability to appreciate fully the role of the Christian in the world.[80] Maritain writes:

> Let us summarize these positions: I hold that while awaiting the "beyond-of-history" in which the kingdom of God will be accomplished in the glory of full manifestation, the Church is already the kingdom of God in the order called *spiritual* and in the state of pilgrimage and crucifixion; and that the world, itself, the order called *temporal*, this world enclosed in history, is a divided and ambiguous domain—at once of God, of man, and of "the Prince of this world."[81]

The relationship between history and the "beyond-of-history," between the church and the kingdom, between the temporal city and the city of God, have of course been the subject of much reflection and research, biblically and theologically.[82] It was precisely a concern of Teilhard de Chardin as well.[83] Is a concrete historical ideal possible? Maritain places

78. Maritain, *Integral Humanism*, 112, 122–25,

79. Maritain, *Integral Humanism*, 54–59, 99–102.

80. Maritain, *Integral Humanism*, 101–11.

81. Maritain, *Integral Humanism*, 126.

82. See the extensive bibliography on biblical eschatology. Today a distinction is clearly made between the church and the kingdom. The church is not simply the kingdom of God on earth.

83. The question of the relationship of the kingdom and the world had to do with one of Maritain's critiques of Teilhard. It is a question to which both Maritain and Teilhard gave much thought. Maritain, late in life, was highly critical of Teilhard (*Peasant of Garonne*, 116–26), as was Etienne Gilson to whose critique Maritain often refers. For

emphasis on the communal, personalist, and peregrinal aspects of the Christian's earthly sojourn.[84] He also acknowledges that the gospel becomes incarnate in the world in plural ways. How one lives the gospel in the world is a question of the rôle of the Christian lay vocation.[85] How are the truths of the gospel refracted in the temporal or cultural order?[86] The

both, Teilhard came across as neo-modernist and gnostic. Both acknowledge some of Teilhard's strengths: Teilhard's experiential and poetic appreciation of the sacred character of creation, the presence of God in the world, as manifest in "the great text of Teilhard, *The Mass on the World*" (*Peasant of Garonne*, 118). Maritain's disapproval of Teilhard, however, is much more animated. He objects to expressions of Teilhard like "meta-Christianity," to his neologisms, and has no sympathy for making the Christ of history into the cosmic Christ. Maritain quotes Gilson: "I am not sure whether an omega point of science exists, but I feel perfectly sure that in the Gospel, Jesus of Nazareth is quite another thing than the 'concrete germ' of the Christ Omega . . ." (*Peasant of Garonne*, 121). All of these are, of course, critiques to which one can reply. Maritain considers Teilhard to be ignorant of Aquinas and yet "he [Teilhard] was, without realizing it, in full agreement with St. Thomas" when it comes to epistemology (*Peasant of Garonne*, 117). We cannot expect Maritain's lack of appreciation for what he sees as Teilhard's poetic imprecision to be reconciled with Teilhard's vision. At the same time, the following text of Maritain's would express a concern vital to Teilhard's project as well: "The whole question here comes down to knowing if one believes that an authentically and vitally Christian politics can arise in history and is now invisibly being prepared. It comes down to knowing if Christianity should incarnate itself to that extent, if the temporal mission of the Christian should go that far, if the witness of love should descend that far; or whether we must abandon the world to the devil in that which is most natural to it—civic or political life. If we believe in the possibility of an authentically and vitally Christian politics, then our most urgent temporal duty is to work for its establishment" (*Peasant of Garonne*, 23). They may in the end have seen the relation between history and eschatology differently, but both struggled with that question in their quest for a renewed transcendent humanism. As critical as Maritain was of Teilhard, others of course were captivated by his vision, e.g., Bishop Fulton J. Sheen (*Footprints*, 69–82). I, of course, following the path I have taken in this book, do not see Aquinas and Teilhard as irreconcilable. Edward Schillebeeckx also addresses some of these same concerns about faith, politics, and mysticism (*Christ*, 762–821; *On Christian Faith*, 47–84).

84. Maritain, *Integral Humanism*, 133–37. Teilhard himself also emphasizes these personal, social, and developmental aspects.

85. Maritain, *Integral Humanism*, 228–29. This too is a question to which Karl Rahner, SJ, gave attention. The first essay I ever read of Rahner's, while an undergraduate student in college, was "Present Situation of Christians." The same theme is also taken up in "The Christian in His World," in *Theological Investigations*, 7:88–99. It is a question many have pondered, e.g., Congar, *Lay People*.

86. Maritain unfortunately used the expression "a new christendom" to probe his insights into the relationship between Christianity and culture although he clearly does not see it as like the Christendom of medieval times. He does see St. Thomas's thought as at the core of a Christian philosophy of culture. See *Integral Humanism*, 75, 127–28, 132, 137–43. Again, a Christian philosophy or theology of culture is a

Christian lives *in history* and yet gives witness to a *suprahistorical world.* For Maritain the question of the relationship between history and the "beyond-of-history" assumes great importance, which is also the question of the relationship between history and the kingdom God.[87] The temporal and the spiritual are distinct, distinguishable, but not separable. One can see the many challenges, dilemmas, and questions, the articulation of a renewed Christian humanism raises. It is to this same dilemma that Teilhard addressed his suggestions for a Christian humanism viable in a post-Christian world. One of Teilhard's major concerns was the Christian's responsibility for the world. He saw the need for a Christian mysticism that valued the world in which Christians find themselves. We do not live for another world only. Maritain also gave more extensive reflection to the role of mysticism in Christian life than many students of St. Thomas. Mystical knowledge is also a way of knowing.[88] For Christian mysticism lay at the core of a theocentric humanism and a renewed Christian evangelization. Given the contemporary reality of many who see themselves as spiritual but not religious, it becomes imperative for the religious to give witness to the mystical core of authentic religious life.

A WORLD-AFFIRMING, SOCIALLY ENGAGED MYSTICISM

"The devout Christian of the future will either be a 'mystic', one who has experienced 'something', or he will cease to be anything at all"—a frequently quoted text of Karl Rahner's.[89] The text raises the complex question of what one means by mysticism and who a mystic might be, intriguing questions widely explored into which we cannot go here. Yet Rahner does say something about what he understands a mystic to be: "one who has experienced 'something.'" Presumably Rahner means some sense of the transcendent, some experience of God, an experiential aspect to one's faith, Thomas Aquinas's "living faith" (*credere in Deum*), not simply belief. Many contemporary Thomists would agree: We are *all*

common concern of post Vatican II theology, e.g., *Gaudium et spes.* With respect to Pope St. John Paul II's philosophy of culture, see n23 above.

87. *Integral Humanism*, 248, 99–126, 54–59.

88. *Degrees of Knowledge*, 247–351.

89. Rahner, "Christian Living Formerly and Today," in *Theological Investigations*, 7:15.

called to the mystical life. Mysticism is not an extraordinary way of being a Christian but the ordinary way. Mysticism does not refer only to the charismatic gifts, the *gratiae gratis datae*, but rather to the fullness of life in the Spirit, the life of the theological virtues and gifts of the Spirit, Aquinas's habitual grace, *gratia gratum faciens*,[90] all of which is ordinary even if challenging, a graced life but not "cheap grace."[91] This is the second Vatican Council's universal call to holiness.[92] Whether we use the word "mystic" or not, whether we see ourselves as "mystics" or not, whether we see our Christian vocation as a call to sanctity or not, pertains more to how we appropriate the language of spiritual theology. However we express it, much of Christian life is lived beneath the surface. Grace is ordinary even if not "of nature" itself, present in the ordinariness of daily life. In that sense we are all called to a "mystical" or supernatural level of living in the Spirit with Christ. Within a Christian humanism, or we might say a Judeo-Christian humanism, or we might say any genuine humanism that recognizes the importance of the transcendent in our lives, within this humanism there lay a mystical current. To this both Thomas Aquinas and Teilhard de Chardin agree, although the word "mysticism" itself was coined long after Aquinas's century itself.[93] Mysticism undergirds a living faith and lay at the core of all religions.

A Christian is not someone who withdraws from the world, but rather someone who immerses himself or herself contemplatively in the world. The Christian life incarnates the divine life, and it becomes something "worldly." As Martin Buber, who saw the need for a believing or biblical humanism, wrote with respect to his Jewish heritage: "If work is to be done in public life, it must be accomplished not above the fray, but in it."[94] The mystical life, we might say, gets messy, but that immersion in the world is what transforms or helps to redeem the world. For Teilhard de Chardin, creation itself becomes diaphanous as it becomes a divine milieu and we sojourners within it. He thus gave attention to the mystical life and

90. E.g., see Arintero, *Mystical Evolution*, esp. vol. 1; Garrigou-Lagrange, *Christian Perfection*, esp. 12–47; and Garrigou-Lagrange, *Three Ages*.

91. Cf., Bonhoeffer, *Cost of Discipleship*, 45–60.

92. See Flannery, *Vatican Council II*, "Lumen Gentium," esp. ch. 5, "The Call to Holiness," ##39–42. O'Malley, *What Happened*, 50–51, 174–75, 274, 310.

93. See McGinn, *Foundations of Mysticism*, 1:266–343.

94. Buber, "Gandhi, Politics, and Us" (1930), in Buber, *Pointing the Way*, 137, quoted in Mendes-Flohr, *Martin Buber*, 254.

reenvisioning it. What does it mean to be a Christian *in* the world? It is not a question of God *or* the world, but of God *and* the world.[95]

Many of Teilhard's essays explicitly use the language of mysticism,[96] while almost a majority deal with the spiritual life in one way or another, and some secondary sources on Teilhard directly addressed the topic of mysticism in the thought of Teilhard.[97] The core spiritual teaching of Teilhard is presented in *The Divine Milieu* which we have already discussed. His "new mysticism" concerns both one's interior life as well as one's engagement with the world. In his essay, "My Fundamental Vision" (1948), he traces the path from "physics" or the science of evolution, to metaphysics, his metaphysics of union, culminating in mysticism, a mysticism for tomorrow, a neo-humanism. Mysticism is the "art of attaining simultaneously . . . the universal and the spiritual" and thus becoming "one with the All."[98]

> For the man who has once thoroughly understood the nature of a world in which cosmogenesis, proceeding along the axis of anthropogenesis, culminates in a Christogenesis—for that man, everything, in every element and event of the universe, is bathed in light and warmth, everything becomes animate, and a fit object of love and worship—not, indeed, directly in itself . . . but at a deeper level than itself: that is, at the extreme and unique term of its development . . . And from all this follows that Christian charity . . . is seen to be the most complete and the most active agent of hominization.[99]

In that essay, as well as in a later one,[100] as well as in others, he contrasts what he calls the road of the East with the road of the West, the latter

95. *DM*, 20–21. "But let there be revealed to us the possibility of believing *at the same time and wholly* in God *and* the World, the one through the other . . ." ("The Heart of the Problem" [1949], *FM*, 268–69).

96. E.g., "The Mystical Milieu" (1917), *WW*, 117–49; "The Mysticism of Science" (1939), *HE*, 163–81; "Some Notes on the Mystical Sense" (1951), *TF*, 209–11.

97. E.g., Duffy, *Teilhard's Mysticism*; Thomas M. King, *Mysticism of Knowing*; Ursula King, *New Mysticism*, along with many other studies that pursue the thought of Teilhard in a more comprehensive way, as well as other studies on the spirituality of Teilhard by Ursula King.

98. "My Fundamental Vision" (1948), *TF*, 199.

99. "My Fundamental Vision," *TF*, 204.

100. "Some Notes on the Mystical Sense: An Attempt at Clarification" (1951), *TF*, 209–11.

being the road he takes.[101] "The mystical sense is essentially a feeling for, a presentiment of, the total and final unity of the world, beyond its present sensibly apprehended multiplicity: it is a cosmic sense of 'oneness.'"[102] It is not only a metaphysics of union and a mysticism thereof as well, but a mysticism of love within which there is the primacy of charity.[103] A mystical current runs throughout the cosmos itself, grounding a humanism for which creation groans, a cosmic, humane, and Christian humanism satisfying the mind and heart of our contemporary world.

Jacques Maritain explored mystical knowledge and experience philosophically, from the vantage point of the thought of Thomas Aquinas, in his classic work, *The Degrees of Knowledge*, wherein he made significant distinctions.[104] Unable to devote more attention to the topic here, we can say that, in accord with Maritain, one needs to distinguish knowledge in the rational order from suprarational knowledge; or distinguish metaphysics, theology, and mysticism proper; that is to say philosophical wisdom, theological wisdom based on revelation or reason illumined by faith, and mystical or infused or experiential knowledge of things divine flowing from the indwelling of the Holy Spirit in the life of the soul. Mystical experience for Maritain refers to experiential knowledge of things divine. Thomas himself did not develop systematically a theology of mysticism or contemplation although he made significant contributions to the topic.[105] Maritain maintains that one can talk *analogously* about mystical or contemplative knowledge in the *natural* order, but not properly speaking, since sanctifying grace undergirds genuine mystical experiences, marking the distinction between the presence of God in all things (the presence of immensity) and God's distinctive presence in the rational creature through the divine indwelling. At the same time, Maritain affirms that there can be authentic mystics in the Hindu, Buddhist, Jewish, and Muslim spiritual traditions because, as Thomas maintains, sanctifying grace is available even apart from the sacraments themselves.[106] Yet the distinction between metaphysics and mysticism

101. See Ursula King, *New Mysticism* for a full discussion of Teilhard's approach to Eastern mysticism.

102. "Some Notes on a Mystical Sense: An Attempt at Clarification" (1951), *TF*, 209.

103. "Some Notes on a Mystical Sense," *TF*, 210.

104. *Degrees of Knowledge*, 247–351.

105. See Tugwell, *Albert and Thomas*, 279–90.

106. *ST*, III, q. 8, a. 3; q. 66, a. 11; q. 67, a. 5, *ad* 2.

must be maintained, as Teilhard himself also did. Metaphysics does not require but opens the door to the mystical. The mystical proper remains a suprasensible or suprarational or graced mode of knowing God. As Josef Pieper stated: "Contemplation is a form of knowing arrived at not by thinking but by seeing, intuition. It is not co-ordinate with the *ratio*, with the power of discursive thinking, but with the *intellectus*, with the capacity for 'simple intuition.'"[107]

One can surmise that Maritain gave more attention to mystical experience because his wife, Raïssa, was clearly a mystic.[108] Thus he articulated, based on the philosophy of Thomas Aquinas, in what mystical, that is supernatural, knowledge consists, a way of knowing available to all of us, although not without grace. Indeed, in one way the mystical is the highest form of human knowledge available to rational creatures while still on earth. Both Thomas Aquinas and Teilhard de Chardin are to be numbered among those mystics, although one may be more known and praised for his philosophical and theological achievements and the other for his synthesis of that knowledge which comes from modern science with Christian faith. Yet the former is also known for his devotion, his poetry, and his "*Non nisi te, Domine*," while the latter is also highly recognized for his experience and awareness of the presence of God in all things, not to mention his "Mass on the World" and a loving surrender to a God with a human and Christic face. What challenges do Christians face as we attempt a world-affirming, socially engaged, Christian mysticism with a human face? I consider next three such challenges, only as examples, which emerged in Charles Taylor's work as well, what in Thomas's day would have been considered disputed questions.

107. Pieper, *Happiness and Contemplation*, 73–74, an excellent study.

108. See Raïssa Maritain, *Raïssa's Journal*, edited and published posthumously by Jacques in 1963. Raïssa died in 1960. For a biography, see Barré, *Beggars for Heaven*; Doering, *French Catholic*. For an excellent study of Maritain's contribution to the study of mysticism, see Arraj, *Mysticism, Metaphysics, and Maritain*.

10

Disputed Questions

Did Jesus die for our sins? Is there an eternal hell? Is the purpose of the human sexual act necessarily procreative? These are only some of the questions with which Catholic theologians are wrestling. Catholic teaching, of course, cannot and does not change to accommodate a *zeitgeist* or placate the times in which it finds itself. Catholic theology has always sought the truth of things, whether that is discerned through reason or in the light of its faith. At the same time, Catholic teaching can change, although not defined doctrines.[1] The Catholic faith encounters the cultures in which it finds itself and their mutual impact on each other. In this chapter I consider three examples in which Christian theology is challenging and challenged. I then return to the topic of what a renewed Christian humanism might ask of us. There could be other examples of course. I am not attempting here to formulate any conclusion to these questions. Rather, I look at one side, then at another, attempting to bring into dialogue varied voices, and not only those of Thomas or of Teilhard. In what does intra-ecclesial, intra-cultural, inter-cultural, inter-religious dialogue consist? That is a basic question which we cannot take further time here to contemplate. As Catholic theology thinks through the challenges that come from a secular world, the question is not how the church's teaching changes but how to present it in a form intelligible to

1. Noonan, *Can and Cannot Change*; Sullivan, *Magisterium*.

our period of history? In the process, we may find at some point a river-bed shifting although it is the same river.

THE DOCTRINE OF ATONEMENT

With respect to the doctrine of the atonement, we find quite contrasting perspectives. For some, God's willing the death of his Son seems incompatible with a God of love. They are thus tempted to abandon this teaching, or even set aside completely the traditional Christian faith. Others have interpreted the teaching such that, although Christ died for all, only a few will in fact be saved. Neither of these opinions is acceptable. Jesus did die for our sins (2 Cor 5:14–15), but the question remains what that means. The doctrine of atonement is crucial, both in terms of the role it has historically played in a Christian's self-understanding, but also in terms of how it is received today. Eleonore Stump begins an extended reflection on the doctrine of the atonement by stating: "The doctrine that Christ has saved human beings from their sins, with all that salvation entails, is the distinctive doctrine of Christianity."[2] It is certainly a core Christian teaching. There are various interpretations of the doctrine of the atonement. Charles Taylor sees the juridical-penal interpretation of the atonement as contributing to the rise of unbelief, "repelling people from the faith."[3] At the same time, according to Taylor, "The Crucifixion cannot be sidelined as merely a regrettable by-product of a valuable career of teaching."[4]

A theology of the cross plays an essential role in how one appropriates the Christian story. Jacques Maritain, in his last writing, offered an inspiring mediation on it.[5] So does Teilhard de Chardin in *The Divine Milieu*.[6] Yet significant issues remain as to how to appropriate it in its fullness. Already in 1920, Teilhard proposed preliminary and challenging thoughts.[7] For Teilhard, evil did not enter the world as the result of a fault

2. Stump, *Atonement*, 3.

3. *A Secular Age*, 78–79. For his emphasis on the importance of the juridical-penal interpretation of the atonement and its contribution to the rise of unbelief, see especially 233, 262, 319, 651–56, 670.

4. *A Secular Age*, 651.

5. Maritain, *Grace and Humanity*, 30–43, 134–44.

6. *DM*, 76–81.

7. "Fall, Redemption, and Geocentrism" (1920), *CE*, 36–44. For reflection on the thought of Teilhard on the doctrine of redemption, refer to my discussion in chapter 7.

committed by an *individual* human being.[8] The fundamental teaching of the church with respect to the history of sin, for Teilhard, has to do with the *universality* of corruption symbolized by an initial human fault. The whole universe from the very beginning has been under the shadow of evil.[9] To that fact, the doctrine of redemption must respond.[10] Teilhard believed that evil was "not a malady specific to the earth."[11] It was even probable that "the conscious layer of the cosmos is not confined to a single point (our mankind) but continues beyond the earth into other stars and other times,"[12] which requires that our doctrine of redemption be multifaceted.[13] Teilhard could appreciate the possibility that "there were worlds before our own, and there will be other worlds after"[14] to which Christ's redemption also applies. Today, even more than in the time of Teilhard, we are aware of the vastness of the universe in which we find ourselves to which Christian theology, Christology, and soteriology must address themselves.[15]

Over twenty years later,[16] Teilhard was continuing to wrestle with these same questions, with which we are concerned today as we continue to proclaim anew the good news about Jesus Christ. What is the relationship between redemption and evolution, or as stated in another way, between redemption and creation? An evolutionary perspective orients us toward "a fantastic future"[17] and not only our historic past. It also invites us to reconsider facets of the redemptive work of Christ which are cosmic in scope and thus reorients our approach to this great mystery.

> For obvious historical reasons, Christian thought and piety have hitherto given *primary* consideration in the dogma of redemption to the idea of expiatory reparation. Christ was regarded

8. "Fall, Redemption, and Geocentrism," *CE*, 37, 39, 42.

9. As indicated in chapter 7, "evil" is an inevitable by-product of the one God's evolving but unfinished universe in the process of seeking its completion.

10. "Fall, Redemption, and Geocentrism," *CE*, 37, 39, 40.

11. "Fall, Redemption, and Geocentrism," *CE*, 40.

12. "Fall, Redemption, and Geocentrism," *CE*, 43.

13. "Fall, Redemption, and Geocentrism," *CE*, 44.

14. "Fall, Redemption, and Geocentrism," *CE*, 44.

15. O'Meara, *Vast Universe* is one attempt to approach some of the theological questions raised by our growing awareness of the vastness of the universe.

16. "Christ the Evolver, or A Logical Development of the Idea of Redemption" (1942), *CE*, 138–50.

17. "Christ the Evolver," *CE*, 143.

> *primarily* as the Lamb bearing the sins of the world, and the world *primarily* as a fallen mass. *In addition*, however, there was from the very beginning another element in the picture—a positive element, of reconstruction or re-creation. New heavens, a new earth: these were, even for an Augustine, the fruit and the price of the sacrifice of the Cross.[18]

Teilhard writes: "No longer *first* to expiate, and then *in addition* to restore; but *first* to create . . . and, in order to do so . . . fight against evil and pay for evil."[19] Whether this reversal of emphasis is in fact what is needed, or whether just the many facets of the doctrine of redemption need to be given their due, remains a disputed question, but our need to think through again the doctrine will be necessary if Christianity is "to be rejuvenated."[20] The doctrine pertains not only to *my* salvation but also to the salvation of *all* as well as to that of *the whole universe.*

Before considering the challenge Teilhard presents, we must present the doctrine of the atonement in a robust contemporary form. Eleonore Stump's *Atonement* is just that. She analyses the doctrine and rethinks it, making the message of the cross credible and relevant. She rejects a commonly articulated approach associated with St. Anselm's soteriology and grounds her reflections instead in the thought of Thomas Aquinas, although moving beyond him as well. At times her text moves more like spiritual reading, at times highly philosophical, with astute interpretations of significant biblical passages such as Jesus's cry of dereliction from the cross, covering a wide range of topics from God as love and mercy to the atonement as a remedy for guilt and shame. "The atonement is a solution to the problem of the human proneness to moral wrongdoing," Stump emphasizes (69).[21] A response to this problem of the human proneness to wrongdoing, however, must not only look backward at humanity's sinful history but also forward to solving present moral dispositions and future wrong acts (76–77). Stump argues that the atonement is not meant to appease God but to transform human hearts. "Penal substitution versions suppose that, without some substitute's bearing the penalty, God must sentence all human beings to damnation as the punishment for their wrongdoing" (73). Stump rejects this penal substitution version of

18. "Christ the Evolver," *CE*, 145. Emphasis in text.

19. "Christ the Evolver," *CE*, 146. Emphasis in text.

20. "Christ the Evolver," *CE*, 147.

21. Stump, *Atonement*. I place page references to Stump's text in the following paragraphs within the text itself.

the Anselmian theory. In its place, building on Aquinas's thought, she retrieves the value of the teaching and illuminates it.

Challenging common assumptions about what the church in fact teaches, e.g., in reference to topics like God's relationship to creation (127, 240, 372), whether God suffers (11, 133–35, 271), and salvation apart from explicit faith (34, 369), she remains traditional. The foundation for her approach is that God *is* a God of love, that God *is* love, that God wills the salvation of all, and that what God seeks in his death on the cross *is* our salvation, transformation, and redemption from bondage to sin. Not, however, by placating an offended God to buy his forgiveness but by allowing our hearts to be stirred so that our union with God may be real and the wounds in our lives healed. The atonement is meant to bring about *at onement* with God. Stump refreshes our appreciation of all that comprises justification, sanctification, and perseverance in the process of our salvation. In the end, she demonstrates both the importance of the doctrine and the need for a renewed interpretation. After being refreshed by Stump's presentation, the doctrine of the atonement is not to be thrown out with the bath water, but neither is it to be handed on in some offensive formulation. Reflecting deeply upon it and appreciating its contribution to what it means to be human aids the process of humanity's transformation. Stump sees Christ's death on the cross as "providing the best means for facilitating human surrender to God," and not as "some kind of payment of a debt or substitutionary punishment for sin" (233).

Whereas Eleonore Stump's approach to the doctrine of the atonement is highly philosophical, Khaled Anatolios's starting point in his *Deification through the Cross* is liturgical. Hers is grounded predominantly in the thought of Thomas Aquinas, his begins with a study of the Byzantine liturgy. Both are attentive to Scripture and Tradition while at the same time being innovative. She puts distance between her philosophical theology of the atonement and that of St. Anselm. Anatolios is sympathetic to Anselm while at the same time recognizing that the element of "necessity" in Anselm's thought needs modification.[22] Along with Charles

22. Anatolios, *Deification*, 272–76, 278–79, 282–83, 303–11, 347–49, 355–61. Anatolios accepts "Anselm's presupposition of humanity's vocation to honor God" (272), while aware of the difficulty in Anselm's thought of his focus on "the intrinsic necessity" of the satisfaction due God (275), this latter being what Stump rejects as unacceptable and not sustainable. Both Stump's and Anatolios's approaches are highly nuanced. Anatolios is favorable to the doxological element in Anselm's thought while recognizing difficulty in Anselm's approach to the "necessity" in how God works salvation (308–9). Stump sees Anselmian approaches as "unsalvageable" (37), primarily

Taylor, penal substitution for Stump is suspect.[23] For Anatolios, some of its insights remain poignant.[24] She writes that "for the doctrine of the atonement there is no analogue to the Chalcedonian formula for the incarnation. That is, there is no creedal formula that specifies the way in which the doctrine is to be interpreted."[25] Anatolios might question that statement since there is "an indispensable datum that must be accommodated in any interpretation of the Christian doctrine of salvation in Christ."[26] Both are true, however. There is in the doctrine of atonement nothing comparable to the Chalcedonian formula but there is also a normative dogmatic core to the doctrine. For the East this is encompassed within the doctrine of deification and for Anatolios deification is not accomplished apart from the cross. Christ's suffering and death are directly efficacious for our salvation. For me, Stump's contribution and those of Anatolios complement each other. Although Anatolios sees his soteriology of doxological contrition as the core of the Christian teaching on the atonement, he nevertheless writes humbly: "Full comprehension of the depths of salvation in Christ will of course always elude not only particular studies like this but indeed all of human comprehension this side of

due to their emphasis on the "necessity" of the atonement in order for God to forgive. For Stump on Anselm, see *Atonement*, 21–22, 31–37, 55–57, 109–10, 233–34, 366–37, 394–96, as well as many other references. Vincent Dávila, OP, who had studied with both Eleonore Stump at St. Louis University and Khaled Anatolios at the University of Notre Dame interprets the contrast between the two as follows: Stump rejects the necessity of atonement because it seems to posit some divine law outside God to which he is accountable—in other words, its necessity ends up meaning that God must fix something in himself, rather than something in us. For Anatolios, necessity in Anselm is the necessity for God to act in accord with his nature (308). Anatolios does seem to find it necessary for God to react to sin—he cannot simply leave sin unaddressed, unchallenged. The key difference, I think, between Stump and Anatolios on this question is that Anatolios appears to accept a form of necessity on God's behalf (God must right the disfiguration of his glory caused by humanity), while Stump emphasizes the need to repair humanity. For Stump the result of sin that needs to be remedied is its effect on us, whereas for Anatolios sin itself must be judged (307–11). David Vincent Meconi, SJ, also offers pertinent insights into the atonement (*On Self-Harm*). In exploring the thought of St. Augustine, Meconi manifests some parallels with the doxological contrition and atonement theology one finds in Anatolios. Eleonore Stump writes the Foreword for his book.

23. Stump, *Atonement*, 76–78, 233.
24. Anatolios, *Deification*, 411–21.
25. Stump, *Atonement*, 3, 234, also 14, 39.
26. Anatolios, *Deification*, 422.

the eschaton."[27] If so, even given a dogmatic core, no soteriology can encompass all that the death of Christ contains within its richness, granted however that right worship and repentance are essential ingredients, as Anatolios maintains. Yet this tells us that the doctrine of salvation cannot be contained in anything like the Chalcedonian formula, other than what the creeds say: Christ died for our sins.[28]

Anatolios emphasizes the doxological motif of giving glory to God, our being drawn into the mystery of the inner-trinitarian life of God,[29] which we can experience in this life in worship.[30] The basic purpose of human life is to give God glory. God's glorification is the core of salvation. Anatolios's conception of Christ "as including the entire cosmos in his glorification of the Father in the Spirit,"[31] is something which Teilhard would rejoice to see. Not only doxology, however, but for us humans, contrition is also at the heart of salvation. Human contrition is our response to the reality of sin. God cannot simply ignore sin but must respond to it.[32] Contrition is the form that the human glorification of God takes in the face of sin, since sin is the "disglorification" of God and contrition the disavowal of that disglorification. Both right worship and repentance are constitutive of Anatolios's soteriology, a soteriology of *both* doxology *and* contrition.[33] Sin, for Anatolios, is anti-doxological; it falls short of the glory and praise that is God's due.[34] Sin distorts God's image by one made in God's image and who ought therefore "represent God."[35]

Both Stump and Anatolios emphasize the transformative side of Christ's salvific work, which for Stump is at the heart of the teaching on atonement, its forward-looking side, a solution to the problem of future wrongdoing, of guilt and shame, for the sake of "the mutual

27. Anatolios, *Deification*, 32.

28. This is not to imply that the Chalcedonian formula encompasses all that can be said about the Incarnation, or that it ends the need for further theological refinement. E.g., see Rahner, "Chalcedon—End or Beginning?," in *Theological Investigations*, 1, 149–200.

29. Anatolios, *Deification*, 60, 88, 230, 234.

30. Anatolios, *Deification*, 24, 30–31, 427–29.

31. Anatolios, *Deification*, 226.

32. Anatolios, *Deification*, 307–12.

33. Anatolios, *Deification*, 32, 83–85, 222–23.

34. Anatolios, *Deification*, 113, 295, 427–29.

35. Anatolios, *Deification*, 297.

indwelling between God and a human person in grace."[36] A question well put to Anatolios's soteriology is whether that which gives glory to God is fundamentally worship or rather action on behalf of the poor (Isa 11–17; Matt 25:31–46), not that these are incompatible. Anatolios does emphasize that "humanity's glorification of God contains an integral obedience to divine commandments."[37] Anatolios looks favorably upon Anselm's emphasis on divine honor, although not on Anselm's focus on the intrinsic necessity of satisfaction. As the West moves cautiously away from an Anselmian interpretation of atonement, Anatolios sees a value in its recognition of the honor due God. It is in Irenaeus, however, as representative of the West, that it is so clear that humanity's salvation is in the glorification of God; the glory of God is humanity's coming to fullness of life.[38] Humanity's ultimate fulfillment, for Anatolios, consists in doxology *and* contrition, a doxological contrition that takes one into an intra-trinitarian glorification. Stump too sees the purpose of the atonement as overcoming the distance between God and human beings so that humanity might be *at one* with God. Anatolios, reflecting on one of Aquinas's contributions to soteriology, speaks of Christ's "interior pain and sadness."[39] On this topic Stump is quite eloquent, making one aware of the extent of Christ's *psychic* pain in his being conscious of the sin of the world.[40] It is in this sense that Christ takes on our sins (Isa 53:5).What makes one unappreciative of the doctrine of the atonement, or less able to personally appropriate it, has been a misrepresentation of its deepest meaning rather than a proper emphasis on its manifestation of the love that Christ has for us.

There is a fitting reverence for the mystery of the cross in the church's never having attempted to define more magisterially the undefinable richness of the cross's revelatory power. It stands before us as a mystery just as his Blessed Mother and beloved disciple stood before the cross in their grief stricken but hope filled and confident way. Its meaning remains inexhaustible and should never be reduced to an act of required appeasement. It was a freely chosen act of love. As I have often put it: Creation itself was an act of perfect love. Greater love than that there

36. Stump, *Atonement*, 339; see 39–69, 339–77. For Anatolios, see *Deification*, 418–21.

37. Anatolios, *Deification*, 282. Ethics itself is ultimately doxological, 409.

38. Anatolios on Irenaeus, *Deification*, 268–72, 274–75, 282–84, 382–83.

39. Anatolios, *Deification*, 332.

40. Stump, *Atonement*, 273–78.

could not be, one might say, for the one who had no need of us to freely choose to share his life with us. Yet greater love than that comes across to us. He not only chose to create but to become one with his creation, a part of it, one of us, in the Incarnation of the Word. Greater love than that there could not be. And yet greater love than that there also was. On the cross God manifested the degree to which he was willing to become one with us. Not only God-with-us (Immanuel) but God-for-us, *totaliter*, on the cross. Greater love than that there could not be, revealing love as a freely chosen self-sacrifice for the sake of the other.[41]

Perhaps with the doctrine of the atonement, more than with any other Christian teaching, the words of St. Ephrem are apropos:

> Lord, who can comprehend even one of your words? We lose more of it than we grasp, like those who drink from a living spring. For God's word offers different facets according to the capacity of the listener, and the Lord has portrayed his message in many colors, so that whoever gazes upon it can see in it what suits him. Within it he has buried manifold treasures, so that each of us might grow rich in seeking them out . . . And so whenever anyone discovers some part of the treasure, he should not think that he has exhausted God's word . . . A thirsty man is happy when he is drinking, and he is not depressed because he cannot exhaust the spring. So let this spring quench your thirst and not your thirst the spring . . . So do not foolishly try to drain in one draught what cannot be consumed all at once, and do not cease out of faintheartedness from what you will be able to absorb as time goes on.[42]

Jacques Maritain, in his own meditation on the cross of Christ, wrote:

> It is the Person of the Word which did and suffered all that Christ did and suffered—through the instrumentality of his human nature. Is it, therefore, necessary for us to say that just as Mary, because she is the Mother of Christ, is the *Mother of God*, so also the death of Christ has been the *death of God?* Yes, it is necessary to say this, although it runs the risk of being terribly misunderstood . . . It remains nevertheless true, provided that one understands correctly that which one says, that on Good Friday *a divine Person died* (a human death), the Word Incarnate died,

41. For this description of love, see Goergen, *Power of Love*, 197, 203, 207, 223, 233.

42. From the Roman Catholic Breviary, *Liturgy of the Hours*, III:199–200 (sixth Sunday in Ordinary Time), from a commentary on the *Diatesseron* by Saint Ephrem.

> died of love and voluntarily. It is a very shocking expression but if one refuses shocking expressions, one renounces glimpsing however little the mystery of the Cross.[43]

At the opposite end of the Christian spectrum from Maritain is Rudolf Steiner (1861–1925), an unorthodox clairvoyant Christian esotericist, founder of anthroposophy, editor of Goethe's scientific writings. I mention him since, from a completely different perspective, he too saw what he called "the mystery of Golgotha" playing a pivotal role in his own life as well as in the history of the universe. It was for Steiner *the* central event in earth's evolution, an objective, cosmic, and historical event. With respect to the role it had in his own spiritual development, he wrote in his autobiography:

> During the period when my statements about Christianity seemed to contradict my later comments, a conscious knowledge of real Christianity began to dawn within me. Around the turn of the century, this seed of knowledge continued to develop. The soul test described here occurred shortly before the beginning of the twentieth century. It was decisive for my soul's development that I stood spiritually before the Mystery of Golgotha in a deep and solemn celebration of knowledge.[44]

With respect to the earth's evolution, he wrote: "This event in Palestine stands in the center, not only of humankind's physical evolution, but also of that of the other worlds to which human beings belong."[45]

Teilhard de Chardin's final sentence in *The Human Phenomenon* reads: "In one way or another, even in the eyes of a mere biologist, it is still true that nothing resembles the way of the Cross as much as the

43. Maritain, *Grace and Humanity*, 139–40. Emphasis in text.

44. Steiner, *Autobiography*,188. Also in that autobiography, in references to the lectures that became a book, *Christianity as Mystical Fact*: "From the beginning I stressed the importance of the words *as mystical fact*. My intention was not merely to present the mystical meaning of Christianity. My purpose was to describe evolution, from the ancient Mysteries to the Mystery of Golgotha, in a way that would reveal forces active in evolution that were not merely earthly, historical forces, but spiritual and extraearthly" (204). It is as a historical as well as a mystical fact that Steiner saw the importance of the mystery of Golgotha in the earth's evolution. See *Christianity*, 69, 85, 114. Also Lindenberg, *Rudolf Steiner*, 324–41. Steiner's high esteem for Thomas Aquinas is manifest in *Redemption of Thinking*, the first work of Steiner's that I read, recommended to me by Sister Adrian Hofstetter, OP.

45. Lindenberg, *Rudolf Steiner*, 337, quoted from Steiner's *Esoteric Science*, 273–74.

human epic."[46] And in a reflection on the meaning of the cross in *The Divine Milieu* he writes:

> It is perfectly true that the Cross means going beyond the frontiers of the sensible world and even, in a sense, breaking with it. The final stages of the ascent to which it calls us compel us to cross a threshold, a critical point, where we lose touch with the zone of the realities of the senses . . . But that agonizing flight from the experimental zones—which is what the Cross means—is only . . . the sublime aspect of a law common to *all* life . . . The royal road of the Cross is no more nor less than the road of human endeavor supernaturally righted and prolonged. Once we have fully grasped the meaning of the Cross, we are no longer in danger of finding life sad and ugly. We shall simply have become more attentive to its incomprehensible gravity.[47]

The cross has led, through the centuries, to profound reflections on the meaning of life. Among those meanings lies the redemptive work of Christ who died for our sins, such as interpreted by Eleonore Stump and Khaled Anatolios. At the same time, equally important is an emphasis on the redemption's cosmic dimensions. Teilhard, in choosing to emphasize the ongoing creative act and the role of the Incarnation within it, may seem to have underemphasized the expiatory aspect of the cross, which he did not deny but chose not to explore. Choosing rather, along lines we recognize today as an emphasis in Eastern theology, he brings to the forefront of his theological reflections the divinization of humanity, the traditional concept of deification as intrinsic to the doctrine of the atonement.[48] Teilhard wrote: "The Christian mind, without losing sight of the 'expiatory' aspect of Christ's saving operation, is much more inclined than heretofore to concentrate its attention on the aspect of 'recasting and building.'"[49] It is in Teilhard's rethinking the doctrine of redemption

46. *HP*, 226.

47. *DM*, 78–79.

48. There are many current biblical, historical, and theological studies on the topic of the atonement. E.g., Finlan, *Problems with Atonement*; and *Options on Atonement*. For an excellent treatment of the biblical background to the notion of debt and satisfaction, Gary Anderson, *Sin*. Taking into consideration the thought of René Girard would be Bartlett, *Cross Purposes*. Also, Robert J. Daly's monumental study of sacrifice, *Christian Sacrifice*. In reference to the doctrine of deification, see Christensen and Wittung, *Partakers*; Meconi, *One Christ*; Lossky, *Image and Likeness*, 97–110; Meyendorff, *Eastern Christian Thought*.

49. "Introduction to the Christian Life" (1944), *CE*, 163. See Rideau, *Thought of Teilhard*, 547–49n125.

within an evolutionary view of the world that his emphasis lay on the divinizing omnipresence of Christ and the universe's re-creation. Within a renewed emphasis on Christian humanism, the traditional Christian teaching on the atoning work of Christ ought not be de-emphasized, but rather needs to be presented as the act of love on God's part that it is. The cross is both a revelation and a celebration of the depth of God's love. I have attempted here to respond to the need for us to think further about our articulation of the doctrine of the atonement. Grounded in a correct interpretation of the thought of Aquinas, a reconstruction such as that presented by Eleonore Stump, along with insights from Teilhard de Chardin, as well as others, the doctrine of the atoning work of Christ becomes not an obstacle but an asset to evangelization. It reflects the degree to which God *cares* about us and about his evolving creation.[50]

PRESENTING THE TEACHING ON HELL

Is there an eternal hell? Is it only a possibility? Is it even a possibility? Will everyone in the end, come Omega, be saved? An ongoing process of continuing purgation in some other realm may not be appealing, nor even multitudinous reincarnations, yet they do challenge us to live a moral life without negating the mercy of God which endures forever as the Psalmist says (136). Whether God would have become incarnate if there had been no tragic history of sin, we will never know, although such would seem to be extremely fitting. Such was the opinion of the early Aquinas as well as his mentor, Albert the Great. Later Thomas saw it equally fitting, and in fact more so, in accord with the teaching of the Scriptures as he understood them, that God became incarnate in order to save us, which manifests not only God's glory and love of creation but also his mercy,[51] which is what both the doctrine of the atonement and the church's teaching on hell is challenged to reveal. We have now spoken about the doctrine of atonement and in chapter 4 about predestination and how Thomas's account is often misrepresented.[52]

Charles Taylor wrote about the doctrine of double predestination:

50. For an excellent collection of essays pertinent to the care of creation, see Meconi, *On Earth*.

51. See chapter 6 above.

52. See chapter 4, esp. n16.

> Needless to say, this wasn't the only way that the double mystery [the Fall and Redemption, or sin and grace] could be articulated. Eastern fathers, like Gregory of Nyssa, put things differently. But Augustine and Anselm shaped the theology of Latin Christendom in this regard, and the Reformation, far from correcting this imbalance, aggravated it. The sense that this language [of damnation and punishment], above all others, has got a lock on the mysteries, is an invitation to drive its logic through to the most counter-intuitive, not to say horrifying conclusions, like the doctrine of the damnation of the majority of humans, or double predestination. The confidence—not to say arrogance—with which these conclusions were drawn anticipates and offers a model for the later humanist hostility to mystery.[53]

Taylor recognized the need to rethink the doctrine of hell.[54] In Roman Catholic circles this challenge was taken up by Hans Urs von Balthasar in *Dare We Hope "That All Men Will Be Saved"?* Von Balthasar places his reflection within the context of a theology of hope. We can hope, we ought to hope, we can pray, that all will be saved, which seems to be God's will as well. Beyond hope, however, we cannot go, and we must let the question rest within the mystery of God.

Those who remain open to eternal damnation as a possibility also leave the door open to universal salvation as a possibility since we cannot affirm in faith that anyone in fact has been damned for all eternity. Hell may be a possibility, but no one may actually be "in hell." Von Balthasar quotes a German catechism written by Walter Kasper: "Neither Holy Scripture nor the Church's Tradition of faith asserts with certainty of any man that he is actually in hell. Hell is always held before our eyes as a *real possibility*, one connected with the offer of conversion and life."[55] Walter Kasper supports what he sees as von Balthasar's balanced approach:

> Thus, the two sets of assertions in Holy Scripture have led to two extreme positions: *massa damnata*, on the one hand, and the redemption of all, on the other. That confronts us with the question whether, and as the case may be, how we can find a way out of this predicament and find a solution that avoids both extremes. Hans

53. *A Secular Age*, 78.

54. *A Secular Age*, 13, 78, 223, 262, 650, 653, 656, 671, 688.

55. From Jordan, ed., *Confession of Faith*, 346. Emphasis in text. Pages 344–52 cover heaven, hell, and purgatory. Quoted in von Balthasar, *Dare We Hope*, 164–65. Also see Kasper, *Mercy*, 107.

> Urs von Balthasar has identified a path, which is supposed to lead us on a course between Origen and Augustine.[56]

David Bentley Hart goes further, however, denying even the possibility of eternal damnation as compatible with the Christian conception of God.[57] He sees it as odious to try and steer a middle path and argues, unlike von Balthasar, that we dare not doubt the salvation of all.[58] For Hart, the traditional Christian view of hell as eternal damnation is "the single best argument for doubting the plausibility of the Christian faith."[59] This remains a strong assertion for anyone concerned about evangelization in a secular age.

Traditional interpretations of the doctrine of hell are what Charles Taylor also sees as contributing to the emergence of unbelief. If one must choose between a God implicated in a doctrine of everlasting torture and no God at all, the latter option becomes more humane. Given how relationality is constitutive of what or who a human person is, Hart maintains that if one is saved, all must be saved, or if one is lost, all will be lost. We cannot separate ourselves out as individuals one from the other.[60] This is a perspective that would resonate with Teilhard de Chardin's thought as well. Hart also places heavy emphasis on the text of St. Paul in 1 Corinthians, chapter 15, verses 24 to 28,[61] which was a pivotal text for Teilhard's eschatological vision. Hart simply sees the salvation of all as being most consistent with the God of revelation and he rejects as morally reprehensible a doctrine of hell associated with a punitive God. Contemporary treatments of the doctrine of hell, however, do not understand it as divine punishment but rather as a freely chosen separation from God in one's refusal to love completely. Can such a choice ever be both free and forever?

56. Kasper, *Mercy*, 106. For Kasper's fuller discussion, see 97–111. Kasper sees mercy as the fundamental attribute of God, 51, 88, 98.

57. David Bentley Hart, *Universal Salvation*. For two critical reviews of Bentley Hart's book, see those by Brotherton and O'Neill.

58. David Bentley Hart, *Universal Salvation*, 66, 102.

59. David Bentley Hart, *Universal Salvation*, 65.

60. David Bentley Hart, *Universal Salvation*, 144–58. Pope Francis, without further explanation, writes in both *Laudato Sí* and *Fratelli Tutti* (##32, 34, 54) that "we can only be saved together."

61. David Bentley Hart, *Universal Salvation*, 104–6, 141, 161, 194.

Von Balthasar's theology takes us back to Thomas Aquinas and the supernatural virtue of hope and discussions on how to reconcile God's justice with God's mercy. As Josef Pieper wrote:

> In theological hope the "antithesis" between divine justice and divine mercy is, as it were, "removed"—not so much "theoretically" as existentially: supernatural hope is man's appropriate, existential answer to the fact that these qualities in God, which to the creature appear to be contradictory, are actually identical. One who looks only at the justice of God is as little able to hope as is one who sees only the mercy of God . . . Only hope is able to comprehend the reality of God that surpasses all antitheses, to know that his mercy is identical with his justice and his justice with his mercy.[62]

The theology of the virtue of hope can also take us to Pope Benedict XVI's encyclical, *Spe Salvi* (*Saved in Hope*) wherein, following de Lubac, he recognizes that hope is a social, not an individualist, reality.[63] To affirm that all *may* be saved leaves the door open to universal salvation but lets it rest within the virtue of hope. To say that all *will* be saved removes us one step from the mystery of salvation but ensures that we leave intact an image of God as love and the Christian conception of God uncompromised.

Gerhard Lohfink, as well as many others, has wrestled with these same questions.[64] His effort to rethink what will happen to us at the moment of death, in the light of Scripture and contemporary science, opens the question of the nature of hell and leaves it an open question. He asks:

> Can God, whose nature is pure love, allow a part of humanity to suffer eternal hell, eternal torment? . . . Can ultimate beatitude, the feast of eternal happiness with God, really exist if at the same time—before the eyes of the blessed—some portion of humanity lives in eternal torment? . . . Has God achieved the purpose of creation if part of that creation has definitely become a hell? Would that not mean that God's creation is a fundamental failure, and that creation's history of salvation and redemption has ultimately fallen short of its intended goal?[65]

62. Pieper, *Faith, Hope, Love*, 128. Quoted in Balthasar, *Dare We Hope*, 156–57.
63. Benedict XVI, *Spe Salvi*, ##13–15. See de Lubac, *Catholicism*.
64. Lohfink, *Is This All*, 166–71.
65. Lohfink, *Is This All*, 167.

For Lohfink, a New Testament scholar, the references about hell in the New Testament must be read within the larger framework of those texts that speak of God's universal will for salvation (1 Tim 2:4, 6; Titus 2:11; Col 1:20; John 12:32; Rom 5:18; Rom 11:32), references that repeat the word *all*.[66] In whatever direction we go, "hell cannot be something that God imposes on people," but "can only be something God does not want, in any case and under any circumstances."[67] Hell must be something that one chooses for oneself. Bentley Hart would ask, is this something that any truly free person who understands the nature of his or her choice would choose? Yet Lohfink avoids saying that we can know for sure that all will be saved. "Talk of hell is required by the sober realism with which we must view history," but "it must always have a counterweight that is much heavier: God's absolute will for salvation."[68] Likewise Charles Taylor maintains: "Hell, the ultimate separation from God, must remain a possibility for human freedom, but all the presumptuous certainty that it is inhabited must be abandoned."[69] Gary Anderson, a specialist in the Hebrew Bible, wisely highlights a biblical truth, that it is never wise to presume on divine mercy.[70]

Universal salvation seems more consistent with Teilhard de Chardin's vision of the universe, his understanding of the nature of the human person, and his emphasis on 1 Corinthians 15, verses 24 to 28. Yet he too lived with the question unanswered. His too was a vision of hope, grounded in faith, that falls short of absolute affirmation of universal salvation, which is clearly what he hopes for, and even in one sense expects. He prays toward the end of *The Divine Milieu:*

> You have told me, O God, to believe in hell. But You have forbidden me to hold with absolute certainty that a single man has been damned. I shall therefore make no attempt to consider the damned here, nor even to discover—by whatsoever means—whether there are any. I shall accept the existence of hell on

66. Lohfink, *Is This All*, 168.

67. Lohfink, *Is This All*, 169.

68. Lohfink, *Is This All*, 171.

69. Taylor, *A Secular Age*, 656.

70. Gary Anderson, *Charity*, 57. His is also an excellent treatment of the doctrine of purgatory, 162–81, wherein he acknowledges that spiritual transformation does not come to closure at death. With respect to purgatory, he writes: "We don't have to pretend that all are saved and by so doing make a mockery of our moral choices, but neither must we consign our beloved to eternal suffering" (181).

> Your word, *as a structural element in the universe*, and I shall pray and meditate until that awe-inspiring thing appears to me as a strengthening and even blessed complement to the vision of Your omnipresence which You have opened out to me.[71]

Perhaps at this point it is best to rely on faith, not dogmatic certitude one way or the other, and to let Jesus simply ask us: Do you love Me? (John 21:15–19). Do you trust me? As one author's meditation has put it: "One is bound to believe either that the mercy of God is limited, i.e., that it extends only to the instant of bodily death, or that it is infinite and never ceases, i.e., that it possesses the means of acting also after the instance of the soul's separation from the body."[72] The mercy of God has no limit. God's love for his creation is infinite. Of those things we can be sure. Thus hell, insofar as there may be a hell come the Parousia, must be an exemplification of God's love, and perhaps the supreme exemplification thereof. It is not God as inflicting torture but God as respecting humanity's nature as conscious and capable of choice, or at least the time it takes for a human being to become free. Greater love than this one could not have, to love and not count the cost to the Lover, to allow the beloved to be free, to mature, and to wait patiently for the beloved's response, while seeing and knowing in one's own eternal life to what end it will come. Perhaps in the end it is to Jesus' approach to the woman taken in adultery where we need to go (John 8:1–11): Let the one who is without sin cast the first stone. And go, and do not sin again.

If creation itself, even given its evolutionary structure, is a supreme manifestation of God's love, and if the Incarnation, God's freely choosing to be one with us, is a further confirmation of the nature of God as love, and if God's Only Begotten Son's freely chosen death on the cross for our sakes manifests a love greater than which there could not be, then the thought of an eternal hell, as inconceivable as it might be, nevertheless held out as possible, is the greatest manifestation of God's love. Greater love there could not be than for the Lover to respect the dignity and freedom of the beloved. God clearly desires the salvation of all. Yet our final destiny also rests within our own hands. As one ponders the mystery of God's love and mercy as well as the consequences of moral evil, one

71. *DM*, 129–30. In the English translation the italics and regular print are reversed in order to give it the character of a prayer or meditation, but the original French text is as in the text above. One can continue to read the meditation as it continues. For his sense of heightened expectation see the epilogue, 133–38.

72. Powell, trans., *Meditations on Tarot*, 322.

becomes willing to entrust our destinies to God's hands, relying on the fact that neither extreme does justice to the whole picture.

THE PHENOMENON OF HUMAN SEXUALITY

The church's soteriological teaching with respect to the death of Christ and its eschatological teaching pertaining to the "last things" probe the mystery of salvation, a mystery to be contemplated, not necessarily resolved. The task of theology is not to eliminate mystery but to bring us to its threshold. At the same time theology is intended to help us understand and appreciate a doctrine as reasonable. How does our exploration, or interpretation, of a doctrine of the faith illuminate for our times who the God of Jesus Christ is? Our next exploration—on human sexuality—has moral implications more than dogmatic ones.

One of the more provocative of Teilhard's insights impacts one's theology of sexuality. As quoted earlier, he wrote in a 1936 essay:

> In its initial forms, and up to a very high stage in life, sexuality seems identified with propagation . . . That the dominant function of sexuality was at first to assure the preservation of the species is indisputable . . . But from the critical moment of hominization, another more essential role was developed for love, a role of which we are seemingly only just beginning to feel the importance.[73]

Does *human* genital sexuality have as its *primary* purpose procreation? Teilhard suggests that something else may be even more fundamental in human sexual love. Teilhard in no way sets aside a traditional understanding of the atonement but seeks to supplement it, and even give a primacy to an undervalued dimension of it. Teilhard's own theology of the atonement is readily compatible with Christian tradition, however. When it comes to universal salvation and the doctrine of an eternal hell, Teilhard also remains traditional, even if he opens for us the question, but in the end does not affirm universal salvation as a fact but only as a possibility, as an object of hope. When it comes to the church's understanding of human sexuality, can the same be said about how Teilhard understands it and what Christian tradition affirms?

When it comes to social ethics, the church's tradition and its social teaching of the past 150 years fits well with Teilhard's orientation to these

73. "Sketch of a Personalistic Universe" (1936), *HE*, 73.

questions. Some have even noted his influence on the Second Vatican Council's Pastoral Constitution on the Church in the Modern World. But what impact does an evolutionary understanding of creation have on our understanding of *human* sexuality? We can quickly become nervous and project varied consequences following upon Teilhard's statement above. We might be tempted to lump together a wide variety of topics from our so-called culture wars, whether those be questions of sexual orientation or gender identity or the nature of marriage. Each of these is a topic deserving reflection. The only question here, however, is whether the vitally important role of procreation is to be considered a *telos* essential for human sexual acts.

Is there a need to reconfigure our understanding of human sexual love in the light of God's creation as evolving? How is sexuality to be understood in the light of Teilhard's emphasis on evolution as amorization? Thinking through difficult theological questions dialogically becomes a moral responsibility. Two contemporary thinkers, along with many others, offer two different approaches to these questions: Paul J. Griffiths and G. J. McAleer. I offer these two to open the door to our reflection. Paul J. Griffiths is a highly respected Catholic theologian. Perceived by most as traditional as well as intellectually independent, he has deference for the church's magisterium.[74] His book, *Christian Flesh*, opens the door for the church to reconsider its approach to sexual morality. We cannot enter deeply into questions of sexual morality here, but Griffiths can be a thought-provoking dialogue partner in this area of moral concern. Language is important for Griffiths. He sometimes uses it in novel although always precise ways.[75] Graham J. McAleer is a professor of philosophy at the Loyola University in Baltimore, Maryland. His 2005 book, *Ecstatic Morality and Sexual Politics*, grounded in the thought of Thomas Aquinas, is replete with insights and is an elaboration of what he calls an Ecstatic Thomism critical of progressive interpretations of Aquinas. Let them for a moment be our partners in dialogue.

McAleer grounds his interpretation of Aquinas's theory of sexuality on the Dionysian principle of *bonum est diffusivum sui* (goodness tends to communicate itself). At the heart of Thomas's thought is his understanding of human desire (*eros*) as other-centered, ecstatic in nature, oriented toward the vision of God. Concupiscence is desire disordered,

74. E.g., see "Theological Disagreement," 23–36; "Under Pressure," 30–37.

75. An excellent introduction to Paul J. Griffiths is his *Intellectual Appetite*.

not reflecting the true nature of desire. McAleer gives a defense of *Humanae Vitae* and its critique of a contraceptive culture in contrast to a culture of the person.[76] *Humanae Vitae* maintained that sex must be oriented to procreation.[77] For McAleer the procreative purpose manifests the biblical theme of "welcoming the stranger."[78] McAleer insights are profound. Yet is it obvious that the human sexual act must be oriented to procreation in order that it be "Christoform"?[79] A Christian theology of marriage is one thing; every human sexual act another. Procreation is one way for sexuality to be fruitful and is a generous gift of self but is it the only way? Procreation does give meaning to the act of giving oneself sexually to another, but that only procreation can make the sexual act meaningful and Christoform is not obvious. Sex is made meaningful through fecundity but is fecundity confined to procreation? That a sexual act be open to welcoming a stranger is an insight to be pondered, but "welcoming the stranger" has significance not only for sexual ethics but also social ethics.

Yet when it comes to social ethics, McAleer is critical of the direction taken by Catholic social teaching since Pope St. John XXIII's encyclical *Pacem in Terris*, which McAleer maintains followed the political philosophy of Jacques Maritain, whose rights-based approach to social questions he considers misguided, a direction however taken by Catholic social teaching since then.[80] McAleer opts for one grounded in the antitotalitarian political philosophy of Aurel Kolnai (1900–1973). McAleer writes: "I will show that the primary goals of Catholic social thought might be better attained by Kolnai's conservative thought than by the 'progressive Thomism' started by Maritain and absorbed by the encyclical tradition."[81] McAleer is also dubious about whether the church's current approach to social questions in the social encyclicals can be helpful in exploring questions of sexual morality. He would not accept Teilhard de

76. *Ecstatic Morality*, 115–36.

77. Paul VI, *Humanae Vitae*, ##3, 9, 11–12.

78. *Ecstatic Morality*, 116, 139, 149, 187.

79. *Ecstatic Morality*, 118.

80. For McAleer's critique of Maritain's approach to natural rights see *Ecstatic Morality*, 153, 160–61, 167–69, 174–77.

81. *Ecstatic Morality*, 138. On Kolnai's political highlighting the value of privilege over that of equalitarianism. see *Ecstatic Morality*, 136, 138, 146–50, 161, 167, 169, 170, 173, 176–79. It would be difficult here to go into more detail on this question.

Chardin's observation and questions whether human ends, given evolution, can change.[82]

For Paul Griffiths, enfleshment is not only *humanly* significant but has a specifically *Christian* dimension. Given the Incarnation, the flesh of Jesus remains the model for understanding flesh as Christians. Sexual acts for Christians ought to deepen one's cleaving to Christ or incorporation into Christ. Griffiths offers a sustained reflection on Paul's First Letter to the Corinthians, chapter 6, verses 12 to 20, which concludes with the words: "Therefore glorify God in your own body." Fornication is not to be understood in terms of acts as such that are permitted and others that are forbidden but rather in terms of the degree to which they glorify the Lord because of the way in which they are done.[83] There can be no simple list of acts in themselves that constitute fornication, no listing of precepts.[84] "There is, no doubt, catechetical and practical utility in so classifying some kinds of fleshly cleaving. But a deeper theoretical consideration still raises doubts."[85]

More effective for moral theology than a list of prohibitions are hagiographies—testimonies to what Christian flesh means: "clear cases of what saints do and don't do, and they do this without resort to the categories of demand or ban or duty."[86] All sexual acts have a potential for wounding. None is exempt. Concupiscence is a word that designates this capacity to do damage, connoting a possessive, expropriative mode of desiring: "concupiscent flesh is concerned principally, and sometimes only, with its own gratification, which is to say not at all with the gifts it may give or the damage it may do to the recipient of its wounding caress."[87] Unfortunately, in our fallen and devastated world, "there are no caresses entirely free of concupiscence; none, therefore, that do not also in some measure wound,"[88] none that is damage-free, not even those that are procreative,[89] except for the caresses that Jesus gives who sets the standard for Christians in contrast to concupiscent flesh.[90] One

82. *Ecstatic Morality*, 97, 62.

83. *Christian Flesh*, 66–70.

84. *Christian Flesh*, 69, 71, 72, 73.

85. *Christian Flesh*, 75.

86. *Christian Flesh*, 77–78.

87. *Christian Flesh*, 125.

88. *Christian Flesh*, 126.

89. *Christian Flesh*, 133–34, 137–38.

90. *Christian Flesh*, 130, 60.

may think that Griffiths lowers the bar with respect to sexual morality, opening the door to a situation ethics, but he in fact raises the bar which becomes Jesus himself.

"Are there particular caresses, particular skin-to-skin fleshly exchanges, forbidden to Christian flesh by precept or command?"[91] Griffiths answers no. He then considers three instances which are most often understood as forbidden to Christians: masturbation, cunnilingus, and sodomy.[92] We cannot go into his analysis here, but he exemplifies an approach to sexual morality that is not tied to the necessity that a sexual act be procreative in order for it to be profoundly Christian. Not all genital pleasure serves a copulatory purpose and need not be restricted to it. "And, theologically, we should expect what we find, which is that our fleshly appetites and capacities generally vastly exceed a single purpose or end: eating isn't just for nourishment, and clothing isn't just for protecting the flesh."[93] What is sexual intimacy for Christians about then? "The point isn't the sex, or gender, of those exchanging caresses; the point is the extent to which the caresses they exchange comport well with their condition as Jesus-cleaved. And that isn't determined by the sex or gender of the participants. There's neither theological nor empirical reason to think so."[94] Griffiths is aware that his carefully thought out but bold approach to these questions may be seen as in contradiction to magisterial teaching which has a high priority for him, but his intent is to open the way for interpretive work on magisterial teaching and perhaps assist doctrinal development in this area.[95] His concern throughout is what makes human flesh, and fleshy acts, profoundly Christian.

Both authors, Griffiths and McAleer, as well as many others, offer significant and thoughtful reflections on a vitally important question. Teilhard de Chardin's contribution comes by raising a question about what the primary purpose of *human* sexuality is. For Teilhard, as we saw in chapter 5, that would be growth in friendship; the development of the universe's affective energies; amorization; the evolution of love.[96] In other words, Christian sexuality is to be focused on the quality of love and

91. *Christian Flesh*, 138.

92. *Christian Flesh*, 138–45.

93. *Christian Flesh*, 141.

94. *Christian Flesh*, 144–45.

95. *Christian Flesh*, 145. Also see Griffiths' "Ulterior Lives."

96. For further reflection on Teilhard's approach to human sexuality, see de Lubac, *Eternal Feminine*, 48–65.

affectionization, more than on the biological function of the affection. This in no way conflicts with the Christian understanding of marriage and its openness to family life.[97] Teilhard's excentration is itself an openness to the stranger. Following upon Charles Taylor's as well as our concern for a theocentric humanism, as Christians face the reality of evangelization in a secular world, how are we to be both faithful to tradition as well as open to a universe that is unfinished? How can we be like the wise scribe who goes into his cellar and brings out something old and something new (Matt 13:52)?

As with the previous theological reflections on the doctrines of atonement and hell, so with human sexuality. Let us consider these as three thought experiments, as three disputed questions, as three topics which Teilhard's vision urges us to consider further, as we contemplate Christianity's future and the future of evangelization. These are only three challenges to be faced in the light of Tradition that are central to the effort to articulate a humanism that is both deeply Christian and responsive to questions of today. My own approach to neuralgic or disputed theological questions, in accord with that of Thomas Aquinas, is to hear varied sides to the question, to see a virtuous life, a truly humane life, to be a graced effort to navigate the delicate balance between extremes. There is always, of course, the individual's discernment of what these extremes are, but this is where a more communal consciousness is of great help. We don't name and navigate the extremes by ourselves alone. We are members of a larger body, the church, in which one finds legitimate diversity. It is important to find a balance between an attitude which approaches sex as suspect and one that places few if any limits on it. Neither Manichaeism nor sexual liberty are healthy, nor do they lead to happiness. In the political world, which appears at present to be in crisis due to the polarization that requires our allegiance to one side or another, do we grow in virtue, charity, or wisdom, if our choices are on the one hand a disregard for traditional moral values or on the other a plea to preserve a premodern consciousness? Neither the prophet of gloom nor the enchantments of

97. One would need to pursue further here the emergence and development of the church's teaching with respect to the procreative purpose of sexual acts. To what degree was this influenced by the social context within which Christianity emerged, a lack of appreciation for human eroticism in a highly ascetic, more dualistic, Neoplatonic, even Manichean world? The constraints placed on sexual acts, the limits within which they could be considered moral, permeated, and predated Christian practice. John Boswell wrote: "Procreative purpose provided an early and influential rationale for controlling sexuality both inside and outside marriage" (*Same-Sex Unions*, 112).

the modern world ring true to what the Incarnation asks of us. Finding that "mean" between extremes is aided if we take a dialogical approach, and we are more likely to be successful the wider the scope of our dialogue partners. Neither traditionalism nor modernism seems the solution we seek.

A CHRISTIAN HUMANISM

Christianity and humanism are not antithetical to each other but rather intrinsic to each other. The Word was made flesh. A human being, Jesus, was God. Teilhard, in *The Divine Milieu*, saw the need for the humanization of the Christian project:

> The great objection brought against Christianity in our time, and the real source of the distrust which insulates entire blocks of humanity from the influence of the Church, has nothing to do with historical or theological difficulties. It is the suspicion that our religion makes it adherents *inhuman*.[98]

A truly integral Christian humanism needs to offer the world a moral vision, respectful of the empirical sciences, that can affirm *both* this world *and* a beyond-this-world, thus "worldly" but with openness to transcendence, *both* person-centered *and* socially conscious, theistic in depth and cosmic in scope. The philosophical theology of Thomas Aquinas and the new directions offered by Teilhard de Chardin, in dialogue with other thinkers and activists, can meet the demand for a Christian humanism that removes a major stumbling block to the church's evangelizing mission. We cannot lock ourselves into "parties"—I am for Paul; I am for Cephas; I am for Apollos (1 Cor 1:12)—I am for Thomas, I am for Teilhard, I am for Rahner, I am for von Balthasar. It is within dialogue between past and present, tradition and modernity, that the Holy Spirit speaks. An understanding of the church's teaching as continually developing goes back as far as St, Vincent of Lérins, in the fifth century, up through St. John Henry Newman, and into the present times. Pope Francis wrote: "Tradition is not a museum, true religion is not a freezer, and doctrine is not static but grows and develops," while at the same time quoting Gustav Mahler that "tradition is not the repository of ashes but the preservation of fire."[99]

98. *DM*, 37. Emphasis in text.

99. *Let Us Dream*, 57. For St. Vincent of Lérins, see Roman Breviary, *Liturgy of the Hours*, 27th Week in Ordinary Time, Office of Readings for Friday. Newman,

Thomas's synthesis has been considered profoundly humanistic by R. W. Southern in his studies of medieval humanism. He wrote:

> Thomas Aquinas died in 1274, and it is probably true that man has never appeared so important a being in so well-ordered and intelligible a universe as in his works. Man was important because he was the link between the created universe and the divine intelligence. He alone in the world of nature could understand nature. He alone in nature could understand the nature of God. He alone could use and perfect nature in accordance with the will of God and thus achieve his full nobility.[100]

Thomas Prudlo, in his contextual study of Thomas Aquinas, wrote: "Thomas still has much to offer. He is the prophet of intelligibility and common sense. In many ways he is the apostle of human integrity and the bearer of optimism about human potentiality that is only born from a profoundly incarnational outlook."[101] The human phenomenon performs this same role in the thought of Teilhard.

If Christian faith is to flourish in a pluralistic society, it must face challenges posed by secular humanisms as well as other religious traditions. What does it mean to be human? Is Christianity's vision of the human convincing? enticing? In a pluralistic world, how do we communicate the truth, beauty, and humanity of the Catholic faith? Pope Francis in both his encyclical *Laudato Sí* ("On Care for Our Common Home") and *Fratelli Tutti* ("On Fraternity and Social Friendship") has expressed a desire for a new or renewed humanism.[102] He wrote: "We urgently need a humanism capable of bringing together the different fields of knowledge, including economics, in the service of a more integral and integrating vision."[103] This integral and integrating anthropological vision needs to be: (1) a moral vision, (2) with a solid philosophical and scientific basis, (3) that values this world, (4) and yet is open to the transcendent realm that is invisible, (5) personalist, in affirming the dignity and value of every

---

Development of Doctrine. Raphael Christianson, OP, while a graduate student at CUA, called to my attention that Juan Arintero, OP, also wrote about the development of doctrine in *Desenvolvimiento y Vitalidad.*

100. Southern, *Medieval Humanism*, 50. See esp. 29–60. Also Southern, *Scholastic Humanism*, esp. I:17–45. Southern also distinguishes varied meanings for the word "humanism."

101. Prudlo, *Environmental Portrait*, 304.

102. *Laudato Sí*, #141. *Fratelli Tutti*, #86.

103. *Laudato Sí*, #141.

human person and his or her relational structure, (6) social, appreciating the relationship between an individual and society with an emphasis on the common good, (7) theistic, grounded in a personal Beyond, and (8) cosmic or cosmological in scope. To this vision both Aquinas and Teilhard have a contribution to make.

A Moral Vision: Jonathan Sacks, the Jewish rabbi to whom I have previously referred, wrote: "The idea of reasoning together was dealt a fateful blow in the twentieth century by the collapse of moral language, the disappearance of 'I ought' and its replacement by 'I want', 'I choose', 'I feel'."[104] There can be no humane world that is not also a moral world, no humanism that is devoid of moral concepts and language. Thomas's virtue ethics provides such a moral vision.[105] Yet Thomas's ethics is enriched by dialogue with the twentieth century's moral challenges and questions, such as we find in insights from Teilhard, the observations of Paul Griffiths, the synodal pastoral approach of Pope Francis, Catholic social teaching, along with many Jewish and Christian interlocutors as well as those of other spiritual traditions. Dialogue does not mean an abandonment of an objective moral order. Thomas remains a foundation on which to build, lest there be no foundation at all. Yet reasoned conversation opens the door to new questions and insights. Can we at least agree that a moral vision and moral wisdom are essential to our future? Is a common moral vision possible in a pluralistic society? What is the Christian moral vision that we offer the world?

A Philosophical and Scientific Foundation: We have emphasized throughout, and certainly Teilhard had emphasized, the importance of a respect for modern science. Both science and theology. Both reason and faith. It was only in the last couple years that I became aware of the foundational work of Georges Lemaître, a Belgian Catholic priest (1894–1966) and professor at the Catholic University of Louvain, who proposed a "big bang theory" of his own, which he called the hypothesis of the primeval atom.[106] A contemporary of Teilhard, there is no evidence of

104. Sacks, *Dignity of Difference*, 3. His latest and last book was *Morality*. Sacks died on November 7, 2020, only months after the latter book was published.

105. See MacIntyre, *After Virtue*.

106. Nicholas Reynolds, OP, did an MA thesis, "Search for Truth," at the Aquinas Institute of Theology in St. Louis, Missouri. Raphael Christianson, OP, also a student at Aquinas Institute at the time, wrote a paper on "Enriching Complementarity," published in *Homiletic and Pastoral Review*. The work of these two students brought Lemaître to my attention.

any mutual interaction between them. He too, however, gives witness to the Catholic commitment to the important role of science in theological reflection. Aquinas's rigorous philosophical work, grounded in the natural philosophy of Aristotle, remains open to development, not resistant to the challenges of evolutionary theory and modern physics.[107] A coherent humanism requires both a metaphysical foundation as well as respect for the natural sciences.

This World as Having Value: Aquinas's anti-Manichean theology of creation emphasizes the goodness of creation and the holiness of the created order. Teilhard's commitment to this world as diaphanous of the divine leads to a world affirming spirituality. The world, its future, the future of the planet, our daily lives, our activities, and our diminishments are all valued by God. As I have often repeated, it is not a question of God *or* the world, but of both God *and* the world. Yet many historic Christian spiritualities created a dichotomy between the secular and the sacred, between this world and the other world, between this life and the life to come. Christian asceticism was seen as a discipline to remove us further and further from the world rather than to immerse ourselves virtuously in the world. For the Christian, ecological concerns are moral concerns. Creation is given to us as a gift and of it we are stewards. We are called upon to engage the world with its unfinishedness and be co-creators of humanity's future. The world is in the hands of God, and in ours as well, to whom God entrusted it.

An Openness to the Transcendent: Granted the emergence of unbelief alongside exclusively immanentist humanisms, Charles Taylor nevertheless notes signs of discontent with the latter. Can one find meaning in a world closed in on itself? Must there not be something other than this world that grounds it? Does not the sense of justice so important to modern moral sensibilities require the belief, at least an openness, to something more than this world alone? Otherwise, no matter what meaning we may find for ourselves, we must admit to this bottom line: The majority live lives of incredible suffering as victims of barbarous injustice. Without something more, beyond us, injustice reigns supreme.

107. The River Forest School of Thomism had always emphasized Aquinas's philosophy of nature and the value of dialogue with modern science. Ashley, *The Way*, 53–54; Ashley, "River Forest School," 1–15. On the continuing important role of Aristotle, see Feser, *Aristotle's Revenge*. On Teilhard, the philosophy of nature and Aristotle, see de Lubac, *Religion of Teilhard*, 97, 169–70. On Thomas Aquinas and evolutionary theory, also see http://www.thomisticevolution.org/.

Their lives do *not* matter; mine does. We find ourselves caught in a socially narrowed network which defines itself in terms of *us* and *them*. The movement, however, must be from "I" to "we."[108] As Teilhard would put it, the direction of development, whether personal or collective, is from centration to excentration to supercentration, from self to others to God. For Aquinas this is what love is, *caritas*, both a love of God and a love of neighbor, as was true for St. Augustine and the Christian tradition before him.[109] A universe without a transcendent dimension is a universe that will eventually collapse upon itself for there is "no exit," to borrow an expression from Jean-Paul Sartre.

Personalist: Christian humanism is person-centered, a person being understood as a relational being, the center of a network of relationships. Personalism, yes; individualism, no. One cannot be, or become, a person, apart from the others who are a part of who we are, which is Teilhard's understanding of personalization. Personalism is associated with the French Catholic philosopher Emmanuel Mounier (1905–1950), who interacted with both Jacques Maritain and Teilhard de Chardin.[110] All three saw the "person" as a social being, as not simply an isolated individual or "self," and as one whose vocation involves a presence to the world, one with inviolable dignity. Mounier's thought also influenced Peter Maurin, Dorothy Day, and the Catholic Worker Movement.[111] Pope St. John Paul II's philosophy was personalist as well.[112]

Socially Conscious: Unfortunately, by way of contrast to "personalist," we cannot here use the word "socialist," for the latter carries with it many unhelpful political and economic overtones. Yet there is something extremely social or communal that is essential to a Christian humanism. The church has an articulate social conscience, as manifest in encyclicals since Pope Leo XIII, who have maintained that neither socialism nor

108. On this theme of "I" and "we," see Sacks, *Morality*, n104 above.

109. Aquinas, *ST*, II-II, q. 23, a. 1; q. 25, a. 1. Augustine, *Teaching Christianity*, 114–26 (Book I, 20–24).

110. On his interaction with Teilhard, see Cuénot, *Teilhard de Chardin*, 249, 260. For a letter from Teilhard to Mounier, see *SC*, 221–23. For Mounier's even stronger relationship with Maritain, see Bernard Doering, *French Catholic Intellectuals*, 60–84, and Amato, *Mounier and Maritain*. Among Mounier's many writings are *A Personalist Manifesto* and *Personalism*.

111. Loughery and Randolph, *Dorothy Day*, 136–41, 159–67.

112. Crosby, *Personalism*.

capitalism responds adequately to society's ills.[113] The Judeo-Christian emphasis has been on the common good.[114] The Pontifical Council for Justice and Peace's *Compendium of the Social Doctrine of the Church*[115] concludes with a section on building a civilization of love.[116] For Teilhard there is no personalization that is not accompanied by socialization, no centration that does not need to be complemented by excentration. One is always a person "in society," in a social context. Catholic social ethics has struggled with social questions, human rights, the option for the poor, and the meaning of money. What does it mean to say that one cannot serve both God and mammon (Matt 6:24)? This latter question has been explored extensively by Eugene McCarraher in *The Enchantments of Mammon: How Capitalism Became the Religion of Modernity*.[117] A social conscience, however, is central to a moral conscience, and the former is not to be severed from the latter.

Theistic: It need not be said that a Christian humanism would be theistic, that there is a God, and that God is a personal God with whom we can have a relationship. Aquinas's arguments that belief in God is a reasonable thing, that what God is remains a mystery, and that we can nevertheless speak meaningfully about God, all these remain cogent. It is not a question of whether God is, but of the picture of God that we present to a world spiritually hungry but often not religiously affiliated. Teilhard

113. John XXIII, *Mater et Magistra*; Paul VI, *Populorum Progressio*; John Paul II, *Laborem Exercens, Sollicitudo Rei Socialis*, #21, *Centesimus Annus*; Pope Benedict XVI, *Deus Caritas Est*. The same is found in Pope Pius XI, *Quadragesimo Anno*. The Church's social teaching, however, is not simply a "modern" doctrine, but goes back to the New Testament. Thomas Schaefgen, OP, illustrates its radical character in his MA thesis, *Come Now, Distribute Your Wealth*. Also see Seseske, ed., *Catholic Social Teaching*.

114. This is true whether one turns to the works of Jonathan Sacks, Robert Bellah, or to the recent writings of Pope Francis.

115. The Pontifical Council for Justice and Peace, *Compendium of the Social Doctrine of the Church* begins by emphasizing an integral humanism and then discusses (1) God's plan of love for humanity; (2) The church's mission and social doctrine; (3) The human person and human rights; (4) The principles of the church's social doctrine; (5) The family, the vital cell of society; (6) Human work; (7) Economic life; (8) The political community; (9) The international community; (10) Safeguarding the environment; (11) The promotion of peace; and (12) Social doctrine and ecclesial action.

116. For a further reflection on this theme, see Carl Anderson, *Civilization of Love*.

117. McCarraher, *Enchantments of Mammon*. The book is a valuable and detailed treatment, close to seven hundred pages of text. David Bentley Hart's review, "Misenchantment," will entice you to read it.

attempts to bring that same God, the God of Jesus Christ, the God whose story Aquinas unfolds, into conjunction with our current knowledge about space and time. God is a God of evolution. What takes time, or is time, for us, is not time at all in God. That a personal God, who is a God of love, whose providence guides the universe, freely chose to create, and create evolutively, is not something insignificant. That same God chose to enter creation itself, by creating for himself a human nature, and thus able to accompany us in our pilgrimages through life. God, for Aquinas, as emphasized by Eleonore Stump,[118] is both Being and a Being, although not a being like any created being since God is Being Itself. God pulls us towards himself, almost like a magnet, as love tends to do, granted our resistances, but the One-Who-Is, that is the One-Who-Is-With-Us, is not a distant deistic deity, but a personal God, who has chosen to reveal himself to us, as a Lover does to his friend, one to whom we pray. It takes time for us to absorb the reality that God *loves* us and desires that we love him in return. He asks us, "Do you love me?" (John 21:15–18).

Cosmic: Our God is not small! As mind boggling as billions of years of evolution might be, and the myriads of galaxies there are, such that we cannot wrap our minds fully around the reality that the cosmos is, so likewise our minds are even less able to grasp fully the mystery of God. As I like to say, however, and as Teilhard said, the human person "finds himself in the grips of what he thought he could grasp."[119] Whatever we discover about the universe or continue to discover, there will always be mystery, that pushes us, pulls us, eludes us, shapes us. Mystery remains a facet of what it means to be human. Mystery is essential to humanism. Mystery lay at the heart of our cosmos, at the heart of God's creation, while we continue to explore it. In the end, physics itself finds itself amid mystery. Albert Einstein himself, neither an atheist nor a believer in a personal God, gave witness to this sense of mystery:

> The most beautiful emotion we can experience is the mysterious. It is the fundamental emotion that stands at the cradle of all true art and science. He to whom this emotion is a stranger, who can no longer wonder and stand rapt in awe, is as good as dead, a snuffed-out candle. To sense that behind anything that can be experienced there is something that our minds cannot

118. See n37 of chapter 4.

119. *DM*, 45.

> grasp, whose beauty and sublimity reaches us only indirectly: this is religiousness.[120]

Let us therefore stand in awe before the universe, whatever it may be that we find. Let there never be an end to our capacity for wonder or our capacity to love, as *Homo sapiens, Homo religiosus, Homo qui amat.*

The eternal God created time (*ST*, I, q. 46, a. 3; q. 66, a. 4). Although our experience of time is only that of the *now*, we are now aware of how extended time is. Robert Francoeur attempted to communicate the evolution of the varied human species, the genus *Homo*, in a comprehensible way by comparison to a calendar year: January first would witness the appearance of *Homo habilis*. Contemporary with the habilenes were the australopithecines who survived until late August or early September. The use of fire seems to have started with early *Homo erectus*. Neanderthal man appeared around November 1. The first indications of religious belief can be found in burial sites of later Neanderthaloids, around December 17. By December 24 all the non-sapiens human forms had died out or been absorbed by more modern Cro-Magnons. Agriculture began around December 28. The whole of our historical period comprises the last two days of our "year." Socrates, Plato, and Aristotle were born about 9:00 a.m. on December 31, Jesus at noon, Columbus around 9:30 p.m. The final hours of December 31 embrace all the nineteenth and twentieth centuries.[121]

Since Francoeur wrote in 1965, much more work has been done by paleoanthropologists pertinent to human origins, the genus *Homo*, which reinforces our awareness of how expansive time is.[122] It is not only a question of human origins now considered to have been two and a half million years ago, however, but the cosmic span of time as well. What is known as the Big Bang, the appearance of matter, energy, time, and space is estimated to have begun 13.5 billion years ago, planet earth as having emerged 4.5 billion years ago, life 3.8 billion years ago. *Homo habilis*

120. From Einstein's credo, "What I Believe," quoted by Isaacson, *Einstein*, 387.

121. Robert T. Francoeur, preface to *AM*, last two pages of the preface. Francoeur at that time judged the appearance of the first humans to have been about one and a half million years ago. Thus a "day" in his "year" was equal to 4,000 years of human history. The taxonomical family into which human beings fall is *Hominidae*, the genus is *Homo*, and our species is *Homo sapiens*.

122. For example, see the delightful story of the anthropological research of Louis and Mary Leakey, and Richard and Meave Leakey, in East Africa (Leakey, *Sediments of Time*). Thousands of fossils have been discovered in the last fifty years that continue to impact the dating of humanity's history.

appears in East Africa 2.5 million years ago, and humans as we know them, our species, *Homo sapiens*, 200,000 years ago. *Homo sapiens* first arrived in the Western hemisphere 16,000 years ago (14,000 BC). Writing was invented between 3500 and 3000 BC. In 1500 AD there were five hundred million people. Today seven billion. On July 20, 1969, Neil Armstrong and Buzz Aldrin landed on the moon.[123] Such is the past. How extended will the future be in this unfinished story?

If we are to align ourselves with the direction that evolution takes, in what direction do we see evolution moving? One of Teilhard's foundational axioms and insights was: Union differentiates. He saw evolution moving in the direction of increased unification. Convergence, emergence, differentiation, unification. Unity for Teilhard was never an undifferentiated mass. The exemplar for human unity was not that of an anthill. His was a cosmology and a metaphysics that stressed unity. All would seem to converge toward Omega, toward the Christ, in whom God would be all in all, in whom our varied identities still remain distinct. Teilhard saw evidence for this in his study of evolution as we do in the theologies of the Trinity.

Today, however, we see more and more proliferation, polarization, pluralization. Many efforts toward increased unity seem to have failed or be challenged—*United* States? *United* Nations? A European *Union*? Which will prevail, unity or plurality? Does evolution tend toward an end of increased fragmentation or a differentiated unification that perfects what it unites? Evolution or entropy? Unity or plurality? Or both, a unity enveloping a wide diversity? For Teilhard, it is as much a matter of choice as it is of evidence. What vision of the universe do we choose? It was a choice that Teilhard addressed early and consciously. Here again, for Teilhard, as within the history of philosophy, there is both the one and the many, which for Teilhard is not an either/or. Yet the end would be the One. In his 1945 essay, ten years before he died, Teilhard addressed the topic in "The Grand Option."[124] These were the choices: Pessimism or Optimism? Optimism of Withdrawal or Optimism of Evolution? Evolution in terms of the many or of the unit? Increased dispersion or increased harmony? Let Teilhard speak for himself.

"In the view of the 'pluralist' the world is moving in the direction of dispersal and therefore of the growing autonomy of its separate elements.

123. For a recent and expert account of this human story, see Harari, *Homo Sapiens*.

124. "The Grand Option" (1945), *FM*, 37–60.

For each individual, the business, the duty and the interest of life consist in achieving, *in opposition to others,* his utmost uniqueness and personal freedom; so that perfection, beatitude, supreme greatness belong not to the whole but to the least part. By this 'dispersive' view the socialization of the human mass becomes a retrograde step."[125] However, "A convergent world, whatever sacrifice of freedom it may seem to demand of us, is the only one which can preserve the dignity and the aspirations of the living being. Therefore, *it must be true.* If we are to avoid total anarchy, the source and the sign of universal death, we can do no other than plunge resolutely forward, even though something in us perish, into the melting-pot of socialization."[126] "It is through love and within love that we must look for the deepening of our deepest self, in the life-giving coming together of humankind."[127]

On the point of the direction of evolution, Yuval Noah Harari would seem to agree with Teilhard:

> Human cultures are in constant flux. Is this flux completely random, or does it have some overall pattern? In other words, does history have a direction? The answer is yes . . . Perceiving the direction of history is really a question of vantage point. When we adopt the proverbial bird's-eye view of history, which examines developments in terms of decades or centuries, it's hard to say whether history moves in the direction of unity or of diversity. However, to understand long-term processes the bird's-eye view is too myopic. We would do better to adopt instead the viewpoint of a cosmic spy satellite, which scans millennia rather than centuries. From such a vantage point it becomes crystal clear that history is moving relentlessly towards unity.[128]

For Thomas Aquinas, creation's plenitude was compatible with its One Source. While there is differentiation, or distinctions, in things, God's universe reflects the One that God is. One God, one creation. All comes from God; all is destined to return to God. The Trinity itself is a

125. "The Grand Option" (1945), *FM*, 45.

126. "The Grand Option" (1945), *FM*, 52.

127. "The Grand Option" (1945), *FM*, 55.

128. Harari, *Sapiens*, 166. On the topic of the future of religion, however, Harari would differ from both Teilhard and Charles Taylor. Although he sees religion as one of the great unifiers of humankind (210–11), he also sees the theistic religions as having increasingly lost their importance (228) vis-à-vis the "humanist religions" of modernity (228–36), which indicates even more the need for a revitalized Christian humanism to meet the challenges of the secular world.

differentiated unity reflected in the cosmos, God's mirror. Both Teilhard and Aquinas contribute insights to our appreciation, understanding, and proclamation of God's gospel for our times.

Epilogue

The Mystery and Power of Love

WHETHER WE GO TO St. Paul or St. John, to St. Augustine or St. Thomas, to Pope Benedict XVI or Pope Francis, the theme of love permeates their understanding of the gospel. St. Paul had written in his great hymn to love: "And now faith, hope, and love abide, these three; and the greatest of these is love" (1 Cor 13:13); and in the Letter to the Romans, "God's love has been poured into our hearts through the Holy Spirit that has been given to us" (5:5). The First Letter of St. John states it most succinctly: "God is love" (4:8,16), and "those who do not love a brother or sister whom they have seen, cannot love God whom they have not seen" (4:20), and therefore "let us love one another, because love is from God; everyone who loves is born of God and knows God" (4:7). The Gospel of John states early on: "God so loved the world that he gave his only Son, so that everyone who believes in him may not perish but may have eternal life" (3:16). Jesus, as reported by the Synoptic Gospels, summarizes the teaching of the Hebrew Bible in a twofold way: "You shall love the Lord your God with all your heart, and with all your soul, and with all your mind, and with all your strength" and "love your neighbor as yourself" (Mark 12:29–31; Matt 22:37–40; Luke 10:27). It is of course Jesus taking his cue here from Moses's teaching of the *Shema* in the book of Deuteronomy (6:4–5) and a text from Leviticus (19:18).

Saint Augustine, in his commentary on the first letter of St. John, emphasizes the centrality of love in the Christian life.

> *Love is from God. God is love.* There, brothers [and sisters], you have the scriptures of God. This epistle is canonical; it is read among all the nations; it is preserved by the authority of

> the whole world; it has built up the whole world. Here you are listening to the Spirit of God: *God is love.*[1]

> Love and do what you want. If you are silent, be silent with love; if you cry out, cry out with love; if you chastise, chastise with love; if you spare, spare with love. The root of love must be within; nothing but good can come from this root.[2]

In another of his sermons, St. Augustine teaches: "There is not one who does not love something, but the question is, what to love. The psalms do not tell us not to love, but to choose the object of our love. But how can we choose unless we are first chosen? We cannot love unless someone has loved us first"; and "God cries out: Love me and you will have me for you would be unable to love me if you did not possess me already."[3] In his *Confessions*, Augustine instructs us that our hearts are restless until they rest in the Lord.[4] It has been said that it was not so much Augustine who was seeking God as it was God who was seeking Augustine.[5] God's love reaching out to us comes first. God desires to be in union with us.

In the tradition of St. Paul's hymn to *agape*, of the beloved disciple's theology of love, of St. Augustine's preaching, for St. Thomas there is no virtue greater than *caritas*. It is the form of all the virtues (*ST*, II-II, q. 23, aa. 6–8). It is supernatural and flows from the gift of a deifying habitual grace freely given. God creates out of love (*ST*, I, q. 20, a. 2). We were created to love, to be like God, to love as God loves, to become love ourselves for we are deifiable. *Caritas* is the life of the soul (*ST*, II-II, q. 23, a. 2, *ad* 2). It is participation in the Holy Spirit (*ST*, II-II, q. 23, a. 3, *ad* 3; q. 24, aa. 2, 7). It is friendship with God. (*ST*, II-II, q. 23, aa. 1, 5; q. 24, a. 2). It denotes a union of affections (*ST*, II-II, q. 27, a. 2). By it one is transformed. By it the lover and the beloved are profoundly united (*ST*, I, q. 20, a. 2, *ad* 1; I-II, q. 28, aa. 1–2). It comprises, as for the Scriptures and St. Augustine, both love of God and of neighbor (*ST*, II-II, q. 25, aa. 1, 12). The more we love God, the stronger our love is (*ST*, II-II, q. 27, a. 6). The "joy of the gospel"[6] as well a peace that surpasses understanding are

1. Augustine, *First Epistle of John*, 107 (Seventh Homily, #5). Emphasis in text.
2. Augustine, *First Epistle of John*, 110 (Seventh Homily, #8).
3. Roman Breviary, *The Liturgy of the Hours*, Office of Readings, Tuesday of Third Week of Easter.
4. Augustine, *Confessions*, 3 (Book I, #1).
5. Turner, *Darkness of God*, 59.
6. To take a reference from Francis, *Evangelii Gaudium*.

among its effects (*ST*, II-II, q. 28, a. 1; q. 29, a. 3). When commenting on Romans 5:5, Thomas writes: "For the Holy Spirit, who is the love of the Father and the Son, to be given to us is our being brought to participate in the love who is the Holy Spirit, and by this participation we are made lovers of God."[7]

For St. Catherine of Siena in the fourteenth century, in tune with the thought of St. Thomas, God is both Truth and Love. She addresses God in *The Dialogue* as "O mad lover!"[8] God has fallen in love with what God has made.[9] In her prayers, Jesus is "gentle Love," as is God.[10]

O immeasurable love!
O gentle love!
Eternal fire!
You are that fire ever blazing,
O high eternal Trinity!
You are direct
without any twisting,
genuine,
without any duplicity,
open
without any pretense.
Turn the eye of your mercy on your creatures.
I know that mercy is your hallmark,
and no matter where I turn
I find nothing but your mercy.
This is why I run crying to your mercy
to have mercy on the world.[11]

St. Thérèse of Lisieux, a doctor of the church as is St. Catherine of Siena, followed in the footsteps of Catherine in imaging God's love as "a mad love" in her "little doctrine," or "science of love." Love was the key to her vocation, as she said, "*I will be love.*" The Blessed Trinity is that "inextinguishable furnace of love" into which she hoped to be swooped up and carried away.[12] The last chapter of her autobiography alone has made her a classic in Western spirituality. It is another love story.

7. Aquinas, *Commentary on Romans*, 132 (chapter 5, lecture 1, #392).

8. Catherine, *Dialogue*, 72 (ch. 30); 325 (ch. 153); 364 (ch. 167).

9. *Dialogue*, 325 (ch. 153); 63 (ch. 25).

10. *Prayers of Catherine*, 6; 48.

11. *Prayers of Catherine*, 72.

12. All the references in quotes come from chapter 11 of Thérèse of Lisieux, *Story of a Soul*, 149–59. Emphasis is in the text.

Christians often tend to contrast a more biblical self-sacrificing *agape* with a more Platonic passionate *eros*. Pope Benedict XVI, however, in acknowledging the centrality of love in any true humanism, in his encyclical letter, *Deus Caritas Est*, understands both *eros* and *agape* as integral to Christian love which is both passionate and a self-offering.[13] They can never be completely separated. The human person cannot live by one alone. God's love itself is passionate, erotic, personal, yet totally *agape*. "God's *eros* for humanity is also totally *agape*."[14] It is a love which is both passionate and forgiving, "God is the absolute and ultimate source of all being . . . but . . . at the same time a lover with the passion of true love."[15] Pope Benedict, as all other spiritual masters before him, sees love as at the heart of things.

One of Pope Francis' mantras is "We were made for love."[16] The humanism to which Pope Francis aspires is grounded in his awareness that "The whole is greater than the part, but it is also greater than the sum of its parts."[17] For Francis, as for many contemporary thinkers and scientists, "Everything in the world is connected;"[18] and "We are part of one another."[19] This latter statement is simply a restatement of St. Paul's Letter to the Romans: "For as in one body we have many members, and not all the members have the same function, so we, who are many, are one body in Christ, *and individually we are members one of another*" (12:4–5, emphasis mine). For Pope Francis, as for Pope Benedict XVI and the New Testament as well, love is at the heart of things. For Pope Francis, as well as for the popes preceding him, we are called to create a "civilization of love." Pope Paul VI coined and first used the phrase. Pope John Paul II used it frequently, at least twenty-seven times, including in two of his encyclicals. Pope Benedict XVI likewise referred to it. It is thus no surprise that Pope Francis used it as well in his encyclical *Fratelli Tutti*.[20]

13. Benedict XVI, *Deus Caritas Est*, 6–16 (##3–11).

14. *Deus Caritas Est*, #10.

15. *Deus Caritas Est*, #10.

16. Francis, *Laudato Sí*, 28 (#58); *Fratelli Tutti*, 39 (#88).

17. Francis, *Evangelii Gaudium*, 114 (#235); *Let Us Dream*, 105.

18. *Laudato Si*, 34, 44, 67, 116 (##16, 91, 138, 240); *Fratelli Tutti*, 16 (#34).

19. *Fratelli Tutti*, 16 (#32).

20. *Fratelli Tutti*, 82 (#183). For all the references to its use by the popes, see Anderson, *Civilization of Love*, 205–17. Pope Paul VI first used it in his homily concluding the 1975 Holy Year. The two encyclicals in which Pope John Paul II used it were *Dives in Misericordia*, #14: and *Evangelium Vitae*, ##6, 27.

For Teilhard de Chardin, love is an energy at the heart of the cosmos, an "energy proper to cosmogenesis."[21] It propels the universe forward and upward. "The most telling and profound way of describing the evolution of the universe would undoubtedly be to trace the evolution of love."[22] It is Alpha; it is Omega. Cosmogenesis is a love story that gives birth to life. Biogenesis a love story that gives birth to human life. Anthropogenesis a love story that gives birth to Jesus Christ. Christogenesis a love story that gives birth to the theosphere. Love is everywhere and in all things.[23] Under the influence of Christ, *caritas* becomes universalized, dynamic, and synthesizing.[24] Everything becomes loveable in God. In interpersonal love we are drawn closer and closer to each other, center to center, soul to soul. "Love alone is capable of completing our beings in themselves as it unites them, for the good reason that love alone takes them and joins them by their very depths—this is a fact of daily experience."[25] In individual acts of love, we contribute to and participate in the one great act of evolutionary love that creation is.

In the well-known quote from "The Evolution of Chastity" which we have previously noted, Teilhard states: "The day will come, after harnessing space, the winds, the tides, gravitation, we shall harness for God the energies of love. And, on that day, for the second time in the history of the world, humanity will have discovered fire."[26] While love is a cosmic and universal energy, it assumes a specific form as human energy,[27] and then again as a Christian phenomenon.[28] The universe, the cosmos, creation is one evolving, ongoing, unfinished process of amorization.[29] Both thought and affectivity, both reflection and affection, both psychogenesis and affectionization contribute to what it means to be human. In an early essay, "The Eternal Feminine," Teilhard wrote: "Only love has the power to move being,"[30] Henri de Lubac compared that prose-poem

21. "Centrology" (1944), *AE*, 119.

22. "The Spirit of the Earth" (1931), *HE*, 33.

23. "The Heart of Matter" (1950), *HM*, 50–51.

24. "Super-Humanity, Super-Christ, Super-Charity" (1943), *SC*, 167.

25. *HP*, 189.

26. "The Evolution of Chastity" (1834), *TF*, 86–87. I have made two adjustments in the translation, from "ether" to "space," and from "man" to "humanity."

27. "Human Energy" (1937), *HE*, 145–60.

28. *HP*, 188–91, 209–15.

29. "The Heart of Matter" (1950), *HM*, 50, 60; "The Christic" (1955), *HM*, 88.

30. "The Eternal Feminine" (1918), *WW*, 200.

about love to Plato's *Symposium*, in which one finds Socrates' praise of the all-powerful energy of love.[31] For Teilhard, whether we look vertically up above, or horizontally up ahead, we find love, Jesus Christ, the mystery of the Trinity, lying in wait for God's creation to be complete. We accept the theological task of looking at the human story from above, from below, from up ahead, and we discover once again that the God of revelation is the God of evolution and Jesus Christ its mediator, Jesus Christ, yesterday, today, and forever (Heb 13:8).

Given the centrality of love within the Judeo-Christian world view, we need to ask: What *is* love? Other languages have varied words for its diverse facets: *eros*, *agape*, *philia* in Greek, *amor*, *caritas*, *amicitia* in Latin, just as we have love, charity, and friendship in English. We use "love" for our desire for union with God, for brotherly and sisterly relationships, for our embrace of those whom we neighbor, for our most intimate friends, as well as being called upon to love ourselves. Love has many faces. It implies an openness toward the other. Elsewhere I have described it as a freely chosen self-limitation for the sake of another.[32] I do not intend to describe it further here. It has an ecstatic, relational, unitive dimension to it. It is the subject of poetry and of philosophy. Plato discussed it. Mystics contemplate it. Friends celebrate it. Saints live it. All three of the disputable questions I raised in the previous chapter—on the Christian understanding of atonement, hell, sexuality—have to do with that question: What *is* love? This is the question of God's having freely chosen to suffer and die *for us*, of whether perfect love is compatible with everlasting separation from God. Love is that which gives meaning to the most personal, most intimate, most physical sexual act. What is love? What does it mean to say that God so loved the world? What is the love that God *is?* We use the word analogously but reverentially.

In the end, the question cannot be answered with words. To answer it, the Christian points to the cross, to the lives of the saints, to profound human friendships. Human love does not become perfected overnight. It is not made perfect in the moment of our baptism, or when we reach the age of reason, or on the evening of one's wedding night or the night of a religious profession. It matures, wounds, forgives. We do as best we can along our pilgrim way, groping towards love, its vision in sight, yet falling short, always learning. Who are you, what are you, O God of Love? Is love

31. Teilhard, "The Eternal Feminine" (1918), *WW*, 192–202. Lubac, *Eternal Feminine*, 31–40, on Teilhard's Christian Platonism. Plato, *Symposium*.

32. Goergen, *Power of Love*, 197.

not simply that to which we give our lives? Something for which we die. Who would say that they could adequately articulate what love is? Yet is there anyone who does not know love when one encounters it? As Pope Francis says, "We are made for love." Because love is sacred, so like God, it is held as sacred, chaste—a gift of self to another.

Love is what God is. Love is self-revealing, self-giving. Love is faithful, compassionate, magnanimous, grateful, generative. Love is the glue that binds us together while at the same time respecting our differences. Love is holy. Love is a cosmic power, the power of attraction, a force that binds, that makes the many to be one and the One many. Love escapes us just when we think we have it within our grasp. We know it, but not quite yet. There is a reciprocity to it. The human animal, the semiotic animal, has a capacity for love that surpasses the forces of attraction found elsewhere in the natural world. The human animal, the animal that loves, is *capax Dei*. Love is divine. Love is a heart-felt desire for something mutual, something unselfish, something everlasting. Love makes me *be*, and to be who I am called to be. It is, as it was for St. Thérèse, our vocation in life.

If we try to understand what love is, it is also important to know what it is not. It is not a feeling, although it can be deeply felt. It is not an idea in the mind, although it is something about which we often think. It is not romance although at times it may have a romantic quality to it. It does not happen instantaneously but requires the test of time. It does not come pain free and yet is deeply satisfying. It is connected to the will, something freely chosen. It allows us to will good for ourselves while not being self-centered. In being oriented outwards towards others, whether toward neighbors and those in need, or toward our brothers and sisters, or towards friends, or towards the tri-personal God, it is self-limiting but not self-diminishing. The more of it we give, the more of it we have. It cannot be measured quantitatively but can be differentiated qualitatively. It is not self-conscious but is self-reflective. It can be ecstatic but not undisciplined.

For Thomas Aquinas, *caritas* is friendship with God. Aelred of Riveaulx suggests that God *is* friendship.[33] For Teilhard, affective energies find their deepest meaning in love directed toward friendship. For Pope Francis friendship is something to be universalized, toward all humankind, and toward the planet itself—a civilization of love, a culture of encounter—akin to Teilhard's emphasis on the affectionization of the

33. Aelred of Rievaulx, *Spiritual Friendship*, 65–66 (##69–70).

universe or Plato's movement of *eros* from a particular love to a more universal love, from the attraction of physical beauty to moral beauty to beauty itself, Beauty Itself.[34] Just as Thomas Aquinas is not only Aristotelian but also Platonic in his doctrine of participation, so is Teilhard Platonic as he sketches the upward and forward *telos* of God's evolving creative act, an act that takes place for us in time but in God is timeless. To our building up, and reflecting upon, this civilization of love, both Thomas Aquinas and Teilhard de Chardin have contributions to make. This has been my conviction. To this, friendships across world views play a major role.[35]

Friendship is the tie, or glue, that binds two lovers together into a union of love. It is from that very particular love that a more universal love unfolds. We cannot say that we love the One we cannot see if we do not love those whom we do see (1 John 4:20). We cannot say that we love everyone in general if we have not loved someone in particular. The move is from the particular to the universal, from particular love to universal love, to a love with planetary and even cosmic dimensions. To love the universe for Christ's sake. To participate in the one great act of giving birth within which the universe groans towards its final fulfillment (Rom 8:22). We are but specks of consciousness in an evolving universe through whom the Savior of the world providentially guides an evolving creation to its completion. It *is* love that makes the world go round. It *is* friendship upon which and from which humankind gains its strength. Where there is friendship, there is God. We were created for friendship with God. We have been structured for friendship, for the other, for ecstasy, for union. Friendship is God's human face. Is friendship in the end not that for which we were made? It is not good for the human one to be alone (Gen 2:18). We are made for others, for the Other, for all others.

The Holy Spirit is the glue that holds the universe together from within. The Holy Spirit is the glue that binds all of humanity together into the one Body of Christ. The Holy Spirit is the glue within the bond of friendship.[36] The Holy Spirit is the bond of unity within the Trinity itself.

34. See Plato, *Symposium*.

35. I referred in chapter 5 to Vernon, *Meaning of Friendship*.

36. Samuel Hakeem, OP, in his MA thesis, "Delightful and Moving Doctrine," brought to my attention Augustine's use of the word "glue" to describe the Holy Spirit's work and which is applied to Augustine's theology of friendship as well. "Augustine argues in *De Trinitate* that the Holy Spirit plays a central role in human friendships as the glue which binds these relationships" (34). See Augustine, *Trinity*, 209 (VI, 1, 7), as well as other such references to the Holy Spirit as glue in Hakeem's thesis.

It is the Holy Spirt that prepares the groaning evolving cosmos to be one great sacrifice of praise.

And God said:
Let us be friends.
And befriend one another
As I have befriended you.

> For this reason, I bow my knees before the Father, from whom every family in heaven and on earth takes its name. I pray that, according to the riches of his glory he may grant that you may be strengthened in your inner being with power through his Spirit, and that Christ may dwell in your hearts through faith, as you are being rooted and grounded in love. I pray that you may have the power to comprehend, with all the saints, what is the breadth and length and height and depth, and to know the love of Christ that surpasses knowledge, so that you may be filled with all the fullness of God. (Eph 3:14–19)

Bibliography

Aczel, Amir D. *The Jesuit and the Skull: Teilhard de Chardin, Evolution, and the Search for Peking Man*. New York: Riverhead, 2007.

Adey, Lionel. *C. S. Lewis' "Great War" with Owen Barfield*. Cumbria, UK: Ink, 2002.

Aelred of Rievaulx. *On Spiritual Friendship*. Translated by Mary Eugenia Laker, SSND. Washington, DC: Cistercian, 1974.

Alison, James. *The Joy of Being Wrong: Original Sin through Easter Eyes*. New York: Crossroad, 1998.

Amato, Joseph. *Mounier and Maritain: A French Catholic Understanding of the Modern World*. Notre Dame, IN: Ave Maria, 2002.

Anatolios, Khaled. *Deification through the Cross: An Eastern Christian Theology of Salvation*. Grand Rapids: Eerdmans, 2020.

Anderson, Carl. *A Civilization of Love: What Every Catholic Can Do to Transform the World*. New York: HarperOne, 2009.

Anderson, Gary A. *Charity: The Place of the Poor in the Biblical Tradition*. New Haven, CT: Yale University Press, 2013.

———. *Sin: A History*. New Haven, CT: Yale University Press, 2009.

Aquinas, Thomas, OP. *The Academic Sermons*. Translated by Mark-Robin Hoogland, CP. Washington, DC: Catholic University of America Press, 2010.

———. *Commentary on the Gospel of St. John*. Translated by J. A. Weisheipl, OP, and F. R. Larcher, OP. Albany, NY: Magi, 1980.

———. *Commentary on the Letter of Saint Paul to the Romans*. Translated by F. R. Larcher, OP. Lander, WY: Aquinas Institute for the Study of Sacred Doctrine, 2012.

———. *Commentary on the Letters of Saint Paul to the Corinthians*. Translated by F. R. Larcher, OP, et al. Lander, WY: Aquinas Institute for the Study of Sacred Doctrine, 2012.

———. *Compendium of Theology*. Translated by Cyril Vollert, SJ. St. Louis: Herder, 1958.

———. *Summa contra Gentiles (On the Truth of the Catholic Faith)*. 5 vols. Translated by Anton Pegis et al. New York: Doubleday, 1955–1957.

———. *Summa Theologica*. 3 vols. Translated by the Fathers of the English Dominican Province. New York: Benziger, 1947–1948. This is the translation I use unless indicated otherwise.

———. *Summa Theologiae*. 60 vols. Edited by Thomas Gilby, OP. New York: McGraw-Hill, 1964–1981. A more recent translation of Aquinas's *Summa* with Latin text and English translation by varied translators.

Arintero, Juan, OP. *Desenvolvimiento y Vitalidad de la Iglesia*. Vol. 2, *Evolución Doctrinal*. Salamanca, Spain: Imprenta de Calatrava, 1975. Originally published in 1911.

———. *The Mystical Evolution in the Development and Vitality of the Church*. 2 vols. Translated by Jordan Aumann, OP. St. Louis: Herder, 1949/1951.

Aristotle. *Nicomachean Ethics*. Translated by Robert C. Bartlett and Susan D. Collins. Chicago: University of Chicago Press, 2011.

Arraj, James. *Mysticism, Metaphysics, and Maritain*. Chiloquin, OR: Inner Growth, 1993.

Ashley, Benedict M., OP. "The River Forest School and the Philosophy of Nature Today." In *Philosophy and the God of Abraham: Essays in Memory of James A. Weisheipl, OP*, edited by R. James Long, 1–15. Toronto: Pontifical Institute of Medieval Studies, 1991.

———. *The Way toward Wisdom: An Interdisciplinary and Intercultural Introduction to Metaphysics*. Notre Dame, IN: University of Notre Dame Press, 2006.

Augustine. *Confessions*. Translated by Henry Chadwick. Oxford: Oxford University Press, 1991.

———. *Homilies on the First Epistle of John*. Translated by Boniface Ramsey. Hyde Park, NY: New City, 2008.

———. *Teaching Christianity (De Doctrina Christiana)*. Translated by Edmund Hill, OP. Hyde Park, NY: New City, 1996.

———. *The Trinity*. Translated by Edmund Hill, OP. New York: New City,1991.

Aurobindo, Sri. *The Integral Yoga: Sri Aurobindo's Teaching and Method of Practice; Selected Letters of Sri Aurobindo*. Pondicherry, India: Sri Aurobindo Ashram, 1993.

Ayala, Francisco J. *Darwin's Gift to Science and Religion*. Washington, DC: Henry, 2007.

Balthasar, Hans Urs von. *Dare We Hope "That All Men Will Be Saved"? With a Short Discourse on Hell*. Translated by David Kipp and Lothar Krauth. San Francisco: Ignatius, 1988.

Barbour, George B. *In the Field with Teilhard de Chardin*. New York: Herder and Herder, 1965.

Barfield, Owen. *Saving the Appearances: A Study in Idolatry*. Middletown, CT: Wesleyan University Press, 1988.

Barré, Jean-Luc. *Jacques and Raïssa Maritain: Beggars for Heaven*. Translated by Bernard E. Doering. Notre Dame, IN: University of Notre Dame Press, 2005.

Bartlett, Anthony W. *Cross Purposes: The Violent Grammar of Christian Atonement*. Harrisburg, PA: Trinity, 2001.

Benedict XVI, Pope. *Deus Caritas Est (God Is Love)*. Washington, DC: United States Conference of Catholic Bishops, 2006.

———. *Spe Salvi (Saved in Hope)*. Washington, DC: United States Conference of Catholic Bishops, 2007.

Bennett, Gaymon, et al., eds. *The Evolution of Evil*. Gottingen, Germany: Vandenhoeck & Ruprecht, 2008.

Bergounioux, Frédéric-Marie, OFM. *The Priestly Heart of Teilhard de Chardin*. Translated by Romano S. Almagno, OFM. *The Cord* 17 (1967) 171–77.

Bonhoeffer, Dietrich. *The Cost of Discipleship*. Translated by Reginald H. Fuller. New York: Macmillan, 1963.

Boswell, John. *Same-Sex Unions in Premodern Europe.* New York: Villard, 1994.

Brotherton, Joshua R. "That All Shall Be Saved: Heaven, Hell, and Universal Salvation." *Nova et Vetera* 18 (2020) 1394–403.

Brown, Raymond, SS. *The Virginal Conception and Bodily Resurrection of Jesus.* New York: Paulist, 1973.

Buber, Martin. *I and Thou.* Translated by Walter Kaufmann. New York: Scribner, 1970.

———. *Pointing the Way: Collected Essays.* Translated by Maurice S. Friedman. New York: Schocken, 1957.

Burrell, David, CSC. *Aquinas: God and Action.* Eugene, OR: Wipf & Stock, 2016.

Carlen, Claudia, IHM, ed. *The Papal Encyclicals, 1958–1981.* Raleigh, NC: Pierian, 1990.

Carroll, James. *Constantine's Sword: The Church and the Jews.* Boston: Houghton Mifflin, 2001.

Casey, Michael, OCSO. *A Thirst for God.* Kalamazoo, MI: Cistercian Studies, 1988.

Catechism of the Catholic Church. New York: Doubleday, 1995.

Catherine of Siena, OP. *The Dialogue.* Translated by Suzanne Noffke, OP. Classics of Western Spirituality. New York: Paulist, 1980.

———. *The Prayers of Catherine of Siena.* 2nd ed. Translated by Suzanne Noffke, OP. New York: Authors Choice, 2001.

Charles, Pierre, SJ. *The Prayer of All Things.* Translated by James Langdale. New York: Herder and Herder, 1964.

Chauchard, Paul. *Man and Cosmos.* New York: Herder and Herder, 1965.

Chenu, M. D., OP. *Toward Understanding Saint Thomas.* Translated by A. M. Landry, OP, and D. Hughes, OP. Chicago: Regnery, 1964.

Chesterton, G. K. *Saint Thomas Aquinas.* Garden City, NY: Doubleday, 1956.

Chik, Janice T. "Thomistic Animalism." *New Blackfriars* 100 (November 2019) 645–62.

Christensen, Michael J., and Jeffery A. Wittung, eds. *Partakers of the Divine Nature: The History and Development of Deification in the Christian Traditions.* Grand Rapids: Baker Academic, 2008.

Christianson, Raphael Joshua, OP. "The Enriching Complementarity of Faith and Science." *Homiletic and Pastoral Review.* https://www.hprweb.com/2019/01/the-enriching-complementarity-of-faith-and-science/.

———. "A Thomistic Model of Friendship with God as Deification." *New Blackfriars* 100 (September 2019) 509–25.

Clarke, W. Norris, SJ. *The One and the Many: A Contemporary Thomistic Metaphysics.* Notre Dame, IN: University of Notre Dame Press, 2001.

Coakley, Sarah. *God, Sexuality, and the Self: An Essay "On the Trinity."* Cambridge: Cambridge University Press, 2013.

Congar, Yves, OP. *Lay People in the Church.* Translated by Donald Attwater. London: Chapman, 1957.

———. *The Mystery of the Temple; or, The Manner of God's Presence to His Creatures from Genesis to the Apocalypse.* Translated by Reginald F. Trevett. London: Burns & Oates, 1962.

Cowell, Siôn. *The Teilhard Lexicon.* Portland, OR: Sussex Academic, 2014.

Cox, Jeffrey. *The English Churches in a Secular Society.* Oxford: Oxford University Press, 1982.

Crean, Thomas, and Alan Fimister. *Integralism: A Manual of Political Philosophy.* Havertown, PA: Casemate, 2020.

Crosby, John F. *The Personalism of John Paul II.* Steubenville, OH: Hildebrand, 2019.

Cuénot, Claude. *Teilhard de Chardin: A Biographical Study*. Translated by Vincent Colimore. Baltimore: Helicon, 1965.

Daly, Robert J., SJ. *Christian Sacrifice: The Judaeo-Christian Background before Origen*. Washington, DC: Catholic University of America Press, 1978.

Dansette, Adrien. *Religious History of Modern France*. 2 vols. Translated by John Dingle. New York: Herder and Herder, 1961.

Davies, Brian, OP. *Thomas Aquinas on God and Evil*. Oxford: Oxford University Press, 2011.

Dávila, Vincent B., OP. "Grace in Romans." Paper submitted as a doctoral student at the University of Notre Dame, May 8, 2020.

Deely, John. *Basics of Semiotics*. Bloomington: Indiana University Press, 1990.

———. *Four Ages of Understanding: The First Postmodern Survey of Philosophy from Ancient Times to the Turn of the Twenty-First Century*. Toronto: University of Toronto Press, 2001.

Dodds, Michael, OP. *Unlocking Divine Action*. Washington, DC: Catholic University of America Press, 2012.

Doering, Bernard. *Jacques Maritain and the French Catholic Intellectuals*. Notre Dame, IN: University of Notre Dame Press, 1983.

Dubarle, André-Marie, OP. *The Biblical Doctrine of Original Sin*. Herder and Herder, 1964.

Dubarle, Dominique, OP. *Scientific Humanism and Christian Thought*. Translated by Reginald Trevett. New York: Philosophical Library, 1956.

Duffy, Kathleen, SSJ. *Teilhard's Mysticism: Seeing the Inner Face of Evolution*. Maryknoll, NY: Orbis, 2014.

Du Mez, Kristen Kobes. *Jesus and John Wayne: How White Evangelicals Corrupted a Faith and Fractured a Nation*. New York: Liveright, 2020.

Dupuis, Jacques, SJ. *Toward a Christian Theology of Religious Pluralism*. Maryknoll, NY: Orbis, 1997.

Durant, Will, and Ariel Durant. *The Lessons of History*. New York: Simon & Schuster, 1968.

Eckhart, Meister, OP. *Meister Eckhart: Teacher and Preacher*. Edited by Bernard McGinn. Translated by Bernard McGinn and Frank Tobin. Classics of Western Spirituality. New York: Paulist, 1986.

———. *Sermons and Treatises*. 3 vols. Translated by M. O'C. Walshe. London: Watkins, 1979.

Edwards, Denis. *Partaking of God: Trinity, Evolution, and Ecology*. Collegeville, MN: Liturgical, 2014.

Eliot, T. S. *The Complete Poems and Plays, 1909–1950*. New York: Harcourt, Brace & World, 1952.

Emerson, Ralph Waldo. *The Essential Writings of Ralph Waldo Emerson*. Edited by Brooks Atkinson. New York: Modern Library, 2000.

Faricy, Robert L., SJ. *Teilhard de Chardin's Theology of the Christian in the World*. New York: Sheed and Ward, 1967.

Farrow, Douglas. "The Problem with Teilhard." *Nova et Vetera* 16 (Spring, 2018) 377–85.

Feingold, Lawrence. *The Natural Desire to See God according to St. Thomas Aquinas and His Interpreters*. 2nd ed. Naples, FL: Sapientia of Ave Maria University, 2010.

Feser, Edward. *Aristotle's Revenge: The Metaphysical Foundations of Physical and Biological Science*. Neunkirchen-Seelscheid, Germany: Editiones Scholasticae, 2019.

Finlan, Stephen. *Options on Atonement in Christian Thought*. Collegeville, MN: Liturgical, 2007.

———. *Problems with Atonement*. Collegeville, MN: Liturgical, 2005.

Flannery, Austin, OP, ed. *Vatican Council II: The Conciliar and Postconciliar Documents*. Rev. ed. Collegeville, MN: Liturgical, 1992.

Francis, Pope. *Evangelii Gaudium (The Joy of the Gospel)*. Washington, DC: United States Conference of Catholic Bishops, 2013.

———. *Fratelli Tutti (On Fraternity and Social Friendship)*. Washington, DC: United States Conference of Catholic Bishops, 2020.

———. *Laudato Sí (On Care for Our Common Home)*. Washington DC: United States Conference of Catholic Bishops, 2015.

———. *Let Us Dream: The Path to a Better Future*. With Austen Ivereigh. New York: Simon & Schuster, 2020.

Frankl, Viktor. *Man's Search for Meaning*. New York: Washington Square, 1965.

Gaine, Simon Francis, OP. *Did the Saviour See the Father? Christ, Salvation, and the Vision of God*. London: Bloomsbury, 2015.

Garaudy, Roger. *From Anathema to Dialogue: The Challenge of Marxist-Christian Cooperation*. New York: Herder and Herder, 1966.

Gardner, Patrick X. "An Inhuman Humanism." In *T&T Clark Companion to Henri de Lubac*, edited by Jordan Hillebert, 225–46. London: Bloomsbury, 2017.

Garrigou-Lagrange, Reginald, OP. *Christian Perfection and Contemplation: According to St. Thomas Aquinas and St. John of the Cross*. Translated by Sister Timothea Doyle, OP. St. Louis: Herder, 1937.

———. *The Three Ages of the Interior Life*. 2 vols. Translated by Sister Timothea Doyle, OP. St. Louis: Herder, 1947/1948.

Gilson, Etienne. *Reason and Revelation in the Middle Ages*. New York: Scribner, 1938.

Goergen, Donald J., OP. "Albert the Great and Thomas Aquinas on the Motive of the Incarnation." *Thomist* 44 (1980) 523–38.

———. *The Death and Resurrection of Jesus*. A Theology of Jesus 2. Wilmington, DE: Glazier, 1988. Reprint by Eugene, OR: Wipf & Stock, 2003.

———. *Fire of Love: Encountering the Holy Spirit*. New York: Paulist, 2006.

———. *The Jesus of Christian History*. A Theology of Jesus 3. Collegeville, MN: Liturgical, 1992. Reprint by Eugene, OR: Wipf & Stock, 2002.

———. *Jesus, Son of God, Son of Mary, Immanuel*. A Theology of Jesus 4. Collegeville, MN: Liturgical, 1995. Reprint by Eugene, OR: Wipf & Stock, 2003.

———. *The Mission and Ministry of Jesus*. A Theology of Jesus 1. Wilmington, DE: Glazier, 1986. Reprint by Eugene, OR: Wipf & Stock, 2003.

———. *The Power of Love*. Chicago: More, 1979.

———. "Prayer in the Dominican Tradition." In *Prayer in the Catholic Tradition*, ed. Robert J. Wicks, 235–52. Cincinnati: Franciscan, 2016.

———. *St. Dominic: The Story of a Preaching Friar*. New York: Paulist, 2016.

Gould, Stephen Jay. *Hen's Teeth and Horses' Toes*. New York: Norton, 1983.

Greene, Graham. *The End of the Affair*. New York: Viking, 1951.

Gregersen, Niels Henrik, ed. *Incarnation: On the Scope and Depth of Christology*. Minneapolis: Fortress, 2015.

Griffiths Paul J. *Christian Flesh*. Stanford, CA: Stanford University Press, 2018.

———. *Intellectual Appetite: A Theological Grammar*. Washington, DC: Catholic University of America Press, 2009.

———. "Theological Disagreement: What It Is & How to Do It." *CTSA Proceedings* 69 (2014) 23–36.

———. "Ulterior Lives: A Review of Richard Rodriguez' *Darling: A Spiritual Autobiography*." *First Things* (April 2014) 58.

———. "Under Pressure." *Commonweal* (May 2020) 30–37.

Gutiérrez, Gustavo, OP. *Las Casas: In Search of the Poor of Jesus Christ*. Translated by Robert R. Barr. Maryknoll, NY: Orbis, 1993.

Hakeem, Samuel, OP. "Delightful and Moving Doctrine: Augustine's Use of Rhetoric in Preaching His Theology of Friendship." MA thesis, Aquinas Institute of Theology, St. Louis, 2017.

Harari, Yuval Noah. *Sapiens: A Brief History of Humankind*. New York: HarperCollins, 2015.

Hart, David Bentley. "Misenchantment." *Commonweal* (January 2020) 47–50.

———. *That All Shall Be Saved: Heaven, Hell, and Universal Salvation*. New Haven, CT: Yale University Press, 2019.

Haught John F. *God After Darwin: A Theology of Evolution*. 2nd ed. Boulder, CO: Westview, 2008.

———. *God After Einstein: What's Really Going On in the Universe?* New Haven, CT: Yale University Press, 2022.

———. *Making Sense of Evolution: Darwin, God, and the Drama of Life*. Louisville: Westminster John Knox, 2010.

———. *The New Cosmic Story: Inside Our Awakening Universe*. New Haven, CT: Yale University Press, 2017.

———. *Resting on the Future: Catholic Theology for an Unfinished Universe*. New York: Bloomsbury, 2015.

———. "Trashing Teilhard: How Not to Read a Great Religious Thinker." *Commonweal* (February 8, 2019) 7–9.

Healy, Nicholas J., Jr. "The Christian Mystery of Nature and Grace." In *T&T Clark Companion to Henri de Lubac*, edited by Jordan Hillebert, 181–204. London: Bloomsbury, 2017.

Hopkins, Gerard Manley. "God's Grandeur." *The Poems of Gerard Manley Hopkins*. 4th ed. Edited by W. H. Gardner and N. H. MacKenzie. Oxford: Oxford University Press, 1970.

Ignatius of Loyola, SJ. *The Spiritual Exercises of St. Ignatius*. Translated by Louis J. Puhl, SJ. Chicago: Loyola University Press, 1951.

Irenaeus. *Against Heresies*. Ante-Nicene Fathers 1. Grand Rapids: Eerdmans, 1885.

———. *Proof of the Apostolic Preaching*. Translated by Joseph Smith. Westminster, MD: Newman, 1952.

Isaacson, Walter. *Einstein: His Life and Universe*. New York: Simon & Schuster, 2007.

Jacobs, Alan. *Original Sin: A Cultural History*. New York: HarperOne, 2008.

Johnson, Elizabeth A., CSJ. *Ask the Beasts: Darwin and the God of Love*. New York: Bloomsbury, 2014.

John XXIII, Pope. "Mater et Magistra" (1961). In Carlen, *Papal Encyclicals*, 59–90.

John Paul II, Pope. "Centesimus Annus" (1991). In Miller, *Encyclicals of John Paul II*, 588–650.

———. "Dialogue between Cultures for a Civilization of Love and Peace." Message for the World Day of Peace. January 1, 2001. https://www.vatican.va/content/john-paul-ii/en/messages/peace/documents/hf_jp-ii_mes_20001208_xxxiv-world-day-for-peace.html.

———. "Dives in Misericordia" (1980). In Miller, *Encyclicals of John Paul II*, 110–50.

———. "Dominum et Vivificantem" (1986). In Miller, *Encyclicals of John Paul II*, 268–339.

———. "Evangelium Vitae" (1995). In Miller, *Encyclicals of John Paul II*, 792–894.

———. "Fides et Ratio" (1998). Boston: Pauline, 1998.

———. "Laborem Exercens" (1981). In Miller, *Encyclicals of John Paul II*, 166–214.

———. "Redemptoris Missio" (1987). In Miller, *Encyclicals of John Paul II*, 494–570.

———. "Slavorum Apostoli" (1985). In Miller, *Encyclicals of John Paul II*, 228–53.

———. "Sollicitudo Rei Socialis" (1987). In Miller, *Encyclicals of John Paul II*, 426–77.

———. "Ut Unum Sint" (1995). In Miller, *Encyclicals of John Paul II*, 914–76.

Journet, Charles. *The Meaning of Evil*. Translated by Michael Barry. New York: Kennedy, 1963.

Jordan, Mark, ed. *The Church's Confession of Faith: A Catholic Catechism for Adults*. Translated from the German Bishops' Conference's Katholischer Erwachsenen Katechismus: Das Glaubensbekenntnis der Kirche by Stephen Wentworth Arn. San Francisco: Ignatius, 1987.

Jordan, Patrick. "A Life of Dialogue: Martin Buber's Path to a Believing Humanism." *Commonweal* (June 2020) 30–33.

Joyce, James. "A Painful Case." In *Dubliners*, 95–105. New York: Vintage, 1993.

Jung, C. G. *Memories, Dreams, Reflections*. Translated by Richard Winston and Clara Winston. New York: Vintage, 1989.

Kasper, Walter. *Mercy: The Essence of the Gospel and the Key to Christian Life*. Translated by William Madges. New York: Paulist, 2013.

Kerr, Fergus, OP. *After Aquinas: Versions of Thomism*. Oxford: Blackwell, 2002.

Kiesling, Christopher, OP. "The Paschal Mystery—Myth, Platonic Idea or History?" *Living Light* 4 (1967) 94–105.

———. "The Seven *Quiet* Gifts of the Holy Spirit." *Living Light* 23 (1986) 137–46.

King, Thomas M., SJ. Foreword to *The Divine Milieu*, vii–xxvi. Translated by Siôn Cowell. Portland, OR: Sussex Academic, 2012.

———. *Teilhard and the Unity of Knowledge*. New York: Paulist, 1983.

———. *Teilhard's Mass: Approaches to "The Mass on the World."* New York: Paulist, 2005.

———. *Teilhard's Mysticism of Knowing*. New York: Seabury, 1981.

King, Ursula. *Spirit of Fire: The Life and Vision of Teilhard de Chardin*. Maryknoll, NY: Orbis, 1996.

———. *Teilhard de Chardin and Eastern Religions*. New York: Paulist, 2011.

———. *Towards a New Mysticism: Teilhard de Chardin and Eastern Religions*. New York: Seabury, 1980.

Kühlewind, Georg. *From Normal to Healthy*. Translated by Michael Lipson. Hudson, NY: Lindisfarne, 1988.

Küng, Hans. *Justification: The Doctrine of Karl Barth and a Catholic Reflection*. Translated by Thomas Collins et al. New York: Nelson, 1964.

Lawson, John. *The Biblical Theology of Saint Irenaeus*. London: Epworth, 1948.

Leakey, Meave. *The Sediments of Time: My Lifelong Search for the Past*. Boston: Houghton Mifflin Harcourt, 2020.

Leroy, Pierre, SJ. *Letters from My Friend Teilhard de Chardin*. Translated by Mary Lukas. New York: Paulist, 1976.

Levering, Matthew. *Engaging the Doctrine of the Holy Spirit: Love and Gift in the Trinity and the Church*. Grand Rapids: Baker Academic, 2016.

Lindenberg, Christoph. *Rudolf Steiner: A Biography*. Translated by Jon McAlice. Great Barrington, MA: SteinerBooks, 2012.

Lohfink, Gerhard. *Is This All There Is? On Resurrection and Eternal Life*. Translated by Linda M. Maloney. Collegeville, MN: Liturgical, 2018.

Lombardo, Nicholas E., OP. *The Father's Will: Christ's Crucifixion and the Goodness of God*. Oxford: Oxford University Press, 2013.

———. *The Logic of Desire: Aquinas on Emotion*. Washington, DC: Catholic University of America Press, 2011.

Lossky, Vladimir. *In the Image and Likeness of God*. Crestwood, NY: St. Vladimir's Seminary Press, 1974.

Loughery, John, and Blythe Randolph. *Dorothy Day: Dissenting Voice of the American Century*. New York: Simon & Schuster, 2020.

Lubac, Henri de, SJ. *Augustinianism and Modern Theology*. Translated by Lancelot Sheppard. New York: Herder and Herder, 1969.

———. *Catholicism, Christ and the Common Destiny of Man*. Translated by Lancelot C. Sheppard and Elizabeth Englund, OCD. San Francisco: Ignatius, 1988.

———. *The Drama of Atheist Humanism*. Translated by Edith M. Riley et al. San Francisco: Ignatius, 1995.

———. *The Eternal Feminine: A Study on the Poem by Teilhard de Chardin*. Translated by René Hague. New York: Harper and Row, 1971.

———. *The Mystery of the Supernatural*. Translated by Rosemary Sheed. New York: Crossroad, 1998.

———. *The Religion of Teilhard de Chardin*. Translated by René Hague. New York: Desclee, 1967.

———. *Teilhard Explained*. Translated by Anthony Buono. New York: Paulist, 1968.

———. *Teilhard Posthume: Réflexions et Souvenirs*. Paris: Fayard, 1977.

Lyons, J. A. *The Cosmic Christ in Origen and Teilhard de Chardin*. Oxford: Oxford University Press, 1982.

MacIntyre, Alasdair. *After Virtue*. 3rd ed. Notre Dame, IN: University of Notre Dame Press, 2007.

Madueme, Hans, and Michael Reeves, eds. *Adam, the Fall, and Original Sin: Theological, Biblical, and Scientific Perspectives*. Grand Rapids: Baker Academic, 2014.

Maloney, George. *The Cosmic Christ*. New York: Sheed and Ward, 1968.

Maritain, Jacques. *The Degrees of Knowledge*. Translated by Gerald B. Phelan. New York: Scribner, 1959.

———. *Integral Humanism: Temporal and Spiritual Problems of a New Christendom*. Translated by Joseph W. Evans. New York: Scribner, 1968.

———. *On the Grace and Humanity of Jesus*. Translated by Joseph W. Evans. New York: Herder and Herder, 1969.

———. *The Peasant of the Garonne*. Translated by Michael Cuddihy and Elizabeth Hughes. New York: Holt, Rinehart and Winston, 1968.

Maritain, Raïssa. *Raïssa's Journal*. Edited by Jacques Maritain. Albany, NY: Magi, 1974.

McAleer Graham J. *Ecstatic Morality and Sexual Politics: A Catholic and Antitotalitarian Theory of the Body*. New York: Fordham University Press, 2005.

McCarraher, Eugene. *The Enchantments of Mammon: How Capitalism Became the Religion of Modernity*. Cambridge: Belknap of Harvard University Press, 2019.

McGinn, Bernard. *The Foundations of Mysticism*. Vol. 1 of *The Presence of God: A History of Western Christian Mysticism*. New York: Crossroad, 1994.

McInerny, Ralph. *Aquinas and Analogy*. Washington, DC: Catholic University of America Press, 1996.

McKenna, John H., CM. *The Eucharistic Epiclesis: A Detailed History from the Patristic to the Modern Era*. 2nd ed. Chicago: Hillenbrand, 2009.

Meconi, David Vincent, SJ. *The One Christ: St. Augustine's Theology of Deification*. Washington, DC: Catholic University of America Press, 2013.

———. *On Self-Harm, Narcissism, Atonement, and the Vulnerable Christ*. New York: Bloomsbury Academic, 2020.

Meconi, David Vincent, SJ, ed. *On Earth as It Is in Heaven: Cultivating a Contemporary Theology of Creation*. Grand Rapids: Eerdmans, 2016.

Meconi, David Vincent, SJ, and Carl E. Olson, eds. *Called to Be the Children of God: The Catholic Theology of Human Deification*. San Francisco: Ignatius, 2016.

Meditations on the Tarot: A Journey into Christian Hermeticism. Afterword by Hans Urs von Balthasar. Translated by Robert Powell. New York: Tarcher, 2002.

Mendes-Flohr, Paul. *Martin Buber: A Life of Faith and Dissent*. New Haven: Yale University Press, 2019.

Meyendorff, John. *Christ in Eastern Christian Thought*. St. Vladimir's Seminary Press, 1975.

Miller, J. Michael, CSB. *The Encyclicals of John Paul II*. Huntington, IN: Our Sunday Visitor, 1996.

Mooney, Christopher F., SJ. *Teilhard de Chardin and the Mystery of Christ*. New York: Harper and Row, 1966.

Mortier, Jeanne, and Marie-Louise Aboux. *Teilhard de Chardin Album*. New York: Harper & Row, 1966.

Most, William G. *Grace, Predestination, and the Salvific Will of God*. Front Royal, VA: Christendom, 1997.

Mounier, Emmanuel. *Personalism*. Notre Dame, IN: University of Notre Dame Press, 1989.

———. *A Personalist Manifesto*. Translated by monks of St. John's Abbey. New York: Longmans, Green, 1938.

Murray, Paul, OP. *Aquinas at Prayer: The Bible, Mysticism and Poetry*. London: Bloomsbury, 2013.

Newman, John Henry. *Apologia Pro Vita Sua*. Garden City, NY: Doubleday, 1956.

———. *An Essay on the Development of Christian Doctrine*. Garden City, NY: Doubleday, 1960.

Niebuhr, H. Richard. *Christ and Culture*. New York: Harper & Row, 1951.

Nogar, Raymond J., OP. *The Wisdom of Evolution*. Garden City, NY: Doubleday, 1963.

Noonan, John T. *A Church That Can and Cannot Change: The Development of Catholic Moral Teaching*. Notre Dame, IN: University of Notre Dame Press, 2005.

North, Robert, SJ. *Teilhard and the Creation of the Soul*. Milwaukee, WI: Bruce, 1967.

O'Malley, John W., SJ. *What Happened at Vatican II*? Cambridge: Belknap of Harvard University Press, 2008.

O'Meara, Thomas, OP. *Vast Universe: Extraterrestrials and Christian Revelation*. Collegeville, MN: Liturgical, 2012.

O'Meara, Thomas, OP, and Paul Philibert, OP. *Scanning the Signs of the Times: French Dominicans in the Twentieth Century*. Adelaide, Australia: ATF, 2013.

O'Neill, Taylor Patrick. "That All Shall Be Saved: Heaven, Hell, and Universal Salvation." *Nova et* Vetera 18 (Fall 2020) 1394–403.

O'Sullivan, James P. "Catholics Re-examining Original Sin in Light of Evolutionary Science: The State of the Question." *New Blackfriars* 99 (2018) 653–74.

Panikkar, Raimon. *Christophany: The Fullness of Man*. Translated by Alfred DiLascia. Maryknoll, NY: Orbis, 2004.

———. *The Cosmotheandric Experience: Emerging Religious Consciousness*. Edited by Scott Eastham. Maryknoll, NY: Orbis, 1993.

Papanikolaou, Aristotle, and George E. Demacopoulos, eds. *Orthodox Readings of Augustine*. Crestwood, NY: St. Vladimir's Seminary Press, 2008.

Paul VI, Pope. *Evangelii nuntiandi (On Evangelization in the Modern World)*. Washington, DC: United States Conference of Catholic Bishops, 1975.

———. *Humanae Vitae (Of Human Life)*. In Carlen, *Papal Encyclicals*, 223–36.

———. *Populorum Progressio (On the Development of Peoples)*. In Carlen, *Papal Encyclicals*, 183–201.

Pieper, Josef. *Faith, Hope, Love*. Translated by Richard Winston et al. San Francisco: Ignatius, 1997.

———. *The Four Cardinal Virtues*. Translated by Richard Winston et al. Notre Dame, IN: University of Notre Dame Press, 1966.

———. *Happiness and Contemplation*. Translated by Richard and Clara Winston. South Bend, IN: St. Augustine's, 1998.

———. "The Negative Element in the Philosophy of St. Thomas Aquinas." In *The Silence of St. Thomas*, 43–71. South Bend, IN: St. Augustine's, 1963.

———. *Scholasticism: Personalities and Problems of Medieval Philosophy*. Translated by Richard Winston and Clara Winston. South Bend, IN: St. Augustine's, 2001.

Pinckaers, Servais, OP. *The Pinckaers Reader: Renewing Thomistic Moral Theology*. Edited by John Berkman and Craig Steven Titus. Washington, DC: Catholic University of America Press, 2005.

———. *The Sources of Christian Ethics*. Translated by Mary Thomas Noble, OP. Washington, DC: Catholic University of America Press, 1995.

Pius XI, Pope. "Quadragesimo Anno" (1931). In Carlen, *Papal Encyclicals*, 415–43. Encyclical on reconstruction of the social order.

Pius XII, Pope. "Mystici Corporis Christi" (1943). In Carlen, *Papal Encyclicals*, 37–63. Encyclical on the mystical body of Christ.

Plato. *Phaedrus and the Seventh and Eighth Letters*. Translated by Walter Hamilton. London: Penguin, 1973.

———. *The Symposium*. Translated by Walter Hamilton. New York: Penguin, 1951.

Pontifical Council for Justice and Peace. *Compendium of the Social Doctrine of the Church*. Washington, DC: United States Conference of Catholic Bishops, 2004.

Porter, Jean. *Nature as Reason: A Thomistic Theory of the Natural Law*. Grand Rapids: Eerdmans, 2005.

Prudlo, Donald S. *Thomas Aquinas: A Historical, Theological, and Environmental Portrait*. New York: Paulist, 2020.

Quasten, Johnannes. *Patrology*. 4 vols. Westminster, MD: Christian Classics, 1983.

Radcliffe, Timothy, OP. *Alive in God: A Christian Imagination*. London: Bloomsbury, 2019.

Rahner, Karl, SJ. "Chalcedon—End or Beginning?" In *Theological Investigations*, vol. 1, translated by Cornelius Ernst, 149–200. New York: Crossroad, 1982.

———. "Christian Humanism." In *Theological Investigations*, vol. 9, translated by Graham Harrison, 187–204. New York: Herder and Herder, 1972.

———. "The Christian in His World." In *Theological Investigations*, vol. 7, translated by David Bourke, 88–99. New York: Herder and Herder, 1971.

———. Christian Living. Formerly and Today." In *Theological* Investigations, vol. 7, translated by David Bourke, 3–24. New York: Herder and Herder, 1971.

———. "The Present Situation of Christians: A Theological Interpretation of the Position of Christians in the Modern World." In *The Christian Commitment*, translated by Cecily Hastings, 3–37. New York: Sheed and Ward, 1963.

———. "Theological Reflections on Monogenism." In *Theological Investigations*, vol. 1, translated by Cornelius Ernst, 229–96. Baltimore: Helicon, 1961.

———. *The Trinity*. Translated by Joseph Donceel, SJ. New York: Herder and Herder, 1970.

Raven, Charles E. *Teilhard de Chardin: Scientist and Seer*. New York: Harper and Row, 1962.

Reynolds, Nicholas, OP. "The Search for Truth: A Unification of Faith and Science in the Spirituality of Msgr. Georges Lemaître." MA thesis, Aquinas Institute of Theology, St. Louis, 2019.

Richardson, Robert D., Jr. *Emerson: The Mind on Fire*. Berkeley: University of California Press, 1995.

Rideau, Émile. *The Thought of Teilhard de Chardin*. Translated by René Hague. New York: Harper & Row, 1967.

Roman Breviary. *Liturgy of the Hours*. 4 vols. Translated by the International Commission on English in the Liturgy. New York: Catholic Book Publishing, 1975/1976.

Sacks, Jonathan. *The Dignity of Difference: How to Avoid the Clash of Civilizations*. London: Bloomsbury, 2003.

———. *Morality: Restoring the Common Good in Divided Times*. New York: Basic, 2020.

Savary, Louis M. *The Divine Milieu Explained*. New York: Paulist, 2007.

———. *Teilhard de Chardin on Morality: Living in an Evolving World*. New York: Paulist, 2019.

Schaefgen, Thomas, OP. "Come Now, Distribute Your Wealth Lavishly: The Social Vision of St. Basil the Great as Preached in Homily 6." MA thesis, Aquinas Institute of Theology, St. Louis, 2012.

Schillebeeckx, Edward, OP. *Christ: The Experience of Jesus as Lord*. Translated by John Bowden. New York: Seabury, 1980.

———. *The Church with a Human Face: A New and Expanded Theology of Ministry*. Translated by John Bowden. New York: Crossroad, 1985.

———. *The Eucharist*. Translated by N. D. Smith. New York: Sheed and Ward, 1968.

———. *On Christian Faith: The Spiritual, Ethical, and Political Dimensions*. Translated by John Bowden. New York: Crossroad, 1987.

Schoonenberg, Piet, SJ. *God's World in the Making*. Techny, IL: Divine Word, 1964.

———. *Man and Sin*. Translated by Joseph Donceel, SJ. Notre Dame, IN: University of Notre Dame Press, 1965.

Schwager, Raymund, SJ. *Banished from Eden: Original Sin and Evolutionary Theory in the Drama of Salvation*. Translated by James Williams. Herefordshire, UK: Gracewing, 2006.

Sertillanges, A. M., OP. *St. Thomas Aquinas and His Work*. Translated by Godfrey Anstruther, OP. London: Aquin, 1957.

Seseske, Daniel, ed. *Catholic Social Teaching Collection*. Park Ridge, IL: Word on Fire, 2020.

Sheen, Fulton J. *Footprints in a Darkened Forest*. New York: Meredith, 1967.

Sheldrake, Rupert. *The Sense of Being Stared At: And Other Aspects of the Extended Mind*. New York: Crown, 2003.

Slattery, John. "Pierre Teilhard de Chardin's Legacy of Eugenics and Racism Can't Be Ignored." *Religious Dispatches*, May 2018. https://religiondispatches.org/pierre-teilhard-de-chardins-legacy-eugenics-racism-cant-ignored/.

Smith, Richard Currie. "Replacing Descartes's 'Thinking Thing' with Deely's 'Semiotic Animal': Resolving Our Species Sustainability Dilemma and Establishing the Semiotic Age." *American Journal of Semiotics* 32 (2016) 143–204. Issue in memory of John N. Deely.

Smulders, Piet, SJ. *The Design of Teilhard de Chardin*. Translated by Arthur Gibson. Westminster, MD: Newman, 1967.

Southern, R. W. *Medieval Humanism and Other Studies*. Oxford: Blackwell, 1970.

———. *Scholastic Humanism and the Unification of Europe*. Oxford: Blackwell, 1995.

Speaight, Robert. *Teilhard de Chardin: A Biography*. New York: Harper and Row, 1967.

Spezzano, Daria. *The Glory of God's Grace: Deification according to St. Thomas Aquinas*. Naples, FL: Sapientia of Ave Maria University, 2015.

Steiner, Rudolf. *Autobiography: Chapters in the Course of My Life, 1861–1907*. Translated by Rita Stebbing. Great Barrington, MA: SteinerBooks, 2006.

———. *Christianity as Mystical Fact and the Mysteries of Antiquity*. Translated by Andrew Welburn. Great Barrington, MA: SteinerBooks, 2006.

———. *An Outline of Esoteric Science*. Translated by Catherine E. Creeger. Hudson, NY: Anthroposophic, 1997.

———. *The Redemption of Thinking: A Study in the Philosophy of Thomas Aquinas*. Translated by A. P. Shepherd and Mildred Robertson Nicoll. Spring Valley, NY: Anthroposophic, 1983.

Steinkerchner, Scott, OP. *Beyond Agreement: Interreligious Dialogue amid Persistent Differences*. New York: Bowman & Littlefield, 2011.

———. "Exploring Other Rivers: A Reflection on Interreligious Dialogue." In *The Parable: Dominican Theological Reflections for the 21st Century*, 9–13. River Forest, IL: Parable Conference, Fall 2006.

Stump, Eleonore. *Aquinas*. New York: Routledge, 2003.

———. *Atonement*. Oxford: Oxford University Press, 2018.

———. *The God of the Bible and the God of the Philosophers*. The 2016 Aquinas Lecture. Milwaukee, WI: Marquette University Press, 2016.

———. "God's Simplicity." In *The Oxford Handbook of Aquinas*, edited by Brian Davies and Eleonore Stump, 135–46. Oxford: Oxford University Press, 2012.

———. "Simplicity and Aquinas's Quantum Metaphysics." In *Die Metaphysik des Aristotoles im Mittlelater: Rezeption und Transformatio*, edited by Gerhard Krieger, 191–210. Berlin: de Gruyter, 2016.

———. *Wandering in Darkness: Narrative and the Problem of Suffering*. Oxford: Clarendon, 2010.

Sullivan, Francis A., SJ. *Magisterium: Teaching Authority in the Catholic Church*. Eugene, OR: Wipf & Stock, 1983.

———. *Salvation Outside the Church? Tracing the History of the Catholic Response*. New York: Paulist, 1992.

Tarnas, Richard. *Cosmos and Psyche: Intimations of a New World View*. New York: Viking, 2006.

Tart, Charles T. *The End of Materialism: How Evidence of the Paranormal Is Bringing Science and Spirit Together*. Oakland, CA: New Harbinger, 2009.

Tauler, Johannes, OP. *Sermons*. Translated by Maria Shrady. Classics of Western Spirituality. New York: Paulist, 1985.

Taylor, Charles. *A Secular Age*. Cambridge: Belknap of Harvard University Press, 2007.

———. *Sources of the Self: The Making of the Modern Identity*. Cambridge: Harvard University Press, 1989.

Teilhard de Chardin, Pierre, SJ. *Activation of Energy*. Translated by René Hague. London: William Collins Sons, 1970.

———. *The Appearance of Man*. Translated. by J. M. Cohen. New York: Harper & Row, 1965.

———. *Christianity and Evolution*. Translated by René Hague. New York: Harcourt Brace Jovanovich, 1971.

———. *The Divine Milieu*. Translated by Bernard Wall. New York: Harper & Row, 1960, the translation from which I quote. There is a later translation by Siôn Cowell. Portland, OR: Sussex Academic Press, 2004.

———. *The Future of Man*. Translated by Norman Denny. New York: Harper & Row, 1964.

———. *The Heart of Matter*. Translated by René Hague. New York: Harcourt Brace Jovanovich, 1978.

———. *Human Energy*. Translated by J. M. Cohen. New York: Harcourt Brace Jovanovich, 1969.

———. *The Human Phenomenon*. Translated by Sarah Appleton-Weber. Portland, OR: Sussex Academic, 2003. The translation from which I quote. Previously translated by Bernard Wall. New York: Harper & Row, 1959.

———. *Hymn of the Universe*. Translated by Simon Bartholomew. New York: Harper & Row, 1965.

———. *Letters from Egypt, 1905–1908*. Translated by Mary Ilford. Preface by Henri de Lubac, SJ. New York: Herder and Herder, 1965.

———. *Letters from Hastings, 1908–1912*. Translated by Judith de Stefano. Introduction by Henri de Lubac, SJ. New York: Herder and Herder, 1968.

———. *Letters from Paris, 1912–1914*. Translated by Michael Mazzarese. Introduction by Henri de Lubac, SJ. New York: Herder and Herder, 1967.

———. *Letters from a Traveller*. New York: Harper & Brothers, 1962.

———. *Letters to Léontine Zanta*. Translated by Bernard Wall. New York: Harper & Row, 1969.

———. *Letters to Two Friends, 1926–1952*. New York: New American Library, 1968.

———. *The Making of a Mind: Letters from a Soldier-Priest, 1914–1919*. Translated by René Hague. New York: Harper & Row, 1965.

———. *Man's Place in Nature*. Translated by René Hague. New York: Harper & Row, 1966.

———. *Science and Christ*. Translated by René Hague. New York: Harper & Row, 1968.

———. *Toward the Future*. Translated by René Hague. New York: Harcourt Brace Jovanovich, 1975.

———. *The Vision of the Past*. Translated by J. M. Cohen. New York: Harper & Row, 1966.

———. *Writings in Time of War*. Translated by René Hague. New York: Harper & Row, 1968.

Teilhard de Chardin, Pierre, SJ, and Maurice Blondel. *Correspondence*. Translated by William Whitman. Commentary by Henri de Lubac, SJ. New York: Herder and Herder, 1967.

Teilhard de Chardin, Pierre, SJ, and Lucile Swan. *The Letters of Teilhard de Chardin & Lucile Swan*. Edited by Thomas M. King, SJ, and Mary Wood Gilbert. Washington, DC: Georgetown University Press, 1993.

Terra, Helmut de. *Memories of Teilhard de Chardin*. Translated by J. Maxwell Brownjohn. New York: Harper & Row, 1964.

Thérèse of Lisieux, OCD. *The Story of a Soul: The Autobiography of Saint Thérèse of Lisieux*. Translated by John Beevers. New York: Doubleday, 1957.

Torrell, Jean-Pierre, OP. *Saint Thomas Aquinas*. 2 vols. Translated by Robert Royal. Washington, DC: Catholic University of America Press, 1996, 2003.

Trouter, Timothy. "The New Integralists: What They Get Wrong, and Why We Can't Ignore Them." *Commonweal* (November 2020) 32–37.

Tugwell, Simon, OP, ed., trans. *Albert and Thomas: Selected Writings*. Classics of Western Spirituality. New York: Paulist, 1988.

Turner, Denys. *The Darkness of God: Negativity in Christian Mysticism*. Cambridge: Cambridge University Press, 1995.

———. *God, Mystery, and Mystification*. Notre Dame, IN: University of Notre Dame Press, 2019.

———. *Julian of Norwich*. New Haven: Yale University Press, 2011.

———. *Thomas Aquinas: A Portrait*. New Haven: Yale University Press, 2013.

Vernon, Mark. *The Meaning of Friendship*. New York: Palgrave Macmillan, 2010.

———. *A Secret History of Christianity: Jesus, the Last Inkling, and the Evolution of Consciousness*. Winchester, UK: Hunt, 2018.

Vogler, Candace. "The Intellectual Animal." *New Blackfriars* 100 (November 2019) 663–76.

Walsh, John Evangelist. *Unravelling Piltdown: The Science Fraud of the Century and Its Solution*. New York: Random House, 1996.

Walsh, Liam, OP. Introduction to *Summa theologiae*, vol. 49, xvii–xxvii. New York: McGraw Hill, 1974.

Weisheipl, James A., OP. *Friar Thomas d'Aquino: His Life, Thought, and Works*. Garden City, NY: Doubleday, 1974.

———. "The Life and Works of St. Albert the Great." In *Albertus Magnus and the Sciences: Commemorative Essays, 1980*, ed. James A. Weisheipl, 13–51. Toronto: Pontifical Institute of Medieval Studies, 1980.

Weldon, Clodagh. *Fr. Victor White, O.P.: The Story of Jung's "White Raven."* Scranton, PA: University of Scranton Press, 2007.

White, Thomas Joseph, OP. *The Incarnate Lord: A Thomistic Study in Christology*. Washington, DC: Catholic University of America Press, 2015.

White, Victor, OP. *God the Unknown and Other Essays*. New York: Harper & Brothers, 1956.

Whitehead, Alfred North. *Adventures of Ideas*. New York: Macmillan, 1933.

———. *Modes of Thought*. New York: Macmillan, 1938.

Wilber, Ken. *Integral Spirituality: A Startling New Role for Religion in the Modern and Postmodern World*. Boston: Shambhala, 2006.

———. *The Marriage of Sense and Soul: Integrating Science and Religion*. New York: Random House, 1998.

———. *Sex, Ecology, Spirituality*. Boston: Shambhala, 1995.

Wildiers, N. M., OFMCap. *An Introduction to Teilhard de Chardin*. Translated by Hubert Hoskins. New York: Harper and Row, 1968.

Williams, A. N. *The Ground of Union: Deification in Aquinas and Palamas*. Oxford: Oxford University Press, 1999.

Wippel, John F. *The Metaphysical Thought of Thomas Aquinas: From Finite Being to Uncreated Being*. Washington, DC: Catholic University of America Press, 2000.

Yeats, W. B. *Selected Poetry*. Edited by A. Norman Jaffares. New York: Macmillan, 1974.

Index of Subjects

Index of Names

Made in United States
North Haven, CT
07 September 2024

57107917R00173